Successful Direct Marketing Methods

Third Edition

Bob Stone
Chairman, Stone & Adler, Inc.

CRAIN BOOKS, an imprint of
NTC NATIONAL TEXTBOOK COMPANY • Lincolnwood, Illinois U.S.A.

To Dorothy, my "one and only" for more than thirty years, who did extra duty in raising five wonderful kids while her husband was almost constantly "in flight." This book is but another manifestation of a wonderful partnership.

1988 Printing
Published by Crain Books, an imprint of National Textbook Company, 4255 West Touhy Avenue, Lincolnwood, Illinois 60646-1975
Manufactured in the United States of America.

890KP 987654

Contents

Section I Getting Started in Direct Marketing

4   Selecting and Selling Merchandise / 73

Section II Choosing Media for Your Message

5   Mailing Lists / 101

Section III Creating and Producing Direct Marketing

12   Techniques of Creating & Marketing Catalogs / 293

13   Techniques of Creating Print Advertising / 327

Section IV Managing Your Direct Marketing Operation

18   Direct Marketing in the Total Marketing Mix / **457**

Foreword

For those companies and organizations interested in direct marketing, there is little doubt that "Bob Stone rewrote the Bible." This third edition of "Successful Direct Marketing Methods" adds significantly to the previous editions and contributes significant new chapters that truly reflect the sophistication of this way of doing business.

Bob Stone's zest for educating people and companies in direct marketing not only spawned the sale of close to 100,000 copies of this book since its original printing in 1975 but also motivated other professionals in the field (Ed Nash, Jim Kobs, and others) to take time out to make their knowledge available in book form. For direct marketing, which was struggling for "its place in the marketing sun" only a few short years ago, these efforts have been more than literary. They have had considerable to do with the advancement of the skills of the profession.

Again, for direct marketing, which cries out for help in the form of more knowledgeable practitioners, this part of the educational process has indeed contributed to more and more of the "Fortune 500" companies entering the arena. Direct marketing, as it is practiced today, grew out of direct mail and mail order. The original, inherent strengths of the direct mail media and the convenience of buying by mail have been harnessed with the addition of other media including broadcast, newspaper inserts, and the dramatic use of telephone marketing. The much-heralded new technology is only beginning to have an impact on business and consumer marketing. Home shopping, although exploding in use, has yet to gain the benefits that the interactive means of ordering eventually will produce. In the business-to-business sector, the transfer of information and the actual selling of products and services through direct marketing has indeed exploded. Financial services, for example, has become a boom industry in direct marketing.

The point of all this is that Bob Stone's book was a landmark. It truly was a launching pad for credibility for direct marketing. There are many other nice things that have happened because this premier educator took the time to do things right. Like the $76,000 in royalties that he has contributed from his book to the Direct Marketing Edcuational Foundation. Again, this has provided motivation for a cause that will produce college graduates and MBA's in direct marketing. This is one of the essential keys to the proper use of this discipline. Many companies will profit from this undertaking. Thank you, Bob Stone.

Robert F. DeLay, President
Direct Marketing Association

About the Author

Position: Chairman of the Board, Stone & Adler, Inc.

Articles: Author of more than 200 articles since 1967 for the feature column on direct marketing appearing in *Advertising Age* magazine published by Crain Communications, Inc.

Awards: Six-time winner of the Direct Marketing Association's Best of Industry Award. His firm, Stone & Adler, has received Direct Marketing Association's highest honor, including the Silver and Gold Echo Awards as well as the International Direct Marketing & Mail Order Symposium's Bronze Carrier Pigeon Award. Member of Direct Marketing HALL OF FAME. Recipient of the Edward M. Meyer Award for contributions to direct marketing education, the Charles S. Downes Award for direct marketing contributions and the John Caples Award for copy excellence.

Affiliations: Former director of the Direct Marketing Association
Former president of the Chicago Association of Direct Marketing
Former membership chairman of the Direct Marketing Association
Former president of the Associated Third Class Mail Users
Member of the Professional Division of Alpha Delta Sigma fraternity
Board member of the Direct Marketing Educational Foundation

Preface

The Bell System is into direct marketing deep. So is AT&T and IBM. And Xerox. And Hewlett-Packard. And American Oil, Hallmark, and American Express. And Time-Life, Grolier, and Disney. And thousands more, big and small. In short—direct marketing is exploding all over the place! But the explosions didn't start in this decade. Lester Wunderman, chairman of the world's largest direct marketing agency—Wunderman, Ricotta & Kline/New York—traces the dynamic evolution back to the 1940s, following World War II. Speaking of this period, Wunderman said,

Looking backward down the long road of direct marketing history one begins to sense a gathering of energy. A charge just waiting for the catalyst which would set off a great explosion.

It happened—and it was not just one explosion, but many. The years and decades following World War II saw explosion after explosion. Each of them changed the way we lived and most of them created new opportunities for direct marketing.

Boom went the population explosion! Suddenly there were more of us. Boom went the new migration! Suburbs grew and some cities got smaller. The retail business exploded as stores followed the population to their new homes.

Then advertising had to take over the selling function the retailer increasingly gave up in his new role as self-service warehouse. Boom!

The women's movement and inflation took an increasing number of single and married women out of the house and into factories and offices. There was less and less time available to everyone who worked. Discretionary time and discretionary income became key items in the family budget. Saving time and effort started to become big business! Boom!

Mass Marketing—in fact, mass anything, started to become an old-fashioned idea. Segmented marketing was becoming the new fact of life, and new media and new entertainment and information systems were being developed to satisfy it. Boom! Boom! Boom! The 1950s, 1960s and 1970s saw explosion after explosion as old ways of doing almost anything gave way to new forms and new needs.

And what *fed* the explosions of the last four decades? Technological breakthroughs and creative breakthroughs—for sure.

Segmented marketing wouldn't be in our vocabulary, but for the computer. Billions of dollars of telephone sales wouldn't be possible, but for the toll-free 800 number. Big ticket merchandise sales—there seems to be no limit to unit of sale—would be but a dream, but for the credit card explosion.

Segmented magazine circulation—*TV Guide* with over 80 editions, for example—became the direct marketer's dream. Newspaper inserts, by the billions, became feasible with the advent of high-speed inserting equipment. Laser beam printing at incredible speed made it possible to personalize direct mail "forty ways from Sunday"—at reasonable cost.

Meanwhile, during these same explosive decades, direct marketers learned how to make television work for them, producing commercials up to the standards of major general advertisers. Concurrent with the mastering of television, it was discovered that multimedia—using two or more media to support the same proposition—greatly increased response. Today it isn't unusual at all to increase response of a newspaper insert by 50 percent or more with the support of TV commercials.

The narrowing of leisure time and the hassle of shopping fed a new phenomena, the upscale catalog, developed to cater to the wishes and perceived needs of the affluent segments of the American population.

Roger Horchow led the way in the early 1970s with the introduction of the Kenton Collection, later to grow into The Horchow Collection catalog. It led to an explosion of upscale catalogs—many successes and many, many failures.

Failures notwithstanding, those who have mastered market segmentation, those who have become astute catalog merchants continue to grow and prosper. And retail merchants have come aboard too—the Bloomingdales, the Saks, the Bergdorf-Goodmans. For the most part they are mailing catalogs instead of opening new stores.

But another phenomenon is a real "switcheroo": catalog entrepreneurs, who lived by catalogs alone, are opening retail stores. Mail order apparel firms like Talbots and Carroll Reed continue to expand their retail store network. Carroll Reed has 15 stores, excluding ski shops.

Talbots has 16 stores. And Fredericks of Hollywood has hundreds of stores.

Market research has proved a boon to catalog marketers, but two of the most vital stimulants to catalog sales have proved to be the 800 toll-free number and credit card ordering privileges. Today it isn't at all uncommon to receive at least 35 percent of catalog orders via the telephone, telephone orders averaging about 20 percent larger than mail orders. That same magic 20 percent increase applies to a credit card order versus a cash order.

Direct marketing explosions have not been limited to the consumer field. The business-to-business category is likewise experiencing explosive growth. There are hundreds of industrial catalogs.

But major growth in business-to-business direct marketing is being fueled more than anything by staggering increases in the cost of industrial sales calls. In 1978 McGraw-Hill estimated the cost of an industrial sales call to be $96.79. By 1982 cost per call was pushing $200.00+—a whopping 106 percent increase. And no relief in sight . . . except *qualified leads.*

Industry has learned the closure rate for qualified leads can be from two to four times as effective as cold calls. So spending $20, $40 to get a qualified lead turns out to be a pittance . . . especially if you are an IBM selling major equipment.

Explosive growth has not been problem-free. There's a dearth of experienced direct marketing talent—especially in the creative area.

Many of today's practitioners are from the old hard-sell school. Ads that are buck horse. Graphics left over from the 1950s and 1960s. Heavy copy. Schlock.

Lamenting the erosion of creative leadership in the U.S.A., Alex Kroll, president of Young & Rubicam, keynoted the Creative Workshop section of ADVERTISING AGE Week on August 11, 1981, with some incisive remarks that could well have been restricted to direct marketing.

The Japanese, Germans, British, and Scandinavians are beating us at our own game. We find that the advertisements that stun and stop, that provoke and outrage, that advance the art of commercial persuasion—the new stuff, the fresh stuff—is not done here, but done there.

Practitioners of American advertising are afflicted with the quitter instinct. Creative managers who grew up in the business in the 1960s and early 1970s became winners looking to be losers, to relieve the pressure of staying on top, to rid themselves of the fierce and relentless concentration it takes to keep winning.

I just think we got comfortable. Perhaps we were on such a winning roll for so long we subconsciously wanted to roll over in the muck and play. Dead. We invented a sop called the norm—a norm to conform to, instead of a grail to search after. We settled for options instead of excellence.

Cynicism and lack of accountability (*accountability* is what sets direct marketing apart) were bred by the practice in the 1960s and early 1970s of hot creatives jumping from agency to agency for higher and higher salaries.

Concerning recruiting, Mr. Kroll said, "We are rutted in the same kind of formula thinking that bogs down much of our advertising. If we want breakthroughs, we could start with a breakthrough in attracting the minds which can break through. Find the eclectic iconoclasts and teach them the trade," he urged. (Let it be noted that direct marketing agencies, in particular, have encouraged agency hopping, often settling for warm bodies in lieu of creative potential.)

Words of wisdom from the head of U.S.A.'s largest general advertising agency, an agency head whose background is in Creative. Riding the wisdom that Kroll expressed at the AD AGE Creative Workshop, Stone & Adler has found, for example, the brightest "eclectic iconoclasts" to be the English majors coming from the leading American universities. They have the inherent talent to create "the new stuff," "the fresh stuff," "the breakthroughs." Teaching them "the trade" is the job of the direct marketing agencies.

A scant decade ago, there were but a handful of major agencies with meaningful direct marketing arms. But today we find practically all the major general agencies with substantial direct marketing units. Y&R with three units, billing in excess of $250 million worldwide. N. W. Ayer, Doyle, Dane, Bernbach, McCann, Ogilvy & Mather—they all have substantial direct marketing arms.

And because big attracts big, it follows the "Fortune 500" types are coming into the fold. Fast. The IBMs. The Xeroxes. The automotive companies. The big financial institutions. Each, seeking out in its own way major income outside traditional channels.

Addressing attendees at the Third Annual John Caples Awards, sponsored by the Direct Marketing Creative Guild, Inc., Lester Wunderman said,

We are no longer in the business of creating an ad or a mailing: we are dealing with information and media systems. We're not just advertising products or services that are in the main created for mail-order selling—we are becoming part of a total marketing mix. The same product that competes for market share in stores will also increasingly compete for a share in direct-to-consumer marketing. We will not be permitted to buy today's result without also building a franchise for tomorrow.

Put simply, I suggest that increasingly direct marketing requires advertising that combines information, persuasion, product positioning, and the triggering of a transaction. New media forms and systems are either ready or imminent which will force these functions to coalesce.

The creative people in our industry today, and those whom I hope we can persuade to enter it tomorrow, will be faced with a unique challenge—to be accountable for results without sacrificing style, taste or touch.

Of all the challenges direct marketers face in the immediate- and long-term future, cable TV has got to be high on the list. The excitement has been there for a long time. Give or take a point or two, the prediction of Y&R media specialist Bill Donnelley—"Major advertisers will get into cable when cable reaches 30 percent of TV households"—is in the "moment of truth" stage.

Direct marketers, for the most part, are expecting cable will create new explosions. But they're not too sure about how best to detonate! There is so little knowledge and so much to learn. Ground rules are being established "as you go."

The ultimate, from the direct marketer's standpoint, is interactive TV, still very much in the experimental stage. QUBE, the U.S. pioneer in interactive TV, makes it possible to order merchandise and services from the convenience of one's home with the use of a hand-held console.

Viewdata, an experiment conducted in the Florida market under the auspices of Knight-Ridder, takes interaction a step further, but lacks the dynamic impact of live "video." With Viewdata you can command advertiser information at will—when you want it. And you can order from the convenience of your home.

Part and parcel of new electronic media is the videodisc, which has built-in direct marketing opportunities for interaction. Sears has already experimented with videodisc owners and using videodisc commercials in major Sears stores.

Where the new electronic media will settle in the total direct marketing mix is pure speculation. But one can be sure that direct marketers will be in the forefront of experimentations.

There are those who say new electronic media will supplant most existing direct marketing mediums: direct mail, the catalog, newspapers, radio, regular TV. Nonsense!

Robert A. Burnett, president and chief executive officer of Meredith Corporation, put the new electronic media in perspective in an address before the Direct Marketing Association when he said, "We see a blurring of the lines that now separate and define media. But let us remember: radio did not displace newspapers. Television did not replace radio. Likewise, future media will not, in our opinion, replace existing media. But they will change and adapt to a new set of marketing conditions."

Then there are those who would have you believe the retail store is dying, that direct marketing will supplant retailing as we know it. More nonsense!

John A. Quelch and Hirotaka Takeuchi, professors at the Harvard Business School, made a strong case for retailers in an essay on nonstore marketing in the July-August 1981 issue of *Harvard Business Review.*

"As noted," they said,

direct marketing threatens the sales of traditional retail outlets—especially those that carry high-margin specialty items. Specialty and department stores are not, however, without defense.

Such prestigious department stores as Neiman-Marcus can hedge their bets by becoming direct marketers themselves and thus expand the geographical base of their sales without investing in new stores. They can control the rate at which their nonstore business expands and prevent any reduction in the ROI of their traditional stores.

Chain stores can minimize sales losses by emphasizing personalized in-store service, by extending store hours, by offering in-store boutiques, by developing a specific image for each local outlet, and by competing with the catalogs of direct marketers through newspaper supplment advertising and direct mailings of their own.

Specialty store chains can also compete against direct marketers on the basis of in-store service, convenience, and breadth of assortment. A specialty shoe retailer such as Edison Bros. can offer customers a wide choice of merchandise at different price and quality levels by locating several outlets with different names in a large mall designed for one-stop shopping and by developing more powerful store images through store design and focused product selection.

Because direct marketers require more lead time for product planning than do retailers and because the product mix listed in a catalog cannot be quickly changed, specialty stores that sell fashion-sensitive merchandise are especially well-equipped to compete with direct marketers by emphasizing the up-to-date nature of their product lines.

No—retailing will not be wiped out by direct marketing. Never. The charter of direct marketing is not to replace traditional distribution channels. Its strength lies in the possibility of establishing new profit centers and in applying its specialized disciplines to expanding sales through traditional channels.

Inherent in all direct marketing activities is the development of a data base, *unique* lists of individuals, of companies who have inquired, or bought. Such lists become prime media for stimulating repeat business, for converting inquiries to sales.

Media available for building data bases stagger the mind. Direct mail. Newspapers. Magazines. Co-ops. Bingo cards. Telephone. radio. TV. Cable. Car cards. Catalogs. Interactive electronic media. Videodiscs. And any combination thereof.

Jimmy Durante used to say, "Folks—you ain't seen nothin' yet." And I believe this is true of direct marketing. Fueled by new technologies. Fueled by ever increasing dual income families, by an expanding over-50 population, by skyrocketing sales call costs, by changes in lifestyles which foretell a boom in home shopping—more explosions are in the air. For sure!

Bob Stone

Acknowledgments

As with both the first and second editions of SUCCESSFUL DI-RECT MARKETING METHODS, the materials in this, the third edition, in no way reflect the sole thinking of the author. Instead this book is a reflection of all that is happening in direct marketing, with generous contributions from a host of people and organizations.

Thanks to Direct Marketing Association for the statistics it has provided. To Pete Hoke, publisher of *Direct Marketing* for his contributions. To Rose Harper, president of the Kleid Co., Inc., for her input on mailing lists. To Stan Rapp and Tom Collins of Rapp & Collins for their contributions on magazines and the techniques of creating print advertising.

And my thanks go likewise to Jo-Von Tucker, president of Jo-Von Tucker & Associates, for her input on catalogs. To Bob Kestnbaum, president of Kestnbaum & Company for his input on the mathematics of direct marketing. And to Paul Murphy, research director of Y&R speciality companies, for his contributions on research for direct marketers.

Numerous present and former staff members of Stone & Adler contributed to this book. Special thanks go to Jerry Wood, president, for his contributions on strategic planning. To Bill Waites for his contributions on electronic media. To Don Kanter for his input on creating mail packages. To Jan Steinert, vice president and account supervisor, for his contributions on telemarketing and managing a lead generation program.

My thanks to Richard Hagle, former publisher of Crain Books and editor of this volume, for his ideas and suggestions on this revised and enlarged edition.

Thanks also go to Frank Daniels for his input on idea development. And finally—a special thank you to Aaron Adler, co-founder of Stone & Adler, for lending his wisdom to the chapter on selecting and selling merchandise.

Section I
Getting Started in Direct Marketing

Chapter One

The Scope of Direct Marketing

Direct marketing, once regarded as an "ugly duckling" in the marketing world, has, in the past decade in particular, taken on all the glamor and wonderment of a Cinderella going to the ball. Its scope has gone beyond the wildest dreams of its most exuberant exponents.

As its scope has enlarged, direct marketing has taken on a new professionalism. This transition from amateurism to professionalism was instigated, for the most part, by a relative handful of visionary direct marketing professionals, visionaries who saw the opportunity to expand the scope from mail order alone to direct response in its totality by applying the special disciplines of direct marketing to all media. And state-of-the-art execution has become more consistent because of the entry of major marketers and major general advertising agencies into the direct marketing stream. Each, in its own way, has brought its knowledge of business planning, its special expertise in graphics, and its know-how in research to the party.

While it can now rightfully be said that direct marketing has earned equal status with all other respected marketing disciplines, it should be carefully noted there are inherent differences in the direct marketing discipline.

Direct Marketing Defined

A hint at the scope of direct marketing and its differences is found in the official definition of the Direct Marketing Association.

> *Direct Marketing* is an interactive system of marketing which uses one or more advertising media to effect a measurable response and/ or transaction at any location.

1

The two most important words in the definition are "measurable response," for if response can't be measured, if cost and income can't be calculated precisely, it's not direct marketing.

The differences between general advertising and direct marketing are quite notable for the objectives are quite different. Here are the basic differences:

Direct Marketing	**General Advertising**
• Selling to individuals. Customers are indentifiable by name, address, and purchase behavior.	• Mass selling. Buyers identified as broad groups sharing common demographic and psychographic characteristics.
• Products have added value or service. Distribution is important product benefit.	• Product benefits do not always include convenient distribution channels.
• The medium is the marketplace.	• Retail outlet is marketplace.
• Marketer controls product until delivery.	• Marketer may lose control as product enters distribution channel.
• Advertising used to motivate an immediate order or inquiry.	• Advertising used for cumulative effect over time to build image, awareness, loyalty, benefit recall. Purchase action deferred.
• Repetition used within ad.	• Repetition used over time.
• Consumers feel high perceived risk—product bought unseen. Recourse is distant.	• Consumers feel less risk—have direct contact with the product and direct recourse.

Distinguishing Marks of Direct Response Ads

So these are the basic differences between general advertising and direct response advertising. But what are the distinguishing marks of direct response ads as contrasted to ads prepared for general advertising?

This question can best be answered by carefully examining the IDS ad shown in Exhibit 1-1. This ad, written by Don Kanter, executive vice president of Stone & Adler, has three distinguishing marks: (1) a definite offer, (2) all the information necessary to make a decision, (3) a response device—in this case a toll-free number and a mail-in coupon. If an ad does not have these three distinguishing marks, it is not a direct response ad.

Exhibit 1-1. IDS: The Right Copy Positioning

What is a Money Market Fund ...and why does it generate such high yields?

IDS
Ideas to help people manage money

How it works

When large corporations, banks, even the federal government need short term cash, they borrow money in what is called the "money market." This is basically a group of institutions and even wealthy individuals who have very large amounts of available money to lend for up to six months.

Because the borrowers want large sums for a short time, and because they put up no security for that money other than their own good name and reputation, they have to pay a higher rate of interest. So it's usually a very profitable investment for the lenders.

But unless you have at least $100,000 of idle cash to spare, forget about being a private lender in the money market. Because that's normally the minimum amount needed to buy a money market "instrument." So it's no wonder the money market has been virtually closed to private individuals, except the very rich.

Until the Money Market Fund came along.

The Money Market Fund operates on a simple principle: Pooling. It receives relatively small amounts of money from a large number of individuals and small businesses...pools that money...and lends it in the money market with the same degree of care and expertise as would any other major lender. The interest earned is then passed along to the Fund's investors, or "shareholders" as dividends. Therefore, you as a shareholder would have the advantage of earning "money market" interest.

Why it's become so popular

Money Market Funds have been around for a number of years. But with the dramatic rise in interest rates, these funds have become enormously popular—not merely with so-called "investors"—but with anyone trying to keep up with inflation. And if a dollar in savings can earn substantially more interest in a Money Market Fund than it can in a regular passbook account, it can mean a mighty big difference—a few months from now, at retirement time, when the kids are ready for college, or whatever.

The advantages of IDS Cash Management Fund II:

1) High current interest rates, earning dividends for you every single day of the year.

2) Liquidity. In plain English, this means you can have your money back—all or part of it—any time you want it, with no interest penalty and no withdrawal charge. That's an important advantage if you need cash in a hurry, or choose to move your money elsewhere.

Compare that to Savings Certificates which require you to tie up your money for months, or even years! In the words of the fine print, there are "substantial interest penalties for early withdrawal." But IDS Cash Management Fund II has no penalty for early withdrawal.

3) Flexibility. Like a checking account. Here's how it works: As a shareholder, you'll receive a book of special draft forms that work just like checks. At any time, you can write a draft for $500 or more against your Fund account to pay bills, make a purchase, pay your taxes, etc. There's no charge for this service. What's more, the money you withdraw *continues to earn interest* until the draft clears the Fund. So the longer your draft remains outstanding, the more interest you earn.

Things you should realize about IDS Cash Management Fund II:

1) There is no guarantee on the interest rate. If you buy an investment sold by a bank or a savings institution, you are guaranteed that the interest rate will not go down during the term of the investment.

But you're also guaranteed that the rate will not go *up* during that term.

Interest rates on IDS Cash Management Fund II fluctuate daily, reflecting what the money market lenders are asking in interest, and what the money market borrowers are willing to pay. If rates go up, you're ahead. If rates go down, to the point where you can do better elsewhere, there's a simple answer: take your money out. Remember, there's no penalty for doing so.

2) In compliance with regulations issued March 14, 1980, by the Federal Reserve Board (as they apply to money market funds), 15% of the investment assets of IDS Cash Management Fund II will be deposited with the Federal Reserve Bank in a non-interest bearing account. This will depress the yield somewhat. Even with this reserve requirement yields are currently in double digits.

3) There is no governmental agency guaranteeing your principal, as there is in a bank or a savings institution. In the unlikely event that the borrowers (corporations, banks, the federal government) default on their money market notes, you could lose part of your investment.

But keep in mind, IDS Cash Management Fund II does not invest your money with "anybody." All our investments are in U.S. government securities, bank securities and issuers who receive the top two credit ratings from Moody's or Standard & Poor's.

How to invest

You need $2,500. That's the minimum investment in IDS Cash Management Fund II. (Once you've opened an account, you can add to it with additional investments as low as $100.)

You also need a prospectus. We try to write our prospectus in plain, clear English—and we maintain a toll-free phone in case you have any questions.

If you decide to invest, you simply mail your application and check to us. We open your account, and as soon as your check clears, you start earning money market interest.

IDS has a unique advantage: We have 160 offices all over the country. You can handle everything by mail or toll-free telephone with our Home Office in Minneapolis...or you're welcome to call or visit an IDS office near your home if you have questions or need further assistance.

About IDS

Before you invest your money *anywhere*, you should know about the company handling your investment.

IDS, headquartered in the IDS Tower, Minneapolis, Minnesota, has been in the money management business for 86 years. Today, it has over six billion dollars of assets under management. IDS is adviser to the Investors Group of Companies which includes IDS Cash Management Fund II.

How to get going

Just call us. We have a toll-free phone that operates 7 days a week, 24 hours a day. The call costs you nothing. We'll send you a prospectus. (If you prefer, you can mail in the coupon.)

Calling us, or mailing the coupon, puts you under *no* obligation whatever. All it does is open up a new opportunity for you. Whether or not you invest is strictly up to you. But wouldn't it make good sense to at least look into it?

Call toll-free for a Prospectus, 800-228-5100.

(Ask for Cash Management Fund II information. Phone any time: 7 days a week, 24 hours a day. In Nebraska, phone 402-571-5200.)

...or mail the coupon today

INVESTORS DIVERSIFIED SERVICES
IDS Tower, Dept 532, Minneapolis, MN 55402

IDS
Since 1894

With over $6,000,000,000 in assets under management, IDS is the investment adviser and the national distributor of IDS Cash Management Fund II Inc.

INVESTORS DIVERSIFIED SERVICES
IDS Tower, Dept 532, Minneapolis, MN 55402

For more complete information, including management fees and expenses, please write or call for a prospectus. Read it carefully before you invest or send money.

Name

Address

City   State   Zip

Home Phone   Business Phone

What the reader of the IDS ad did not see or know was that the unique copy positioning Don Kanter took was not a hunch. Instead the positioning came out of research—professional direct marketers rely heavily upon research (See Chapter 17)—which showed conclusively at the time that a surprising number of business people and consumers really didn't know what a money market fund was. The wisdom of Don Kanter playing off of research was confirmed by the fact that this particular direct response ad became the control ad for IDS. And it won out time after time when new ads were tested against it.

Direct Marketing Flow Chart

The total scope of media from which direct marketers can choose today appears on the direct marketing flow chart (Exhibit 1-2) published by *Direct Marketing* magazine. Interspersed with the media scope are the disciplines involved in a successful direct marketing operation.

Inherent in the direct marketing process is the development of a data base of both prospects and customers who have responded to direct response offers, regardless of media employed. The data base, replete with supporting data such as media source, date of response, type of order or inquiry, etc., serves as the basis for all future promotion.

Direct Response Advertising Expenditures

To a large extent it is the mastering of multimedia, discovering and proving the synergism between media, that has earned direct marketing equal status with other respected marketing disciplines. And I personally believe the dramatic growth of direct marketing—from $60 billion in 1978 to $137.9 billion in sales in 1982—stemmed largely from the increased use of multimedia approaches.

Table 1-1 shows expenditures by media. The most dramatic growth in the media mix has occurred with telephone. As new electronic media become viable, one can expect the media mix to take on an even more exciting potential.

Direct Mail
Costs

One might conclude, with considerable "logic," that because of spiraling postage, printing, and mailing costs, other media are growing at the expense of direct mail. Surprisingly, such is not the case.

Table 1-2 charts media costs, including direct mail, over a five-year period. Costs for direct mail were computed by getting a quote on an identical mailing package in a million quantity for each of the five years, including lettershop and postage costs. Statistics for all other media came from *Marketing & Media Decisions* magazine.

Surprisingly, direct mail shows the smallest increase over five years—33 percent. Daytime network TV, on the other hand, shows a 45 percent increase; evening network TV—60 percent; spot TV—40 percent; mag-

Exhibit 1-2. Direct Marketing Flow Chart

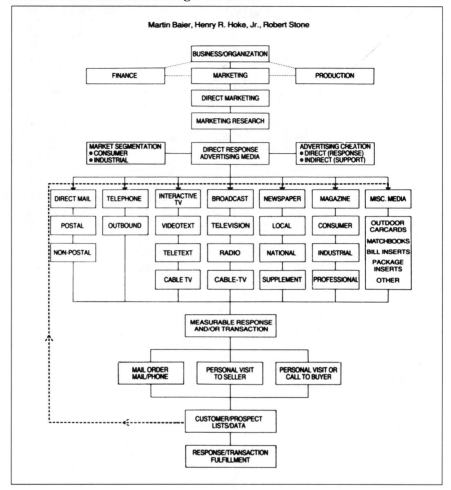

azines—45 percent; R.O.P. newspapers—43 percent; and newspaper supplements—42 percent. DMA reports that the cost of producing an average direct mail package in a 250,000 quantity actually dropped slightly in 1982 over 1981: $289.93 per 1,000 vs. $291.48.

The Uniqueness of Direct Mail

New electronic media notwithstanding, it is safe to say direct mail will never phase out. Even if direct mail costs were rising faster than all other media, direct mail would not phase out. There are important reasons for this.

Table 1-1. Total Direct Marketing Advertising Expenditures—1981
(In Millions)

	1982	1981
Coupons	$ 127.1	$ 94.6
Direct Mail	11,359.4	10,566.7
Consumer Magazines	167.0	150.0
Business Magazines	66.0	59.0
Newspapers	70.6	73.0
Newspaper Preprints	2,500.0	2,288.5
Telephone	12,935.6	11,467.0
Television	339.0	295.0
Radio	33.0	29.0
Total	**$ 27,597.7**	**$25,022.8**

The most important reason of all is that direct mail is the only print medium—bar none—which can guarantee *no waste circulation*. None. The only way, outside of telephone of course, to "talk" with all your customers to the exclusion of prospects is via direct mail. The only print medium available for following up on inquiries is direct mail. The only print medium available for getting renewals for magazine subscriptions is direct mail. The same is true when it comes to reaching donors to charities, association members, and members of fraternal organizations.

Direct mail is unique in another way. It is the *only medium* with practically no restriction on format. A circular can be as large as a printing press will accommodate. A mailing package can include stamps, tokens, gadgets. A letter can be personalized to the limit of one's imagination. A letter is not limited in number of pages.

Contrast the flexibility of direct mail with other media. Radio and TV commercials are limited by time. Magazines and newspapers are restricted by page sizes.

Dramatic Application of Direct Mail

Direct mail has one other inherent quality that does not exist for any other media—its *privateness*. This is true even if the identical mailing is sent to millions. No other print medium lends itself as well to a one-on-one dialogue between writer and reader. Thus it is that the "personal" aspect of a mailing, a letter in particular, can motivate people to respond beyond the most hopeful expectations. And I can't think of a better example of the power of direct mail than a fund raising effort on behalf of The Direct Mail/Marketing Educational Foundation.

Table 1-2. Media Costs Over a Five-Year Period

Index of Unit Costs	*Direct Mail	**Network TV		**Spot TV	**Mags.	**News- papers	**Supple- ments
		Day	Evening				
1977	100	100	100	100	100	100	100
1978	107	111	112	102	109	110	108
1979	115	121	126	117	118	118	117
1980	124	137	148	131	131	131	129
1981	133	145	160	140	145	143	142

Source: *Stone & Adler—August, 1981
    **Marketing & Media Decisions*—August, 1981

But before you read the five-page letter that brought pledges in excess of $227,000 for each 1,000 prospects, let me give you a little background. The Direct Mail/Marketing Educational Foundation was founded in 1965. A study of college curriculums at the time showed conclusively that advertising and marketing students were being taught practically nothing about direct marketing. Therefore, the first priority of the Foundation was to find a way to acquaint college students with the uniqueness of the direct marketing discipline. The five-page letter and pledge card shown in Exhibits 1-3 and 1-4 tell the rest of the fascinating story.

Special note should be made of the pledge card, which was enclosed in a stamped reply envelope (Exhibit 1-4). The name and address of the recipient were typed on the card, and a suggested contribution was checked. The wisdom of suggesting an amount for each prospective contributor was confirmed by the fact that only a handful of contributors pledged an amount different from what was suggested.

The Foundation could have ended its campaign with this one very successful mailing. But good direct mail procedure dictates otherwise. So the Foundation sent a followup mailing to all who did not respond. The followup consisted of a handwritten memo (Exhibit 1-5) and an exact copy of the original letter. The followup mailing worked too. Not as profitable as the first mailing, of course, but still highly profitable.

Still short of the goal, the Foundation applied another direct marketing technique—telemarketing. (See Chapter 10.) Using a taped message from Bob DeLay, President of DMA, yours truly, and CCI—a major telemarketing organization—phoned all remaining prospects who had not responded.

Telemarketing paid out too. Handsomely! So there you have a campaign with direct mail at the forefront which produced over $227,000 in pledges for each 1,000 prospects contacted. The power of direct mail never ceases to amaze me.

Exhibit 1-3. Direct Mail Letter

STONE & ADLER INC.

150 NORTH WACKER DRIVE • CHICAGO, ILLINOIS 60606 • TELEPHONE 312/346-6100

ROBERT STONE, *Chairman of the Board*

July 28, 1982

Mr. John Jones
Jones Manufacturing Co.
1621 Main Street
Ottumwa, Iowa 52501

Dear John,

Remember when you were a kid. A "dreamer" was put down
as someone who would never amount to anything -- destined
to be a "non-achiever" for life.

What a myth!

Let me tell you about some "dreamers" who became super
achievers in direct marketing. They succeeded beyond
their wildest dreams.

There's the thrilling story of L. L. Bean in Maine. For
years they ran a successful mail order business...catering
to outdoorsmen.

But Leon Gorman dreamed of new horizons...a new world out
there of men and women who never fished or hunted -- dressed
the way outdoors people dress. A pipe dream? Hardly. Leon
Gorman turned dream to reality. Sales - plateaued at the
$50 million level - boomed past the $100 million level in a
few short years.

What about the legendary "kitchen table" people? Len
Carlson, out in California, is a part of the legend.

Len and his wife Gloria shared a dream. They dreamed they
could put together a catalog of hard-to-find gadgets that
would appeal to the masses. Thus Sunset House was born.

Fifteen years and a customer base of 6.5 million names
later, the press announced Sunset House had been acquired
by a major corporation for a price reported to be in the
millions.

The most remarkable dream story on the agency side is that
of Lester Wunderman. Les was an account person with the
Max Sackheim agency. He dreamed of having his own agency.

But an agency that would apply sophisticated direct response

Exhibit 1-3. Direct Mail Letter (continued)

-2-

techniques to all media -- including a "new" medium called
television. Today his firm - Wunderman, Ricotta & Kline -
has billings in excess of $100 million, with offices in New
York and 12 foreign countries.

As you read of these dreams-come-true I hope you are recall-
ing your own. The dreams you have had which have helped you
to get to where you are today.

> But of all the dreams-come-true which I have
> witnessed over the years there is one which
> supersedes all others. A dream-come-true
> which has touched all our lives, a dream
> which will live on beyond our lifetimes.

The year was 1965. Lewis Kleid, a leading list broker in
his day, was a close friend of Edward N. Mayer, Jr., known
around the world as "Mr. Direct Mail."

Lew made a proposition to Ed. He said, "Ed - if you will
devote time to teaching the rudiments of direct marketing to
college kids, I'll provide the seed money to make it happen."

Thus, with the simplicity that was a trademark of Ed Mayer,
the Lewis Kleid Institute was launched. Today, almost 17
years later, The Direct Mail/Marketing Educational
Foundation, a non-profit organization which sponsors Kleid
Institutes, continues in the Ed Mayer image.

> Over the past 17 years over 1,000 bright college
> students have taken the 5-day intensive course,
> sponsored by the Foundation...all expenses paid.
> It is estimated that over 50% of these students
> have entered into a direct marketing career.

As one of the privileged few who has had the honor of lectur-
ing each new group of candidates over many years -- I only
wish you could witness, as I have, the excitement that comes
to each as they are introduced to the wonders of direct
marketing disciplines.

"I learned more in five days than in my four years as a
marketing major," is a somewhat typical statement from one
of these exuberant students.

But let me give you just a few quotes from hundreds in file.

"I learned so very much -- the week just set my spark for
direct marketing into a big roaring fire!"

                                    Marilee Gibson Yorchak
                                    New Mexico State University

Exhibit 1-3. Direct Mail Letter (continued)

-3-

"The Institute has greatly increased my awareness and understanding of direct marketing, and furthered my career interest."

Tim Harrison
University of North Carolina

"If one of your objectives was to stimulate young, ambitious
people to enter your field, you succeeded with me."

Paula Miante
College of William and Mary

I guess from all of this one would have to conclude our dream
has truly come true. Well - not exactly.

None of us ever dreamed that direct marketing would have the
explosive growth we have all experienced. (As an aside -
when I wrote my first book I trumpeted that total sales of
goods and services via the direct marketing method had reached
the staggering figure of $300 million. The estimated figure
for 1981 is $120 <u>billion</u>!)

So now we realize that if our true dream is to be realized -
growing our own at the college level to people our future
growth - we are going to have to raise our sights beyond the
far horizon.

Where we are bringing the gifted student to the Institute -
only one each from about 35 colleges twice each year - we've
got to get Direct Marketing taught on the college campus in
full semester courses. Not to three score and ten for five
days. Instead - to hundreds for full semesters.

Is this "The Impossible Dream"? No!

I'm now going to tell you about what some regard to be an
emerging "miracle," which is in the process of happening as
I pen this letter.

At a Board of Directors meeting a few months ago in the
offices of The Direct Mail/Marketing Educational Foundation,
Richard L. Montesi, President, made a startling proposal.
A proposal which he stated would make our ultimate dream
come true.

The ultimate dream, as he expressed it, is to establish a
Chair for a Direct Marketing Center in three major universities: one in the Middle West; one in the East; and one in
the West.

The full-scale curriculums will be structured to earn a
degree in Direct Marketing for each graduate, carrying with

Exhibit 1-3. Direct Mail Letter (continued)

-4-

them a stature similar to that enjoyed by a graduate from
the Wharton School of Business or Harvard Business School.

"An exciting idea," we said. "But how are we going to fund
these centers?" "From a capital fund of $1.2 million," Dick
said. "$1.2 million. Good God!" was the reaction.

Well then the miracle started happening. Andy Andrews, one
of the directors, said — "Why don't we go around the table
right now and see how much commitment we can get over the
next three years from the small group of directors at this
table?"

Would you believe we raised $120,000.00 - 10% of our goal -
within five minutes!

When we left that day a few of us agreed to write some
letters and make some phone calls. And what happened as
a result surpasses anything in my experience.

Remember those "dreamers" I talked about earlier? Well let
me tell you what happened with some of them.

Remember Leon Gorman of L. L. Bean? He's committed $15,000
over three years. And Len Carlson — another $15,000. And
Les Wunderman - $15,000. They're putting their money where
their dreams are.

The list goes on. "Dusty" Loo of Looart Press - a major
commitment. John Flieder of Allstate Insurance - "Count
us in." Kiplinger Washington Editors. The Kleid Company.
Jim Kobs of Kobs & Brady - "Absolutely!" Publishers
Clearing House. Grolier. Colonial Penn. Rodale Press.
Spiegel. American Express.

John Yeck of Yeck Brothers Group - "You can count on us."
Eddie Bauer. Rapp & Collins. Ogilvy & Mather. Alan Drey.
The DR Group. Hanover House. And on and on.

   To this moment, these people and some others we
   have contacted bring total commitments to
   $725,000. So we have reached 60% of our goal!

This is exciting in itself, but equally exciting is the
fact that we have two formal proposals from two major
universities detailing how a Chair would be established
for Direct Marketing. And the cost.

One proposal is from UMKC - University of Missouri, where
Martin Baier of Old American has taught Direct Marketing
classes for a number of years. The other proposal is from

Exhibit 1-3. Direct Mail Letter (continued)

-5-

New York University. Both universities are ready when we are.

So we are this close to bringing off a 20th Century miracle!

Now we come to you to ask you to share in this dream of dreams. There is a pledge card inside of the enclosed envelope. The amount suggested is just that. A suggestion. You are the best judge of what your company should pledge against the future.

I have asked for and have gotten approval to have your response come back to me personally. I'd like to hear from you even if there is some unforseen circumstance under which you cannot make a pledge.

We must decide very soon upon the first university to establish a Direct Marketing Center. Therefore I will appreciate it if you will reply within the next 10 days. Thank you so very much.

Sincerely,

Bob Stone

P.S. It is my fondest dream that you and I will be there to witness the commencement exercises of the first graduating class with a degree in Direct Marketing.

Exhibit 1-4. Pledge Card

"A Margin of Excellence"

THE DIRECT MAIL/MARKETING EDUCATIONAL FOUNDATION
CAPITAL FUND RAISING PROGRAM

Our organization wishes to participate in the DMMEF Capital Fund Raising Program. Our 3-YEAR PLEDGE is indicated to the right.

　　　　Mr. John Jones

Company　**Jones Manufacturing Co.**

　　　　1621 Main Street

Officer Name **Ottumwa, Iowa 52501**

_____
Address

_____
Signature

YOUR TAX DEDUCTIBLE GIFT WILL MAKE A DIFFERENCE

Contribution Category		Payment Schedule
☐ Leadership Gift $10,000 annually	$ _____	payable by Sept. 15, 1982
☐ Major Gift $5,000 annually	$ _____	payable by 1983
☐ Special Gift $2,500 annually	$ _____	payable by 1984
☑ Supporting Gift $1,000 annually		

Pledges are for three years only and are nonbinding commitments. Reminders will be mailed thirty days prior to the payment dates indicated above.

Exhibit 1-5. Completing the Package: The Personal Note

From the Desk of
Bob Stone

June 8

Fred —

I'm sure you've been too busy to get to the attached letter.

But the response has been so great that I'm confident I will get a favorable reply from you too.

Sure hope you will be participating.

Best Wishes,
Bob Stone

The Impact of Credit Cards

One of the major factors in increasing the scope of direct marketing has been the credit card, whether the medium through which credit is offered be direct mail, print, or broadcast. Offering charge privileges through travel and entertainment cards (American Express, Diners Club, and Carte Blanche) as well as through bank cards (VISA and Master-Card) has become commonplace.

In addition to travel-and-entertainment cards and bank cards, consider the fact that scores of retail stores offer their own credit cards. As of 1979 the Nilson Report estimated that there were 119 million oil company credit cards in circulation. Breakouts for travel-and-entertainment cards and bank cards are shown in Table 1-3. Charge card arrangements offer two advantages to the direct marketer: (1) the opportunity to sell bigger ticket items, and (2) freedom from credit problems. And the frosting on the cake is that when charge privileges are offered, the average catalog mail order is 20 percent larger than the average cash order.

Table 1-4 shows the results of a DMA survey regarding consumer vs. business charge orders. The DMA survey revealed the percentages of those who accept various charge cards:

- Consumer Marketers:
  - 97.88 percent accept Mastercard and VISA
  - 30.4 percent accept American Express in addition to MasterCard and VISA
  - 19.5 percent accept Diners Club and American Express in addition to MasterCard and VISA
  - 2.0 percent accept an Other card only
  - 2.0 percent accept an Other card in addition to MasterCard and VISA

- Business Marketers:
  - 33.3 percent accept MasterCard, VISA and American Express
  - 23.1 percent accept only MasterCard and VISA
  - 19.0 percent accept Diners, American Express plus MasterCard and VISA
  - 4.7 percent accept American Express only
  - 4.7 percent accept MasterCard and American Express only

Six Big Keys to Direct Marketing Success

The expanded scope of direct marketing begs the question, "What does make direct marketing successful?" An oversimplified answer might be: *offering the right products or services via the right media, with the most*

**Table 1-3. Number of Credit Cards in Circulation
in the United States, 1980-1981**

Credit Card	No. in Circulation
American Express	8,500,000
Carte Blanche	725,000
Diners Club	910,000
MasterCard	51,111,603
VISA	64,571,000

*enticing propositions, presented with the most effective formats, proved
successful as a result of the right tests.*

Sounds pretty simple. But, of course, it isn't! Let's explore the six
big keys to direct marketing success and some basic questions relating
to them.

1. *Right product or services.* Success in any endeavor starts with the
product. No matter what the selling medium, no business can long
survive unless the product is *right.* Time was when direct sale of
products via mail, space, or broadcast advertising was looked upon as a
means of "dumping" merchandise that did not sell well through retail
channels. Time was when off-brand merchandise, which couldn't get
shelf space in retail stores, was offered direct to the consumer. That's all
changed today. Successful direct marketers offer quality merchandise of
good value.

2. *Right media.* Some authorities give half or more of the credit for the
success of a mailing to the lists that are used. You can't prove the figure.
But you can bet on this: one of the most important keys to success is
lists! Likewise, selection of the publications used for print ads and the
stations used for broadcast are vital keys to success. (Chapters 5 through
10 cover each major medium in depth.)

3. *Right offer.* There is no key to success more important than the offer.
You can have the right product, the right mailing lists, the right print
and broadcast media. But you still won't make it big if you don't have
the right offer. You've got to overcome human inertia, whatever the
medium. (Chapter 3 covers 28 different offers designed to overcome
human inertia.)

4. *Right formats.* The number of formats for presenting offers is almost
endless. This is particularly true of direct mail, where there are few
restrictions on format. The marketer can use anything from a simple
post card to a 9 x 12 mailing package which could include a giant four-
color brochure, letter, giant order card, tokens, stamps, pop-ups, and so
on.

Table 1-4.

	Consumer	Business
Average Order Value	$58.43	$175.00
Median Order Value	30.00	120.00
Mode Order Value	30.00	$100 to $150.00
Order Value Range	$5 to $300.00	$12 to $900.00

Restrictions on print and broadcast advertising are, of course, more stringent, because of controls by the publishers and the stations. But the important point is that there is a *right* format for a given mailing package, a given ad, and a given commercial. Depending on format selected, the results can be anywhere from disastrous to sensational.

5. *Right tests.* With literally thousands of chances to do the wrong thing, the way to achieve direct marketing success is to test to determine the *right* thing. Indeed, direct marketing is the most *measurable* type of marketing there is.

Mailing packages can be tested scientifically to determine such vital factors as best offer, best format, best lists, best copy, best postage, and so on.

The print medium, with the advent of regional editions, has also made an endless variety of tests possible. Direct marketers now test by regions. They test for size and color. They test for position. They test bind-in cards, bingo cards. They test special against general interest magazines. Newspapers can be tested to learn all you have to know.

It is also possible to test the efficiency of broadcast on a control basis. Testing is likewise possible when the telephone is used as a selling medium. (Chapter 16 clearly spells out the techniques that enable you to test for the right answers.)

6. *Right analyses.* The final element essential to a successful direct marketing program is right analyses. Direct marketers live by figures, but misinterpretation of figures often leads to erroneous conclusions. Fortunes have been lost by counting *trial orders* instead of counting *paid-ups.* Fortunes have been lost by *averaging* response, by not really knowing break-even points, by never determining the value of a customer, by never preparing cash-flow charts.

Chapter 15 is devoted to applying the mathematics of direct marketing properly.

Checklist for Applying the Six Big Keys to Direct Marketing Success

1. The product or service you offer
  ☐ Is it a real value for the price asked?

☐ How does it stack up against competition?
☐ Do you have exclusive features?
☐ Does your packaging create a good first impression?
☐ Is the market broad enough to support a going organization?
☐ Is your product cost low enough to warrant a mail order markup?
☐ Does your product or service lend itself to repeat business?

2. The media you use
Customer lists
☐ Is your customer list cleaned on a regular basis?
☐ Do you keep a second copy of your list in a secure place to avoid loss?
☐ Have you developed a profile of your customer list, giving you all the important demographic characteristics?
☐ Have you coded your customer list by recency of purchase?
☐ Have you worked your customer list by the classic mail order formula: recency-frequency-monetary?
☐ Have you thought of what other products or services may appeal to your customer list?
☐ Do you mail your customer list often enough to capitalize on the investment?

Prospect lists
☐ Do you freely provide facts and figures to one or more competent mailing list brokers, enabling them to unearth productive lists for you?
☐ Have you worked with competent list compilers in selecting names of prospects who match the profile of those on your customer list?
☐ Do you test meaningful, measurable, projectable quantities?
☐ Have you measured the true results of prospect lists, computing for each list the number of inquiries, the quantity of returned goods, net cash receipts per thousand mailed, and repeat business?
☐ Have you determined how often you can successfully mail to the same prospect lists?

Print
☐ Have you matched your offers with your markets and used print publications with good direct response track records?
☐ Have you measured the true results of print media, computing for each newspaper or magazine the number of inquiries, the amount of returned goods, net cash receipts per insertion, and repeat business?
☐ Have you determined how often you can successfully use the same print media?

Broadcast

☐ Have you selected broadcast media that best fit your objective: (a) to get inquiries or orders; (b) to support other advertising media?

☐ Have you measured the true results of broadcast media, computing for each station the number of inquiries, the amount of returned goods, net cash receipts per broadcast schedule, and repeat business?

☐ Have you determined the proper times and frequency for broadcast schedules?

3. The offers you make

☐ Are you making the most enticing offers you can within the realm of good business?

☐ Does your offer lend itself to the use of any or all of these incentives for response: free gift, contest, free trial offer, installment terms, price savings, money back guarantee?

☐ Does your offer lend itself to the development of an "automatic" repeat business cycle?

☐ Does your offer lend itself to a "get-a-friend" program?

☐ Have you determined the ideal introductory period or quantity for your offer?

☐ Have you determined the ideal introductory price for your offer?

☐ Have you determined the possibility of multiple sales for your offer?

4. The formats you use

Direct mail

☐ Are your mailing packages in character with your product or services and the markets you are reaching?

☐ Have you developed the ideal format for your mailing packages, with particular emphasis on mailing envelope, letter, circular, response form, and reply envelope?

☐ Do you work with one or more creative envelope manufacturers?

☐ Are your sales letters in character with your offers?

☐ Are your circulars graphic, descriptive, and in tune with the complete mailing package?

☐ Does your response form contain the complete offer? Is it attractive enough to grab attention and impel action?

Print

☐ Are your ads in character with your product and services and the markets you are reaching?

☐ Have you explored newspaper inserts, magazine inserts, bind-in cards, tip-on cards, Dutch door newspaper inserts, plastic records?

Broadcast
- ☐ Are your commercials in character with your products and services and the markets you are reaching?
- ☐ Have you determined the efficiency of stand-up announcer commercials vs. staged commercials?
- ☐ Have you explored the efficiency of noted personality endorsements?

5. The tests you make
- ☐ Do you consistently test the big things: product, media, offers, and formats?
- ☐ Have you tested to determine the best timing for your offers, the best frequency?
- ☐ Have you determined the most responsive geographical areas?
- ☐ Do you consistently test new direct mail packages against control packages, new ads against control ads, new commercials against control commercials?
- ☐ Do you use adequate test quantities?
- ☐ Do you follow your test figures through to conclusion, using net revenue per thousand as the key criterion?
- ☐ Do you interpret your test figures in the light of the effect on the image and future profits of your company?

6. The right analyses
- ☐ Do you track results by source, computing front-end response, returned goods factors, and bad debt factor for each source?
- ☐ Do you analyze results by ZIP codes, by demographics?
- ☐ Do you compute the level of repeat business by original source?

Ten Major Responsibilities

The world of direct marketing is a big world, an exciting world, an awesome world for those who have never operated within it. And the scope keeps expanding.

As more and more major corporations and agencies enter direct marketing (and they are doing so at a rapidly accelerating rate), it is becoming clear that those who are succeeding are doing so by setting up direct marketing separate and apart from other marketing and advertising functions.

It is safe to predict that in the next decade all major corporations and agencies will have staffs of direct marketing experts. Following is a detailed list of the 10 major responsibilities of the direct marketing executive—a total of 78 individual functions.

Exhibit 1-6
Direct
Marketing
Evaluations
and Functions
Checklist.

1. Product selection and
   development
   Market potential
   Competition
   Reliability of sources
   Value comparison
   Packaging
   Shipping costs
   Unit of sale
   Profit margin
   Ease of use
   Instructions
   Refurbishing costs
   Repeat potential
   Evaluation of syndication

2. Strategic planning
   Establishing objectives
   Developing planning models
   Doing business planning
   Developing strategies
   Implementation of
   strategies

3. Markets and media selection
   Mailing lists
   Magazines
   Newspapers and
   supplements
   Radio and television
   Co-ops
   Telemarketing
   Car cards, match books, etc.

4. Creative development and
   scheduling
   Strategy and concept
   Offers
   Copy
   Layouts
   Formats
   FTC regulations
   Scheduling of ads and
   mailing packages

5. Research
   Exploratory research
   Pre-testing
   Evaluative research
   Qualitative research
   Quantitative research
   Focus groups
   Survey research

6. Testing procedures
   Compiled vs. direct response lists
   Regional testing
   Testing by ZIP codes
   Testing by socioeconomic factors
   Seasonal testing
   Price testing
   Offer testing
   Establishing control ads and
   control mailing packages
   Determining media duplication
   Using probability scales
   Preevaluation of ads and mailing
   packages
   Measuring readership

7. Fulfillment
   Shipping facilities
   Replacement procedures
   Returned goods procedures
   Distribution centers
   Shipping method (carriers)

8. Budgeting and accounting
   Cash flow charts
   Bad debt reserves
   Financing costs
   Attrition scales
   Forms and systems
   Commercial credit card
   affiliations
   Credit and collection procedures
   Recency, frequency, and monetary
   criteria

9. Customer service
   Sales correspondence
   Complaints and adjustments
   Activation and reactivation

10. Personnel and supplier relations
    Advertising department
    Fulfillment sources
    Accounting department
    Customer service
    Advertising agency
    List brokers
    Space reps
    Suppliers of merchandise and
    services
    Printers, engravers, and
    typesetters
    Artists and art studios
    Envelope houses

Self-quiz

1. Define direct marketing.

_____

_____

_____

_____

2. What are the three distinguishing marks of a direct response ad?

a. _____

b. _____

c. _____

3. Name the two leading media in the total media mix for direct response advertising.

a. _____

b. _____

4. Name two unique attributes of direct mail as contrasted to print and broadcast media.

a. _____

b. _____

5. Name the five major credit cards widely offered by direct marketers.

a. _____   d. _____

b. _____   e. _____

c. _____

6. What are the six big keys to direct marketing success?

a. _____   d. _____

b. _____   e. _____

c. _____   f. _____

7. What are the 10 major responsibilities of direct marketing executives?

a. _____   f. _____

b. _____   g. _____

c. _____   h. _____

d. _____   i. _____

e. _____   j. _____

Pilot Project

You have been given the chore of developing a direct response ad for your company. The objective of the ad is to get qualified leads for your sales force who sell roofing to home owners.

Applying the three distinguishing marks of a direct response ad, outline your answers to these three questions:

1. What will your offer be?
2. What information will you include in your ad?
3. What means of response will you provide?

Chapter Two

Strategic Business Planning

With the new professionalism that has come to direct marketing the discipline is being treated more and more as a "business." And with this new viewpoint the need for strategic business planning has emerged. Major traditional marketers who have established direct marketing units as separate profit centers have insisted upon strategic business planning for these centers just as they do for their traditional operations. But strategic business planning is quite foreign to those who have built businesses based solely upon direct marketing methods. Yet the rewards that can come from strategic business planning can be as great proportionately for the entrepreneur as for the giant corporation.

When facing the reality that large- and medium-size companies have been the stimulus for recent growth, it behooves today's direct marketer to take heed to the signals and make sure that their approaches are as contemporary as their potential targets. Since accountability is one of the key elements in direct marketing programs, it is necessary for us to ensure that we remain on track with our own marketing plans, up to date with the emerging technologies, and, finally, with optimizing our own organization's resources.

Strategic Business Planning Defined

First of all, let's define our terms. *Strategic business planning* is a formal method to consider alternatives related to the growth, development or other options of an enterprise, organization, or business. It has application for large and small companies in direct marketing, ranging from fund raising to lead generation to product sales. When properly developed, a strategic business plan should provide:

- A comprehensive review of the current business
- A description of the problems and opportunities that must be dealt with in the short term
- Clear direction
- A practical action plan

A strategic business plan is *not* a marketing plan. It is much broader in scope, but it does address marketing issues related to a business or company. A well-designed plan will permit much greater control over one's business, enabling the individual to deal with critical situations in a proactive rather than a reactive manner.

Direct marketers have countered the strategic planning issue with a number of comments such as:

- "It's expensive and time-consuming."
- "My plan is based on past experience and current expectations."
- "We don't have the availability of talent in our organization to make planning work."

These comments seem quite valid, especially for smaller firms. Many are hard pressed to look out further than three months at a time. However, when the following questions are asked, companies of all sizes are likely to agree on the impact:

- Has your company felt the impact of new or revised federal regulations over the past few years?
- Is the current economic environment having an impact on profitability?
- Are sales increasing at the rate you forecasted?
- Are you comfortable with your organization's ability to adapt to change?

These questions, and many more like them, apply to virtually every business endeavor. Managing these responses and affiliated actions are the key to success in direct marketing today.

How to Develop a Plan

After disposing of the questions on what strategic business planning entails and how it applies to direct marketers, the next step is how to develop a plan and what should be included. Let's agree on one more fact. There are countless methods used for developing strategic business plans. They range from the efforts of a single, specially trained planning executive to extensive committee approaches. The range of the information developed is equally broad. A plan in some industries may dictate a company's action for a 10-year period, whereas in other cases, it may suggest very specific actions for a 12-month period. Depending upon the purpose and expectations, any approach may benefit an organization.

There does not seem to be any evidence that better results are achieved through any one methodology. However, for direct marketers, I feel that a more simplified and practical approach will yield the most actionable information. Further, while it would be nice to be able to project, with infinite wisdom, what will happen to our industry and organization or company over the next five years, it is next to impossible. Just review recent growth, technological change, and new applications of direct marketing and you will understand the difficulty of accurate long term planning. Also, the array of information to be included in a strategic business plan should be subject to the criteria of what is absolutely necessary, rather than what you would like to include. The simpler the plan and the process for developing it, the higher the likelihood of success.

To provide a clearer understanding of a business plan, look at the planning model in Exhibit 2-1. It has proven successful with a number of direct marketing operations. Initial examination of the model suggests a planning time span of three years. However, the meat of the plan is in the annual action plan that covers a 12-month time frame. As stated, a 12-month planning horizon seems to provide more than enough opportunity to manage change.

Let's examine each of the components of the model in more detail.

Exhibit 2-1. A Model for Strategic Business Planning

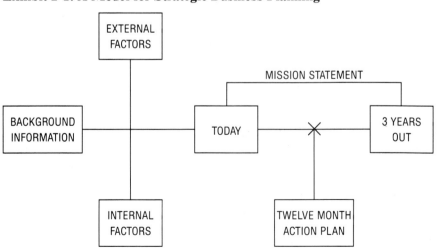

Background
Information

In order to develop a strategic business plan, it is necessary to carefully and thoroughly investigate a company's performance. In effect, you are trying to take a "snapshot" of activities covering the current situation and extending back two or three years. As this is performed, you can separate data into two categories: (a.) Financial and Marketing/Sales and (b.) Organizational Data.

In the first case, you are looking for the following types of information:

- Growth
- Market share
- Expenditures in specific categories
- Seasonality of sales
- Profit levels
- Product/service line
- Financial resources
- Allocation of resources
- How you rate against your competition

In the second case, you must review how the organization and staff conduct the business. You must determine how the organization works rather than how it looks on the formal organization chart. You must get a "fix" on the company's personality.

For example, is the good work being accomplished on a daily basis spread evenly across the staff or is it really accomplished by a core of dedicated people. Or, do the key employees understand what the business is trying to accomplish, rather than just reporting the "party line." This case is every bit as important as knowing the financial operations of the business. However, it is the one most often overlooked in business planning.

After collecting the raw data on business, marketing and organizational issues, we are ready to proceed to the next step in the model.

External
Factors

Simply stated, *external factors*, sometimes referred to as exogenous factors, are all of those activities and actions that have an impact on your business, but are out of your immediate control. You might quickly say, "If we cannot exert any control over these factors, why include them at all?" The answer to that is twofold: positioning and contingency.

Examples of external factors are:

- Current economy
- Federal regulation
- Competition
- Availability of resources

- Postal rates
- Technology
- and countless others

If we examine one external factor, you will get a clearer understanding of why it is important to determine what they are and how they impact your business:

The current economy. We certainly cannot control this complex and far-reaching situation. However, consider for a moment the action we can take to optimize our position. To name just a few, we can:

- Better manage cash flow
- Reduce inventory
- Tighten receivables

As you can see, we have been able to reduce some of the impact of this external factor on our business.

When developing a list of external factors, two considerations are important:

1. Limit the list to the most important factors only. For many companies, 10 or less. There is nothing more frustrating or less rewarding than considering all of the perils outside of your control and never getting to the major issues that affect your firm directly.

2. As you discuss and decide on each major external factor, be specific in defining what impact it has on your business. If this is impossible, discard the factor.

After looking outside your company or business and sifting through the relevant information, it is time to move to the next phase of plan development.

Internal Factors   Internal factors are those you do have control of and influence over. Such factors are probably best described as the strengths and weaknesses of your company. The identification of strengths and weaknesses are often referred to as the "building blocks" of a sound strategic business plan. Experience has indicated it is easier and more productive to start with the positive aspects—therefore the strengths.

Basically stated, they include those activities that you consistently complete extremely well—the things that give you an edge on your competition. They can include, but are not limited to:

- Technology
- Product
- Marketing
- Process
- Service
- Systems

- People
- Organization
- Attitude
- Flexibility
- Management
- Communication
- Leadership

For example, in direct marketing, a company might refer to its preeminence in product development, production innovations, back-end service and performance, etc. All of these are significant attributes and must be defined. This will allow for leveraging real strengths against stated goals. One note of caution. Make sure your description of a strength is accurate. Oftentimes the definition of these considerations is completed in a cavalier manner, and what is described by some as being a strength turns out to be of less value than previously reported.

The next move in the development of internal factors is defining weaknesses. Actually, this is the toughest part in developing a strategic business plan. However, this part of the inspection will yield the greatest return. It is difficult to elaborate on the shortfalls of a business. In this case, we are often getting at sub-par performance levels. How many executives really want to define what's wrong with the operation, the staff, or even their direction of them? Weaknesses can be described as what a company does poorly and can include the following:

- Technology
- Product
- Marketing
- Process
- Service
- Systems

- People
- Organization
- Attitude
- Flexibility
- Management
- Communication
- Leadership

A comprehensive review of internal factors will provide an accurate picture of the company as it is today. More often than not, when completed objectively, it is quite revealing. In content alone, it can include a number of documents and summary sheets. Gathering the data is only one step. The next is to condense it into an accurate, readable document. And that brings us to the next component of the planning model.

**Mission
Statement**

The *mission statement* is a condensation of what the company is today and what we want (expect) it to be tomorrow. Let's separate the mission statement into those parts and describe each individually.

Mission Statement—Today The purpose of this statement is to accurately define in business shorthand the position of the company as it now exists. It is derived from the microscopic review discussed earlier. It usually is restructured in length to one or two typewritten pages. If it is honest, it will probably sound somewhat pessimistic. But that's okay. Actually, more often than not, where the company is today is not where it wants to be tomorrow.

Let's take a look at a mission statement. After considerable discussion, one direct marketing company, which for the sake of this discussion we'll call Leisure Time Activities, developed this statement of where they are today:

LEISURE TIME ACTIVITIES Today—1983

Today we are an established mail order company operating in the U.S. and Canada with a preeminent niche in the leisure activities market. In 1982, we had sales of $17 million and an embarrassing shortfall of $1.5 million in profits. Our recent growth has been sluggish and has not met our expectations. We have limited information on the market, but we do know we have a dominant share of the hobby segment. We have not extended this strength into the larger market of sporting goods.

The competition is intensifying especially for sporting goods. Major companies have an edge and they are expanding the market. This is all taking place in a market where there is little current product innovation. We feel technological change is coming, but don't know when. As a company, we have moved from a leadership position to a company that follows.

Although we have good products and a good customer base, we have become complacent. We have not leveraged our small size and financial strength to the best advantage. Our marketing approach is lackluster. We have experienced a breakdown in leadership, management and communications. This has confused our direction and has had a negative impact on company spirit and teamwork; and as a result, we have had a breakdown in company performance in several areas.

Although we perceive our company and organization to be in a growth mode, we have not taken effective actions to make it happen. We have discussed an appetite for change and have developed a consensus on the major issues that must be resolved.

In summary, we are at a turning point. We must leverage our good name and products which have enabled us to become a major force in this industry, develop innovative marketing plans and move in one direction, collectively.

Mission Statement—Tomorrow The purpose of this statement is to define reasonable goals to be achieved within a specific period. The length of time to cover for this type of statement varies. A three-year period for goal setting is often an agreeable compromise.

But let's take a look at Leisure Time Activities again—where do they see themselves in three years?

LEISURE TIME ACTIVITIES—Three Years Out

By the end of 1985 we will be recognized as an aggressive, multi-line direct marketing company. We will have demonstrated state-of-the-art marketing programs, a collective winning attitude and financial results in line with written plans. We will have a sales volume of $20 million with a minimum of 25% R.O.I. And will generate a profit on sales of 10%.

Our growth will be carefully planned. We will have expanded our capabilities and increased our share of the sporting goods market. Our product lines will include but not be limited to, equipment and supplies, clothing, related gift items and tend to have more proprietary products.

Our management has become a cohesive team which is directing a qualified, experienced and motivated staff. This collective effort has provided a competitive edge and the flexibility to use our strengths in the best possible way.

Our financial performance has enabled the company to easily secure capital for further investment opportunities.

In summary, we have turned Leisure Time Activities around. This has been recognized by our stockholders, our employees and the industry. We have replaced our former complacency with a demonstrated winning attitude.

If you manage to plan correctly, you will revisit these goals on an annual basis to make sure you remain on track and that changing conditions are updated. Remember, a plan is not a document that is put on the shelf and dusted off each December. In developing this section of the mission statement, you may wish to include:

- Sales/Income
- Markets
- Technology

- Organization/Size
- New Products
- Position in Market

The checklist in Exhibit 2-2 is provided to assist in structuring your mission statement.

You are now at a critical point in the planning model—you have developed:

What You Are Today ⟵⟶ What You Want To Be In Three Years

The next step is to deal with the "gaps" in the mission statement. The differences between your strengths/weaknesses now and your expected position in three years.

Action Plans

The fundamental output from any good strategic business plan is the identification of those actions or activities that must be accomplished in order to reach your intended position. These actions or activities

Exhibit 2-2. Mission Statement

General Information	Today	Three Years Out
Volume		
Profit		
Growth		
Market Position		
External Factors		
Competition		
Industry Factors		
Geography		
Internal Factors		
Strengths		
Weaknesses		
Product		
Summary		

spring forth from your examination of internal and external factors and are summarized in the today section of the mission statement.

The question is, how do you prepare an action plan that guarantees progress against your stated goals? There may be several ways to develop this kind of plan. However, there are a few fundamentals to success:

- Top management endorsement
- Clearly stated tasks
- Complete understanding by those who must implement the plan
- Realistic and attainable actions

If the above criteria can be met, the likelihood of success is greatly increased. Now, let's move on to the development of an action plan. An action plan defines the "must-do" tasks for completion, usually over a 12-month period. These are the problems or opportunities that must be handled in order to achieve planning goals. They must be specific and precisely worded to ensure that those responsible for achievement have a clear understanding of the tasks to be accomplished. Participants must know *what* is to be accomplished, *how* it will be accomplished, by *whom*, and *within what time frame*. Anything short of these conditions will negatively impact performance against the plan.

There are some guidelines for developing objectives and strategies that detail the action plan. Let's start out the right way and clearly define what we mean when using the following terms:

- *Objective*. A statement that accurately describes *"what"* is to be accomplished over the next 12 months. In almost all cases, it is a must-do task.
- *Strategies*. A listing of methods, events, etc., that describe *"how"* an objective will be achieved. Completed strategies always list who is responsible, for what, and when.

To simplify the discussion, let's divide it into two parts:

- How to develop good objectives
- How to develop effective strategies

How to Develop Good Objectives

The very first step in moving toward the development of action plan objectives is to review any notes developed during the strength and weakness identification. Determine the problems, not the symptoms. After this is completed, review the problems and define them as clearly as possible. It is necessary at this stage to move from the general to the specific. It is easier to reduce a general concept by listing all situations or actions relating to the problem prior to specifically pinpointing it. Perhaps the following example will make this clearer.

Example 1 Let's take a look at the Leisure Time Activities company again. In the general area, one of the problems is the need to increase profits.

"A definite need to increase profit"

If we dig deeper, we can expand this area to include:

1. We need a 10 percent profit on all sales made in 1983-84.
2. We must improve our marketing approach.
3. We must regain our leadership position.
4. We lack specific controls—financial, purchasing, inventory, marketing programs.
5. We need to develop systems to accurately project our financial future.
6. We need a minimum of 25 percent R.O.I.

While all of the above comments are valid, they do not relate directly to the same specific problem: (1) gets at the heart of the problem—how much and when. It further describes the scope of what is to be done. The others, steps (2)-(6), may either be strategies (how to do it) or may be related to another problem.

It is necessary to use this process for all problem areas so that accurate descriptions of the problems are developed.

The next step is to take the refined list for each problem and write an objective. As this is completed, consider whether the problem or task is realistic and achievable. If you should feel that nothing can practically be done in a given situation, why continue working on it? While this situation doesn't happen very often, it should be acknowledged. Let's assume that the problem can be dealt with. You must now put it in a clear statement that describes what is to be accomplished. We have found that there are three integral parts in defining problems. They are:

1. A clear, concise statement of the *task*
2. The *purpose* for completing the task
3. Reasonable *time* measurement(s)

Further, we have found that when these factors are included, the probability of successful completion is greatly increased.

The outline method seems to be the easiest approach in applying the factors. Here's an example:

Task	**Purpose**	**Time**
What do we want to do?	Why are we doing it?	When do we want it completed or what interim time checks should we use?

Going back to an earlier situation, we can develop an objective that meets the criteria. (For sake of discussion, we have stated the real problem as the need to increase profits through planning.)

Task	**Purpose**	**Time**
• Achieve a sales volume of $20MM with a minimum 25% ROI	• To increase profits	• Within next 12 months
	• Regain leadership position	• By December 1985
• Develop short and long term plans		• Monitor progress quarterly

Using this information, we can develop an objective statement that clearly reflects our intention:

<u>By December, 1985</u>   we must develop short and long term plans
      TIME   TASK

<u>to achieve a sales volume of $20MM with a minimum 25% R.O.I.</u>
                          PURPOSE

<u>and retain a leadership position</u> in our market. Progress on this

will be <u>formally monitored on a monthly basis.</u>
                ADDITIONAL MEASUREMENTS

At this point you may ask the question—is all this really necessary? The best answer is simply this: if you do not take the time to clearly select and write the plan objectives, not much will happen. One other example might help.

Example 2. Leisure Time Activities found that after a comprehensive assessment, there were a number of internal problems related to morale and communications. As they focused on the problem, it seemed that improved communications would really clear up the situation. They then developed this objective:

"We must improve company internal communications."

From this point, they further identified five strategies that would be necessary to achieve the objective. After additional discussion, they felt that even if all of the strategies were implemented, they would only, at best, achieve a partial solution to the problem. In re-analyzing the objective, they found some critical flaws as listed below:

1. Only part of the task was identified.
2. The purpose of the action was not specified.
3. There were no time measurements or checkpoints.

They went back to discuss the objectives. The following revision makes the point quite well:

> Within six months, we will improve the interchange of information and ideas throughout the company about plans and activities affecting operations and policies, in order to encourage feedback and involvement of all employees.

You will notice when we move into strategy development that a clear objective reduces the difficulty of strategy selection.

How to
Develop
Effective
Strategies

Now that you know what must be done, we will discuss approaches and methods to describe *how* it should be done. Strategies are events, methods, etc., that crisply define the kinds of actions that should be taken to solve a problem; i.e., complete an objective. If an objective has been clearly written, the strategies are easily developed.

One way to look at strategies is to think of an action plan. What kind of actions should you take to rectify this problem or improve a given situation. At this point, you are not trying to get down to details. Rather, you are looking for a logical sequence of activity that will outline actions for the next 12 months or so. By the way, some strategies may extend beyond a 12-month period. To get a better fix, let's continue with the objective just discussed in Example 2:

> Within six months, we will improve the interchange of information and ideas throughout the company about plans and activities affecting operations and policies, in order to encourage feedback and involvement of all employees.

While this objective may be typical of any number of companies, the methods used to achieve it may vary considerably. A group must consider all of the problems, resources, and other considerations. Let's list some facts that seem apparent:

1. We know when we want to accomplish it.
2. We know the type of communication we want to disseminate (plans and activities).
3. We know what areas it will affect (operations and policies).
4. We know we need to encourage feedback and involvement.

What seems to emerge is that Leisure Time Activities needs to improve interchange of information on a companywide basis. They now know what they want to do and need to develop how they are going to do it. In discussing the matter further, they came up with the following action recommendations:

- Set up a departmental activities program
- Set up an Operations Improvement Committee to answer questions and get employee feedback
- Provide a forum for departmental information interchange
- Meet informally with employees
- Deliver a "State of the Company" message
- Provide feedback on progress of plans and activities

These were refined and expanded as shown in Exhibit 2-3.

As you can see, the group went from the general to the specific. When approaching it in this manner, you can see where the plan stands at all times. This company turned a normal problem into a reasonable and practical opportunity.

How to Manage the Plan

Once a strategic business plan is written, there is a tendency to forget about it and to return to the normal everyday grind. This happens in spite of the fact that the objectives that were developed during the process were *must-do* tasks. To assure that must-do tasks are acted upon and to make certain the plan functions as a road map, proceed as follows:

1. Set up a small planning coordination function (1-2 people). This function is responsible for managing the plan from the meeting to back on the job. The function should:
   A. Coordinate with each person responsible for an objective and make sure their assigned objective is in final form with realistic due dates, strategy assignments, etc. (During the planning meeting, appoint one or two people to be responsible for each objective developed.)
   B. Consolidate all objectives and review background data (developed in the meeting).

C. Submit it for management approval.
D. Develop a short typewritten overview of the planning meeting which describes the highlights of the plan (no confidential information) for all employees. After the management's approval, this should be discussed with all employees as appropriate.
E. Stay on top of the plan. The coordination group should establish a practical method to evaluate progress against strategies. This should be put into a two-page report and presented to Management on a quarterly basis.

Exhibit 2-3. Executing Strategies

Strategies	Responsibility	Due Date
1. Company orientation to department activities: set up program and schedule	Personnel & Div. Managers	Monthly
2. Operations Improvement Committee to be set up to answer questions and obtain feedback from employees.	A representative from each department	5/15
3. Management Committee will be the forum for interchange of departmental information and in turn inform their department and get feedback.	Management Committee	3/23
4. "State of the Company" message —Where we are, how we are doing, etc.	President	4/1 and Annual
5. Informal meeting of all employees.	Executive Committee	6/1 and 12/1 and Semi-Annual
6. Memo from Executive Committee to employees on how we are doing.	Executive Committee	Monthly
7. Staff luncheons with informal meetings—opportunity for employees to ask questions.	Management Committee	When necessary
8. New employee orientation.	Personnel & department peer level	5/1
9. Social/Athletic activities a. set up program b. schedule an "activity day."	Personnel Personnel Management Committee	5/1 4/15

2. There are a number of other practical approaches which can be utilized. These range from getting lower level organizational participation on strategies to individual departmental plans.

In summary, strategic business planning is a management tool that enables an organization to focus on problems and opportunities, on current position and future direction, and, finally, on what to do about it. Participating in the development of a strategic business plan is only one phase. Making it work is another.

Self-quiz

1. Define strategic business planning.

_____

_____

_____

_____

2. What are the two types of data required for background information pertinent to developing a strategic business plan?

a. _____

b. _____

3. List six external factors that can have an impact on a direct marketing operation, but can not be directly controlled.

a. _____   d. _____

b. _____   e. _____

c. _____   f. _____

4. List six internal factors over which a direct marketing operation can exercise control.

a. _____   d. _____

b. _____   e. _____

c. _____   f. _____

5. Define a mission statement.

_____

_____

_____

_____

6. What are the four fundamentals to making an action plan work?

a. _____

b. _____

c. _____

d. _____

7. Define an objective as it relates to a business plan.

_____

_____

_____

_____

8. Define a strategy as it relates to a business plan.

_____

_____

_____

_____

9. In moving toward the development of action plan objectives one should determine the _____, not the

_____.

10. What are the three integral parts involved in defining a problem?

a. _____

b. _____

c. _____

Pilot Project

PROBLEM: Your company has had a mail order catalog for three years that offers ladies apparel, home furnishings, and gift items. You are no match for competitors like Horchow, Neiman-Marcus, and Sakowitz. Your resources, both personnel and financial, are limited. It is obvious that you are fighting a losing battle as you are now positioned.

OBJECTIVE: Your objective is to change direction and establish a clearly defined niche in the marketplace, changing your merchandise mix to items not generally available from your competition.

YOUR
ASSIGNMENT: It is your assignment to develop strategies and an action plan that will reposition your catalog in the marketplace over the next 12 months. (Among the strategies you might consider are: positioning your catalog as *the source* for apparel, home furnishings and gifts for the career woman, or positioning your catalog as *the source* for apparel and gift items for those engaged in outdoor activities.)

Chapter Three

Importance of the Offer

We said at the outset of this book that if an ad, TV or radio commercial, or direct mail piece doesn't have an offer, then it's not direct marketing. The propositions you make to customers—more often referred to as *offers*—can mean the difference between success or failure. Depending on the offer, differences in response of 25, 50, 100 percent, and more are commonplace.

Not only is the offer you make the key to success or failure, but the manner in which an offer is presented can have an equally dramatic effect. For example, here are three ways to state the same offer:

1. Half price!
2. Buy one—get one *free!*
3. 50% off!

Each statement conveys the same offer, but statement number 2 pulled 40 percent better than statement number 1 or number 3. Consumers perceived statement number 2 to be the most attractive offer.

Offers With Multiple Appeals

Exhibit 3-1 illustrates what appears to be a very innocent order card. But the multiple appeals used are certain to have a strong effect on front-end response. And the "conditions" for accepting are certain to have an immediate and long-term effect on how well the publisher does both front-end and back-end.

Let's examine the appeals and conditions. "Please send me, free, the Premier issue of GEO." That's strong: You can't beat the appeal of something free. But note the slight condition ". . . and reserve a money-saving Charter Subscription in my name."

The first appeal is followed by another appeal and a condition: "At the end of thirty days, if I have not instructed you to cancel my reservation, you may enter my subscription at the Charter Rate of $36 for one year (12 more monthly issues)—a savings of $12 off the annual cover price of $4 per issue."

So the *basic* offer breaks out like this: First issue free (appeal); right to cancel at the end of 30 days (appeal); enter 12-month subscription at $36 unless instructed otherwise (condition); save $12 off the annual cover price (appeal).

But the offer doesn't end there. "As a Charter Subscriber, I am entitled to renew annually at savings of 25% off the newsstand price." (Appeal.) "Please bill me automatically each year." (Condition.) "If at any time, for any reason, I elect to cancel my subscription, I will receive a full refund on all unmailed issues. The Premier issue is mine to keep in any case." (Appeal.)

Finally, "In addition, when I pay for my Charter Subscription, as a special gift I will receive a limited-edition copy of the GEO Premier

Exhibit 3-1. Offer with Multiple Appeals and Conditions.

GEO

FREE PREMIER ISSUE / CHARTER SUBSCRIPTION RESERVATION

Please send me, free, the Premier Issue of GEO, and reserve a money-saving Charter Subscription in my name. At the end of thirty days, if I have not instructed you to cancel my reservation, you may enter my subscription at the Charter Rate of $36 for one year (12 more monthly issues)—a savings of $12 off the annual cover price of $4 per issue.

As a Charter Subscriber, I am entitled to renew annually at savings of 25% off the newsstand price. Please bill me automatically each year. If at any time, for any reason, I elect to cancel my subscription, I will receive a full refund on all un-mailed issues. The Premier Issue is mine to keep in any case.

In addition, when I pay for my Charter Subscription, as a special gift I will receive a limited-edition copy of the GEO Premier Issue Cover Poster.

00507

Please make any necessary corrections in your name or address. Return this reservation form in the postage-paid reply envelope enclosed.

MR ROBERT STONE

H-PF-R   P.O.BOX 2552, BOULDER, COLORADO 80322

Issue Cover Poster." (Both a condition and an appeal.) In total, a brilliantly conceived and well thought through offer.

The Effects

This offer, one of many tested by *Geo* in the introduction of its international magazine, can have a tremendous effect on immediate and long-term results.

Geo and its agency know that offering the premier issue free will almost certainly bring a greater response than "tighter" offers that don't allow for cancellation after the first issue. But it also knows that, historically, its "loose" offer can result in cancellations as high as 65 percent. So, to be determined is whether the superb quality of its magazine will overcome the historically poor conversion rate of this type of offer.

Guaranteeing in perpetuity a renewal rate of 25 percent off the newsstand price is a "safe" offer in that it is a more or less standard discount for the publishing industry. I don't see any long-term problems with that offer.

But—"Please bill me automatically each year"—could be a problem, or a bonanza. This condition allows *Geo* to bill automatically without employing a renewal series, often six to eight efforts. Yet to be determined, however, is whether (a) the cancellation rate will be the same, better or worse than when a renewal series is used and (b) whether the pay-ups will be the same, better or worse than when a renewal series is used.

The sign-off offer—"In addition, when I pay for my Charter Subscription, as a special gift I will receive a limited-edition copy of the Premier issue Cover Poster"—is smartly conceived. It is clear recognition on the part of *Geo* and its agency that not only do "loose" offers like this one historically result in a low conversion rate, but that pay-ups for those who don't cancel tend to be lower than for "tighter" offers. To be learned is whether the lure of the free cover poster upon payment will hype the conversion rate and the payment rate.

So this "innocent" offer is loaded with immediate and long-term implications. And so it is with all direct response offers. That's why no direct response person worth his salt would consider starting creative until offers are clearly thought through.

Factors to Consider

Basically, there are 10 factors to consider when creating an offer.

1. *Price.* This is a toughie. Does the price you settle upon allow for a sufficient markup? If you have competition, is the price competitive? Is the price you settle upon perceived by the consumer to be the right price for the value received?

If you want to sell your item for $7.95 each, how about two for $15.90 (same price, but you get twice the average sale)? How about selling the first for $11.95 and the second for $3.95 (same total dollars if you sell two units—and if you don't sell two units you get a higher price for a single unit)?

Pricing. There's nothing more important. Testing to determine the best price is vital to maximizing long-term payoff.

2. *Shipping and handling.* Where applicable (and it's usually not applicable when selling a publication or service), shipping and handling charges can be an important factor in pricing. It's important to know how much you can add to a base price without adversely affecting sales.

Many merchandisers follow a rule of thumb that shipping and handling charges should not exceed 10 percent of the basic selling price. But again, testing is advisable.

3. *Unit of sale.* Will your product or service be offered "each?" "Two for?" "Set of X?" Obviously, the more units you can move per sale, the better off you are likely to be. BUT—if your prime objective is to build a large customer list fast, would you be better off to offer single units if you got twice the response over a "two for" offer?

In the case of *Geo,* suppose it had offered six months for $18? Would it be better off long term?

4. *Optional features.* Optional features include such things as special colors, outsizes, special binding for books, personalization.

Optional features often increase the average order. For example, when the publisher of a dictionary offered thumb indexing at $2 extra, 25 percent of total purchasers opted for this added feature.

5. *Future obligation.* Subscribers to *Geo,* returning the illustrated order card, have agreed to automatic billing, if they don't elect to cancel.

More common are book and record offers that commit the purchaser to future obligation. ("Take 10 records for $1 and agree to buy six more in the coming 12 months.") A continuity program offer might state: "Get volume one free—others will be sent at regular intervals."

Future obligation offers, when successful, enable the marketer to "pay" a substantial price for the first order, knowing there will be a long-term payout.

6. *Credit options.* Many marketers feel a major factor in the direct marketing explosion during the past decade has been the proliferation of credit cards. It's rare today to receive a catalog that does not contain one or more of these credit options: "Charge to American Express, Diners Club, Carte Blanche, VISA, MasterCard." It pays: The average order is usually 15 percent or more larger than a cash order.

Offer Credit

Some major direct marketers offer credit for 30 days (*Geo* is doing this), others offer installment credit with interest added (oil companies are a good example). Whether it be commercial credit cards or house credit, history says credit options increase revenue.

7. *Incentives.* Incentives include free gifts, discounts, and sweepstakes. (*Geo* offered two incentives, the premier issue free with a conditional subscription and a free poster upon payment.)

Toll-free ordering privilege is likewise an incentive—ease of ordering. Not unlike credit options, toll-free ordering privileges tend to increase the average order 15 percent and more.

But incentives must be tested front-end and back-end. Are people "buying" the free gift or sweeps? Will they be as good repeat customers as those who bought in the first instance without incentive?

8. *Time limits.* Time limits add urgency to an offer. (*Geo,* for example, could have applied a time limit to its charter offer—with good logic.)

One word of caution: If you establish a time limit, stick to it!

9. *Quantity limits.* One of the major proponents of quantity limits is the collectibles field. ("Only 5,000 will be minted. Then the molds will be destroyed.") There is something in the human psyche that says, "If it's in short supply, I want it!" Even "Limit—two to a customer" often outperforms no limit.

But, if you set a limit, stick to it.

10. *Guarantees.* Of the 10 factors to be considered in structuring an offer, there is one which should never be passed up—*the guarantee. Geo* has two guarantees: Cancel the subscription if not pleased with the free Premier issue and "if at any time, for any reason, I elect to cancel my subscription, I will receive a full refund on all unmailed issues."

Hundreds of millions of people have ordered by phone or mail over the decades with the assurance their satisfaction is guaranteed. Don't make an offer without a guarantee!

Nothing should happen in the creative process until you have structured an offer, or offers, which will make the creative process work. But let's remember this—what you offer is what you live with!

Checklist of Basic Offers

The following checklist briefly describes 28 basic offers that may be used singly or in various combinations, depending on the marketer's objectives. Variations on some of these basic offers are illustrated in Exhibits 3-2 through 3-6.

1. *Free information.* This is often the most effective offer, particularly when getting leads for salespeople is the prime objective or nonprospects must be screened out at low cost before expensive literature is sent to prime prospects.

2. *Samples.* A sample of a product or service is often a very effective sales tool. If a sample can be enclosed in a mailing package, results often more than warrant the extra cost. Consideration should be given to charging a nominal price for a sample. The recipient's investment in a sample promotes trying it, and this usually results in a substantial increase in sales.

3. *Free trial.* Bellwether of mail order. Melts away human inertia. Consider fitting the length of the trial period to the nature of the product or service, rather than the standard 15 days.

4. *Conditional sale.* Prearranges the possibility of long-term acceptance based on a sample. Example: "Please send me, free, the Premier issue of *Geo,* and reserve a money-saving Charter Subscription in my name. At the end of thirty days, if I have not instructed you to cancel my reservation, you may enter my subscription at the Charter Rate of $36 for one year (12 more monthly issues)—a savings of $12 off the annual cover price of $4 per issue."

5. *Till forbid.* Prearranges for continuing shipments on a specified basis. The customer has the option to forbid future shipments at any specified time. Works well for business services offers and continuity book programs.

6. *Yes-no.* An involvement offer. The prospect is asked to respond, usually through a token or stamp, indicating whether he accepts or

Exhibit 3-2. Involvement Device

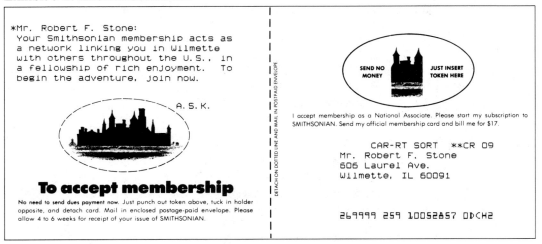

Order form, with personal message from Smithsonian, includes an involvement device.

rejects the offer. Historically, more favorable responses are received with this offer than when no rejection option is provided.

7. *Time limit.* Setting a time limit on a given offer *forces* action, either positive or negative. Usually it is more effective to name a specific date rather than a time period. It is important to test for the most effective time limit because a short period may not allow sufficient time for deliberation. Too long a period, on the other hand, may promote inertia.

8. *Get-a-friend.* Based on the axiom that the best source for new customers is one's present list of satisfied customers. Many get-a-friend

Exhibit 3-3. Postcard Mailing with Multiple Devices

Simple postcard mailing from Newsweek includes sales message, yes-no offer, discount offer, and subscription card.

SAVE 75% WITH NEWSWEEK'S GOLDEN ANNIVERSARY SUBSCRIPTION OFFER!

Dear Mr. Stone,
No big sales pitch. Subscribe to Newsweek now and take advantage of our special 50th Anniversary Offer -- the lowest rate available -- a full 75% off the cover price and 50% off the basic subscription rate. Act now!

Mr. Robert Stone
606 Laurel Ave
Wilmette, Il. 60091

☐ **I do**
☐ **I do not**

34471215   Offer ends 7/15/82

accept this special invitation to receive **26** weeks of Newsweek for **$9.75** (only 37.5¢ a copy)—75% off the $1.50 cover price, 50% off the 75¢ basic subscription rate. I prefer this alternate term ☐ **52** weeks for **$19.50** (I still pay only 37.5¢ a copy).

Please check one: ☐ Bill me ☐ Payment enclosed   ☐ Charge ☐ American Express   ☐ Diners
                              (put form in envelope)   (put form in envelope) ☐ VISA ☐ Master Card

Card # _____ Expires _____   1159714485

Interbank # (Master Card) _____ Signature _____
                                    Good only in the 50 states of the U.S.A.

Newsweek
P.O. BOX 411 • LIVINGSTON, N.J. 07039
Tell us, Mr. Stone,
whether you will
accept this special
HALF-PRICE OFFER!

FIRST CLASS PRESORTED

Mr. Robert Stone
606 Laurel Ave
Wilmette, Il. 60091

Exhibit 3-4. Three-Tier Offer

FREE SOCIAL SECURITY FACT KIT

Here is what you get in your FREE Fact Kit:

50-page Handbook tells you all about your rights, benefits, and privileges under Social Security. It even explains how to collect the money you're entitled to.

Benefits Computer makes it easy to calculate the approximate monthly benefits you'll collect.

Official Social Security Request Form Send it in, and the government reports directly to you on the Social Security earnings credited to your account for each of your working years. It's important to check this report for accuracy, since there's a 3-year time limit for correcting any errors.

As a free gift to you, Old American invites you to accept a 3-piece Social Security Fact Kit. To receive this no-obligation gift, place Label A here.

**BOX A
AFFIX LABEL A HERE**

TRIP-AID ACCIDENT POLICY CERTIFICATE

☐ **YES** Send me your policy. I have enclosed 10¢ with my application.

Date of Birth _____
　　　　　Month　　　Date　　　Year

Beneficiary _____
　　　First Name　Middle Initial　Last Name

Relationship of Beneficiary _____

To the best of my knowledge and belief, I am sound mentally and physically. I understand that the policy (Series ID3077) becomes effective when issued.

Signature X _____
　　　First Name　Middle Initial　Last Name

Licensed Resident Agent, if applicable
ID2000   Old American Ins. Co. • 4900 Oak • PO Box 573 • K.C., MO 64141

**BOX B
AFFIX LABEL B HERE**

Indicate any change to name and/or address by crossing out and inserting correct information.

**OLD AMERICAN
TRIP-AID ACCIDENT POLICY**

For persons 40 to 85 years of age
30 DAYS COVERAGE FOR 10¢
(Regular premium is $5.40 monthly)

TRIP-AID ACCIDENT POLICY CERTIFICATE

☐ **YES.** Send me your policy. I have enclosed 10¢ with my application.

Date of Birth _____
　　　　　Month　　　Date　　　Year

Beneficiary _____
　　　First Name　Middle Initial　Last Name

Relationship of Beneficiary _____

To the best of my knowledge and belief, I am sound mentally and physically. I understand that the policy (Series ID3077) becomes effective when issued.

Signature X _____
　　　First Name　Middle Initial　Last Name

Licensed Resident Agent, if applicable
ID2000   Old American Ins. Co. • 4900 Oak • PO Box 573 • K.C., MO 64141

**THIS APPLICATION FOR USE
BY SPOUSE OR OTHER
FAMILY MEMBER, AGE 40 TO 85,
WHO ALSO WISHES TO APPLY**

Name _____
　　　Please Print

Address _____

City _____

State _____ Zip _____

DP:AP1082:25T

Three-tier offer from Old American Insurance Company offers: (1) a free Social Security Fact Kit; (2) an opportunity for the mail recipient to accept a 10¢ introductory offer for a Trip-Aid Accident Policy; and (3) the same opportunity for a spouse or other family member.

offers get new customers in a large volume at low acquisition cost. The best response for a get-a-friend offer usually results from limiting the number of friends' names requested and offering a reward for providing names or securing new customers.

9. *Contests.* These create attention and excitement. Stringent FTC rules apply. Highly effective in conjunction with magazine subscription offers and popular merchandise offers.

10. *Discounts.* A discount is a never-ending lure to consumers as well as businessmen. Discounts are particularly effective where the value of

Exhibit 3-5. Get-A-Friend Offer

Get-a-friend offer from the Literary Guild: Member encourages a friend to fill in new application. Member fills in the balance of card, indicating bonus desired as a reward for acquiring a new member.

The Literary Guild   231-3

New Applicant: Choose 4 books for $1 with membership!

Please accept my application for membership in The Literary Guild. Send me the 4 books indicated and bill me just $1, plus shipping and handling. I agree to the membership plan described in the enclosed circular and understand that I need buy only 4 more books at the regular low club prices whenever I want them. After buying 4 more books I may resign or remain a member for as long as I wish without further obligation to purchase books.
SATISFACTION GUARANTEED: If not completely satisfied with your Introductory package, return all four books within ten days. Your membership will be canceled and you'll owe nothing.

Write in code numbers of your 4 books here

Mr.
Mrs.
Miss
Ms.
_____
(please print)
Address _____ Apt. _____
City _____ State _____ Zip _____

Present Member: Take 2 books FREE for each friend who becomes a member!
Write in code numbers of your 2 books here:

SPECIAL BONUS: Take one of these gifts free for each friend you introduce to The Literary Guild. Check one box for each friend:
☐ 88278 "Foot Notes" Memo Board
☐ 81075 The Literary Guild Book Jacket
☐ 85597 The Literary Guild Mini-Bag

81075
88278
85597

PRESENT MEMBER: In addition to your 2 FREE books, take one of these gifts free for each member recruited.

IMPORTANT: To avoid delay, please enter your current book club account number.

Name _____
(please print)
Address _____ Apt. _____
City _____ State _____ Zip _____

53   Order cannot be processed unless this card is filled in by both Present Member and New Applicant   FG033

a product or service is well established. Three types of discounts are widely offered: (a) for cash, (b) for an introductory order, and (c) for volume purchase.

11. *Negative option.* This offer prearranges for shipment if the customer doesn't abort the shipment by mailing the rejection form prior to deadline date. In popular use by book and record clubs. FTC guidelines must be followed carefully.

12. *Positive option.* Every shipment is based on a *direct action* by the club member, rather than a *nonaction* as exemplified by the negative option feature of most book and record clubs. Front-end response to a positive option is likely to be lower, but long-pull sales are likely to be greater.

13. *Lifetime membership.* Under this plan, the member pays one fee, $5, for instance, at the time of becoming a member. In return the member is guaranteed substantial reduction from established retail prices. There is no requirement that the respondent make a specified number of purchases. But the safeguard to the marketer is that the member is more likely to make purchases because of his front-end investment.

14. *Load-ups.* This proposition is a favorite of publishers of continuity series. Example: The publisher offers a set of 12 books, one to be released each month. After the purchaser has received and paid for the first three books, the publisher invites him to receive the remaining nine, all in one shipment, with the understanding that payments can

Exhibit 3-6. Use of Token with Free Offer

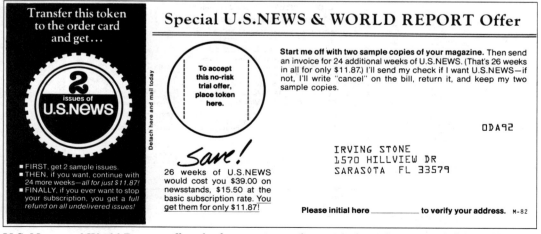

U.S. News and World Report *offers the first two issues free, with the right to cancel the conditional subscription for 24 additional issues. Token dramatizes the free offer.*

continue to be made monthly. This load-up offer invariably results in more *complete sets* of books being sold.

15. *Free gift.* Most direct response advertisers have increased response through free gift offers. For best results, you should test several gifts to determine the most appealing. There's no set criterion for the cost of a gift as related to selling cost. The most important criteria are: (a) appropriateness of the gift; (b) its effect on repeat business; and (c) net profit per thousand circulation or distribution including cost of the gift.

16. *Secret gift.* Lester Wunderman, Chairman of Wunderman, Ricotta & Kline, invented the secret gift offer, commonly known as the "Gold Box offer." Conceived to measure the impact of TV upon the pull of a newspaper or magazine insert, the viewer was told that there was a secret gold box on the insert order form and that by filling in the box the prospect would reserve an extra free gift over and above the regular free gift offer.

17. *Cash-up free gift.* Used primarily by publishers, cash-up offers stimulate cash with order. Incentives for advance cash payment usually involve one or two extra issues of a publication, or a special report not available to charge subscribers.

18. *Add-on offers.* One of the most innovative offers ever developed for increasing the unit of sale was first developed, I believe, by the "Horchow Collection." The offer was directed to catalog buyers about to place a phone order, toll-free. The direction was, "When you place your phone order ask about our Special-of-the-Month." The special was always a discount on a catalog item. One catalog marketer I know of adapted this idea and consistently sold the "special" to 10 percent to 15 percent of phone order inquirers.

19. *Deluxe alternative.* Related to the famous Sears tradition of *good, better, best* are offers for deluxe alternatives. A classic example would be a dictionary offered in a regular edition or in a thumb-indexed edition for $2 more. By giving the prospect the choice, the advertiser often increases total response and total dollars.

20. *Charters.* A charter offer by its very nature denotes something special. The offer plays on the human trait that many people want to be among the first to see, try, and use something new. The most successful charter offers include special rewards or concessions for early support.

21. *Guaranteed buy-back.* "Satisfaction guaranteed" is the heart of mail order selling. But the guaranteed buy-back offer goes much further. This guarantee pledges to buy back the product (if the customer so requests) at the original price for a period of time after original purchase.

22. *Multiproduct.* Multiproduct offers may take the form of a series of postcards or a collection of individual sheets, each with a separate order form. Each product presentation is structured to stand on its own feet.

23. *Piggybacks.* These are "add-on" offers that ride along with major offers at no additional postage cost. The unit of sale is usually much smaller than the major offer. Testing is advocated to determine whether piggybacks add to or steal from sales of the major offer.

24. *Bounce-backs.* Bounce-back offers succeed on the premise, "the best time to sell a person is right after you have sold him." Bounce-back order forms are usually included in shipments or with invoices or statements. Bounce-backs may offer (a) more of the same, (b) related items, or (c) items totally different from those originally purchased.

25. *Good-better-best.* The essence of the offer is to give the prospect a choice between something and something. Example: For their State of the Union series, the Franklin Mint gave the prospect three choices: 24k gold on sterling at $72.50 monthly, solid sterling silver at $43.75 monthly, and solid bronze at $17.50 monthly.

26. *Optional terms.* The technique here is to give the prospect the option of choosing terms at varying rates. The bigger the commitment, the better the buy.

27. *Flexible terms.* A derivative of optional terms is flexible terms. The potential subscriber to a magazine is offered a bargain weekly rate of, say, 25 cents a week for a minimum period of 16 weeks. But, if he wishes, the subscriber may choose to enter his subcription for any number of weeks beyond the minimum at the same bargain rate.

28. *Exclusive rights.* This is an offer made by publishers of syndicated newsletters. Under the terms of such an offer, the first to order—an insurance broker, for example—has exclusive rights for his trading area so long as he remains a subscriber.

Some of these 28 basic offers warrant additional explanation.

Free Gift

Giving free gifts for inquiring, for trying, and for buying has got to be as old an incentive as trading stamps. It is not unusual at all for the right gift to increase response by 25 percent and more. On the other hand, a free gift offer can actually reduce response or have no favorable effect on the basic offer. This is particularly true where the unit of sale or amount of sale consideration overshadows the appeal of the free gift.

What's more, there is a tremendous variance in the appeal of free gifts. For example, the Airline Passengers Association tested two free gifts along with a membership offer: an airline guide and a carry-on suit bag. The suit bag did 50 percent better than the guide.

A fund-raising organization selling to schools tested three different gifts: a set of children's books, a camera, and a 30-cup coffee maker. The coffee maker won by a wide margin; the children's books came in a poor third.

Testing for the most appealing gifts is essential because of the great differences in pull. In selecting gifts for testing purposes, follow this good rule of thumb: Gifts that are suited to personal use tend to have considerably more appeal than those that aren't.

There is yet another consideration about free gifts: Is it more effective to offer a selection of free gifts of comparable value than to offer only one gift? The answer is that offering a selection of gifts of comparable value usually reduces response. This is perhaps explained by the inability of many people to make a choice.

Adopting the one-gift method (after testing for the one with the most appeal) should not be confused with offering gifts of varying value for orders of varying amounts. This is quite a different situation. A multiple-gift proposition might be a free travel clock for orders up to $25, a free transistor radio for orders from $25 to $50, and a free Polaroid camera for orders over $50.

Offering gifts of varying value for orders of varying amounts is logical to the consumer. The advertiser can afford a more expensive gift in conjunction with a larger order. His prime objective is accomplished by increasing his average order over and above what it would be if there were no extra incentive.

The multiple-gift plan works for many, but it can also boomerang. This usually happens when the top gift calls for a purchase over and above what most people can use or afford. The effect can also be negative if the gift offered for the price most people can afford is of little value or consequence. The multiple-gift plan tied to order value has good potential advantages, but careful tests must be conducted. An adaptation of the multiple-gift plan is a gift, often called a "keeper," for trying (free trial), plus a gift for keeping (paying for the purchase). Under this plan the prospect is told he can keep the gift offered for trying even if he returns the product being offered for sale. However, if the product being offered is retained, the prospect also keeps a second gift of greater value than the first.

Still another possibility with gift offers is giving more than one gift for either trying or buying. If the budget for the incentive is $1, for example, the advertiser can offer one gift costing $1, two gifts costing $1, combined, or even three gifts totaling $1. From a sales strategy standpoint, some advertisers spell out what one or two of the gifts are and offer an additional "mystery gift" for prompt response. Fingerhut Corporation of Minneapolis is a strong proponent of multiple gifts and "mystery" gifts.

Free gifts are a tricky business, to be sure. Gift selection and gift tie-ins to offers require careful testing for best results. The $64 question always is, "How much can I afford to spend for a gift?" Aaron Adler, co-founder of Stone & Adler, maintains that most marketers make an erroneous arbitrary decision in advance, such as "I can afford to spend 5 percent of selling price." He maintains that a far more logical approach is to select the most appealing gift possible, without being restricted by an arbitrary cost figure, than to be guided by the net profit figures resulting from tests. For example, Table 3-1 shows a comparison of net profits for two promotions, one with a gift costing $1.00 and the other with a gift costing $2.00 on a $29.95 offer, given a 50 percent better pull with the $2.00 premium.

It is interesting to note that, in this example, when the $1.00 gift was offered, the mailing just about broke even. But when the cost of the gift was doubled, the profit jumped from $4.52 to $52.16 per thousand mailed.

Another advantage of offering more attractive gifts (which naturally cost more) is to offer gifts of substantial value tied to cumulative purchases. This plan can prove particularly effective when the products or services being offered produce consistent repeat orders. A typical offer under a cumulative purchase plan might be: "When your total purchases of our custom-made cigars reach $150, you receive a power saw absolutely free."

Get-A-Friend Perhaps one of the most overlooked and yet most profitable of all offers is the get-a-friend offer. If you have a list of satisfied customers, it is quite natural for them to want to let their friends in on a good thing.

The basic technique for get-a-friend offers is to offer an incentive in appreciation for a favor. Nominal gifts are often given to a customer for the simple act of providing friends' names, with more substantial gifts awarded to the customer for friends who become customers.

Based on experience, here is what you can expect in using the get-a-friend approach: You will get a larger number of friends' names if the

Table 3-1. Comparison of Profits from Promotions with Free Gifts of Different Costs.

Item	$1 Gift	$2 Gift
Net pull of promotion	1%	1.5%
Sales per thousand pieces	$299.50	$449.25
Less:		
Mailing cost...........................	$120.00	$120.00
Merchandise cost (45%)........	134.98	202.16
Administrative cost (10%)....	30.00	44.93
Premium cost.......................	10.00	30.00
Total costs...............................	294.98	397.09
Profit per thousand pieces........	$ 4.52	$ 52.16

customer is guaranteed that his name will not be used in soliciting his friends. Response from friends, however, will be consistently better if you are allowed to refer to the party who supplied their names.

To get the best of two worlds, therefore, you should allow the customer to indicate whether his name may be used in soliciting his friends. For example: "You may use my name when writing my friends," or "Do not use my name when writing my friends."

Response from friends decreases in proportion to the number of names provided by a customer. One can expect the response from three names provided by one person to be greater than the total response from six names provided by another person. The reason is that it is natural to list the names in order of likelihood of interest.

Two safeguards may be applied to getting the maximum response from friends' names: (1) limit the number of names to be provided, for example, to three or four, and (2) promote names provided in order of listing, such as all names provided first as one group, all names provided second as another group, and so forth. Those who have mastered the technique of getting friends' names from satisfied customers have found that, with very few exceptions, such lists are more responsive than most lists they can rent or buy.

Short- and Long-Term Effects on Offers

A major consideration in structuring offers is the effect a given offer will have on your objectives.

- Is it your objective to get a *maximum* number of new customers for a given product or service as quickly as possible?
- Is it your objective to determine the *repeat business factor* as quickly as possible?
- Is it your objective to break even or make a profit in the shortest possible period?

So, the key question to ask when designing an offer is, "How will this offer help to accomplish my objective?"

Offers Relate to Objectives

Say you are introducing a new hobby magazine. You have the choice of making a short-term offer (3 months, for instance) or a long-term offer (say 12 months). Since you want to determine acceptances as quickly as possible (your objective), you would rightly decide on a short-term offer. Under the short-term offer, after 3 months you will be getting a picture of renewal percentages. If you have made an initial offer of 12-month subscriptions, you would have to wait a year to determine the publication renewal rate. In the interim, you would be missing vital information important to your magazine's success.

If the 3-month trial subscriptions are renewed at a satisfactory rate, you could then safely proceed to develop offers designed to get initial long-term subscriptions. It is axiomatic in the publishing field that the longer the initial term of subscription, the higher the renewal rate is likely to be. Professional circulation men know from experience that if they are getting, say, a 35 percent conversion on a 3-month trial, they can expect a conversion of 50 percent or more on 12-month initial subscriptions. This knowledge, therefore, can be extrapolated from the short-term objective to the long-term objective.

Sol Blumenfeld, a prominent direct marketing consultant, when addressing a Direct Mail/Marketing Association convention, made some pertinent remarks about the dangers of looking only at front-end response. Blumenfeld stated, "Many people still cling to the CPA (cost per application) or CPI (cost per inquiry) response syndromes. In their eagerness to sell now, they frequently foul up their chances to sell later."

He then asks, "Can the practice of those who concern themselves only with front-end response at least partially explain book club conversions of only 50 to 60 percent? Magazine renewal rates of only 30 percent? Correspondence school attrition factors of as much as 40 percent?"

Blumenfeld gives us a case in point. A control for the Britannica Home Study Library Service (a division of Encyclopaedia Britannica) was run against several test ads developed by the agency. Control ads offered free the first volume of *Compton's Encyclopedia.* Major emphasis was placed on sending for the free volume; small emphasis was placed on the idea of ultimately purchasing the balance of the 24-volume set. Front-end response was excellent; the rate of conversion to full 24-volume sets was poor. Profitability was unacceptable.

Against the control ad, the agency tested several new ads that offered Volume I free but also revealed the cost of the complete set—right in the headline. Here's what happened: The cost per coupon for the new ads was 20 percent higher than the control ad, but conversions to full sets improved a full 350 percent!

Ways to Hype Response

Once you have decided on your most appealing offer, either arbitrarily or by testing, you should ask a very specific question: How can I hype my offer to make it even more appealing? There are several ways.

Terms of
Payment

Where a direct sale is involved, the terms of payment you require can hype or depress response. A given product or service can have tremendous appeal, but if payment terms are too stringent—beyond the means of a potential buyer—the offer will surely be a failure. Five general categories of payment terms may be offered: (1) cash with order, (2) C.O.D., (3) open account, (4) installment terms, and; (5) revolving credit.

If a five-way split test were made among these categories, it is almost certain that response would be in inverse ratio to the listing of the five categories. Revolving credit would be the most attractive and cash with order the least-attractive terms. With each loosening of terms, the appeal of the offer is hyped. In a four-way split test on a merchandise offer, here's how four terms actually ranked (the least-appealing terms have a 100 percent ranking): cash with order, 100 percent; cash with order—free gift for trying, 144 percent; bill me offer (open account), 177 percent; and, bill me offer (open account) and free gift, 233 percent.

As the figures disclose, the most attractive terms (bill-me offer and free gift) were almost two-and-one-half times more appealing than the least attractive terms (cash with order).

While C.O.D. terms are generally more attractive than cash-with-order requirements, the hazard of C.O.D. terms is refusal on delivery. It is not unusual to sustain an 8 percent refusal rate when C.O.D. terms are offered. (Many C.O.D. orders are placed emotionally, and emotion cools off when the delivery man or letter carrier calls and requests payment.)

When merchandise or services are offered on open account, payment is customarily requested in 15 or 30 days. Such terms are naturally more appealing than cash with order or C.O.D. Open account terms are customary when selling to business firms. When used in selling to the consumer, however, such terms, while appealing, can result in a high percentage of bad debts, unless carefully selected credit-checked lists are used.

The best appeals lie in installment terms and revolving credit terms. Both mechanisms require substantial financing facilities and a sophisticated credit collection system. Installment selling in the consumer field is virtually essential for the successful sale of "big ticket" merchandise—items selling for $69.95 and up.

One can have the best of two worlds—most appealing terms and no credit risk—by making credit arrangements through a sales finance firm or commercial credit card operations, such as American Express, Diners Club, Carte Blanche, or one of the bank cards—VISA, or MasterCard.

Bank cards and travel-and-entertainment cards have proved a boon to mail order operations, especially catalog operations. It is not unusual to hype the average order from a catalog by 20 percent when bank card privileges or travel-and-entertainment card privileges are offered. Not only do these privileges tend to increase the amount of the average order, they also tend to increase the total response.

When arrangements are made through commercial credit card operations, any member may charge purchases to his card. The credit of all members in good standing is ensured by the respective credit card operations. The advertiser is paid by the agency for the total sales charged less a discount charge, usually about 1 to 3 percent for bank cards and 3 to 7 percent for travel-and-entertainment cards.

Sweepstakes

Perhaps the most dramatic hype available to direct marketers is sweepstakes. A sweeps overlayed on an offer adds excitement and interest. Two major direct marketers who have used sweepstakes through the 1960s and 1970s and on into the 1980s are *Reader's Digest* and Publishers Clearing House. The techniques they use are the ultimate in sophistication.

Both *Reader's Digest* and Publishers Clearing House use TV support as an integral part of their sweepstakes promotions. Success depends upon (1) heavy market penetration of the printed materials, (2) time-controlled delivery of the printed offer to coincide with TV support, and (3) sufficient TV impact to excite interest in the printed promotion. Careful testing is required to determine the most cost-efficient amount of TV laid over the print offer. "Keep TV commercials simple," cautions Publishers Clearing House. Current PCH commercials prove they practice what they preach: They feature the sweepstakes, using past winners to carry the message, leaving the magazine savings story to the mailing package.

Astute direct marketers like RD and PCH know incentives for prompt response tend to increase total response. Each has built incentives for prompt response into its sweepstakes contests. *Reader's Digest*, for example, has offered the following bonus award incentive: "$1,000 a day for every day your entry beats the deadline of January 31." This means that, if the grand prize is $50,000 and your entry is postmarked before January 21, you, as the grand prize winner, will win an extra $10,000. Another technique is reader involvement. "Seven Chances to Be a Winner," PCH announces in promoting a $400,000 sweepstakes. The entrant was given seven prize numbers.

Umbrella Sweepstakes

A big sweepstakes requires a bushel of money for prizes and administration. Direct marketers, bottom-line people that they are, have found ways to overlay a major sweeps on more than one proposition. *Reader's Digest,* for example, can overlay the same sweeps on a magazine subscription offer, a book club offer, and a record offer—each falling under the umbrella of one prize budget.

Thomas J. Conlon, president of D. L. Blair, the largest sweepstakes judging agency in the country, points out that there are many questions to be answered for anyone contemplating a sweepstakes. Here are the questions we put to Mr. Conlon and his replies.

Q. Currently, what are the most popular prize structures?

A. Cash, automobiles, travel and home entertainment appliances—in that order—continue to be the most appealing and popular prize structures. According to our most recent research, apparel (fur coats, designer dresses) has virtually no appeal. As for other merchandise, we generally prefer to eschew the use of merchandise prizes except when we have conclusive research indicating greater consumer preference for the prize item than for its equivalent cash value.

Q. When a sweeps is tested against a nonsweeps, what range of increase might be expected for a magazine subscription offer or catalog offer?

A. Using a sweepstakes overlay, we have never seen less than a 15 percent increase in orders for either a catalog or a magazine subscription. The greatest increase we have ever seen is 350 percent. Generally, the increment falls between 30 and 100 percent.

Q. Can a low-budget sweeps be successful?

A. Though it is generally true that the success levels of any sweepstakes are importantly impacted by prize budget, we have seen low-budget programs work extremely well when directed at special interest groups. Thus, while a $3,500 value grand prize would provide little or no motivation to most broad audience segments, a $3,500 home flight simulator would be highly appealing to an audience comprised solely of private pilots; a $3,500 hunting carbine would be highly appealing to NRA members; a $3,500 one-of-a-kind Wedgwood bud vase would be extremely appealing to Wedgwood collectors.

Q. From a legal standpoint, must all prizes be awarded in a sweepstakes offer?

A. Speaking solely from the narrow area of what is strictly legal, it is only necessary to award prizes to those who have submitted entry numbers that the judges have preselected as winning numbers. There are however, very compelling business and ethical reasons that strongly suggest that any direct marketer would be ill-advised to consider awarding fewer than the full number of prizes which he has advertised.

Q. Is the average order from a catalog, for example, likely to be smaller with a sweeps entry?

A. It depends on whether the order is from a former buyer or a new customer. The average order from former buyers tends to be larger.

Exhibit 3-7. Sweepstakes Offer.

Playboy Great Escape Sweepstakes offers a $72,235. grand prize and an array of lesser prizes on the front cover of a four-page folder and personalized entry coupon for the same group of prizes.

Playboy's "Biggest Ever"...

THE $165,000.00 GREAT ESCAPE SWEEPSTAKES
GRAND PRIZE: $72,235.00

Why the odd amount?
Because the Grand Prize is the equivalent of a ribbon of dollar bills — stretched over 7 miles. Isn't that enough to stir the imagination? And you could be the winner. It's entirely possible. Right now — you're probably conjuring up all sorts of things you could do with this kind of cash...a whole season of getaway weekends...that new condominium you've had your eye on...a college fund for the children...a visit to Europe's famed capitals...a carefree Caribbean cruise...even your own pleasure cruiser.

1ST PRIZE

DATSUN 280-ZX

2 lucky winners will receive this Grand Luxury 2+2—a sophisticated sports car with air conditioning; steel-belted radial tires; fuel-efficient, 5-speed overdrive transmission; split fold-down, rear seat backs; posh carpeting; and power operation for the windows and antenna which goes up as you turn on the AM/FM digital 4-speaker stereo. All the Datsun magic.

3RD PRIZE

2ND PRIZE

HONDA CB750K

6 people will win this superbike and feel as if they are riding on air. The 749 cc. DOHC, 16-valve, 4-cylinder powerhouse is noted for its dependability and performance. It also boasts a 5.3 gallon gas tank, requiring fewer fill-ups. Other subtle refinements: a new 55/60 watt halogen headlight; 4 megaphone-type mufflers; powerful, 11.6" front disc brake. Jump aboard the saddle and fly.

PANASONIC VIDEO ENTERTAINMENT CENTER

10 winners will receive the finest in audio/visual equipment—a VCR system with a 6-hour record/playback capability—and a 19" wireless remote control color TV. A 24-hour timer starts the recorder when you're not at home to catch your favorite show.

4TH PRIZE—25 WINNERS

Soloflex Exerciser

The complete gymnasium! The 6' tall frame with attachments converts with ease to several different stations to accommodate situps, bench presses, dips, chins and more. Sturdy construction. The ultimate in exercise equipment for home use.

5TH PRIZE—30 WINNERS

Cosina CX-2 35mm Camera

This ultra-compact camera goes anywhere handily. Features a 5-element f2.8 lens. Exposure is automatic with a programmed electronic shutter. Speeds are up to 1/500 of a second. Winder and flash unit included. Your photography will reflect the Cosina touch.

6TH PRIZE—1000 WINNERS

Playboy Guides to Casino Gambling

Thorough and authoritative, these 4 no-nonsense volumes on Roulette, Craps, Blackjack and Baccarat are the books you'll need to become a crafty player. A foremost gambling authority brings his considerable knowledge and expertise to these Guides.

"Early Bird" Cash Prize —

$5,000.00

Mail Before March 9th

Exhibit 3-7. Sweepstakes Offer.

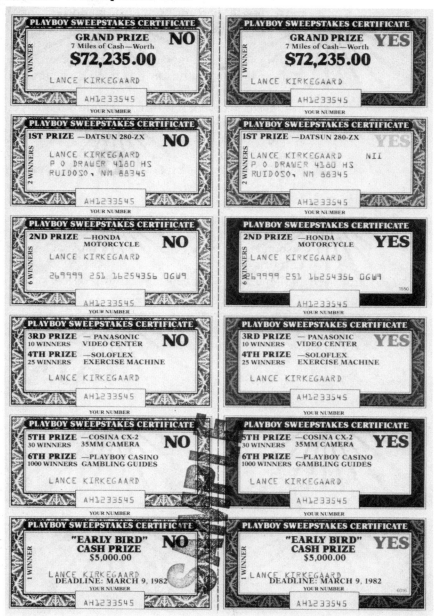

I've seen a sweepstakes increase the value of each catalog order by more than 40 percent. New customer orders, on the other hand, tend to be lower than average, probably because these are fringe buyers coming in as a result of the sweepstakes overlay.

Q. Having acquired a new customer with a sweepstakes contest, would you say that repeat business is likely to depend on additional sweepstakes contests?

A. Yes, to some degree it is true that continuing sweepstakes promotions might be necessary to maintain a normal level of repeat business. I would say this is true to the same extent that a customer first acquired with incentives such as price-off coupons, free gifts, discount offers, and the like would be conditioned to such offers in the future.

Q. What is the profile of sweepstakes entrants these days?

A. It's becoming broader with more geographic, economic, and educational homogeneity. This "flattening" process extends to the sex of respondents: men account for almost 47 percent of sweepstakes entrants.

Q. Is the appeal of sweepstakes to direct marketing customers increasing, declining, or holding flat?

Exhibit 3-8. Devices to Hype Response.

Included in the Playboy Great Escape Sweepstakes mailing package are two devices: a "Publisher's Letter" and an "Early Bird" bonus offer.

A. Almost without exception, our direct mail marketing clients are reporting greater new customer and current buyer penetration from their sweepstakes programs. Since we are seeing comparable response increases in programs run by our package goods clients, it would appear that there is significantly more consumer interest in sweepstakes than has ever been the case before.

Telephone

Toll-free telephone response (800 numbers) offers the opportunity to hype the response from just about any offer, particularly offers involving free information or the sale of merchandise. (See Chapter 10—Telemarketing.)

Publisher's Letter

Another innovative device that has been developed for hyping responses during the past decade is an extra mailing enclosure known as the "publisher's letter." It gets its name from its first usage—a short letter from a magazine publisher enclosed in the basic mailing package.

The publisher's letter usually carries a headline: "If you have decided not to respond, read this letter." The letter copy typically reinforces the offer made in the basic mailing package, assures the reader it is valid, and guarantees the terms. This extra enclosure often increases response by 10 percent and more. While the publisher's letter was originated for subscription letters, this device was soon adopted by other direct marketers selling goods and services. Results have been equally productive.

The Guarantee

No matter what the terms or basic offer may be, a strong guarantee is essential when selling products or services direct. For more than 90 years, Sears, Roebuck and Company has guaranteed satisfaction for every article offered. Over the years, no one else has ever succeeded in mail order operations without duplicating the Sears guarantee or offering a similar assurance.

The importance of the guarantee is perhaps best understood by recognizing a negative fact of life. It is this. Over 90 years after Sears first established its ironclad guarantee, it is still a fact of human nature that one is hesitant to send for merchandise unless one knows that the product may be returned for full credit it if does not meet expectations. Guaranteed satisfaction should be a part of any offer soliciting a direct sale.

Many marketers have developed unique guarantees that go beyond the trial period. Madison House, for instance, advertised a new fishing lure in a March issue of *Family Weekly*. The company knew, of course, that in northern areas, lakes were frozen over and that there would be no opportunity to test and use this lure before spring. Madison House overcame the problem beautifully by urging the fishing buff to send for the lure *now*, with the proviso that the lure could be returned any time within six months for a full cash refund. This guarantee had two advantages: It assured the fishing buff that, even though he was ordering the lure out of season, he could return it after he tried it in season; and it enabled Madison House to advertise and get business out of season.

One of the most successful manuals ever produced at National Research Bureau was the 428-page *Retail Advertising and Sales Promotion Manual.* It was offered on a 10-day free trial basis with the guarantee: "If this manual isn't all we say it is, you may return it any time within twelve months for full refund." National Research Bureau sold over 20,000 manuals at $19.95. It is significant that, after several years, no one has ever asked for a refund!

Many marketers reinforce their own guarantees with a "third party" guarantee. "Approved by Underwriters Laboratory" can make the difference where electrical appliances are concerned. The *Good Housekeeping* Seal of Approval has long been accepted as a guarantee of validity of claim.

Publishers Clearing House has made this statement: "In addition to the publisher's own warranties, Publishers Clearing House makes you this unconditional guarantee: You may have a full cash refund at any time, or for any reason, on the unused part of any subscription ordered through the clearing house. This guarantee has no time limit. It is your assurance that you can order from Publishers Clearing House with complete confidence."

In direct sales, the right proposition and the right terms of payment are only two-thirds of the impetus. A clear, strong guarantee completes the equation.

Exhibit 3-9. Sears Guarantee

SEARS GUARANTEE

Your satisfaction is guaranteed or your money back.

We guarantee that every article in this catalog is accurately described and illustrated.

If, for any reason whatever, you are not satisfied with any article purchased from us, we want you to return it to us at our expense.

We will exchange it for exactly what you want, or will return your money, including any transportation charges you have paid.

SEARS, ROEBUCK AND CO.

Danger of Overkill

The power of an offer cannot be overestimated. But there's such a thing as too much of a good thing—offers that sound too good to be true or that produce a great front-end response but make for poor pay-ups or poor repeat customers. Here are two thought-provoking examples:

A comprehensive test was structured for a fund-raising organization to determine whether response would best be maximized by (a) offering a free gift as an incentive for an offer; (b) offering a combination of free gift plus a cash bonus for completing a sale; or (c) offering a cash bonus only. The combination of free-gift-plus-cash-bonus pulled the lowest response by far; the free-gift proposition far outpulled the cash-bonus proposition.

The second example: A $200 piece of electronic equipment was offered for 15-day free trial. This was the basic proposition. But half the people on the list also were invited to enter a sweepstakes contest. The portion of the list who were not invited to enter a sweepstakes responded 25 percent better than the portion who were invited to enter.

In both these examples, the more generous offer proved to be "too much." One must be most careful not to make the offer so overwhelming that it overshadows the product or services being offered. Another important consideration in structuring offers is the axiom, "As you make your bed, so shall you lie in it." Here's what we mean. If you obtain thousands of new customers by offering free gifts as incentives, don't expect a maximum degree of repeat business unless you continue to offer free gifts. Similarly, if you build a big list of installment credit buyers, don't expect these buyers to respond well to cash-basis offers, and vice versa.

Given offers attract given types of customers. Make sure these are the types you really want. Here is an illustration of our axiom. A firm selling to businesses built a large customer list based on a series of soft-sell offers. The firm then went into another product line, offering products to their customers and to cold prospect lists. Three offers were tested: (1) a free gift for ordering, (2) a discount for ordering, and (3) no incentive. The results of the three offers against cold lists and against the customer list are provided in Table 3-2.

Table 3-2. Results of Testing Three Types of Offers with Both Cold and Customer Lists.

	Results (In Percent)	
	Cold Lists	Customer List
Free gift	2.2	3.2
Discount	5.2	3.1
No incentive	2.5	3.9

Note the dramatic differences in response between cold lists and the customer list. The discount offer was more than twice as attractive to cold lists. But, to the customer list, not nurtured in this manner, the discount offer was the least attractive. Note also that the offer with no extra incentive was the most attractive to the customer list.

Effect on Bad Debts

It is rarely mentioned that a misleading offer can have a devastating effect on bad debts. A misleading offer causes the consumer, without consciously thinking about it, to feel that he has been rooked and often leads him to conclude, "They can whistle for their money." The justice, if it may be called that, is that those who would mislead usually end up paying dearly for their misdeeds.

The fact that it is poor business to make misleading offers is underscored by the following true story. For many years two large publishers exchanged mailing lists—each making noncompeting offers to the list of the other. The two publishers exchanged bad-debt lists. Time after time, the publisher known for its misleading offers would send the other publisher a list of customers with whom it had bad-debt experience. When the names were compared, it was found that, in over 80 percent of the cases where both publishers had the same customers, the publisher who practiced forthrightness had no bad-debt experience with the identical customers. Honesty does pay.

Make It Easy To Order

The structure of an offer should not be taken lightly. The impact an offer can have on immediate and long-term results can be tremendous. Sad, but true, some of the most brilliant offers fail, not because the offers aren't appealing, but because they are poorly presented, verbally or graphically, or both. The greatest sins of execution are to be found in coupon space ads.

Tony Antin, who directed creative services for *Reader's Digest,* laid down this mandate for coupon order forms: "A coupon (order form) should be—*must be*—an artistic cliché. Rectangular. Surrounded by dash lines. Not even dotted lines. Because one connects dots. One cuts along dashes. Moreover, the coupon should be where it belongs, at the lower outside. The coupon should stand out from the rest of the ad."

So, construction of offers boils down to this: Your primary job is to overcome human inertia. Your offers should relate to objectives. Consider the short- and long-term effects. And, by all means, make it easy to order!

Self-Quiz

1. An ad, TV or radio commercial, or direct mail piece can't be regarded as direct marketing unless there is a(n)_____.

2. Basically, there are 10 factors to consider when creating an offer. They are:

a. _____   f. _____

b. _____   g. _____

c. _____   h. _____

d. _____   i. _____

e. _____   j. _____

3. Of the 10 factors, which one should *always* be applied to a direct sale offer?

_____

4. What is a "till forbid" offer?

_____

_____

_____

5. What is the difference between a "negative option" and a "positive option"?

_____

_____

_____

6. What is the basic rule to follow in testing a variety of free gifts to determine which is most appealing?

_____

_____

_____

7. Here are five terms of payment: (1) cash with order, (2) C.O.D., (3) open account, (4) installment terms, and (5) revolving credit. Which is likely to have the most appeal?

_____

8. What is an "Umbrella Sweepstakes"?

_____

_____

_____

9. Currently, what are the most popular prize structures for sweepstakes?

_____

_____

_____

10. Define a "Publisher's Letter."

_____

_____

_____

11. Why is the guarantee in direct sale offers so essential?

_____

_____

_____

12. What is a "third party" guarantee?

_____

_____

_____

13. Under what conditions can an offer be "too attractive"?

_____

_____

_____

14. Check the requirement for an effective coupon (order form):

Coupons should be ☐ rectangular ☐ oval. Coupons should be surrounded by ☐ dotted lines ☐ dash lines.

Pilot Project

You have been given an important assignment: to launch a new publication for the over 50 market called *Prime Time.*

This is to be a monthly publication carrying a cover price of $2.50, with a mail subscription rate of $24 a year. The publisher is anxious to: (a) reach a subscription base of 100,000 subscribers before the first issue appears and (b) determine the renewal rate as quickly as possible. There will be no newsstand distribution.

Keeping the publisher's objectives in mind, develop three different offers that might be tested.

Chapter Four

Selecting and Selling Merchandise

The urge to enter the mail order business is an urge that just won't go away for thousands of entrepreneurs. Yet most who enter the arena fail—miserably. The reasons for failure are multitudinous. A false belief one can get rich quick. Lack of intuitive feelings about mail order products. No sense of necessary ratios of cost to selling price. Failure to test properly. A dearth of knowledge about appropriate media. Poor merchandise sources. Insufficient capital. And on and on and on.

How then does one find hot mail order items? Where do you go? What do you look for? What should you avoid? How do you start?

There is no greater authority to answer these questions than Len Carlson of Los Angeles who has pioneered and marketed about 10,000 mail order items over the past 30 years. His sage advice could pay the cost of this book hundreds of times over.

The first tip from Len Carlson is that you look for items whose benefits you can demonstrate with photos and graphics and copy that dramatize the end use.

And where do you find such items? Rarely in general merchandise stores. More often in boutiques—off-beat stores that offer the unusual. Boutiques in this country and particularly boutiques abroad.

Then, there are the trade shows, the Housewares Show in Chicago, the hardware and stationery shows, the premium shows. And the foreign trade shows, too. He calls his escapades "treasure hunts."

He doesn't just look. He asks questions: "What items are you selling to mail order companies now?" "Can you add this feature?" "What are the requirements for getting an exclusive on this item?" "What kind of a backup inventory can you guarantee?"

Most manufacturer's representatives are startled when he asks, "What do you have in your big briefcase that doesn't sell well?" Often he finds items that bombed out on retail shelves that he can bring to life in catalogs and promote with demonstrable benefits.

Along the same line, he recommends resurrection of oldies but goodies, taking them out of mothballs for new generations of buyers. An analogy he gives is a technique Walt Disney employed to bring back his successful kid movies every seven years.

The tips for finding mail order items continue. "You have to become a great reader, subscribing to jillions of consumer and trade magazines," says Mr. Carlson. "Not only U.S. magazines, but foreign magazines, as well." Many of the magazines are available in libraries. Then there is what he calls "the rule of two." Here's how that works. You religiously accumulate mail order catalogs. When you see a new item, you record it as a test. If you see the same item in a subsequent catalog, you assume the test worked and your interest should be piqued. If you don't see the item a second time, you can assume the item bombed.

One of the top mail order secrets Mr. Carlson learned years ago is the appeal of personalization. Few stores personalize. So a mail order operation can take a standard stock item, personalize it and change the appeal from "ho-hum" to "exciting." Such mundane items as dog and cat dishes, floor mats, and paper napkins are good examples.

But there is one rule for selecting hot mail order items he uses that is my favorite. It goes like this: Show all new items to your wife. If she says "no"—go with them!

Gloria Carlson, based upon years of experience, agrees with Len.

The checklist that follows summarizes the sources for discovering viable mail order items.

Where to Discover Mail Order Items

1. Study competitive catalogs and solo offers.
2. Read Consumer Magazines.
3. Subscribe to Pertinent Trade Journals.
4. Cover U.S. Trade Shows.
5. Browse Retail Stores Constantly.
6. Write to Manufacturers Listed in Directories.
7. Talk to Manufacturers' Representatives.
8. Periodically Visit Book Stores and the Library.
9. Attend Foreign Trade Fairs; Shop Foreign Stores.
10. Read Foreign Magazines and Catalogs.
11. Contact Foreign Commercial Attachés.

12. Revive Your Old Successes.
13. Set Up and Refer to Your 'Idea File' Frequently.
14. Add on Features to Existing Items.
15. Personalize if Pertinent to Product.

- Use your instincts!
- Keep your eyes open!
- Hustle! Work!
- Innovate!
- Think MERCHANDISE—all the time!
- *The search never ends!*

One of the most invaluable checklists developed by Mr. Carlson is his list of 34 factors to consider when selecting mail-order items. This checklist follows.

34 Factors to Consider When Selecting Mail Order Items

1. Is there a perceived need for the product?
2. Is it practical?
3. Is it unique?
4. Is the price right for my customer or prospect?
5. Is it good value?
6. Is the markup sufficient to assure profit?
7. Is the market large enough? Does it have broad appeal?
8. Or . . . are there specific smaller segments of my list that have a strong desire for the product?
9. Is it new? Or . . . will my customers perceive it to be new?
10. Will it photograph/illustrate interestingly?
11. Are there sufficient unusual selling features to make the copy exciting?
12. Is it economical to ship? Too fragile? Odd-shaped? Too heavy? Too big?
13. Can it be personalized?
14. Are there any legal problems to overcome?
15. Is it safe to use?
16. Is the supplier reputable?
17. Will backup merchandise be available for fast shipment on re-orders?
18. Might returns be too huge?
19. Will refurbishing of returned merchandise be practical?
20. Is it, or can it be, packaged attractively?
21. Are usage instructions clear?

22. How does it compare to competitive products?
23. Will it have exclusivity?
24. Will it lend itself to repeat business?
25. Is it consumable (for repeat orders)?
26. Is it faddy? Too short-lived?
27. Is it too seasonal for mail order selling?
28. Can an add-on to the product make it more distinctive and saleable?
29. Will the number of stock-keeping units (sizes and colors) create inventory problems?
30. Does it lend itself to multiple pricing?
31. Is it too readily available in stores?
32. Is it like an old, hot item that guarantees its success?
33. Or . . . is it doomed because similar items failed before?
34. Does my mother/wife/brother/husband like it? (If so, it probably should be discarded!)

Let's take checkpoint number 6, for example: Is the markup sufficient to assure profit? On this Mr. Carlson says, "The books say you need four or five times cost in order to sell profitably. I don't think that's necessarily true. Certainly you need to more than double the cost of an item to come out."

On checkpoint number 24: Will it lend itself to repeat business? Here is what he says: "You should search for items that lend themselves to repeat business. Otherwise you've got to keep coming up with new items for repeat business. Consumable items are the ideal."

Knowing how to evaluate products is a key to mail order success. But not the only key. Finding a niche for yourself in the marketplace is at the top of the list.

"Your first question," says Mr. Carlson, "should be: 'What's missing from the market?'" When he launched Sunset House, he perceived a void in the marketplace that could be filled by bringing hundreds of gadgets together in one catalog. A multi-million-dollar business grew from the recognition of this void.

Years later another entrepreneur perceived there was no one place in the market where one could buy hard to find tools. Thus the highly successful Brookstone Catalog operation was born.

Finding a void and the right items to fill that void are key. But even these steps are short of achieving success. The entrepreneur, in particular, must be a total businessman. The final checklist from Len Carlson is the coup de grâce. It's the "moment of truth" for would-be mail order millionaires. Careful study of this comprehensive checklist could lead many to conclude "mail order is not for me." And that could be good!

Merchandise Selection & Product Development

1. Set marketing objective.
2. Select products.
3. Perform market research.
4. Evaluate potentials.

Media Selection

1. Make budget decisions.
2. Decide on direct mail circulation.
3. Select appropriate house list segments.
4. Arrange rental/compilation of outside lists (list brokers).
5. Decide timing of campaign.
6. Buy space/time (ad agencies, reps, media).
7. Arrange for inserts/co-ops/package inserts/other media.
8. Consider telephone selling.

Creative Decisions

1. Develop the offers and formats.
2. Get copy prepared.
3. Arrange for photography/illustrations.
4. Typography, design, and layout considerations.
5. Production and scheduling.
6. Set printing and mailing program.
7. Buy envelopes.
8. Work with creative consultants.

Testing Projects

1. Offers
2. Prices
3. Lists
4. Geographic Areas
5. Formats

Buying Procedures

1. Negotiate with vendors and purchase products.
2. Follow up vendors for delivery.
3. Re-buy.
4. Maintain inventory control.
5. Control inspection of incoming merchandise.
6. Dispose of overstock inventory.

Management Functions

1. Estimate costs, potentials, and profitability.
2. Analyze response and sales.
3. Check legal aspects re merchandising.
4. Double-check record-keeping and data-capture activity.
5. Decide if credit/credit cards to be offered.
6. Decide if telephone orders should be accepted.
7. Study if foreign sales are possible.
8. Sell house products, wholesale, to others.
9. Maintain liaison with fulfillment, accounting, and customer service departments.

An Entrepreneurial Success Story

With caution hopefully well established, it's time to give living proof that entrepreneurs can succeed in spite of the hazards involved. Let me tell you about a beautiful, intelligent, and charming young lady by the name of Annie Hurlbut. She is a classic example of getting into mail order by serendipity. A neophyte in every sense, but she has performed like she wrote Len Carlson's checklists!

Annie Hurlbut is an anthropologist who, when she was at Yale, spent her sophomore summer working at an archeological dig in Peru. There she encountered the alpaca, a cameloid animal related to the vicuna and the llama. Although the alpaca has an unpleasant disposition (it spits at people, she says), it is the mainstay of the economy of the Andes, serving as food and, along with the llama, as beast of burden. (The alpaca can carry up to a 50-lb. load. "Put 51 lbs. on it and it balks," Ms. Hurlbut says.) But the alpaca is raised mainly for its extraordinary wool, which is lightweight, warm, and grows naturally in a variety of colors, from white to beige, brown, and gray.

Ms. Hurlbut returned to Peru again as a graduate student in anthropology, but this time for her thesis research on women who sell in primitive markets. Among their wares were handloomed alpaca garments, which were warm and practical but not exactly stylish.

So, Annie Hurlbut turned designer. She worked with the Peruvians to design sweaters with more flair so they would be more acceptable to North American women. With her first stock, she returned to the Hurlbut farm in Tonganoxie, Kansas, and started a mail order catalog business called, "The Peruvian Connection," with her mother as a partner. They produced a catalog and did some ads. And with this, Annie Hurlbut was in the mail order business.

Some of Annie's early ads were as primitive as the natives. And the first "catalog" was really no more than an amateurish flyer. But the first ads and catalogs sold enough merchandise to pay the bills with some left over to reinvest. Clearly, alpaca styled by Peruvians overcame any lack of sophistication in mail order techniques. Annie Hurlbut's sense of style, plus alpaca's uniqueness, worked. Annie learned quickly that the secret to building a mail order business was in developing a customer file as quickly as possible. Then to offer those customers other items.

Peruvian Connection's first offering outside of apparel was pure alpaca blankets. (See Exhibit 4-1).

There are a couple of other noteworthy tried-and-true mail order techniques that Annie Hurlbut used in conjunction with this mailing. Enclosing a swatch of the blanket was a brilliant stroke. (I couldn't resist running my finger over the swatch—it is really soft!) Also, Annie encouraged ordering by phone and charging to a credit card.

Would you like to guess what the pull was from the customer list? Five percent? No. Ten percent? No. Twenty-five percent? No. It pulled 43 percent—a pull the "professionals" would give up their birthright to get.

Expanding Existing Mail Order Operations

It has been said with considerable validity—"No mail order item, or mail order line is forever." It is certainly a truism that every mail order item—not unlike items sold through traditional channels—is subject to product life cycles. (See Exhibit 4-2.) Hence there is the ever-present need to come up with new products and services. How does one do that?

When someone asks Aaron Adler, co-founder of Stone & Adler, how to determine what new product or service to offer, he asks, "What business are you in?" Nine times out of ten, the person will say, "Oh, I'm in the catalog business," or, "I sell collectibles," or, "I sell books," or, something similar. That type of answer is true, of course, so far as it goes. But it probably doesn't go far enough if you really want to explore all the possibilities of your operation. The executive of a company who thinks of himself as being in the "catalog business" or in the "record

Exhibit 4-1. The Peruvian Connection

December 26th, 1979

Dear Special Customer:

   In early December, on a trip to Peru for Christmas orders, I stumbled across some extraordinary 100% alpaca blankets, a swatch of which I'm enclosing in this envelope. I was astonished by the quality of the fibre used and impressed with the workmanship, even to the blanket-stitched edges. When I heard the prices (under half of what we pay for the $250 Mon Repos blankets we import), I called the States to consult with my partner, and bought up every one. A few hours later The Peruvian Connection was launched into the market of luxury blankets. As far as I know, we are the first and only U.S. importers of 100% alpaca blankets, although they have been exported to Europe for some time.

   Our plan is to sell these blankets at direct-importer WHOLESALE prices in order to compete with the $75 to $95 prices of the 50% alpaca/50% sheep's wool blankets currently available in stores and through catalogues such as Gumps, Brookstone, Shopping International and others. These half alpaca blankets are beautiful, warm and sturdy. We know, we've been importing them for years. But for weightless warmth and silky softness, no natural fibre-- not mohair, not angora, not even cashmere-- competes with pure alpaca. The secret lies in the high lanolin content of this wool from the Andes.

   The reason you rarely see 100% alpaca blankets in this country is simple: Alpacas, which live almost exclusively in the Andes, produce a limited amount of wool (they are sheared only once every two years during the rainy season). The global demand for scarce alpaca fibre, however, is insatiable. In the four years

distributed in the united states by

canaan farm tonganoxie kansas 66086 (913) 845-2750

Two-page letter gets attention at the outset, and quickly establishes value through the technique of favorable comparison.

Exhibit 4.1. The Peruvian Connection

of our import business, the Peruvian market price of alpaca has
more than quadrupled.

Since Inca times, when by law only nobility could wear clothing
of fine alpaca, alpaca has been valued over the hair of its coarser
cousin, the llama. Now even lesser quality llama sells for astound-
ing prices. In the December, '79 issue of <u>Smithsonian</u>, the domestic price of llama was quoted at $32 a pound, compared to the 75¢
a pound price quoted for sheep's wool. The article didn't mention
alpaca, probably because even in Andean marketplaces, the latter
sells for considerably more than the highest grade of llama. Predictions are that the price of this once royal fibre will continue
to climb. Alpaca is, in effect, Peru's golden fleece.

The small number of blankets I brought back in December were
bought just ahead of a substantial mid-December price rise. As
a test market, between now and January 31st, we are offering 64
of these blankets at prices well below our own Wholesale prices.
Because our supply at this price is limited, we are offering this
special discount to only a fraction of our mailing list, most of
whom are old customers. You are one of 100 people in on this
sneak preview.

If you love alpaca, don't wait for the price rise to buy one
of these blankets. As are all of our exotic exclusives from Peru,
our new 100% alpaca blankets are fully guaranteed.

We at the Peruvian Connection send you our warmest, softest
wishes for a Happy New Year.

SPECIAL PRICE
THROUGH Jan 31st

WHOLESALE PRICES FOR 100% ALPACA BLANKETS:

Blanket (86"x65") .... $140.00 $125.
  (pictured, in natural alpaca stripes)

Throw Blanket (75"x57") $103.50 $92.50
  (pictured, in natural alpaca stripes)

Lap robe (or child's blanket) (43"x35")...... $42.00 $37.50
  (not pictured, in solid color soft brown)

Exhibit 4-1. The Peruvian Connection

Four-color circular was included with 2-page letter.

business" limits his options severely. His thinking is confined so narrowly that it becomes difficult to come up with new offers for customers. On the other hand, if he gives serious thought to the total character of his business, new avenues of possibility are opened, perhaps leading to the development and promotion of a wider range of products and services.

To illustrate: Is a mail order insurance company merely in the business of selling insurance? Not at all. It is really in the business of helping to provide financial security to its policyholders and prospects. From that perspective, management of an insurance company can think of offering not only other kinds of insurance policies but also financial planning services, loans, and the sale of mutual funds, assuming, of course, there is no conflict with insurance or investment laws and regulations.

More and more successful mail order companies have adopted this kind of thinking. A classic example is the Franklin Mint, whose management recognized that the company was not simply in the business of selling limited-edition medallions. Franklin Mint was actually in the business of producing fine art objects on a limited-edition basis for

Exhibit 4-2. Concept of the Product Life Cycle

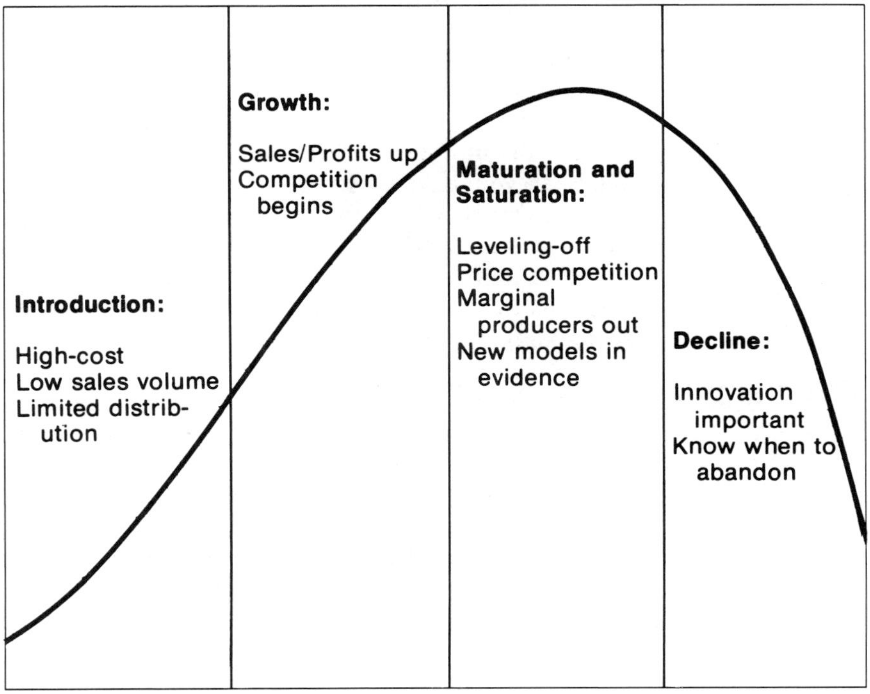

those who enjoy the pleasure and status provided by owning handsome objects not available to the majority of the general public. In addition, the possibility existed that the value of these objects would increase as time went on. As a result, the company has successfully offered limited-edition art prints, books, glassware, porcelain, and a myriad of other items. (See Exhibit 4-3.)

Another example is Baldwin Cooke Company. This firm for many years had offered an executive planner (desk diary) that businesspeople found made an excellent Christmas gift for their clients and friends. Then came the realization that the company was not simply in the business of selling desk diaries, but rather was in the business of selling executive gifts. This led to the development of a broad line of successful new products. The company's gift catalog today runs 32 pages with a circulation of one million plus.

An outstanding example of this broad-based thinking is the Meredith Publishing Company, publishers of *Better Homes and Gardens,* among other publications. Recognizing that the company was not simply in the magazine publishing business but rather in the business of disseminating useful, helpful information to large segments of middle America, management moved into such product areas as geographic atlases, world globes, gardening books, cookbooks, and a whole range of similar materials.

So, if you are exploring new products or services you can offer your customers or those you can use to reach new prospects, think about what kind of business you are really in. When you make that determination, you'll find that many new areas will open for you.

For the moment, let's pursue the idea that you are in direct marketing, that you have a list of customers built by offering products or services that they have found eminently satisfactory, and that you would like to expand your sales to those customers with new offerings. Let's also assume that you have answered the question of what business you are really in and have concluded that there are broader areas of endeavor available than you had previously realized. What then?

What are your capabilities?

First, review your capabilities and those of your organization and, again, try to think in the broadest possible terms.

The G.R.I. Corporation, which originally launched the World of Beauty Club, decided to utilize the ability it had developed in working with cosmetic manufacturers to set up a similar arrangement of sampling with a group of food manufacturers. In this case the market consisted of large numbers of people who wanted to sample new foods and save money on a regular basis.

Exhibit 4-3. Expanding Your Product Line

Ad from Franklin Porcelain typifies new product expansion program.

Other companies that have looked at their own expertise and facilities to determine what new products and services they could develop range all the way from the Donnelley Company, which utilized its co-op mailings to include the sale of its own products, to Time-Life, which used its editorial and photographic expertise to produce probably the most successful series of continuity books in the publishing industry.

So along with determining the business you're in, probably the second most important factor to investigate is your company's capabilities. As you can see, determining what business you are in and examining your capabilities go hand in hand in helping you pinpoint new

Table 4-1. Leading Mail Order Businesses (Worldwide Sales)

Name of Business	Sales ($MM's)	Sales Segments
1. Sears, Roebuck	$1,780	Catalog Retail
2. J.C. Penney	1,200	Catalog Retail
3. Montgomery Ward	780	Catalog Retail
4. United Services Automobile Association	940	Insurance
5. Geico	660	Insurance
6. Colonial Penn	580	Insurance
7. Time-Books	500	Books
8. Spiegel	450	Catalog Retail
9. Reader's Digest Magazines	400	Magazines
10. Reader's Digest—Multi-Products	400	Multi-Products
11. Franklin Mint	374	Collectibles
12. National Liberty	330	Insurance
13. Aldens	280	Catalog Retail
14. Fingerhut	275	Multi-Products
15. Reader's Digest Books	270	Books
16. New Process	231	Apparel
17. Time—Magazines	216	Magazines
18. Signature	200	Multi-Products
19. Columbia Record Club	195	Records
20. Lane Bryant	168	Apparel
21. Doubleday	160	Books
22. American Express	150	Multi-Products
23. Grolier	135	Books
24. L.L. Bean	132	Sporting Goods
25. TV Guide	124	Magazines
26. Physician's Mutual	120	Insurance
27. Olan Mills	100	Photography
28. Old American Insurance	100	Insurance
29. RCA Music Service	100	Records
30. Union Fidelity	100	Insurance
31. National Geographic Society	98	Magazines
32. Ambassador	90	Multi-Products
33. United Equitable	90	Insurance
34. Unity Buying Service	90	Multi-Products
35. Commerce Clearing House	89	Business Services
36. Bradford Exchange	86	Collectibles

Source: Adapted from *Direct Marketing* magazine—July 1982

This chart lists 72 firms engaged in mail order. Sales volume figures are estimates, except for public companies. Sales segments indicate the diversity of goods and services sold via mail order.

Table 4-1. Leading Mail Order Businesses (Worldwide Sales)—*cont.*

Name of Business	Sales ($MM's)	Sales Segments
37. Avon Fashions	80	Apparel
38. Eastern Numismatics	76	Collectibles
39. Meredith	76	Magazines
40. Department of Commerce	75	Educational
41. Dreyfus Corp.	74	Financial Services
42. Federal Express	72	Business Services
43. Garden Way	72	Gardening
44. Warshawsky	70	Automotive
45. Comp-U-Card	60	Multi-Products
46. Shopsmith	58	Hardware/Tools
47. Looart	55	Stationery
48. AT&T Long Lines	54	Business Services
49. Spencer Gifts	50	Gifts
50. Swiss Colony	50	Food
51. Union Fidelity	50	Insurance
52. Xerox Family Service	50	Books
53. Jackson & Perkins	46	Gardening
54. Eddie Bauer	43	Sporting Goods
55. Harry & David	41	Food
56. Burpee	40	Gardening
57. Haband	40	Apparel
58. Sunset House	40	Gifts
59. Figi's	36	Food
60. Rodale—Magazines	36	Magazines
61. Miles Kimball	35	Gifts
62. Sharper Image	35	Consumer Electronics/ Science
63. Talbot's	35	Apparel
64. SAVE	33	Multi-Products
65. Hirchene Photo Products	32	Photography
66. Eastern Mountain Sports	31	Sporting Goods
67. Brookstone	30	Hardware/Tools
68. C&H Materials Handling	30	Industrials
69. Drawing Board	30	Business Supplies
70. Healthkit	30	Consumer Electronics/ Science
71. Hudson Pharmaceuticals	30	Health
72. Sturdee	30	Health

merchandise or services. But there are significant differences between these areas and they must be considered individually. By doing so, you will be able to broaden your horizons even more.

What is your image with your prospect?

A third area to consider in this entire process is one that, paradoxically, instead of expanding your horizons is more likely to limit them or at least put some boundaries on them. Unlike the first two considerations—determining the business you are really in and examining your capabilities—this third area requires you to carefully analyze the "image" customers have of your company.

Every customer has an image of the company he or she deals with. This image may differ from customer to customer (and probably does in degree if not in kind), based on the relationship each customer has had with that company. If one customer has had nothing but satisfactory dealings with a company, that customer's image would differ from that of one who may have had an unsatisfactory experience, regardless of the cause. But the company's basic image will vary only slightly from customer to customer and will be essentially the same for all customers.

For example, General Motors has a particular image with most Americans. That image exists even for those who have never owned a GM car. The buyer of a GM car who was not happy with his or her purchase may have a somewhat different image of that company based on how his or her complaints were treated. But, in general, the American public believes that General Motors is a responsible, reputable company selling various forms of transportation among which are cars they enjoy using and driving.

Another example in an entirely different field is International Business Machines. Here is a company with which, I dare say, the majority of Americans have never had direct contact. But the image of IBM with most people is probably that of a major American, multinational corporation with unsurpassed technical and scientific skill in the development of the most advanced computers. As in the case of Henry Ford of an earlier day, IBM is probably regarded by most Americans as the developer and the most advanced proponent of a particular technology. In the case of IBM, this technology is concerned with sophisticated computers and with office equipment such as typewriters.

This perceived image is a vitally important factor when you are considering what new products or services to offer your customers or your prospects, if your company is sufficiently well known. It has been proved over and over in direct marketing as well as in other distribution channels that a company has great difficulty selling merchandise or services that do not fit the public's preconceived image of that company. This can be illustrated in the case of one company that built its customer list on the sale of power tools and then failed dismally in an offer of books of general interest to the same audience.

Let's take the case of the Minnesota-based Fingerhut Company. This firm has built a fine reputation by offering good values in medium- to low-priced merchandise ranging from power tools to tableware. While the company was able successfully to sell medium- to low-priced men's and women's wear to the same audience, it is highly doubtful that they could just as successfully sell fine bound books or Yves St. Laurent clothing. This is true not only because the demographics of the Fingerhut list probably are not suited to the higher-priced category, but also because the Fingerhut image does not conform to that high-priced merchandise.

Unless your customers or prospects are willing to believe that you are a qualified source for the products you are offering, they are unlikely to buy. But if those prospects *expect* certain products from you, because they fit your company image, your chances of success are vastly enhanced.

Thus, it is extremely important that you fully recognize the image you present to your customers and that you select offerings that are appropriate to that image. This recognition, as mentioned earlier, narrows your choices. But it narrows them to your ultimate advantage if it keeps you from going so far afield that what you offer will stand little chance of success.

At this point we might discuss the kinds of factors that tend to create a company's image. The combination of such factors consists of approximately equal parts of the following:

- The products or services offered in the past.
- The style and quality of the new product itself.
- The price level.
- The presentation of the product, whether it is an ad, a commercial, or a mailing piece. The "sound" of the copy and the appearance of the graphics send a definite message to the prospect.
- The "look" of the merchandise package received by the customer.
- The "sound" and appearance of any other communication with your customer, e.g., the invoice, the way complaints are handled, and the way telephone communications are conducted.
- The "tone" of any publicity your company receives.

An excellent example of the difference a company's image can make can be given in a comparison of two companies featuring outdoor products: L. L. Bean of Maine and Norm Thompson of Seattle, Washington. Just as they are at opposite ends of the country, both companies successfully present different, yet equally acceptable, images. L. L. Bean's image is that of an old-line, conservative company with the Yankee habit of underplaying its product, a company featuring timeless styles that appeal primarily to a mature audience. Norm Thompson, on the

Exhibit 4-4. The Importance of Image

This classic McGraw-Hill ad, directed to prospects for business publication advertising, applies with equal force to those who would enter the mail order field.

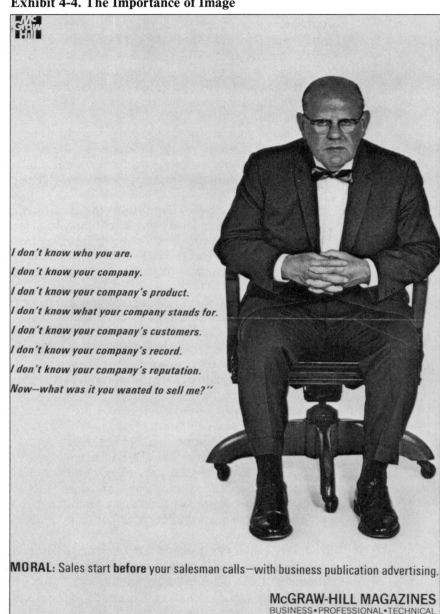

other hand, shows an image of a company that appeals to men and women with a more youthful lifestyle. The company prides itself on its ability to come up with interesting, often exotic new products from abroad.

Examine the characteristics of your customer list	Another most important "mine" to explore for products or services is your own customer list. Study your list from a number of different perspectives, such as:

- How your list was developed
- How your customers have been "educated"
- What they are buying, if you give them choices
- The demographics and psychographics of your customers
- The "product experience" of your list

Let's start with the first point, how your list was developed. In other words, what type of merchandise have your customers been buying? At what prices? How have they paid: cash, charge, time payment? These may appear to be obvious questions, but it is surprising how often they are overlooked when new product planning is under consideration.

Your customers are constantly "telling" you what they like and are interested in every time they make a purchase. Catalog companies are following this rule every time they analyze each product in their catalog for profitability. By doing this, they automatically determine which products are most popular and, as a corollary, which new products they should add to their line and at what prices.

If you are successfully selling a vacuum cleaner through direct marketing, it is likely your customers would be logical prospects for such products as sets of dishes, tableware, glassware, and similar items. If you are selling clothing through the mail, as does the Haband Company and New Process, your customers might well be tempted by offerings of economical housewares, luggage, towel sets, and so forth.

Moreover, the price levels of your merchandise are standards by which to judge any new offering. There is one proviso: You should be constantly testing higher price levels to determine the upper pricing limits of your customer list. Just a 10 or 15 percent increase in the price level your customers will accept may open many more profitable products or services for you to offer.

This, of course, raises the question of methods of payment used by your customers. If they pay in cash or by credit card, they will probably prefer to continue to purchase on that basis. This will probably add to the difficulty of introducing a new item that requires a higher purchase price. On the other hand, if your customers are used to paying on the installment plan, they more likely will be willing to purchase higher-priced merchandise, especially if you can increase the number of install-ments. Customers who prefer to pay for their merchandise on a monthly basis are, generally speaking, more likely to be concerned with the amount of the individual payment rather than the total price of the product.

The second point is, "How have your customers been educated?" The way in which you first got your customers has an important influ-ence on what they expect of you in future offers. An example of the power of this "educating" process is the Fingerhut Company, whose customers have been conditioned to expect a host of free gifts with every purchase. It is unlikely that Fingerhut would be successful with a new offering that did not include such free gifts.

The Grolier Corporation has built a large list of book customers by offering free the first volume of a set of books, whether or not the prospect decides to continue with the series. Again, an offering to these customers of a new series without the free volume would probably fail. At the same time, Time-Life Books has been extremely successful in a program of selling books with an offer that only permits the prospect to examine a new volume for a limited time, without getting it free.

Especially if you are just starting in business, give serious thought to your front-end offer. Be sure you are clear on how you want your customers "educated." The way you start out is probably the way you will have to continue. If you'd rather not adopt the pattern of free gifts, free volumes, and sweepstakes, you probably ought not to start with such an offer.

What is the lifestyle of your customers?

Now we get to your customers themselves. What kind of a lifestyle do they have? If you haven't already, you should do a comprehensive analysis to develop a "profile" of your "typical customer."

More and more we are finding that the demographic profiles of customers combined with their psychographic (lifestyle) profiles give many clues to successful new product development and sales.

With such a profile, you will find all kinds of "road signs" to new products or services. How your customers live, the kinds of vacations they take, the type of entertainment they enjoy, whether they prefer books to movies, as well as their income level, education, size of family, whether they live in a house or apartment, and other demographic characteristics—all are hints as to the new products or services they might be interested in.

Obviously, people who live in an apartment are less likely to be prospects for a set of power tools than people who live in a house. Similarly, people who prefer movies to books are not very good pros-pects for a best seller.

| What new products are people buying? | When you want to determine whether an offering will work in direct marketing, review the products that people are currently buying at retail. Examples are LED watches and paperback books. |

Formerly, direct marketers tended to shy away from products available at retail. But that is no longer true. A wide variety of products ranging from Polaroid cameras to General Electric toasters have been and are being sold through the direct response method in increasing volume. Only a few years ago the Quality Paperback Book Club was started, successfully, on a direct response basis, to take advantage of the tremendous popularity of paperbacks. When you consider that paperbacks are sold in virtually every drugstore, cigar shop, candy store, railroad station, and airport—as well as every bookstore—QPB's success can be seen as a tribute to the convenience and acceptance of direct marketing.

| Look at the new lifestyles | American lifestyles seem to be changing more rapidly all the time. A few years ago the women's liberation movement initiated a continuing change in the lifestyles of many women that influences the lifestyles of a great many men as well. Over half of all women in America now work outside the home. Obviously, employed women have different needs from those who don't work. More convenient food preparation products, for instance. The number of unmarried women who head households also keeps growing. Their needs, too, are different. Their need for financial advice, for example, is certainly different from that of married women. For many years senior citizens have constituted a growing segment of U.S. society. Older people have many needs that differ from those of younger age groups. An example of how one group is addressing those needs is the American Association of Retired Persons. The association offers people over 55 a wide variety of services ranging from travel opportunities to insurance. Membership is over 6,000,000. All of these groups have particular needs that frequently can be met by the perceptive direct marketer. |

Price/value relationships

Once you have selected your product or service, you are faced with the problem of pricing it. How much can you get for it? Whatever price you select, it must appear to the prospect as the "right" price for that item. He or she must perceive your price as being a value. And that perception depends on the item and the person to whom you are appealing.

A person earning $250 per week has one set of price/value relationships. Another earning $750 per week has a different set. To the first person, a $7 tie may have just the right price/value relationship. To the second, the tie may seem "cheap."

A piece of merchandise in itself has a perceived price/value relationship with the consumer. One expects a set of cookware to cost less than a set of bone china dishes. A price of $49 for a set of cookware might sound just right. But $49 for bone china dinnerware set sounds suspiciously inexpensive.

As an example of how people establish a price/value relationship for a product, here's a test conducted by a direct marketer selling a set of four kitchen knives. Five offers were tested with the results indicated.

- Offer 1—four knives at $19.95 plus $1.00 shipping and handling. Pull: 1.3 percent.
- Offer 2—four knives at $19.95, plus hanging board at $1.50 (optional), plus $1.00 shipping and handling. Pull: 1.3 percent; 80 percent took the hanging board.
- Offer 3—four knives, plus hanging board, plus shipping and handling at $24.95. Pull: 0.9 percent.
- Offer 4—three knives at $19.95, plus $1.00 shipping and handling. Pull: 0.8 percent.
- Offer 5—five knives at $29.95, plus hanging board at $1.50, plus $1.00 shipping and handling. Pull: 0.7 percent.

As you can see, the prospects saw offer 2 as the best in terms of price and value, far better than offer 3, which was only $2.50 more.

We have been through this time after time, and we have found that the assumption that there is a right price for every item invariably holds true. Certain cookware sets can only be sold at $39.95. Certain clock radios can only be sold at $49.95. Certain sets of stainless tableware can only be sold at $24.95.

Conversely, we have also found that the customer will, in some cases, accept a higher price than you would have chosen as the proper price/value relationship. For example, a paint gun was tested at both $49.95 and $59.95. And sales at the $59.95 price were better. So, while you may think you have a good idea what the right price for an item should be, you should test that price, but also test at a higher and lower price. You may be pleasantly surprised.

Price/value relationships change, too. Inflation has an effect on them. So does competition. And the relative popularity of the item is important. The same paint gun that sold successfully at $59.95 now sells for $89.95 in about the same quantities as it did at the lower price. Remember when Sharp came out with the first electronic calculator? It was only a four-function model, but American Express sold thousands at $300. Today you'd be lucky to get $15 for it.

Other areas to consider

Finally, let's consider several other marketing factors apart from the product or service itself. These are such factors as the offer, the advertising medium to be used, and how to use research in reaching your decisions.

So far as the offer is concerned, regard it as an opportunity to say to the prospect, "Here is a special reason for acting now rather than waiting to order at a future date." The best offers flow from the product or service being offered. A good example is the original Franklin Mint five-year buy-back guarantee, an offer that corresponded perfectly with the firm's assumption that their products might increase in value. Book club and record club offers of X number of books or records for as little as 10 cents are other examples. Free gift offers, limited time or quantity offers, free trial periods, and a wide variety of others can be useful. Try to develop an offer that relates to the general character of your merchandise best. It can pay big dividends.

Products may determine media

When it comes to deciding which advertising medium to use, a number of basic factors must be considered. Generally speaking, if the product doesn't carry at least a $15.00 profit at a $29.95 retail price, you probably won't be successful in a solo mailing, unless the pull is really sensational.

A further consideration in your decision as to whether to use the direct mail system is the amount of copy and illustration you need. The more of both you require, the more likely your product belongs in the mail. If your item is suited to a visual demonstration, television becomes a likely medium, especially if the item's price is under $29.95.

Newspaper inserts should not be overlooked as a viable medium today. Inserts have brought a new dimension that offers as much copy space as needed with a wide variety of interesting formats, plus a return envelope, quality reproduction, and, often, market segmentation. Newspaper inserts have opened opportunities for a wide range of offers—from insurance to limited-edition commemoratives and free credit cards.

The use of research

Over the past few years an activity that has been receiving more attention in determining product selection is market research. For many years, direct marketers believed that the only way to determine the appeal of a product or service was to put it in the mail or run an ad and see if it sold. Today, sophisticated direct marketers are more and more turning to research as a means of helping to determine whether an item stands a chance of success. (See Chapter 16.)

Consider the various research techniques available to help in selecting your product or service so as to increase your prospects for success. Research such as focus group testing can give you valuable insights into the appeal (or lack thereof) of your offering. It can also help you determine which one of two or more items have the strongest appeal. Often this procedure can even help you add to the appeal of your product or service by suggesting benefits to be added.

Reliable sources

Everything we've said so far presupposes that you have a dependable source for supplying your product or that you will have a supplier once you determine what you are going to sell. Seasoned direct marketers always make certain they are ready to deliver when they put a promotion in the mail, or advertise in a magazine, or offer the item via broadcast. A cardinal point to remember is: the product must be on hand before you start your promotion. Once you have mailed or placed your ad, you have committed yourself fully. You can't recall the mailing or magazine. And in the direct response business, if you can't deliver in a reasonable length of time, you will lose a large percentage of your orders. You will create much expensive, time-consuming correspondence. You will engender a lot of ill-will and undoubtedly lose the bulk of your investment.

Mining your customer base

While direct marketers must be on a relentless, continuous search for new products and services, there is the ever-present danger that the excitement of new product development will take attention from the product or products that built the business in the first place. No established direct marketer can afford to overlook this danger because their customer bases are the lifeblood of their businesses.

One could travel the world over, but could not find a direct marketer more aware of the value of this customer base than Garden Way, a 15-year-old company in New England doing over $60 million a year. Garden Way is a place where the principal product is a 300-pound, $700 rotary garden tiller called a Troy-Bilt, a tiller with an automatic-type transmission with powered wheels and powered tines in the rear. Over the past 10 years Garden Way has attracted over 2,500,000 inquiries, converted 16 percent to owners—over 400,000 happy gardeners—who are the cornerstone of their business.

If there is one thing that distinguishes the Garden Way marketing program from others it's got to be its owner program, a program that doesn't make sense on the surface. Here we have 400,000 customers who spent $700 each for a Troy-Bilt tiller, about as unlikely a group for repeat business as one could expect.

Yet, in the face of this, Garden Way developed a program completely dedicated to nurturing and wooing these 400,000 Troy-Bilt owners in what it refers to as its "Intensive Care Department." Every other month all 400,000 receive the "Troy-Bilt Owner News," a gardening newspaper that costs over $600,000 a year to produce. Regular surprise gifts and mailings carrying planting charts, service charts, booklets, and bulletins go to this choice list. In addition, there is a free, continuing course in gardening and factory service tips. Now are you ready for this? Not once during the process of the owner program does Garden Way ask for the order!

So what happens? Would you believe that 25 percent of Garden Way sales come from owners, their families, friends, and neighbors each year. The way I figure it, that's about $15 million. It might be said, "That's what happens when people talk to their best friends—their customers."

As Garden Way points out, the keynote to new product development and after-market development for the future will be its loyal customer base. Its guiding question at all times will be—what's best for our customer?

Self-Quiz

1. The first tip in selecting mail order items is that you should select items whose benefits you can _____ with photos and graphics.

2. List 10 sources for discovering mail order items:

a. _____   f. _____

b. _____   g. _____

c. _____   h. _____

d. _____   i. _____

e. _____   j. _____

3. List 10 factors to consider when selecting mail order items:

a. _____   f. _____

b. _____   g. _____

c. _____   h. _____

d. _____   i. _____

e. _____   j. _____

4. What are the four phases of the product life cycle?

a. _____   c. _____

b. _____   d. _____

5. In attempting to expand your business with new products or services, what is the first question you should ask yourself?

_____

_____

6. How does the image of your company influence your selection of products?

_____

_____

7. In determining what other products you might offer your customers, you should look at your house list from five different angles. They are:

a. _____

b. _____

c. _____

d. _____

e. _____

8. Define price/value relationships.

_____

_____

_____

_____

9. The more copy and illustration you need to adequately present your product, the more likely it is that:

☐ space is your best medium.

☐ direct mail is your best medium.

10. A major source of gaining new customers is _____

_____.

Pilot Project

You are Annie Hurlbut. You have developed a customer base of 20,000 women who have purchased handloomed alpaca garments made in Peru.

The question you face is, "What else might I offer to my customer list?" Make a list of 10 products you think would be most attractive to this customer base.

Section II
Choosing Media for Your Message

Chapter Five

Mailing Lists

Mailing lists are the media in direct mail.

What is a list? The *Random House Dictionary* defines a list as "a series of names or other items written or printed together in meaningful groupings so as to constitute a record." The operative words are "meaningful groupings." The list, then, is simply a way to organize otherwise random material into market segments.

In general terms, there are three things that are both central and indispensable to direct marketing through lists:

1. Identifying the best customers on internal (house) lists
2. Finding more of them through outside lists
3. Selling to them at a maximum profit with minimum waste

Types of Lists

There are two broad categories of lists: internal (house) lists and external (outside) lists. *Internal lists* (a company's own files) include customers, former customers, subscribers, former subscribers, donors, former donors, inquiries, prospects, warranty cards, etc. *External lists* include compiled and direct response lists from sources outside the company.

Your best customer is the one you already have. Internal lists, popularly known as house files, should be considered an *information data base*. It is essential, in the data collection process, to include as much relevant information as possible about your customers. Remember that this data base (house file) is a company asset as valuable to direct marketers as any asset the company has.

In every instance, the first expense—and usually the most costly— is the acquisition cost. Over the life of the customer, subscriber, member, contributor, etc. the acquisition cost isn't really the payoff—the revenue will come from persistency—its lifetime value. Therefore, the data base must be structured to serve as a marketing information system. This will enable you to make marketing decisions based on facts.

With certain exceptions, if a product or service can't be sold to your in-house names, it can't be sold anywhere. But even a house file is not effective unless you have the ability to segment it productively and use it selectively.

House File Segmentation

Let's start with the definition of *segment*: one of the constituent parts into which an entity or quantity is divided as if by natural boundaries.

With lists, then, segmentation works on the theory that parts of a list have more sales potential for a particular product or service than other parts of a list. The art in getting more sales from existing customers is to be able to match offers to the customers' buying preferences. It goes without saying that segmentation is practical in relation to the size of a list. If the list constitutes only a few hundred names, segmentation is hardly worthwhile. But if a list runs as few as 5,000 names, segmentation can prove very worthwhile. And if the list runs into the hundreds of thousands, segmentation becomes essential to maximizing profits. In the classic questions of journalism, each mailer must continually ask:

- *Who* are my customers?
- *What* do they buy from me?
- *Why* do they respond to my mailings?
- *How* do I retain them and increase their purchases?
- *Where* do I find others like them?
- *When* do I sell them more effectively?

The answers to these questions can only be found in careful attention to the specifics of planning. In list utilization, planning is defined in three basic areas: selection, analysis and budgeting (forecasting). These subjects will all be covered later in this chapter.

The first of this vital trio—selection—begins with the internal lists.

Customer value or definition of a good customer depends on the dynamics of the company. The function of the marketing effort must be geared to converting first-time buyers into loyal, repeat customers. This can be described as target marketing. One approach to target marketing is to use the customer's past history to project future purchases.

If the data base is programmed to store certain bits of information about each customer, the data base is not just a list of customers—it's a gallery of portraits. The art is to get more sales from existing customers by being able to match your offers to their buying preferences.

The behavioral characteristics of your customers can best be catered to by applying the RFM formula. The *R* stands for *recency.* Did the customer order anything recently? The *F* stands for *frequency* of purchases (a very significant factor). The *M* stands for the *monetary* value of the purchases.

Application of the RFM formula might reveal that one big order every three years yields a satisfactory profit. A series of small orders at odd intervals may or may not yield profit.

Bob Kestnbaum, president of Kestnbaum & Co., and an authority on the mathematics of direct marketing (see Chapter 15), expands the RFM formula slightly, using the acronym FRAT. *F* stands for frequency. *R* stands for recency. *A* stands for amount (monetary). *T* stands for *type* of purchase. Kestnbaum puts particular emphasis on frequency—the number of purchases within a season or a calendar period.

As Bob points out, if you select only frequency of purchase names from a customer base, you will be dealing with a smaller number of names than you would with recency of purchase names. But you would be almost certain to hype response. Commenting upon type of purchase—what the customer bought—Kestnbaum counsels that the data base containing this information should be very specific. It is not enough, for example, to record that a customer bought shirts. The data should indicate type of shirts—dress shirts or sport shirts. (This says something about lifestyle.)

In addition to the behavioral characteristics of RFM, or FRAT, other psychodynamic factors that should be included are:

- *Mode of payment:* cash, open account, installments, credit card.
- *Geographics:* not only where your customer lives, but also correlating recency, frequency, monetary to geographic areas.
- *Type of product purchased:* labeled by product categories—household, leisure, recreation, fashions, gourmet, travel, sports, do-it-yourself, etc.
- *Length of time on the file:* an indication of interest in your publication, book club, catalog, etc.
- *Source:* direct mail, radio, TV, space, telephone, cable TV, inserts, co-ops, etc. It is important to note that the use of multimedia contributes another lifestyle statistic to the data base.
- *Date of last transaction:* includes payment, change of address, correspondence, renewal, unsolicited contributions, etc.

These are just some of the variables. Others should be determined based on what the company sells. A magazine publisher for example, will not use the same factors as a catalog company or a fund-raising organization.

Several mathematical regression techniques allow the marketer to relate each element of customer data on the file to other transactional data and, thus, to predict customer behavior. It is important to realize that there is no universal equation that applies to all types of regression analysis. Every equation must be custom-designed based on the dynamics of the particular company and must be used, evaluated, and updated on a continuing basis.

Properly structured, this type of research will lead to customer demand analysis and segmentation on the theory that parts of a list have more sales potential (hence more profit) for a particular product than others. You must do all you can to optimize the segmentation of your customer file for internal use and for list rental to others because both aspects will contribute substantially to your profit picture.

External Lists

This information developed from your house file can be extended to your use of outside lists. There are two basic kinds of outside or external lists: compiled lists (usually by some common interest) and lists of inquiries and/or customers from other companies. With literally thousands of lists to choose from, the dominant characteristics of the internal file will prevail and establish direction for selection of external lists. (See Table 5-1.)

Lists of other companies' customers have one advantage over compiled lists if those companies sell by direct response: they have one discriminant characteristic—they are direct mail buyers. While compiled lists do not necessarily represent direct response buyers, they do have discriminant characteristics. There are extensive compilations in the business, professional, educational, technical, agricultural markets—and the consumer market. If you want to reach college students, the biggest universe is represented by compiled lists. If you want to reach presidents of firms by number of employees, compiled lists will give you the most complete coverage. If your market is to "new mothers," compiled lists offer the biggest universe. And likewise for accountants, engineers, farmers, and scores of categories.

In the business category (used by business-to-business advertisers, mail order companies selling to the business community, and business and financial services), these compilations offer the opportunity to reach any segment of U.S. industry. Selections are available by SIC (Standard Industrial Classification) code, size of company, number of employees, occupational level, by individual name, by title, and almost any configuration of selection factors required for the particular promotion.

In the professional market, there exists a multitude of choices. For example: doctors (by specialty, age, in private practice, intern, affiliated with hospital practice, hospital administrator, etc.); lawyers (by size of

firm, specialty, one-man firm, senior partners, ABA members, etc);
educators (by discipline, elementary, secondary, college teachers, administrators, pupil enrollment, etc.).

Most business/professional compilations are derived from printed
sources: directories, rosters, registrations at trade shows, Dun & Bradstreet. There is a *Directory of Directories* that lists over 5,200 directories

Table 5-1. Better Homes & Gardens Available List Selections

	No. of Names
(1) Subscribers (5-Year Length of Residence)	1,200,000
(2) Subscribers (10-Year Length of Residence)	800,000
(3) Monthly Changes of Address	75,000
(4) Subscribing Gift Subscription Donors	275,000
(5) Non-Subscribing Gift Subscription Donors	200,000
(6) Multiple Purchasers (Actives who purchased one-plus book within last 2 years)	500,000
(7) Super Spot Subscribers	875,000
(8) Ethnic	
British	3,476,000
Irish	901,000
Scottish	217,000
Spanish	244,000
Italian	169,000
French	130,000
German	764,000
Chinese	10,267
Japanese	15,187
Polish	62,000
Dutch	60,000
Swedish	178,000
Norwegian	55,000
Jewish	143,000
(9) Religious	
Jewish	205,000
Catholic	1,540,000
Protestant	4,718,000
Oriental	26,118
(10) Families With Three or More Children	525,000
(11) Female-Headed Households	1,500,000
(12) Retirees	1,100,000

This table shows the multiplicity of selections (12) available from a major list—
Better Homes & Gardens.

of various types. (Note: Since lists deteriorate rapidly, it is important to find out *when* the list was compiled.)

In the consumer market, companies such as Polk, Metromail, and Donnelley, among others, offer the capability of reaching almost every household in the U.S. with an overlay of Census tract statistics. Census tracts are comprised of relatively small areas with the purpose of making each tract as homogeneous as possible. One important use of compiled lists is to match external files against the house list to get a better feel for the demographics of the external file for segmentation purposes. For example, one group that can be segmented is super spot subscribers—those who live in high-income areas. With properly structured tests and in-depth analysis, you can establish a market for your product by demographics such as income, education, number of children in the family, and so on. This type of compilation usually can't be tested with small quantities and/or without carefully structured response analysis. This will be discussed at greater length later in this chapter.

Why do companies rent their lists? Profit. And the recognition that there is no such thing as a "captive audience." The fact that a person buys by mail is an indication of a "mail order buying characteristic." That person is likely to appear on many lists, which is why duplication elimination is an established technique used by most volume mailers (see merge/purge).

Let's look at potential profit. Assuming a list of 500,000 names, turned over 20 times per year:

> 10,000,000 names at a net to the list owner of $36 per M ($45 per M, less 20% broker's commission) = $360,000. At a running cost of about $2/M, we are talking about $340,000 that goes right down to the bottom line. Depending on the quality and size of the list, this could really be a very conservative estimate.

How does outside list rental affect internal sales? There have been very carefully structured tests conducted over the years to answer this question. Results show over and over again that there is no effect or, at the most, a minimal effect upon internal sales. The number of kinds of lists available for rental boggles the mind. To get a feel for list availability, refer to Table 5-2: Review of Consumer Lists by Category.

Demographics

People of like interests tend to cluster ("birds of a feather flock together"). While the impact of societal changes does affect this theory, demographics is still a valid method by which to add another dimension to the customer profile.

Table 5-2. Review of Consumer Lists by Category

	No. of Lists	Universe (000)
Hobbies & Special Interests		
Special Interest Reading	17	1,348
Female How-To (includes Cook Book, Recipe Cards)	111	25,243
Sports/Outdoors/Camping/Boating	334	40,587
Automotive	69	14,903
Photography	53	10,794
Men's Reading	16	4,909
Men's How-To	102	18,225
Gardening	70	16,909
Collectibles, Antiques	145	11,629
Sub-Total	917	144,547
Entertainment		
Records, Tapes	57	19,765
Music Mdse. & Publications	26	3,989
Gourmet Foods & Mdse.	77	13,006
Travel	49	5,588
Theatre/Concerts/Ballet/etc.	97	7,772
Games & Intellectual Recreation	7	790
Sub-Total	313	50,910
Reading		
General & Cultural	91	25,889
Nature & Science	49	6,269
Arts	39	3,371
History	35	3,438
News & Politics	58	12,859
Regional Magazines	116	7,456
Escapist	17	2,891
Sub-Total	405	62,173
Self-Improvement		
Opportunity Seekers	222	45,248
Health	170	27,416
Insurance & Maturity Market	33	50,851
Religious/Ethnic	119	74,838
Occult, Metaphysical, Astrology	23	9,491
Sub-Total	567	207,844
Home Interest/Family		
Catalogs & General Mdse.	214	86,568
Parents/Children/Students	206	71,910
Women's Clothes & Beauty Aids	149	50,139
Shelter & Other Women's Books	41	29,002
Men's Clothing & Accessories	46	6,435
Sub-Total	656	244,050
TOTAL ALL CATEGORIES	2,858	709,524

ZIP codes, which many mailers once feared, have proven to be a boon instead of a burden. They brought list maintenance into the computer age. This step made it possible to identify duplicate names in a mailing and also led to analysis of response by ZIP codes.

It then led to a further refinement in geographical analysis by *Census tract overlays.* Unlike geopolitical districts (cities, counties, states, and even ZIP codes) Census tracts are relatively small and homogeneous. Most residents in the Census tract will exhibit more demographic similarities than differences—age, marital status, income, occupation, education, home ownership, home value, number of children in the household, etc. As mentioned previously, this type of analysis can lead to further house file segmentation. In some instances, inferential lifestyle values are added based on the resulting demographics.

Psychographics (Lifestyle)

Veblen's theory of "conspicuous consumption" at one point in time was a sharp behavioral definition. But now we see that consumers, although demographically related, have been showing marked tendencies to spend their discretionary income quite differently. To identify our target market, it is essential to capture lifestyle details. This concept is not new—it has been recognized for a long time that societal changes have *influenced demographics.*

If we look at "The Target is Moving" (Table 5-3), we see that these socio-economic changes are quite evident. The significance of these trends can't be ignored. In a highly advanced and rapidly expanding technological environment, we must recognize that socioeconomic changes will come even more rapidly. In marketing, societal change is a subject you can never know enough about.

List Brokers and List Selection

A broker, as the name implies, serves two sides: the client (mailer) and the list owner. If you have a product or service that is to be sold to a vertical market—for example, doctors, lawyers or accountants or any other pinpointed, highly-specialized market—finding the right lists is simple. In almost every field, there is a compiler, trade publication, or list owner who has the precise list.

It gets decidedly more complex when you are selling a product that has a broader appeal. Here is where the broker can offer invaluable assistance in suggesting those lists that appear to represent the market you are trying to reach. You get the benefit of experts who make mailing lists their full-time specialization.

A professional relationship doesn't work if the list consultant is asked to operate in a vacuum or in abstract terms. You must view the broker as part of the total marketing process. You must specify your needs and objectives well enough in advance to permit the broker to research the list marketplace. (This research is also a valuable tool for the creative people. Working without a clear, complete knowledge of the list market makes it difficult to properly focus the promotional copy.)

To emphasize—here are some factors necessary to establish a competent working relationship with a list broker:

1. Bring the list broker into the picture at an early stage to help define the market.

Table 5-3. The Target Is Moving

Working Women
(1) Half the labor force
(2) More than half of all married women work. Over 50% of married couples have dual income
(3) By 1990—only one out of four married women will be a full-time homemaker.

Families (Preliminary Report from Census 1970 vs. 1980)
(1) Number of children in a household decreasing
(2) Number of children increasing (more women of child-bearing age)
(3) Size of household declined sharply since 1970. Nearly 23% of all U.S. households consist of one person
(4) Total number of households increased from 63.4 million to 80.4 million
(5) Surprising number of single people living in units which once accommodated families.
(6) Households maintained by women increased by 51% vs. 11% growth in families. Families maintained by a man increased by 33.6%. Over 8,000,000 men and women are raising children alone.

Age Distribution of the Population
(1) Majority of U.S. population (as a result of 'baby boom' between 1946 & 1954) is past 30 years old and represents about 53.4 million.
(2) 45-54 market represents 25% of spending in U.S. The over-45 group represents the largest pool of *purchasing power* ever to impact on U.S. economy.

Geographical Shifts (where of the market)
(1) Distant *ex*urbs are growing residential areas
(2) Rural areas now have executive homes where pastures once were
(3) Some states struggling with industrial decline—others trying to cope with industrial growth

Recreation
(1) More leisure time makes relaxation one of America's most serious businesses. Represents about 8-9% of gross national product.
(2) *Recreational learning* a major trend.
(3) *Electronic recreation room* with mini-computers linked to the TV set.

2. Give the broker *time* to do a professional job. Specific, targeted list recommendations take time. Information such as balance counts, selectivity, segmentation, geographical counts, etc. is essential to proper list selection.
3. List rental orders (accompanied by the mailing piece and a requested specific mail date) must be cleared for approval with the list owner. Allow time for this process.
   (Refer to List Tests, Market Tests for further list selection strategies.)

List Managers

During the past few years there has been a trend toward list management whereby a given list broker takes over the complete management of a list for rental purposes. Under this arrangement, the list manager performs all or almost all of the following functions:

1. Handles contacts with list brokers.
2. Clears sample mailing piece and mail date with list owner.
3. Processes list rental orders.
4. Follows up on completion of list rental orders to assure delivery of order within the specified return date.
5. Bills the broker on behalf of the list owner.
6. Collects payment and remits to list owner less broker's commission and list management fee.
7. Assumes responsibility for all promotions of the list and sales activity without charge (over and above the established fee) to the list owner.
8. If the list owner so desires, the manager assumes responsibility for the maintenance of the list either in-house or with an outside computer service bureau.
9. Provides the list owner with a detailed activity report—including billing and collecting information—on a predetermined time frame.

The list rental business is, for some list owners, a part-time activity. Being relieved of the voluminous details involved and the time required to promote the list usually more than warrants the extra compensation the manager receives for the specialized services rendered.

List Information

List brokers and list managers present list information on what is known as a data card. The *data card* shows the price of the list. The rate is quoted on a per-thousand-name (per M) basis. The price range averages $40 to $50 per thousand for direct response lists, exclusive of selection charges. Compiled lists usually rent at a far lower rate per thousand. Exhibit 5-1 typifies specific data available to the prospective list renter.

List Rental Procedures

Lists can be ordered directly from a list owner, but most list rental orders are placed through list brokers. The broker handles all the details with the list owner: clearances, order placement, followup for order completion, billing, collecting, and payment to the list owner, less the usual 20 percent commission that accrues to the list broker.

The rental of lists involves certain conditions:

1. The names are rented for *one time use* only. No copy of the list is to be retained for any purpose whatsoever.
2. Usage must be cleared with the list owner in advance. The mailing piece which is approved is the only one that can be used.
3. The mail date approved by the list owner must be adhered to.
4. List rentals are charged on a per-thousand-name basis.
5. Net name arrangements vary, but most list owners will specify the percentage (of the names supplied) for which the full list rental charge per M must be paid plus a specific running cost for the names not used.
6. Most list owners charge extra for selections such as: sex, recency, ZIP, state, unit of sale, or any segmentation available on the particular list. Prices vary.

List Tests

Test: The means by which the presence, quality or genuineness of anything is determined, a means of trial. As any crossword puzzle fan knows, a test is an experiment, an attempt to determine by small-scale trial, whether something will or won't work consistently or universally.

How big should a sample be? The proper sample size is determined by two factors: sampling tolerance (or deviation) and the degree of risk that the user is willing to accept. As long as we have perfect random samples, we can keep sampling tolerance small by taking large samples. This part of the equation is scientific.

The risk factor is much harder to deal with because this involves subjective judgments. Some people can't tolerate much risk.

Some practitioners advocate that the sample size should be based on the number of responses needed. The caution here is that some mailers, particularly on a new product, have what might be termed "unreasonable expectations." The higher the price of the product, the lower the response is likely to be. Under these circumstances, a small test quantity will not yield the numbers needed to project with a degree

Exhibit 5-1. Architectural Digest—Interior Design Magazine

All of these descriptive factors are important in selecting lists. Demographics and even psychographic detailing can be inferred on: (1) the nature of the product, (2) unit of sale, (3) media used to acquire the names, (4) recency of purchase.

380,455 Paid Direct Response Subscribers @ **$60/M**
Can Select:

273,419	Long-Term Subscribers	@ $60/M
50,629	Multi-Subscribers (to both Architectural Digest & Bon Appetit)	@ $65/M
22,928	Business Address Subscribers (mostly company-only)	@ $60/M
7,522	Canadian Subscribers	@ $60/M
** 10,800	Foreign Subscribers	@ $60/M
** 50,000	Expires (Last 6 Months)	@ $35/M
** 5,000	Address Changes (Monthly)	@ $65/M
**Monthly	Hotline Paid Subscribers (20,000 Average)	@ $65/M

July 1982   K01 Y02
                    D01 Z01

Minimum: 5,000
Architectural Digest
Service Center
Att: F. Yates (no cc)
8460 Higuera Street
Culver City,
  CA 90230

—or—

**Neodata Services
Att: Larry R.
  Cline (cc)
2500 Broadway
Boulder, CO 80302

Complete Sample Reqd.
Allow 3 weeks for processing orders.

Air Freight shipments will be sent collect unless otherwise specified.

Magtape Return:
Above address where applicable.

Net Name Payment:
85% + $5/M
(50,000 minimum).

**STATE COUNTS
ON
REVERSE SIDE**

DATA	Homeowners & professionals interested in interior design, furnishings & decorative arts. Beautifully illustrated, articles include reviews of outstanding homes & features on antique collecting, art & restoration.
UNIT	$36 yearly (12 issues) $19.95 introductory rate (8 issues).
SEX	67% women. Can select identifiable names @ N/C: 170,808 women; 103,496 men.
PROFILE	Median age 44.7; 84% attended college; 31.7% own a second home. Average household income $114,790. 66.5% professional/managerial.
MEDIA	100% Direct Response.
FILED	Zip sequence/4-up Cheshire/9T/1600 Magtape. DMMA Mail Preference Service used.
SELECTIONS	Nth name @ N/C. State / SCF @ $3/M. Zip @ $3/M (*only* using Zip tape.) Pressure-Sensitive labels @ $3/M.
KEYING	To 10 digits @ N/C; except Neodata (**) can only do up to 4 digits).
NOTE	Fund Raising offers subject to advance approval of complete *actual* mailing piece.

of confidence. If, for example, you expect 3 orders per thousand, you should test 20,000 to give you a sense of response validity.

Some others advocate the ideal sample as a constant percentage of the entire list. This is impractical and expensive when the list is a large one. Believe it or not, your sampling tolerance is hardly affected at all by the size of the list.

List testing, unfortunately, is not conducted under laboratory conditions. For starters, we can't get a true random sampling in most instances. The best we can do is systematic sampling—an nth name sample. And even this is not always executed properly.

For example, here are the results from a total mailing of 35,000 pieces, all mailed to the identical list, all mailed the same day, but broken out under five different keys.

Key Code	Quantity	% Response
91035	7,500	1.48
91036	7,500	1.29
91037	7,500	1.39
91038	7,500	1.48
91039	7,500	1.25

Theoretically, the percent of response should have been identical for all five keys, but actually there was a variation of 18 percent from high to low response. So one way to get a feeling for the validity of a test is to use a checking system whereby you give a separate key to each one-fifth of a test quantity. If the response is quite equal, you can feel comfortable. If there are substantial variations within the subsets, you must proceed cautiously.

Another universal practice is to reconfirm the test with a larger sample. Actually, this type of sequential sampling is the most reliable schematic because you can schedule quantities on each successive usage in an orderly fashion, supported by monitored results. Thus you are able to control and minimize the risk.

Another very important factor to be considered in the "how big" question is the back-end (persistency) factor. If you must track these customers (frequency of purchase, collections, conversions, renewals, average take), you need to test in larger quantities. For example, if each test list is 5,000 names and response is 2 percent, tracking future activity of an average of only 50 respondents from each list can prove unreliable from the standpoint of mathematical analysis. In tracking studies of book, record, and tape clubs, the number of *starts* to be analyzed is critical to the evaluation process.

In general terms, then, based on experience, a 5,000 quantity is usually adequate and more than 10,000 doesn't seem to be worthwhile.

I'm afraid that the testing question of "how many" will always be with us. It can't be answered in an absolute way because there are no consistent elements that are universally applicable to every product or service being sold by mail. When you think about it, continuation mailings rarely yield the same response as the test because there are variables from test to continuation that cannot be controlled—time lapse, seasonality, change in list sources, economics, weather conditions, consumer behavior, and a host of other factors.

Market Tests

If you are introducing a new product, it is essential to use the direct mail test to determine the potential universe for the product. Initial preconceptions about ultimate sales penetration and about target markets are usually restrictive and rarely accurate.

In addition, the initial test mailing is sometimes too small to be projectable to a large continuation mailing. For example, an initial test of 50,000, which usually will include offer and package tests, is not projectable to a continuation mailing of 500,000 or more. Yet in many instances, this is the stated objective. So, it is recommended that no less than a 100,000 quantity be used and preferably 150,000, particularly if tests, other than the market test, are being conducted.

To be able to identify the market, a "spectrum test" is recommended. Working with 20 to 30 lists, you construct a ladder of three tests—a sort of X, Y, Z arrangement. Your middle group, the Y of the spectrum, is drawn from lists that appear to be right on target. Your X panel is drawn from those which, because of certain affinity factors, could be considered good prospects. The Z group, while it reflects a very different profile, inferentially could have reasons for being interested. This type of spectrum testing yields clues about how deeply you can mail because it is a two-dimensional sample. You are sampling the universe of lists as well as the people on the particular lists chosen.

Then there is always the question of what to do on a test mailing of, say, 150,000. Are we better off testing 30 lists with 5,000 or 15 lists with 10,000? This depends on the growth pattern established in the original forecast plan.

Let's run through as an example, a magazine called *The Glory of Art*.

The first step was an "Overview of List Markets." The intention of this overview is to provide a feel for the potential universe—and to decide on the specific lists to be selected from each category. (See Table 5-4.) On the *Glory of Art* it was decided to go with 30 lists, because the market testing was most crucial in determining whether or not this was a viable publication in the marketplace. (See Table 5-5.)

You will note that, while the schedule is concentrated in the more targeted categories, other categories, such as women's fashions, were explored with an eye toward market evaluation and expansion.

In analyzing by category in the initial stages, it is better to look at the number of lists tested in each category and the success ratio—rather than averaging response on each category. Averages can be misleading.

Table 5-4. Overview of List Markets (Glory of Art)

Category	No. of Lists	Potential Universe
Art / Antiques / Collectibles	31	2,995,900
Up-Scale Gifts & Decorating Items	24	2,088,600
Luxury Foods & Gifts	16	3,316,200
Photography	5	968,900
Women's High Fashions	8	843,500
Cultural Books & Magazines	31	5,232,200
Regional Publications	20	2,732,100
Cultural Arts	7	485,400
Miscellaneous (credit card)	5	1,732,000
TOTAL:	147	20,394,800*

© Copyright by Rose Harper, The Kleid Company, Inc.

*Can be reduced by approximately 25% due to the duplication factor.

Table 5-5. Glory of Art List Test Schedule 150,000

Category	Universe	Test Quantity	No. of Lists
Art / Antiques / Collectibles	1,215,600	45,000	9
Up-Scale Gifts & Decorating Items	383,000	20,000	4
Luxury Foods & Gifts	1,871,900	25,000	5
Photography	150,000	5,000	1
Women's High Fashions	185,000	5,000	1
Cultural Books & Magazines	876,900	25,000	5
Regional Publications	267,000	10,000	2
Cultural Arts	245,000	10,000	2
Miscellaneous (credit card)	125,000	5,000	1
	5,319,400	150,000	30

© Copyright by Rose Harper, The Kleid Company, Inc.

One list in a particular category that responded dramatically higher or lower than the other lists can influence the overall average.

This type of analysis should be considered directional—and not an absolute. In some instances the ratios are reliable, in some instances they're not. For example, where only one list was tested in a category and it proved responsive, that category must be approached more cautiously than the category where five lists were tested and they were all responsive. (See Table 5-6.)

The most important element to consider, however, is that the dynamics of each testing situation are dissimilar—particularly the objectives, the time frame, and the financials. These variables must be studied and given consideration in structuring the initial test.

Duplication Elimination

The advent of the ZIP code in 1967 forced list owners into the computer age. This led to the breakthrough in the ability to remove duplicate names (dupes) within a mailing. The popular term is "merge/purge"— and what it means is the matching of two or more mailing lists by electronic means to remove duplication and to insure that each addres-

Table 5-6. Glory of Art Analysis Success Factor By Category

	No. of Tests	No. of Continuations	% Success
Y (of the Spectrum)			
Art, Antiques, Collectibles	9	7	77.8
Cultural Books & Magazines	5	5	100.
Cultural Arts	2	1	50.
Sub-Total	16	13	81.3
X			
Upscale Gifts & Decorating Items	4	1	25.
Photography	1	1	100.
Regional Publications	2	2	100.
Sub-Total	7	4	57.1
Z			
Luxury Foods & Gifts	5	2	40.
Women's High Fashions	1	1	100.
Miscellaneous (Credit Card)	1	—	—
Sub-Total	7	3	42.9
TOTAL	30	20	66.6%

© Copyright by Rose Harper, The Kleid Company, Inc.

see receives only one mailing piece. This is accomplished by the use of a match code that is a series of characters extracted on a consistent basis from the name and address which fully identifies that person to the computer.

Aside from avoiding the irritation to the recipient of receiving several of the same mailings at almost the same time and sending a solicitation to a present customer, there are considerable dollar savings involved. (See Table 5-7.)

Another factor that needs to be considered because of merge/purge is the resulting true or actual list cost per thousand. This is essential information in projecting a mailing plan—and an *actual* list cost per order. (See Table 5-8.)

In most instances the house file (or segments of the house file) is the primary list against which the rental lists are matched. Then, all lists are matched against each other. In the process, intralist duplication is also discovered. Since the mailing tape, after the match, is in ZIP code sequence, it provides the opportunity to:

1. Analyze response by ZIP code by matching the tape of response against the mailing tape.
2. Omit all ZIP codes which, from previous experience, have not been responsive or have proven to have a high bad-pay factor.

At what quantity it makes sense to merge/purge against the house file is a knotty question. Some managements maintain a strict policy against any duplication of their house file regardless of the quantity of the rental names. In such instances merge/purge is an imperative.

Table 5-7. Dollar Savings On Dupe Removal

Percent Duplication	Mailing Quantity			
	1,000,000	2,500,000	5,000,000	10,000,000
5	$10,000	$25,000	$50,000	$100,000
10	20,000	50,000	100,000	200,000
15	30,000	75,000	150,000	300,000
20	40,000	100,000	200,000	400,000
25	50,000	125,000	250,000	500,000
30	60,000	150,000	300,000	600,000
35	70,000	175,000	350,000	700,000

© Copyright by Rose Harper, The Kleid Company, Inc.

Savings achieved by eliminating duplicate names from a mailing (based on a mailing cost of $200 per thousand pieces).

Judgment dictates that the larger your house file becomes, the higher the percentage of duplication you can expect from rented lists. Thus if a direct marketer has a house list of 1,000,000 names, for example, merge/purge is almost always advisable, no matter what the quantity of rented names. On the other hand, if the house list is, say, only 50,000 names, it hardly makes sense to merge/purge 5 lists of 5,000 each against the house file because the duplication factor would be very small.

However, the duplication factor should not be the sole consideration in deciding for or against merge/purge. A firm with a house file of 50,000 names might elect to build its house file fast and, therefore, test 20 lists of 5,000 names simultaneously. The chances of heavy duplication between these 100,000 names could be in the 25 percent range. Therefore, merge/purge would make sense even though duplication against the house file would probably be small.

Tape-to-tape matching offers other marketing opportunities. For example, an insurance company has been reaching "golden age" prospects via Census tract addressing by using tracts with the highest density of older people. There was waste, however, in reaching everyone in a Census tract. By tape-to-tape matching against a list of families with young children in the same areas, it was possible to refine the selections by suppressing the young families. Tape-to-tape matching also allows for file overlay analysis to take advantage of various types of information available on consumer files. For example, refer back to the selections available on the *Better Homes & Gardens* file. Much of this detailing was accomplished in this manner.

Table 5-8. Actual List Cost per Thousand After Merge/Purge Assuming Gross Quantity of 50,000 Names and a 25% Duplication Factor

Gross Quantity	List Cost per M	Running Charges per M	Selection Charges per M	Billing 85% on Basic List Rental	Running Costs	Selection Charges	Total Billing	Actual List CPM (assuming 75% qty. mailed)
50,000	$40.00	$5.00	—	$1,700.00	$37.50	—	$1,737.50	46.33
50,000	$40.00	$5.00	$6.50	1,700.00	37.50	$325.00	2,062.50	55.00
50,000	$45.00	$5.00	—	1,912.50	37.50	—	1,950.00	52.00
50,000	$45.00	$5.00	$4.50	1,912.50	37.50	225.00	2,175.00	58.00
50,000	$50.00	$5.00	—	2,125.00	37.50	—	2,162.50	57.67
50,000	$50.00	$5.00	$7.50	2,125.00	37.50	375.00	2,537.50	67.67
50,000	$55.00	$5.00	—	2,337.50	37.50	—	2,375.00	63.33
50,000	$55.00	$5.00	$6.50	2,337.50	37.50	325.00	2,700.00	72.00

Another example is the overlay on the *McCall's* magazine subscriber file that was done by Donnelley Marketing. This enabled selection by age, income, dwelling unit size, length of residence, ethnic, and religious preference. Lifestyle Selector (Denver, CO), through the information they collect on consumer information cards, will overlay their master file on your house file. The names that match are then analyzed to produce a lifestyle profile of your house file—demographically by age, income, occupation, marital status, home ownership, etc.—plus a lifestyle profile including 48 interest and hobby categories, such as foreign travel, gardening, cooking, photography, physical fitness, among others.

PRIZM, a division of Claritas Company, Roslyn, VA, represents a new generation of market targeting systems made possible through the massive data resources of the U.S. Census and some important developments in the field of demographic research. The PRIZM (Potential Rating Index by Zip Markets) service was formed by combining two independent data bases: The Claritas Cluster System (a "geodemographic" market segmentation system that has classified all of the thousands of neighborhoods and communities in the United States into 40 different homogeneous types or "clusters") and The Simmons Market Research Bureau Annual Surveys (a series of syndicated surveys of product usage and media readership/viewership). Using the address of every respondent in the SMRB surveys, the respondents were assigned to their respective clusters. These subsets of respondents then provided measurements of cluster behavior towards all major products, services, and media. The thrust of this system is "a new way to use ZIP codes for market targeting."

Some of the terminology used in the merge/purge process is:

- Contribution to Multibuyers—names appearing more than once that are transferred to the multibuyer file
- Quantity ordered—by the mailer
- Gross Input—actual quantity processed into the system
- Unordered names—(could involve requested omits such as state, SCF, ZIP)
- Edit Errors—usually mistakes in the address (City, State, ZIP)
- Net Records into Merge/Purge—after omitting unordered names and edit errors
- Internal Duplication—also described as intrafile duplicates that represent names and addresses appearing more than once within one file
- Pander File Matches—usually from the DMA Mail Preference Service tape. (These are people who have written to DMA indicating that they prefer *not* to get any mail.)

- Suppression Matches—usually an internal file of customers, plus those people who requested that their name not be used for list rental purposes, bad-pay file, etc.
- Unique Records—names that remain on the mailing tape only one time.

Scheduling and Analysis of Direct Mail Programs

The attraction of direct mail is its *measurability*. Direct mail is not inexpensive. On a cost per thousand exposure, aside from telephone, it is probably the most expensive medium. But unlike most media, the response per thousand is not extrapolated. It is an arithmetical fact.

Let's go back to the *Glory of Art*, where 30 lists were tested in the initial mailing.

In order to plan the continuation mailing, there is the need to analyze the test results. Here are the factors considered—and a review of the overall test mailing:

Actual Mail Quantity	150,040
Number of Orders	3,256
Percent Response	2.170
Package Cost per M	$180
List Cost per M	$45.56
Total Cost per M	$225.56
Total Cost	$33,843
Gross Cost per Subscriber	$10.39
Percent Credit	90.40
Percent Bad Pay	28.10
Net Subscribers	2,428
Net Percent Response	1.61
Net Cost per Subscriber	$13.93
Total Revenue (on Net)	$43,702
Net Revenue (total Revenue minus Total Cost)	$9,859
Net Revenue per Subscriber	$4.06

Important: These same factors were considered on a *list-by-list basis.*

Another important step is to consider the assumptions that need to be applied when projecting the roll-out response. This qualifier is necessary for a variety of reasons: the test quantity of 5,000 on each list; the test mailing was made at a different time (see seasonality); the increase in merge/purge factor due to the larger mailing quantity.

In this instance the following assumptions were used:

1. 12% loss through merge/purge
2. 10% lift for seasonality
3. 7% decrease for test to continuation
4. Credit and Bad-Pay at Actual for each list

These assumptions were applied on a *list-by-list* basis with the starting point being previous response. (See Table 5-9—*Glory of Art Continuation Mailing*—which shows a sampling of the list-by-list analysis).

Now let's look at the summary of the continuation mailing (see Table 5-10), using the same factors that were used to analyze the test mailing.

You will note that 100,000 in new list tests was included. In order to sustain a continuing and ongoing direct mail program, it is essential to develop an inventory of profitable lists. Therefore, in most instances, 10 percent of the total mailing should be devoted to list testing.

Remember that mailing plans are budgets or pro-forma profit plans. And, in direct mail, it all starts with list history. The ability to review the history of a list on an each-time-used basis is critical to structuring a sound mailing plan because in direct mail, the list is the medium.

One of the most helpful evaluation tools is the use of "break-even" analysis. This measures the response needed for total revenue to meet total promotional cost. At this point, obviously there is no profit. Each company, then, must add other constants (overhead, cost of money, cost of product, bad-pay, returns, refurbishing, customer lifetime value, etc.,) to determine how much you can afford to pay for an order.

There are many variations in the analytical process. The charts refer to magazines—but with some variations, could apply to books, catalogs, etc. It all boils down to the abolute necessity of measuring results within the parameters of the financial dynamics of the particular situation. If direct mail is measurable, then the message must be loud and clear. And it doesn't stop with front-end response.

One precaution: There is a danger in working with averages. The "average" is a handy mathematical device, but remember, there are several kinds of averages, all different and each revealing a wholly different aspect of the same set of figures. Let's look at how a group's typical income would be, computing just four of the more simple averaging methods. (See Table 5-11.)

There is no intention here to dispute the use of averages. That would be impractical. What is being suggested is that the nuances behind averages be observed. You need, to use a statistical term, to be

Table 5-9. Glory of Art—Continuation Mailing

Art / Antique / Collectibles

	Mail Qty.	% Resp.	Mail Qty.	# Orders	% Resp.	Pkg. C.P.M.	List C.P.M.	Total C.P.M.	C.P.O.	% Credit	% Bad Pay	Net Orders	Net % Resp.	Net C.P.O.	Total Cost	Total Revenue	Net Revenue	Net Revenue per Subs.
List #1	5,004	2.90	44,300	1,315	2.97	$180	$45.45	$225.45	$7.59	91.0	27.6	985	2.22	$10.15	9,987	17,730	7,743	7.86
List #2	4,950	3.10	35,250	1,117	3.17	180	63.85	243.85	7.69	88.0	28.1	841	2.38	10.24	8,595	15,138	6,543	7.78
List #3	5,007	3.00	44,000	1,350	3.07	180	45.47	227.47	7.34	89.0	23.0	1,074	2.44	9.32	10,008	19,332	9,324	8.68
List #4	5,100	2.90	43,200	1,278	2.96	180	63.66	243.66	8.23	91.0	29.3	937	2.17	11.22	10,562	16,866	6,304	6.72
List #5	4,999	2.80	43,100	1,232	2.86	180	50.72	230.72	8.06	82.0	21.0	1,020	2.37	9.74	9,944	18,360	8,416	8.25
List #6	5,060	3.00	47,600	1,461	3.07	180	63.02	243.02	7.91	85.0	26.0	1,138	2.39	10.17	11,567	20,484	8,917	7.83
List #7	4,975	3.10	30,800	976	3.17	180	51.13	231.13	6.72	92.0	28.0	725	2.35	9.84	7,118	13,050	5,932	8.18

Sample of List-by-List Evaluation

aware of the "outliers," the freaks, that can influence the average unduly and lead to incorrect interpretation of results.

Seasonality

Seasonality has been a priority subject in direct mail for a long time. Have seasonality patterns been changing? During the past five years it appears so, from the seasonality study conducted by The Kleid Company, Inc. (See Table 5-12.)

While the dynamics of budgeting and other considerations can, and do, influence mailing periods, there are strong reasons why seasonality studies should be conducted by companies using direct mail on a consistent basis. The same type of names (such as changes of address), the same quantity, offer, and mailing package should be mailed at the same time each month to measure seasonality.

Statistical and Analytical Techniques

Statistics is a branch of mathematics dealing with the collection, analysis, and interpretation of masses of numerical data. In some instances, it is easy. For example, descriptive statistics. These represent numbers that yield an efficient summary of some type of information. For example, batting averages, unemployment rates, Dow-Jones averages.

Table 5-10. Glory of Art—Continuation Mailing

	Continuations	List Tests	Total
Mail Quantity	866,702	100,000	966,702
Number of Orders	23,759	2,000	25,759
Percent Response	2.74	2.00	2.66
Package CPM	$180.	$180.	$180.
List CPM	$51.73	$45.	$51.03
Total CPM	$231.73	$225.	$231.03
C.P.O.	$8.45	$11.25	$8.67
Percent Credit	89.4	89.3	89.4
Percent Bad Pay	26.6	27.3	26.6
Net Orders	18,105	1,513	19,618
Net Percent Response	2.09	1.51	2.03
Net C.P.O.	$11.09	$14.90	$11.38
Total Cost	$200,842	$22,500	$223,342
Total Revenue	$325,890	$27,234	$353,124
Net Revenue	$125,048	$4,734	$129,782
Net Revenue per Subscriber	$6.91	$3.12	$6.61

©Copyright by Rose Harper, The Kleid Company, Inc.

In direct mail, it is essential to segment and define our market. And to do this, it becomes necessary to look at the techniques available for use in analysis and as market research tools.

Multivariate methods are not new, but the proliferation of these techniques in marketing research has been spurred by the ability of the computer to perform enormous numbers of calculations in a short time. Factor analysis, a member of the family of multivariate methods, is based on the following proposition. If there is a systematic interdependence among a set of variables, it must be due to something fundamental that created the interdependence. These underlying factors will tend to cluster the variables into categories. The categories are not mutually exclusive. Factor analysis will perform the identification of underlying factors and the grouping of manifest (observed) variables under each factor.

Table 5-11. Family Income

(1)	$40,000	
(2)	$30,000	
(3)	$25,000	
(4)	$20,000	
(5)	$15,000	
(6)	$12,500	
(7)	$12,500	
(8)	$12,500	
(9)	$12,500	
(10)	$10,000	
	$190,000	

Here is the group's "typical" income computed using 4 of the more simple averaging methods:

Arithmetic Mean—$19,000
The most common kind of average. Computed by taking the sum of all the families. In this example, four families earn more than the mean and six earn less.

Mid-Range—$25,000
The richest earns 4 times more than the poorest. Add the bottom and top and divide by 2. Two families earn more than the mid-range and 7 earn less.

Median—$13,750
If you want to represent the group by what a family in the exact middle gets, you must locate the median—the income that will be higher than the incomes of the lower half and lower than the upper half. If there were 11 families, the median income would be the sixth highest. With only 10— no family is in the middle, so you find the dividing line by adding the fifth and sixth and dividing by 2. In this example, the median is less than both the mid-range and the mean.

Mode—$12,500
Also called the Norm. Mode in statistical work equals that value, magnitude or score which occurs the greatest number of times in a given series of observations. In this example, the modal income is $12,500. If there had been no set of 2 or more, there would have been no mode.

For example, Old American Insurance Company of Kansas City, Missouri, has a unique data bank that stores up to 103 bits of manifest data about each ZIP code. The data bank lists potential marketing units (ZIP code areas) in terms of their environmental characteristics which, when combined into factors, provide the inferential dimension of lifestyle and are thus used to predict consumer behavior. Using factor analysis, Old American can mathematically correlate the 103 environmental variables of the ZIP code areas of interest with each other and thus condense them into a dozen or more uncorrelated factors, that are much more meaningful and manageable in subsequent analysis.

Regression analysis and correlation analysis enable us to deal with variables that are stated in terms of numerical values rather than in qualitative categories. These methods provide the bases for measuring the strength of the relationships among the variables. The term *regression analysis* refers to the methods by which estimates are made of the values of a variable from a knowledge of the values or one or more other variables and to the measurement of the errors involved in this estimation process. The term *correlation analysis* refers to methods for measuring the strength of the association (correlations) among these variables. Equations are used in both instances to express the relationship among the variables.

There are many variations of these mathematical, analytical systems. The direct marketer must be aware of the importance of statistical analysis for decision making. And, to make it worthwhile, the direct marketer needs to establish the marketing concepts or criteria so that

Table 5-12. Seasonality Study Showing Top Three Months Covering Two 12-Month Periods.

	1980-81			1980-82		
	1	**2**	**3**	**1**	**2**	**3**
Business / Finance	Jan	Dec	Sept	Dec	Jan	July
Cultural Reading	Dec	July	June	Dec	June	Sept
General Reading	July	Dec	Jan	July	Dec	Jan
Self-Improvement	Jan	Dec	July	Dec	Sept	Jan
Home Interest	Jan	Feb	Dec	Feb	Jan	July
Parents & Children	Dec	July	Jan	July	Jan	Dec
Hobbies / Related Subjects	July	Jan	Dec	July	Dec	Jan
Entertainment	Jan	Sept	July	July	Aug	Sept
Education / Technical / Professional	Dec	July	Aug	June	Dec	July
Fund Raising	Jan	Sept	Oct	Nov	Oct	Aug

©Copyright by Rose Harper, The Kleid Company, Inc.

the statisticians can decide on the technique to be used in order to get actionable information—information from the data base that will help you manage your other resources better.

Mathematical Modeling

Modeling techniques have been used in direct mail for some time now, but today's advanced technology allows for marketing information systems with predictive capabilities. In the magazine field, for example, the Promotion Evaluation Model (designed by Policy Development Corp., LaJolla, CA), is a tool for source evaluation. The initial gross cost of acquiring a new subscriber is not the key to the real value of the subscription. Back-end performance (pay-ups, conversion, renewal rates) provide the definitive measurement of response. Source evaluation is a method for examining the renewability and profitability of a new subscriber/product through a variety of sources within a particular time frame.

Then there are marketing decision models. In general, a "model" allows exploration of various alternatives by profit ratios, return on investment, and any other pertinent statistics. You can play the "what if" game by making a number of changes to see their effect on the overall plan. It's a simulation technique. And it all starts with a data base of past experience, data, and history. The data collection and processing activity is extremely important and will be directional in the selection of the model to be developed.

The heart of every direct marketing operation is a data base. The degree of success you achieve in the use of mailing lists will be measured by your ability to extract the most profitable segments from your data base and those of others.

Self-Quiz

1. What three things are both central and indispensable to direct marketing through lists?

a. _____

b. _____

c. _____

2. The two broad categories of lists are _____

and _____.

3. Your best customer is _____.

4. The art of getting more sales from existing customers is to be able to

match _____

to customer buying _____.

5. Define the RFM formula:

<u>R</u> stands for _____.

<u>F</u> stands for _____.

<u>M</u> stands for _____.

6. Define Super Spot Subscribers:

_____

_____

7. More than _____ of all married women work.

8. List brokers serve two sides: the _____

and the _____.

9. In testing a new list a _____

quantity is usually adequate.

10. However, if a mailer is testing offers and mailing packages simultaneously, a quantity of at least _____ names is recommended.

11. Define a "spectrum test."

_____

_____

_____

12. Define "merge/purge."

_____

_____

_____

13. How does one best establish the seasonality factor of his mailing program?

_____

_____

_____

Pilot Project

You are the circulation director of a consumer magazine. You have agreed to conduct a mailing list seminar for the marketing class of a leading university.

In preparation for this seminar define all aspects of the following outline.

A. Definition of a list
B. The three things central and indispensable to direct marketing through lists
C. Definition of internal and external lists
D. The theory of segmentation
E. Definition of RFM formula
F. Value of Census Tracts

G. Value of ZIP codes

H. Functions of a list broker

I. Functions of list managers

J. Components of list data cards

K. Purpose of list tests

L. Test quantities

M. Theory of a "spectrum test"

N. Duplication elimination

O. Break-even analysis

P. Seasonality

Q. Factor analysis

R. Regression and correlation analysis

S. Modelling techniques

Chapter Six

Magazines

Where Do You Go First?

The advertising pages of magazines are to the direct response advertiser what the retail outlet is to the manufacturer selling through the more traditional channels. A magazine that performs consistently well for a variety of direct response advertisers is like a store in a low-rent, high-traffic location. It's far more profitable than a store selling the same merchandise on the wrong side of town.

Such a magazine just seems to have an atmosphere that is more conducive to the mail response customer. The mail order shopping reader traffic is high in relation to the publication's cost per thousand. Magazines in this category (and this is by no means a complete list) are *National Enquirer, Parade,* and the mighty *TV Guide.* Women's publications also doing well for mail order advertisers are *Family Circle, Better Homes and Gardens, Good Housekeeping, Cosmopolitan, Woman's Day, Seventeen,* and *Redbook.* Men's publications include *Mechanix Illustrated, Moose, Playboy,* and *Penthouse.* (For a comprehensive list of magazines that provide a structured mail order atmosphere, see Table 6-1.)

But just as retail locations come into and go out of favor with each passing decade, so do the trends that determine which publications work well in the mail order marketplace at a particular time. For example, coming into favor right now are *New Yorker, Country Living, Family Circle,* and *Smithsonian.* In the 1960s there was much greater interest in such publications as *McCall's, Ladies' Home Journal, House & Garden, House Beautiful,* and the *National Observer.* And I can remember in the 1950s looking to *Living for Young Homemakers, Harper's/Atlantic,* and *Saturday Review*—and the *Saturday Evening Post* could be counted on for good results.

There are some publications that one might assume at first glance to be just great for the mail order advertiser. But close examination of performance figures for many different advertisers in these publications causes a red flag to be raised for the direct marketing advertiser. Here are a few places to go right now at your own risk: *Reader's Digest, National Geographic, New York,* and *Town & Country.* Some of these publications, though, have done well for high-ticket items like collectibles.

Regional Editions: When Is the Part Bigger Than the Whole?

For the buyer of space in magazines today, most publications with circulations of over 1.5 million offer the opportunity to buy a regional portion of the national circulation. But it was not always so.

Although it has been said that the *New Yorker* was the first to publish sectional or regional editions in 1929, it wasn't until the late 1950s that major magazines began selling regional space to all advertisers, not just to those who had distribution limited to a particular section of the circulation area.

The availability of regional editions for everyone opened important opportunities to the mail order advertiser. Here are a few of the things you can do with regional buys:

1. You don't have to invest in the full national cost of a publication to get some indication of its effectiveness for your proposition. In some cases, such as *Time* or *TV Guide,* by running in a single edition you can determine relative response with an investment 20 percent less than what it costs to make a national buy.

2. Some regions traditionally pull better than others for the mail order advertiser. For many mail order products or services, nothing does better than the West Coast or worse than the New England region. You can select the best response area for your particular proposition.

Remember, in most publications you will be paying a premium for the privilege of buying partial circulation. If you are testing a publication, putting your advertising message in the better-pulling region can offset much of this premium charge.

3. Availability of regional editions makes possible multiple copy testing in a single issue of a publication. Some magazines offer A/B split-run copy testing in each of the regional editions published. For example, in *TV Guide,* you can test one piece of copy against your control in one edition, another against your control in a second edition, another against your control in a third, and so on. As a result, you can learn as much about different pieces of copy in a single issue of one publication as you could discover in several national A/B copy splits in the same publication over a time span of two years or more.

4. When testing regionally, don't make the mistake of testing too small a circulation quantity. It is essential that you test a large enough circulation segment to provide readable results that can be projected accurately for still larger circulations.

Warning: Buying regional space is not all fun and games. You will have to pay for the privilege in a number of ways. As mentioned, regional space costs more. How much more? You can get an idea of what to expect from these representative examples: *Woman's Day* from 59 to 148 percent; *Time* from 7 to 305 percent; *Popular Science* from 21 to 54 percent; *TV Guide* from 5 to 179 percent; and *Reader's Digest* from 39 to 215 percent.

The minimum and maximum figures relate to the number and circulation size of regions you may be buying for any one insertion.

Another factor to keep in mind is the relatively poor position regional ads receive. The regional sections usually appear far back in the magazine or in a "well" or signature of several consecutive pages of advertising with no editorial matter to catch the reader. As you will see later in our discussion of position placement, the poor location of an ad in a magazine can depress results as much as 50 percent below what the same advertisement would pull if it were in the first few pages of the same publication. If you are using regional space for testing, be certain to factor this into your evaluation.

An example of how various factors must be weighed in utilizing regional circulation for test purposes follows.

Regional Test Schedule for XYZ Yarn & Craft Company

	REDBOOK
Space:	Full-page four-color insert
Position:	Third card position
Issue:	May, 1982
Space Cost:	$13,955. (printing cost not included)
Editions Used:	Central (746,800)
	North Central (327,500)
Total test circulation:	1,074,300 (20.0 percent of total circulation)
Regional premium:	30 percent
	FAMILY CIRCLE
Space:	Full-page four-color insert
Position:	Back of main editorial (regional forms)
Issue:	June, 1982
Space Cost:	$4,058. (printing cost not included)
Editions Used:	Los Angeles (600,000)
	San Francisco (348,000)
Total test circulation:	948,000 (12.8 percent of total circulation)
Regional premium:	None. This publication offers a special prorated test rate for full-page inserts.

Since full-page four-color inserts have been extremely profitable for some of the larger mail order advertisers, this size unit was tested for the XYZ Yarn & Craft Co. to see if such inserts could bring in a lower lead cost than obtained from a black-and-white page and card.

Because women's publications are the most successful media for this advertiser, the company went to two that offered the mechanical capabilities for regional testing of such an insert. Although May and June are not prime mail order months, it was necessary to test then in order to allow turnaround time for the next season's scheduling. Therefore, the following factors would have to be taken into consideration in projecting test results to learn whether this unit would be successful in prime mail order months with full circulation: (1) regional premium, (2) month of insertion, (3) position in book, and (4) relative value of specific media.

Pilot Publications: The Beacons of Direct Response Media Scheduling

When planning your direct marketing media schedule, think about the media universe the way you think about the view of the sky in the evening. If you have no familiarity with the stars, the sky appears to be a jumble of blinking lights with no apparent relationship. But as you begin to study the heavens, you are soon able to pick out clusters of stars that have a relationship to one another in constellations.

You will recognize the stars that make up the Big Dipper in Ursa Major, the Hunter, the Swan, the Bull, and other familiar constellations. If you were to go on to become a professional astronomer, you would eventually recognize 89 distinctly different groups. Once you know the various constellations, a star within a particular grouping inevitably leads your eye to the other related stars.

The magazine universe is no different. There are nearly 400 consumer magazines published with circulations of 100,000 or more. The first step in approaching this vast list is to sort out the universe of magazines into categories. Although this process is somewhat arbitrary, and different experts may not agree entirely as to which magazines fall into which category, we are going to set down a chart of the major publications that you can use like a chart of the skies to map out particular magazine groupings. Once you begin to think of magazines as forming logical groupings within the total magazine universe, you can begin to determine the groupings offering the most likely marketplace for your product or proposition. Table 6-2 is a basic magazine category chart and lists some of the publications currently available for the direct response advertiser.

Table 6-1. U.S. Consumer Magazines with Mail Order
and/or Shopping Advertising Pages

Class	Publication	Class	Publication	Class	Publication
	A	2	Art Express	24	Better Homes and Gardens Low-Calorie Recipes
23	Accent on Living	2	Art Gallery, The		
8	Across the Board	2	Artnews	24	Better Homes and Gardens Quick and Easy Entertaining Ideas
42	A. D. Magazine	22	Asia		
8B	Adirondack Life	43	Astronomy		
21A	Advocate, The	30A	Atlantic City Magazine	24	Better Homes and Gardens Remodeling Ideas
4	Aero	22	Atlantic, The		
41	Africa Report	22	Attenzione	24	Better Homes and Gardens Traditional Home
17A	After Dark	33	Audio		
31	Air Force Times	35	Audubon	24	Better Homes and Gardens Window and Wall Ideas
4	Air Line Pilot	24	Austin Homes & Gardens		
4	Air Progress	3	Auto Racing Digest		
1	AirCal Magazine	3	Autobuff	14	Better Homes and Gardens 100's of Needlework and Craft Ideas
1	Alas Inflight Group	3	AutoWeek		
19	Alaska	4	Aviation		
49	Alaska Woman		**B**	22A	Better Living
1	Alaskafest	20	B'nai B'rith International Jewish Monthly, The	45	Bicycling
9B	Alcalde			45	Billiards Digest
30A	Aloha	5	Baby Talk	35	Bird Talk
2	American Artist	8B	Backpacker	35	Bird Watcher's Digest
5	American Baby	25	Backstretch, The	8	Black Enterprise
8	American Business	33	Bam	24	Blair & Ketchum's Country Journal
17A	American Classic Screen	8	Barron's-National Business and Financial Weekly		
2	American Collector			25	Blood-Horse, The
25	American Cowboy	45	Baseball Digest	1A	Blum's Farmers & Planters Almanac and Turner's Carolina Almanac
13	American Field	45	Basketball Digest		
17A	American Film	19	Bassmaster Magazine		
19	American Handgunner, The	6	Bay & Delta Yachtsman	45	BMX Action
		23	Bestways	6	Boating
23A	American History Illustrated	24	Better Homes and Gardens	30A	Boca Raton
				18	Bon Appetit
21	American Horticulturist	24	Better Homes and Gardens All-Time Favorite Recipes	19	Bowhunter
19	American Hunter, The			51	Boys' LIfe
20	American Legion Magazine, The			7	Bride's
		7	Better Homes and Gardens Brides' Book	23A	British Heritage
31A	American Motorcyclist			8	Business Week
41	American Opinion	11	Better Homes and Gardens Christmas Ideas	43	Byte
39	American Photographer				**C**
19	American Rifleman	24	Better Homes and Gardens Country Cooking	20	CAA Magazine
21	American Rose Magazine			30A	California
26	American Scholar, The	11	Better Homes and Gardens Country Crafts	39	Camera Arts
19	American Shotgunner, The			22	Caminos
		24	Better Homes and Gardens Country Home and Kitchen Ideas	41	Campaigns & Elections
41	American Spectator, The			8A	Camping Hotline
12	American Square Dance Magazine			8B	Canoe
		24	Better Homes and Gardens Decorating Ideas	24	Capper's Weekly
1	American Way			3	Car and Driver
22	American West	24	Better Homes and Gardens Do-It-Yourself Home Improvement and Repair	3	Car and Driver Buyers Guide
24	Americana				
1	Amtrak Express			3	Car Collector/Car Classics
28	Antaeus	21	Better Homes and Gardens Garden Ideas and Outdoor Living		
2	Antique Monthly			3	Car Craft
2	Antique Trader Weekly, The			3	Car Exchange
		21	Better Homes and Gardens Gardener's Handbook	3	Cars
4	AOPA Pilot			13	Cat Fancy
8B	Appalachia			42	Catholic Digest
25	Appaloosa News	24	Better Homes and Gardens Holiday Cooking & Entertaining Ideas	42	Catholic Twin Circle
25	Arabian Horse World			13	Cats Magazine
45	Archery World			47	CB Magazine
24	Architectural Digest			45	Century Sports Network
36A	Argus	11	Better Homes and Gardens Holiday Crafts	11	Ceramic Arts & Crafts
31	Army Times			41	Channels of Communications
31	Army Times Military Group				

Table 6-1. U.S. Consumer Magazines with Mail Order and/or Shopping Advertising Pages

Class	Publication
42	Charisma
10	Charlton Comics Group
6	Chesapeake Bay Magazine
11	Chess Life
43B	Chic
38	Chicago Tribune Magazine
42	Christian Century, The
42	Christian Herald
42	Christian Life
42	Christianity Today
25	Chronicle of the Horse, The
42	Church Herald, The
30A	Cincinnati
33	Circus Magazine
23A	Civil War Times Illustrated
15	Classified, Inc.
30A	Cleveland Magazine
44	Club Living
49	Co-ed
7	Co-Ed's Guide To Getting Married
11	Coin World
11	Coins
2	Collectibles Illustrated
2	Collector Editions Quarterly
2	Collectors Mart
2	Collectors News
24	Colonial Homes
20	Columbia
8	Commodities
41	Commonweal
43	Compute
30A	Connecticut Magazine
46	Connecticut Motorist
24	Consumer LIfe
22	Consumers Digest
33	Contemporary Christian Music
1	Continental Extra
25	Continental Horseman
18	Cook's Magazine, The
49	Cosmopolitan
50	Cosmopolitan's Beauty Guide
50	Cosmopolitan's Super Diet & Exercise Guide
24	Country Gentleman
24	Country Living
30A	Country Magazine
45	Court Club Sports
11	Crafts 'N Things
11	Crafts Magazine
8	Crain's Chicago Business
43	Creative Computing
11	Creative Crafts
33	Creem
41	Crisis, The
45	Cross Country Ski Magazine

Class	Publication
45	Cross Country Skier
6	Cruising World
31A	Custom Bike
3	Custom Rodder
31A	Cycle
31A	Cycle Buyers Guide
31A	Cycle Guide
31A	Cycle News
31A	Cycle Street and Touring Guide
31A	Cycle World
31A	Cycle World Test Annual & Buyer's Guide

D

Class	Publication
30A	D Magazine
24	Dallas-Fort Worth Home & Garden
17A	Dancemagazine
39	Darkroom Photogrpahy
39	Darkroom Techniques
34	Davis Digests
11	Decorating & Craft Ideas
30A	Denver Magazine
30A	Desert
30B	Dial, The
31A	Dirt Bike
46	Discovery
46	Diversion
13	Dog Fancy
13	Dog World
33	Down Beat
30A	Down East
17A	Dramatics/Dramatics' Curtain
33	Drum Corps World
19	Ducks Unlimited
8	Dun's Business Month
3	Dune Buggies & Hot VWs
43A	Dynamic Years

E

Class	Publication
20	Eagle Magazine
24	Early American Life
24	Earth Shelter Living
30B	East Central Florida Public Broadcasting Monthly
22	East West Journal
1	Eastern Review
31A	Easyriders
49	Elan
16	Electronic Learning
20	Elks Magazine, The
41	Encore
6	Ensign, The
42	Episcopalian, The
25	Equus
30A	Erie Magazine
30	Esquire
49	Essence
49	Everywoman

Class	Publication
F	
31	Family
49	Family Circle
49	Family Circle Great Ideas
11	Family Circle Great Ideas Christmas Helps
18	Family Circle Great Ideas Entertaining at Home
14	Family Circle Great Ideas Fashions & Crafts
50	Family Circle Great Ideas How To Be Pretty & Trim
24	Family Circle Great Ideas Remodeling & Decorating Made Easy
21	Family Food Garden, The
24	Family Handyman, The
8A	Family Motor Coaching
34	Fate
20	Federal Times
2	Fiberarts
19	Field & Stream
43A	50 plus
8	Financial World
24	Fine Homebuilding
11	Fine Woodworking
19	Fins and Feathers
19	Fisherman Group
19	Fishing and Hunting News
19	Fishing Facts
19	Fishing in Maryland, New Jersey, New York
19	Fishing World
45	Florida Golfweek
45	Florida Racquet Journal
19	Florida Sportsman
21	Flower & Garden Magazine
19	Fly Fisherman
19	Fly Tyer
4	Flying
11	Flying Models
45	Football Digest
8	Forbes
30A	Forecast
41	Foreign Affairs
41	Foreign Service Journal
8	Fortune
3	4 Wheel & Off-Road
3	Four Wheeler
8	Frequent Flyer
19	Full Cry
19	Fur-Fish-Game
43	Fusion
9A	Future
22	Futurist, The
G	
45	Gambling Times
11	Games
21	Gardener, The
30	Genesis
43B	Gentleman's Companion

Table 6-1. U.S. Consumer Magazines with Mail Order and/or Shopping Advertising Pages

Class	Publication	Class	Publication	Class	Publication
30	Gentlemen's Quarterly	3	Hot Rod Magazine	14	McCall's Needlework & Crafts
22	GEO	13	Hounds and Hunting	24	Mechanics & Home Repair
30A	Georgetown	24	House Beautiful		
7	Getting Married: A Planning Guide	24	House Beautiful's Home Decorating	29	Mechanix Illustrated
49	Girl Scout Leader	17	Houston Arts Magazine	43	Mechanix Illustrated Computers '83
50	Glamour	24	Houston Home & Garden	49	Medical/Mrs.
45	Glider Rider	41	Human Events	24	Metro Home & Garden Magazines
22A	Globe	19	Hunting		
30A	Gold Coast of Florida	19	Hunting Annual 1983	30A	Metro—Newark!
45	Golf Digest	43B	Hustler	24	Metropolitan Home
45	Golf Magazine			30A	Miami Magazine
45	Golf World		**I**	30A	Miami Mensual
49	Good Housekeeping	16	Image	19	Michigan Out-Of-Doors
24	Good Ideas	8	Income Opportunities	43	Microcomputing
8B	Good Sam's Hi-Way Herald	30A	Indianapolis Magazine	11	Miniature Collector
		30A	Indianapolis Monthly	11	Model Railroader
18	Gourmet	8	Industry Week	7	Modern Bride
49	Graduate Woman	46	Inn America Magazine	33	Modern Drummer
19	Gray's Sporting Journal	16	Instructor	43A	Modern Maturity
30A	Greenville Magazine	33	International Musician & Recording World	39	Modern Photography
1A	Grier's Almanac			8	Money
22	Grit	46	International Travel News	22A	Moneysworth
42	Group	17	International Traveler	30A	Monthly Detroit
19	Gun Dog		**J**	18	Monthly Magazine of Food & Wine, The
19	Gun Week	30A	Jacksonville Magazine		
30	Gung-Ho	51	Junior Scholastic	1A	Moon Sign Book
19	Guns & Ammo		**K**	20	Moose Magazine
19	Guns & Ammo Annual 1983	3	Keepin' Track Of Vettes	25	Morgan Horse, The
		33	Keyboard World	22	Mother Earth News, The
19	Guns Magazine		**L**	22	Mother Jones
	H	1A	Ladies Birthday Almanac, The	5	Mothers' Manual
20	Hadassah Magazine			31A	Motocross Action
47	Ham Radio Magazine	49	Ladies' Home Journal	6	Motor Boating & Sailing
14	Handmade	49	Lady's Circle	3	Motor Trend
46	Happy Wanderer, The	6	Lakeland Boating	31A	Motorcycle
50	Harper's Bazaar	21	Landscaping Homes and Gardens	31A	Motorcyclist Magazine
22	Harper's Magazine			8A	Motorhome
49	Hartford Woman	11	Lapidary Journal	46	Motorland
9B	Harvard Magazine	42	Leadership	3	Motortech
23	Health	16	Learning	24	Moving House and Home
23	Health Protection	23	Let's Live	49	Ms.
21	Herb Quarterly, The	11	Linn's Stamp News	45	Muscle Digest
33	High Fidelity	42	Living Church, The	33	Music City News
43	High Technology	30A	Los Angeles Magazine		**N**
27A	High Times	38	Los Angeles Times Home Magazine	41	Nation, The
23A	Highlander, The			2	National Calendar of Indoor-Outdoor Art Fairs
45	Hockey Digest	8B	Lost Treasure		
45	Hockey News, The	42	Lutheran Standard, The	42	National Catholic Register
24	Home	42	Lutheran, The		
49	The Homemaker of the National Extension Homemakers Council		**M**	22A	National Enquirer
		42A	Macfadden Women's Group	25	National Horseman, The
24	Homeowners How To			11	National Knife Collector
25	Hoof Beats	50	Mademoiselle	45	National Masters News
17A	Horizon	2	Magazine Antiques, The	35	National Parks
25	Horse Illustrated	34	Magazine of Fantasy and Science Fiction, The	45	National Racquetball
25	Horseman			41	National Review
25	Horesemen's Journal	6	Marine and Recreation News	51	National 4-H News
25	Horseplay			22	Natural History
25	Horsetrader, The	10	Marvel Comics Group	31	Navy Times
21	Horticulture, The Magazine of American Gardening			46	Negro Traveler and Conventioneer
				30A	Nevada Magazine

Table 6-1. U.S. Consumer Magazines with Mail Order and/or Shopping Advertising Pages

Class	Publication	Class	Publication	Class	Publication
46	New England Guide, The	11	Plastercrafts	6	Rudder
30A	New Hampshire Profiles	30	Playboy	45	The Runner
30A	New Jersey Monthly	30	Players	45	Runner's World
30A	New Mexico Magazine	49	Playgirl		
41	New Republic, The	33	Polyphony		**S**
24	New Shelter	3	Pontiac	30A	Sacramento Magazine
36A	New York Magazine	11	Popular Ceramics	25	Saddle and Bridle
46	New York Motorist	47	Popular Electronics	6	Sail
38	New York News	3	Popular Hot Rodding	6	Sailboat & Equipment
	Magazine	11	Popular Magazine Group		Directory
28	New York Review of	29	Popular Mechanics	6	Sailing
	Books, The	39	Popular Photography	8	St. Louis Business
38	The New York Times	39	Popular Photography's		Journal
	Magazine		Photography Annual	30A	St. Louis Magazine
22	New Yorker, The	39	Popular Photography's	6	Salt Water Sportsman
19	North American Hunter		Photography Buying	30A	San Francisco
2	North Light		Guide	30B	San Francisco Focus
8B	Northeast Outdoors	29	Popular Science	22	Saturday Evening Post,
35	Not Man Apart	2	Portfolio		The
43A	NRTA/AARP News	45	Powder	22	Saturday Review
	Bulletins	6	Powerboat	49	Savvy
22	Nuestro	25	Practical Horseman	51	Scholastic Magazines
11	Numismatic News	42	Presbyterian Survey		Groups
24	NY Habitat	23	Prevention	29	Science & Mechanics
		22	Prime Time	43	Science Digest
	O	45	Private Country Club	43	Scientific American
31	Off Duty		Guest Policy Directory	20	Scouting
3	Off-Road	4	Private Pilot	6	Sea & Pacific Skipper
34	Official Detective Group,	45	Pro Quarterback	49	Self
	The	1	PSA Magazine	43A	Senior Publishers Group
30A	Ohio Magazine	22	Psychology Today	22	Sepia
1A	Old Farmer's Almanac,	13	Pure-Bred Dogs Ameri-	49	Seventeen
	The		can Kennel Gazette	33	Sheet Music Magazine
34	Old West	51	Purple Cow	30A	Shenandoah Valley
3	On Track				Magazine
24	1,001 Home Ideas		**Q**	19	Shooting Times
21	Organic Gardening	47	QST	19	Shotgun Sports
42	Our Sunday Visitor	25	Quarter Horse Journal,	35	Sierra
19	Outdoor Life		The	46	Signature
19	Outdoor Press, The	25	Quarter Racing Record,	33	Sing Out!
8B	Outside		The	33	Singing News, The
33	Ovation			19	Skeet Shooting Review
3	Owner Operator		**R**	45	Ski
1	Ozark	11	Railfan & Railroad	45	Ski America
		11	Railroad Model	45	Ski X-C
	P		Craftsman	45	Skiers Directory
30A	Pacific Northwest	41	Reason	45	Skiing
25	Paint Horse Journal	49	Redbook Magazine	45	Skin Diver Magazine
1	Pan Am Clipper	50	Redbook's Be Beautiful	45	Skydiving
20	Paraplegia News	5	Redbook's Young Mother	6	Small Boat Journal
49	Parents	1	Republic Scene	43C	Snow Goer
11	Passenger Train Journal	31	Retired Officer, The	43C	Snow Week
19	Pennsylvania Sportsman,	36A	Review of the News, The	43C	Snowmobile
	The	31A	Rider	43C	Snowmobile News
25	Performance Horseman	3	Road & Track	49	Soap Opera Digest
43	Personal Computing	31A	Road Rider	45	Soccer Digest
6	Petersen Marine Group	44	Robb Report, The	30	Soldier of Fortune
39	Petersen's Photographic	11	Rock & Gem	6	Soundings
	Magazine	30A	Rocky Mountain	46	South American Travel
30A	Philadelphia Magazine		Magazine		Guide
30A	Phoenix Magazine	34	Rod Serling's The Twi-	6	Southern Boating
24	Phoenix Home/Garden		light Zone Magazine	17	Southern California
3	Pickup, Van & 4WD	45	Rodeo News		Coast
30A	Pittsburgh	33	Rolling Stone	17	Southern California Guide
4	Plane&Pilot	9A	Rotarian, The	24	Southern Living

Table 6-1. U.S. Consumer Magazines with Mail Order and/or Shopping Advertising Pages

Class	Publication
19	Southern Outdoors
2	Spinning Wheel
45	Sport
4	Sport Aviation
36A	Sporting News, The
45	Sports 'N Spokes
19	Sports Afield
19	Sports Afield/Special Publications
19	Sports And Recreation
3	Sports Car
45	SportsWise New York
41	Spotlight, The
49	Spring
12	Square Dancing
45	Starting Line
46	State, The
33	Stereo Review
31A	Street Chopper
3	Street Rodder
22	Success
24	Sunset
3	Super Chevy
30	Survive

T

Class	Publication
30A	Tampa Bay Magazine
30A	Tampa Magazine
43	Technology
43	Technology Illustrated
43	Technology Review
49	'Teen
45	Tennis
19	Texas Fisherman, The
21	Texas Gardener
24	Texas Homes
19	Texas Hunters Directory
30A	Texas Monthly
46	This Week On Oahu
25	Thoroughbred Record, The
51	Tiger Beat Group
20	Toastmaster, The
13	Today's Animal News
39	Today's Photographer
11	Tole World
31A	Touring Bike
22	Town & Country
45	Track & Field News
1A	Trail Blazer's Almanac and Pioneer Guide Book
6	Trailer Boats
8A	Trailer Life
11	Trains
19	Trap & Field
19	Trapper, The
46	Travel & Leisure
46	Travel/Holiday
11	Tropical Fish Hobbyist
33	Trouser Press
3	Truckin'
34	True West
1	TWA Ambassador
30A	Twin Cities

U

Class	Publication
44	Ultra Magazine
4	Ultralight Flyer
1	United
22	USA Today
1	USAir Magazine
30A	Utah Holiday Magazine

V

Class	Publication
20	V.F.W. Magazine
46	Vacationland
22	Vanity Fair
23	Vegetarian Times
45	Velo-News
8	Venture
24	Victorian Homes
47	Video
47	Video Review
47	Videoplay Magazine
50	Vogue
14	Vogue Patterns
25	Voice of the Tennessee Walking Horse
3	VW & Porsche

W

Class	Publication
49	W
30A	Washington Dossier, The
41	Washington Monthly, The
46	Washington Motorist, The
38	Washington Post Magazine, The
30A	Washingtonian Magazine, The
45	Water Skier, The
6	Waterfront
36A	Weekly, The
49	Weight Watchers Magazine
4	Western Flyer
25	Western Horseman, The
19	Western Outdoor News
1	Western's World
30A	Wichitan, The
11	Winning
30A	Wisconsin Monthly
49	Woman's Day
11	Woman's Day Best Ideas for Christmas
49	Woman's Day Dessert Lover's Cookbook
49	Woman's Day Diet & Exercise Guide
14	Woman's Day Granny Squares and Needlework Ideas
49	Woman's Day Great Holiday Baking Ideas
24	Woman's Day Home Decorating
49	Woman's Day Home Entertaining Ideas
24	Woman's Day Home Improvements

Class	Publication
24	Woman's Day Kitchen & Bath Guide
24	Woman's Day Kitchen and Family Rooms
50	Woman's Day Make Yourself Beautiful
14	Woman's Day 101 Needlework & Sweater Ideas
24	Woman's Day Remodeling Ideas
49	Woman's Day Simply Delicious Meals in Minutes
49	Woman's Day Special Interest Publications
49	Woman's Day 101 Ways To Lose Weight And Stay Healthy
49	Women's Sports
8B	Woodall's Campground Directory
43A	Woodall's Retirement Directory
8A	Woodall's RV Buyer's Guide
6	WoodenBoat
20	Woodmen of the World Magazine
24	Woodstove, Coalstove, and Solar Equipment Directory
24	Woodworker's Journal, The
49	Workbasket
24	Workbench
49	Working Mother
49	Working Woman
45	World of Rodeo and Western Heritage, The
41	World Press Review
45	World Tennis
28	Writer's Digest

Y

Class	Publication
6	Yacht Racing/Cruising
6	Yachting
6	Yachting's Boat Buyers Guide
22	Yankee

Within each category there are usually one or more publications that perform particularly well for the direct response advertiser at a lower cost than other publications in the group. We call those magazines the pilot publications for the group. If you use the pilot publications and they produce an acceptable cost per response, you can then proceed

Table 6-2. Basic Consumer Magazine Categories

Demographic	Category	Sample Publications
Dual audience	General editorial/ entertainment	Grit, National Enquirer, National Geographic, New York Times Magazine Section, Parade, People, Reader's Digest, TV Guide
	News	Time, Newsweek, Sports Illustrated, U.S. News & World Report
	Special Interest	Architectural Digest, Business Week, Elks, Foreign Affairs, Hi Fidelity, Modern Photography, Natural History, Ski, Travel & Leisure, Wall St. Journal, Yankee
Women	General/service/ shelter (home service)	Better Homes & Gardens, Cosmopolitan, Ebony, Family Circle, Good Housekeeping, House Beautiful, House & Garden, Ladies' Home Journal, McCall's, Redbook, Sunset, Woman's Day
	Fashion	Glamour, Harper's Bazaar, Mademoiselle, Vogue
	Special interest	Brides, MacFadden's Women's Group, McCall's Needlework & Crafts, Parents
Men	General/ entertainment/ fashion	Esquire, Gentlemen's Quarterly, Penthouse, Playboy
	Special Interest	Cars, Field & Stream, Mechanix Illustrated, Outdoor Life, Popular Mechanics, Popular Science, Road & Track, Sports Afield
Youth	Male	Boys' Life
	Female	Teen, Young Miss
	Dual audience	Scholastic Magazines, National 4-H News

to explore the possibility of adding other magazines in that category to your media schedule.

In selecting the pilot publications in a category, keep in mind that you are not dealing with a static situation. As indicated earlier, a publication's mail order advertising viability changes from year to year, and what is a bellwether publication this season may not be the one to use next year. What is important is that you check out your own experience and the experience of others in determining the best places to advertise first in each category, and the next best, and the next best, and so on.

Think of your media buying program as an ever-widening circle, as illustrated in Exhibit 6-1. At the center is a nucleus of pilot publications. Each successively larger ring would include reruns in all profitable pilot publications plus new test books. In the same way, you can expand from campaign to campaign to cover wider levels of the various media categories until you have reached the widest possible universe.

Exhibit 6-1. Circle Approach to Media Selection

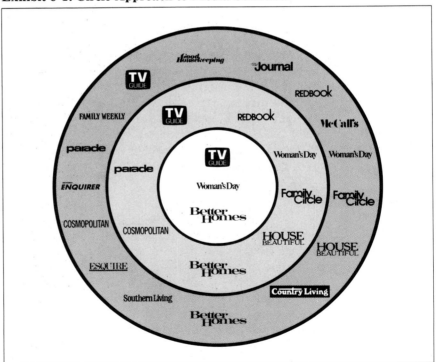

Bind-In Cards

The reason for the success of the insert card is self-evident. Pick up a magazine, thumb through its pages, and see for yourself how effectively the bound-in-cards flag down the reader. Each time someone picks up the publication, there is the insert card pointing to your message. Another reason is the ease with which the reader can respond. The business reply card eliminates the trouble of addressing an envelope, providing a stamp, and so on.

Before the development of the insert card, the third and fourth covers of a magazine were the prime mail order positions and were sold at a premium. The bind-in insert card has created a world in which three, four, five, or more direct response advertisers can all have the position impact once reserved for the cover advertisers alone.

When you go to purchase space for a page and an accompanying insert card, you must face the fact that the best things in life are not free. Insert card advertising costs more. You must pay a space charge for the page and the card and sometimes a separate binding charge, and you must then add in the cost of printing the cards. How much you pay, of course, depends on the individual publication, the size of the card, and a number of other factors. There is no rule of thumb to follow in estimating the additional cost for an insert card. Space charges alone for a standard business reply card can be as little as 40 percent of the black-and-white page plus additional binding charges.

When the cost of the insert unit adds up to as much as four times the cost of an ordinary black-and-white page, you will have to receive four times the response to justify the added expense.

For most direct response advertisers, the response is likely to be six to eight times as great when pulling for an order and as much as six to eight times as great in pulling for inquiries. As a result, you can expect to cut your cost per response by 50 percent or more with an insert card as opposed to an ordinary on-page coupon ad.

Bingo Cards

While insert cards have a dramatic effect upon response, so do bingo cards. Bingo cards, often referred to as "information cards," are a unique device developed by magazine publishers, both consumer and business, to make it easy for the reader to request more information. "Bingo card" is really a generic term for any form—a reply card or printed form on a magazine page—on which the publisher prints designated numbers for specified literature. The reader simply circles the number designated for the literature desired. (See Exhibit 6-2.)

Typically an advertiser placing a specified unit of space in a magazine is entitled to a bingo card in the back of the publication. Ads reference these bingo cards with statements such as, "For further information circle Item #146." The cards are sent directly to the publisher who, in turn, sends compiled lists of inquiries to participating advertisers. The respective advertisers then send fulfillment literature to all who have inquired.

A neat system, to be sure, but a caveat is in order. "We get tons of requests for literature from bingo cards, but they're not worth a damn," is a frequent advertiser complaint.

Exhibit 6-2. Bingo Card for *Better Homes & Gardens*

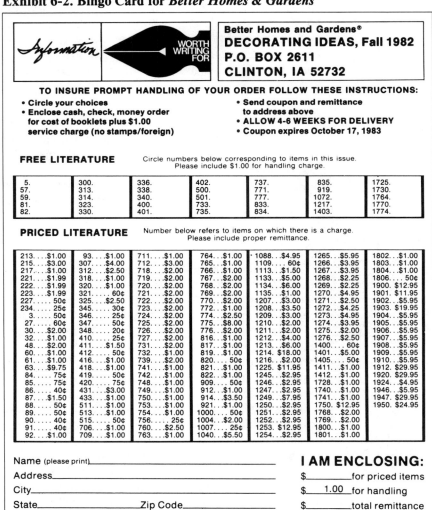

On the other hand, "Bingo cards can be very productive," states Adolph Auerbacher, publisher of 22 special interest publications, for *Better Homes & Gardens*. Auerbacher points to two prime reasons for poor sales conversion: (1) failure of advertisers to respond to inquiries quickly (2) failure of advertisers to qualify prospects properly. Pointing to a survey by *Better Homes & Gardens* among 203 companies to whom they responded, Auerbacher reports the following response times. During the first week 13 percent sent literature. At the end of the first month they had heard from 62 percent. Thirty-eight percent of the companies had not responded a month after the first response was received. And 10 percent were never heard from. (For maximum effectiveness all advertisers should have responded within two weeks.)

To the question of qualifying prospects properly for a better likelihood of sales conversion, Auerbacher gives some interesting theories and facts. To the age old question, "Should the advertiser charge for literature or send it free?", he makes this key point:

> If an air conditioner advertiser, for example, has a literature cost of $1, he has a natural tendency to want to get his dollar back. But he may lose sight of the fact that his real objective is to sell a $500 air conditioner.
>
> Even taking into account that those who pay $1 for the literature might be more qualified, the ratio of free requests to dollar payments may be so overwhelming that more air conditioners in total might be sold to consumers who requested free literature.

But often it is best to charge for literature as a qualifier. The "$64 question" is "how much?" Here Adolph Auerbacher provides some hard facts. Citing Table 6-3, he refers to three titles among their stable of special interest books with the details of response by amount charged for literature. Free literature requests had the greatest response in every case, as one would expect. But note the differences in response between varying amounts requested. For *Remodeling Ideas*, for example, a 10¢ request pulled 22 percent as many requests as free. But 25¢ pulled more requests than 10¢. And in the case of *Building Ideas*, a 50¢ request pulled as well as a 25¢ request. With the exception of *Decorating Ideas*, both a $1 and a $2 request got a very poor response, suggesting upper limits of resistance perhaps.

So, as Mr. Auerbacher points out, success in the use of bingo cards depends, to a major degree, upon rapid fulfillment of literature requests and qualifying prospects in the most cost-efficient way. Two additional factors must be taken into account: (1) the closer the literature offered ties to the special interest of the book, the better the response is likely to be; (2) advertiser awareness is an important response factor (an Armstrong will most always outpull a Joe Blow).

Magazine Advertising Response Pattern: What Do These Early Results Mean?

There is a remarkable similarity from one insertion to another in the rate of response over time for most magazines. Monthly publications generally have a similar pattern for the rate of response from week to week. However, the pattern of response for publications in different categories can vary. For example, a mass circulation weekly magazine *(TV Guide* or *Parade)* will pull a higher percentage of the total response in the first few weeks than a shelter book (such as *House & Garden* or

Table 6-3. Tabulation of Literature Requests

Price	Median Response	% of Free	*High	**Low	***Ratio H/L
Better Homes & Gardens Remodeling Ideas, Spring '80					
Free	672		1171	192	6:1
10¢	148	22	373	113	3:1
25¢	213	32	408	51	8:1
50¢	130	19	540	51	10:1
$1	82	12	240	3	80:1
$2	19	3	129	2	65:1
Better Homes & Gardens Building Ideas, Spring '80					
Free	781		1501	252	6:1
10¢	108	14	199	60	3:1
25¢	298	38	430	109	4:1
50¢	297	38	722	97	7:1
$1	95	12	431	3	143:1
$2	31	4	164	3	55:1
Better Homes & Gardens Decorating Ideas, Spring '80					
Free	491		1420	21	67:1
10¢	62	13	72	49	1.5:1
25¢	193	39	400	68	6:1
50¢	138	28	646	35	18:1
$1	102	21	282	17	16:1
$2	79	16	123	19	6:1

"Information Worth Writing For" section arranged to show median, highest response, lowest response and ratio between highest and lowest response.

Definitions: ***HIGH** means the highest number of requests for the literature of a given advertiser in a particular issue. ****LOW** means the lowest number of requests. *****RATIO H/L** means the ratio of response of the best puller contrasted to the worst puller.

Better Homes & Gardens). A shelter book has a slower response curve but keeps pulling for a long period of time because it is kept much longer and is not so short-lived as a mass circulation magazine.

Also, subscription circulation will pull faster than newsstand circulation. Subscribers usually receive their copies within a few days while newsstand sales are spread out over an entire month. Consequently the response pattern is spread out as well.

If you are running an ad calling for direct response from a monthly magazine, here is a general guide to the likely response flow:

After the first week....................	3-7%	After two months..................	75-85%
After the second week...........	20-25%	After three months...............	85-92%
After the third week..............	40-45%	After four months.................	92-95%
After one month	50-55%		

From a weekly publication, such as *Time* or *TV Guide,* the curve is entirely different; 50 percent of your response usually comes in the first two weeks.

These expectations, of course, represent the average of many hundreds of response curves for different propositions. You may see variations up or down from the classic curve for any single insertion.

As a general rule for monthlies, you can expect to project the final results within 10 percent accuracy after the third week of counting responses. If you are new to the business, give yourself the experience of entering daily result counts by hand for dozens of ads. Before long you will develop an instinct for projecting how an ad for your particular proposition is doing within the first 10 days of measured response.

Timing and Frequency: When Should You Run? How Often Should You Go Back?

Once you determine where you want to run, timing and frequency are the two crucial factors in putting together an effective print schedule.

Of course, there are some propositions that have a time of the year when they will do best, e.g., novelty items are likely to be purchased in October and November or even as early as late September for Christmas gifts. But for the nonseasonal items, you can look forward to two major print advertising seasons for direct response.

The first and by far the most productive for most propositions is the winter season, which begins with the January issue and runs through the February and March issues. The second season begins with the August issue and runs through the November issue.

The best winter months for most people are January and February. The best fall months are October and November. For schools and book continuity propositions, September frequently does as well or better.

If you have a nonseasonal item and you want to do your initial test at the best possible time, use a February issue with a January sale date or a January issue with a late December or early January sale date of whatever publication makes the most sense for your proposition.

How much of a factor is the particular month in which an ad appears? It could make a difference of 40 percent or even more. Here is an example of what the direct response advertiser may expect to experience during the year if the cost per response (CPR) in February were $2: January, $2.05; February, $2; March, $2.20; April, $2.50; May, $2.60; June, $2.80; July, $2.60; August, $2.40; September, $2.60; October, $2.20; November, $2.20; December, $2.40.

These hypothetical relative costs are based on the assumption that the insertion is run one time in any one of the 12 issues of a monthly publication. But, of course, if you are successful, you will want to run your copy more than once. So now we are faced with the other crucial question: What will various rates of frequency do to your response? Should you run once a year? Twice? Three times? Or every other month?

The frequency factor is more difficult to formulate than the timing factor. Optimum frequency cannot be generalized for print media advertising. Some propositions can be run month after month in a publication and show very little difference in cost per response. At one time, Doubleday & Company had worked out optimum frequency curves for some of its book club ads that required a 24-month hiatus between insertions.

How, then, do you go about determining ideal frequency of insertions? Try this procedure. The first time your copy appears in a publication, run it at the most likely time of the year for your special appeal. If you have a nonseasonal proposition, use January or February issues.

If the cost per response is in an acceptable range or up to 20 percent better than expected, wait six months and follow with a second insertion. If that insertion produces results within an acceptable range, you probably are a twice-a-year advertiser.

If the first insertion pulls well over 20 percent better than the planned order margin, turn around and repeat within a three or four-month period.

If the response to the test insertion in January or February was marginal, it usually makes sense to wait a full year before returning for another try in that publication.

The best gauge of how quickly you can run the next insertion aimed at the same magazine audience is the strength of the response from the last insertion. What you are reading in the results is a measurement of the saturation factor as it relates to that portion of the circulation that is interested in your selling message.

Of course, like all the other factors that affect response, frequency does not operate in a vacuum. The offer of a particularly advantageous position in a particular month or a breakthrough to better results with improved copy can lead you to set aside whatever carefully worked out frequency you had adopted earlier.

Determining Proper Ad Size: How Much Is Too Much?

A crucial factor in obtaining an acceptable cost per response is the size of the advertising unit you select. Ordinarily, the bigger the ad the better job the creative people can do in presenting the selling message. But there is one catch. Advertising space costs money. And the more you spend, the greater the response you need to get your money back.

What you want to find is the most efficient size for your particular proposition and for the copy approach you have chosen. Just as with frequency, there is no simple rule of thumb here.

Generally speaking, advertising for leads or prospects or to gain inquiries requires less advertising space than copy that is pulling for orders. Many companies seeking inquiries or running a lead item to get names for catalog followup make use of advertising units of less than one column. Only a handful of companies looking for prospects can make effective use of full-page space. Going one step further and using a page and insert card to pull for leads runs the risk of being too effective. This unit can bring in inquiries at very low cost, but there is always the danger that the quality will be very poor. Find out at your own peril.

For example, if you use a black-and-white page with a tear-off coupon that generates leads at $5 each and that convert at a 10 percent rate, then your advertising cost per sale is $50. Take the same insertion and place it as a page and insert card, and the cost per response may be as low as $3. If the conversion rate held up at 10 percent, the advertising cost per sale would be only $30. But it is more likely that the advertiser would experience a sharp conversion rate drop to perhaps 5 percent, with a resultant $60 cost per sale plus the cost of processing the additional leads.

When a direct sale or a future commitment to buy is sought, the dynamics usually are different from those when inquiries are sought. As a general rule, the higher the unit of sale or dollar volume commitment, the larger the unit of space that can be afforded, right up to the double page spread with insert card. However, there are a number of additional factors to be considered as well:

1. The nature of the product presentation may inherently require a particular space unit. For example, in record club and book club advertising, experience has shown that a maximum number of books and records should be displayed for best results. As a consequence, many of these clubs run a two-page spread as their standard ad unit. And in a small-size publication such as *TV Guide,* they may take six or even eight pages to display the proper number of books and records.

2. Some propositions, such as Time-Life Books in the continuity book-selling field, require four-color advertising in order to present the beautiful color illustrations that are an important feature of the product being sold.

3. Usually full-page ads appear at the front of a publication and small-space ads at the back. So going to a full-page unit is often related to the benefits you can expect from a premium, front-of-book position.

4. If you are successful with a single-page ad with coupon, test using an insert card before you try to add a second page. If the page and insert card work for you, give the spread and card a try.

5. Most mail order advertising falls into one of three size categories: (a) the spectacular unit—anything from the page and standard card insert to the four-page preprinted insert; (b) the single full-page unit; and (c) the small-space unit less than one column in size.

The awkward sizes in pulling for an order appear to be the one-column and two-column units. These inserts seldom work better than their big-brother pages or little-sister 56-line, 42-line, and 21-line units, although a "square third" (2 columns by 70 lines) can be a very efficient space unit.

Always remember, space costs money. The objective is to take the minimum amount of space you need to express your proposition effectively and to return a profit.

Start by having the creative director at your advertising agency express the proposition in the amount of space needed to convey a powerful selling message. Once you have established the cost per response for this basic unit, you can experiment with other size units.

If you have two publications on your schedule that perform about equally well for the basic unit, try testing the same ad approach expressed in a smaller or larger space size in one of those two publications while running the basic control unit in the same month in the other publication.

Four-Color, Two-Color, Black-and-White: How Colorful Should Your Advertising Be?

All magazines charge extra for adding color to your advertising. And remember there will be additional production expense if you go this route.

Usually the cost of adding a second color to a black-and-white page does not return the added costs charged by the publication for the space and the expense of producing the ad. If the copy is right, the words will do their job without getting an appreciable lift from having headline set in red or blue or green. An exception might be the use of a second color tint as background to provide special impact to your page.

It is with the use of four-color advertising that the direct response advertiser has an opportunity to profit on an investment in color.

A number of publications (for example, *Esquire, Time, Woman's Day, Ladies' Home Journal*) allow you to run a split of four-color vs. black-and-white, in an alternating copy A/B perfect split-run. Test results indicate an increase of anywhere from 30 percent to almost 60 percent where there is appropriate and dramatic utilization of the four-color process.

Given a striking piece of artwork related to the proposition or an inherently colorful product feature to present, you can expect an increase in response when you use four-color advertising. Since you will need more than a 20 percent increase in most publications to make the use of color profitable, it is wise to pretest the value of this factor before scheduling it across the board. Some products such as insurance simply do not require color.

Now just what can you expect the cost of four-color advertising to be? Table 6-4 shows four-color charges from a representative group of consumer publications.

Table 6-4. Four-Color Rate Examples

Publication	Black-and-White Page Rate	Four-Color Page Rate	Percentage Increase for Four-Color
Woman's Day	$53,720	$64,310	19.7
Family Circle	44,767*	51,375*	14.8
Ladies' Home Journal	39,000	48,000	23.1
Seventeen	13,325	19,250	44.5
Redbook	32,270	42,675	32.2
McCall's	48,670	59,830	22.9
Good Housekeeping	39,300*	46,416*	18.1
Glamour	17,250	24,340	41.1
Newsweek	40,930	63,850	56.0
Time	55,045	85,870	56.0
Sports Illustrated	35,725	55,730	60.0
Popular Mechanics	12,219*	20,568*	68.3
Mechanix Illustrated	11,985*	17,970*	49.9
Reader's Digest	81,300	97,700	20.2
Esquire	9,675*	14,475*	49.6

*Mail order rates

If you plan to use four-color advertising, the increase in publication space cost is only one of the cost factors to be weighed. The cost of the original four-color engravings for a 7×10 page runs from $3,000 to $5,000 depending on the copy and artwork being used. This compares with a black-and-white engraving cost that could be from $200 to $300. In addition, any dye transfers or other four-color preparatory work will probably increase mechanical preparation costs by 50 percent or more over a comparable black-and-white insertion.

The Position Factor Can Mean As Much As What You Say

Position in life may not be everything, but in direct response it often means the difference between paying out or sudden death. By "position" we mean where your advertisement appears in the publication. There are two rules governing the position factor. First, the closer to the front of the book an ad is placed, the better the response will be. Second, the more visible the position, the better the response will be.

The first rule defies rational analysis. Yet it is as certain as the sun's rising in the morning. Many magazine publishers have offered elaborate research studies demonstrating to the general advertiser that an ad in the editorial matter far back in a publication gets better readership than an ad placed within the first few pages of the publication. This may well be true for the general or institutional advertiser, but it is not true for the direct response advertiser.

Whatever the explanation may be, the fact remains that decades of measured direct response advertising tell the same story over and over again. A position in the first seven pages of the magazine produces a dramatically better response (all other factors being the same) than if the same insertion appears farther back in the same issue.

How much better? There are as many answers to this question as there are old pros in the business. However, here is about what you might expect the relative response to be from various page positions as measured against the first right-hand page arbitrarily rated at a pull of 100.

First right-hand page	100	Back of book (following main	
Second right-hand page	95	body of editorial matter)	50
Third right-hand page	90	Back cover	100
Fourth right-hand page	85	Inside third cover	90
Back of front of the book		Page facing third cover	85
(preceding editorial matter)	70		

The second rule is more easily explained. An ad must be seen before it can be read or acted on. Right-hand pages pull better than left-hand pages, frequently by as much as 15 percent. Insert cards open the magazine to the advertiser's message and thereby create their own "cover" position. Of course, the insert card introduces the additional factor of providing a postage-free response vehicle as well. But the response from insert cards, too, is subject to the influence of how far back in the magazine the insertion appears. Here is what you can expect in most publications (assigning a 100 rating to the first card):

First insert card position	100
Second insert card position	95
Third insert card position	85
Fourth insert card position	75*
Fifth insert card position	70*

*If position follows main editorial matter.

The pull of position is as inexorable as the pull of gravity. Well, almost, that is. There are a few exceptions. In the fashion and the mechanics magazines, card positioning seems to make little or no difference. Another exception may involve the placement of an ad opposite a related column or feature article in a publication (for example, a *Home Handyman's Encyclopedia* ad opposite the Home Handyman column). Another exception may involve placement of your ad in a high-readership shopping section at the back of a magazine.

How To Buy Space

Since mail order advertising is always subject to bottom-line analysis, the price you pay for space can mean the difference between profit and loss. Mrs. Florence Peloquin, mail order advertising director for *Woman's Day,* provides some basic questions the advertiser should ask the publisher or his agency before placing space.

1. Is there a special mail order rate? Mail order rates are usually 10 to 30 percent lower than general rates.
2. Is there a special mail order section, a shopping section where mail order ads are grouped? Usually the back of the book.
3. Does the book have remnant space available at substantial discounts? Many publishers offer discounts of up to 50 percent off the regular rate.
4. Is there an insertion frequency discount, or dollar volume discount? Is frequency construed as the number of insertions in a time period or consecutive issues? Many publishers credit more than one insertion in an issue towards frequency.

5. Do corporate discounts apply to mail order? Sometimes the corporate discount is better than the mail order discount.

6. Do you have seasonal discounts? Some publishers have low-volume advertising months during which they offer substantial discounts.

7. Do you offer spread discounts when running two pages or more in one issue? The discount can run up to 60 percent on the second page.

8. Do you have a publisher's rate? Is this in addition to or in lieu of the mail order rate? It can be additive.

9. Will you accept a per-inquiry (P.I.) deal? Under P.I. deals the advertiser pays the publisher an amount for each inquiry or order, or a minimum flat amount for the space, plus so much per inquiry or order.

10. Do you accept "umbrella contracts"? Some media buying services and agencies own banks or reserves of space with given publications and can offer discounts even for one-time ads.

11. Do you barter for space? Barter usually involves a combination of cash and merchandise.

When bought properly, tested properly, and used properly, magazine advertising represents a vast universe of sales and profit potential for the direct response advertiser.

Self-quiz

1. Name five magazines that provide a conducive atmosphere for direct response advertisers.

a. _____

b. _____

c. _____

d. _____

e. _____

2. Name the four major advantages of using regional editions of magazines.

a. _____

b. _____

c. _____

d. _____

3. What are the two negative factors involved in buying regional space?

a. _____

b. _____

4. Name five basic consumer magazine categories.

a. _____

b. _____

c. _____

d. _____

e. _____

5. Give the definition of a pilot publication.

_____

_____

_____

6. What is the theory of an expanded media-buying program based on an ever-widening circle?

_____

_____

_____

_____

7. What is the principal advantage of an insert card in a magazine?

_____

_____

_____

8. When direct response advertisers use insert cards, the response is likely to be: _____ to _____ times as great when pulling for an order and as much as _____ to _____ times as great in pulling for inquiries.

9. What are the two prime reasons for poor sales conversions to "bingo cards"?

a. _____

b. _____

10. As a general rule, when a direct response advertiser uses a monthly magazine, he or she can usually expect to have about 50 percent of his or her total response after _____ weeks.

11. For weekly publications 50 percent of total response can be expected after _____ weeks.

12. From a timing standpoint, which is the most productive season for most direct response propositions?

_____

_____

13. Which is the second most productive season?

_____

14. When is the best possible time to test a nonseasonal item?

_____

_____

15. How much is the cost per response (CPR) likely to vary between the best pulling month and the poorest pulling month? _____
_____ percent

16. Provide guidelines for frequency factors in magazine advertising.

a. If the cost per response is in an acceptable range or up to 20 percent better than expected, wait _____ months and follow up with a second insertion in the second half of the year.

b. If the first insertion pulls well over 20 percent better than allowed order margin, turn around and repeat within a _____ or _____ month period.

c. If response to the test insertion in January or February was marginal, it usually makes sense to wait _____ before returning for another try in that publication.

17. Generally speaking, which requires more space for effective direct response advertising?

_____ Pulling inquiries

_____ Pulling orders

18. What is the prime advantage of a full-page ad vs. a small ad in a magazine?

_____

_____

19. If a single-page ad with coupon is successful, what is the next logical test?

_____

_____

_____

_____

20. What are the three size categories for most mail order advertising?

a. _____

b. _____

c. _____

21. When four-color vs. black-and-white is tested, results indicate an increase of anywhere from _____ percent to almost _____ percent where there is appropriate and dramatic utilization of the four-color process.

22. What are the two rules governing the "position" factor for the direct response advertiser?

a. _____

b. _____

23. Right-hand pages pull better than left-hand pages by as much as _____ percent.

24. If a 100 rating is assigned to a first insert card position in a publication having five insert card positions, what would the fifth insert card rating be?

_____

25. Mail order rates are usually _____ percent to _____ percent lower than general rates.

Pilot project

You are the advertising manager for a publisher of children's books. It is your assignment to test market a new continuity series of 10 books written for age levels 6 to 10. Each book in the series will sell for $4.95. Outline a plan for test marketing in magazines.

1. What pilot publications would you schedule for testing?

2. Will you use any regional editions?

3. Do a circle approach to media selection indicating what additional publications you will expand to if the pilot publications prove successful.

4. Prepare a timing schedule, indicating when your pilot ads will break and when your expanded media-buying program will take place.

5. What ad size will you use and will the ad be black-and-white, two color, or four color?

Chapter Seven

Newspapers

For sheer circulation in print, there is nothing to compare with the daily and Sunday newspapers. There were 1,730 daily newspapers in the United States with an average daily circulation of 61,400,000 as of January 1, 1982. Thus the circulation available through newspapers offers an exciting opportunity for direct response advertisers. It is significant that many direct response advertisers spend all or a major portion of their budgets in newspapers.

Newspapers are unique in that they can serve as a vehicle for carrying direct response advertising formats foreign to their regular news pages. Remarkable results have been achieved by using these special formats.

Newspaper Preprints

Use of preprints by direct response advertisers is a phenomenon of this decade. The Newspaper Advertising Bureau of New York estimates that 28.7 billion preprints circulated in 1981. Preprints became a viable method for direct marketers in 1965. In the first five months of that year there was only one preprint mail order advertiser (Time-Life Books) in million-circulation newspapers.

Columbia Record Club followed Time-Life Books in 1965. Wunderman, Ricotta & Kline, the club's agency, first tested preprints in newspapers in six markets (*Akron Beacon, Dallas Times Herald, Des Moines Register, Minneapolis Tribune, Peoria Journal Star,* and *Seattle Times*). Hundreds of millions of preprints have since been run in newspapers by Columbia Record Club. There are two obvious advantages to preprints such as those used by Columbia. First, they provide abundant space for the detailed listing of items available. Second, a perforated postpaid return card may be imprinted, which, because of the weight of the stock used, closely resembles an ordinary post card and can be easily mailed by the respondent.

The dramatic impact of preprints in a newspaper must be measured against the greatly increased cost. Comparing a four-page preprint with a fourth cover in a syndicated Sunday supplement, one finds the preprint costs almost four times as much. The tremendous volume of preprints found in the Sunday newspaper is good evidence that the increased cost often is more than warranted.

Newspaper Advertising Bureau furnishes the following estimated space costs for inserts for the top 100 markets based on a tabloid size of 10¾ × 12¾. Two pages plus flap, $29.34 per M; four pages, $30.37 per M; six pages, $33.41 per M; eight pages, $35.17 per M; twelve pages, $40.41 per M; sixteen pages, $45.67 per M; twenty-four pages, $54.40 per M.

It should be noted that these estimated costs in the 100 top markets are for *space only.* Printing costs of the inserts must be added. A breakdown of costs for space, depending on the sizes of preprint, for 39 representative newspapers is given in Table 7-1. Careful note should be taken of the fact that the CPM tends to be lower for large metro papers. Thus, if a direct marketer has a proposition that appeals only to small towns, the chances for successful use of preprints are greatly diminished. Other facts about preprints and their use and trend as provided by Newspaper Preprint Corporation are listed in Table 7-1.

Acceptable Size

Size depends on the newspaper's policy and equipment, but, generally speaking, minimum sizes are 5½ × 8⅛. Maximum size is 10¾ × 14½. These minimum and maximum sizes are folded sizes—unfolded size could be larger. For example, a standard format size of 21½ × 14½ printed on heavy stock could fold in half to 10¾ × 14½.

Sunday vs. Weekday Inserts

Figures for 1981 show that weekday preprints have increased to the point that they constitute about 48.3 percent of total preprint circulation in the top 100 markets.

Card vs. Multipage Insert

A survey shows that 87 percent of total preprints used are of multipage formats. Because just about all Sunday newspapers accept preprints and between 80 percent and 90 percent of daily newspapers accept inserts, it behooves all direct marketers who have products or services appealing to mass markets to explore this selling vehicle.

Syndicated Newspaper Supplements

Imagine placing three space insertion orders and buying newspaper circulation of 50 million plus! This is indeed possible if you place insertion orders in the three major syndicated newspaper supplements.

Branham Newspapers, Inc., major newspaper representative, presents the figures in Table 7-2.

Distribution of the three syndicated supplements breaks down about this way. Sunday Mag/Net is distributed by about 57 member newspapers. Those carrying Sunday Mag/Net supplements offer a choice of 43 top metro areas for advertising.

Family Weekly is generally carried by the newspapers with smaller circulations, many of which publish within the top metro areas but basically "C" and "D" counties. The majority of the newspapers distributing *Family Weekly* are outside the top 150 metro areas.

Parade is included in some of the Sunday Mag/Net newspapers, but generally it is more evenly distributed among the top 100 metro areas. Obvious advantages of syndicated supplements are their relatively low cost per thousand circulation and the possibility of reaching top metro areas as well as smaller cities, depending on the supplement used.

One thing going for the syndicated supplements is their mail order atmosphere. *Parade*, for instance, points out that 60 percent of its advertising carries some kind of coupon that enables the advertiser to get a measurement of results. For example, four major mail order concerns, Franklin Mint, Columbia House, Haband, and Doubleday Book Club, are currently spending $1.2 to $2 million dollars each on 16 to 20 pages of color advertising in *Parade*.

Among the syndicated supplements, *Parade* and *Family Weekly* offer a mail order booklet inserted on a regular basis. This booklet, commonly called a Dutch Door, usually runs 12 pages. Its page size is one-half that of the supplement. Some issues are taken over entirely by one advertiser. Other issues contain a variety of small mail order ads.

It is obvious that a direct marketer who has not previously placed space in one of the syndicated supplements would not go full run without testing. *Parade*, for example, offers remnant space to mail order advertisers at 33 percent discount. Remnant space is advertising space left over when package goods advertisers buy only in those markets where they have distribution. Second to testing in remnant space is testing in regions.

With about 650 Sunday and weekend magazines, both syndicated and locally edited, a direct response advertiser has an incredible amount of distribution available at low cost.

Comics As a Direct Marketing Medium

Perhaps the biggest sleeper as a medium for direct marketers is the comic section of weekend newspapers. Comics are not glamorous, nor are they prestigious. But their total circulation, readership, and demographics constitute an exciting universe for the direct response advertis-

Table 7-1. Facts About Newspaper Preprint Inserts.

Newspaper	Single-Sheet Insert		Four-Page Insert		Six-Page Insert		Eight-Page Insert		Sunday Circulation
	Gross Rate	CPM	Gross Rate	CPM	Gross Rate	CPM	Gross Rate	CPM	
Asheville Citizen Times Asheville, North Carolina (Available daily • CPM based on circulation day of insertion)	850 lines or less $	24.00	850 lines or less $	26.00	850 lines or less $	27.50	850 lines or less $	29.00	68,000
Atlantic City Press Atlantic City, New Jersey (CPM based on circulation day of insertion)		25.00		30.00		30.00		30.00	78,000
Bangor Daily News Bangor, Maine (CPM based on circulation day of insertion)		21.00		23.00		27.00		30.00	88,000
Charleston Gazette Daily Mail Charleston, W. Va.	$ 3,099	28.96	$ 3,099	28.96	$ 3,099	28.96	$ 3,435	32.10	107,000
Chicago Zone Newspapers									
Aurora Beacon News Aurora, Ill.	$ 1,976	47.00	$ 1,976	47.00	$ 1,976	47.00	$ 1,976	47.00	42,000
Elgin Courier News Journal & Wheaton Journal	$ 1,927	47.00	$ 1,927	47.00	$ 1,927	47.00	$ 1,927	47.00	34,000 (Elgin) 7,000 (Wh'tn)
Joliet Herald News Joliet, Illinois	$ 2,350	47.00	$ 2,350	47.00	$ 2,350	47.00	$ 2,350	47.00	50,000
The Cincinnati Enquirer Cincinnati, Ohio (Available daily)	$10,676	32.83	$11,071	37.15	$11,863	39.81	$13,840	46.44	298,000
Dayton News & Journal Herald, Dayton, Ohio (Available daily; eight-page minimum)	$ 6,727	30.30	$ 7,351	33.11	$ 7,928	35.71	$ 9,070	40.86	222,000
The Detroit News Detroit, Michigan (Envelope inserts *not* accepted—available daily)	$27,225	33.00	$27,225	33.00	$27,225	33.00	$27,225	33.00	825,000
Green Bay Press Gazette, Green Bay, Wis. (Available daily)	$ 2,448	34.00	$ 2,448	34.00	$ 2,448	34.00	$ 2,448	34.00	72,000
The Record Hackensack, N.J. (CPM based on circulation day of insertion)		24.71		24.71		24.71		31.77	215,000
The Houston Chronicle Houston, Texas (CPM based on latest publisher's statement; available daily Wed/Thurs)		29.50		29.50		29.50		29.50	481,000
The State Journal Lansing, Mich. (Available daily)	$ 2,293	28.66	$ 2,293	28.66	$ 2,293	28.66	$ 3,104	38.80	80,000
The Arkansas Gazette Little Rock, Ark. (Available daily)	$ 4,846	30.67	$ 4,846	30.67	$ 5,114	32.37	$ 5,383	34.07	158,000
Manchester Union Leader, Manchester, N.H. (Available daily)	$ 1,770	24.58	$ 1,770	24.58	$ 2,100	29.17	$ 2,100	29.17	72,000

Source: Newspaper Preprint Corporation

Table 7-1. Facts About Newspaper Preprint Inserts (continued).

Newspaper	Single-Sheet Insert		Four-Page Insert		Six-Page Insert		Eight-Page Insert		Sunday Circulation
	Gross Rate	CPM	Gross Rate	CPM	Gross Rate	CPM	Gross Rate	CPM	
Newport News Press & Times Herald		39.00		42.00		47.00		51.00	105,000
(CPM based on actual paid circulation of previous Sunday rounded to nearest thousand.)									
The Sunday Oklahoman Oklahoma City, Okla. (Available daily)	$12,438	41.46	$12,438	41.46	$12,438	41.46	$15,939	58.13	300,000
The Omaha World Herald, Omaha, Neb.	$ 7,317	26.51	$ 7,317	26.51	$ 8,232	29.83	$ 9,697	35.13	276,000
Palm Beach Post-Times W. Palm Beach, Fla. (Available daily)		24.00		28.00		32.00		34.00	156,000
Richmond News Leader & Times Dispatch Richmond, Va. (Available daily)	$ 5,893	26.91	$ 6,859	31.32	$ 7,805	35.64	$ 8,757	39.96	219,000
San Bernardino Sun-Telegram, San Bernardino, Calif. (CPM based on latest SRDS; available daily)		24.00		26.00		31.00		34.00	84,000
San Diego Union Tribune, San Diego, Calif. (Available daily)	$ 9,860	29.00	$ 9,860	29.00	$ 9,860	29.00	$ 9,860	29.00	340,000
San Francisco Chronicle Examiner, San Francisco, Calif. (CPM rate based on latest publisher's statement rounded to nearest thousand.)		35.00		37.75		37.75		37.75	673,000
The Scranton Times Scranton, Penna. (Available daily)		23.00		24.00		27.00		27.00	49,000
Springfield Sun News Springfield, Ohio (No daily)	$ 1,677	39.93	$ 1,767	42.07	$ 1,867	44.45	$ 2,070	49.29	42,000
The Tacoma News Tribune, Tacoma, Wash. (Available daily)	$ 2,500	22.12	$ 2,832	25.06	$ 3,150	27.87	$ 3,532	31.26	113,000
Tampa Tribune & Times Tampa, Fla. (CPM rate based on press run day of insertion; available daily)		32.50		35.00		38.50		40.50	256,000
The Trenton Times Trenton, N.J. (CPM based on circulation day of insertion; available daily)		25.57		25.57		30.79		37.58	79,000
The Washington Post Washington, D.C.	$28,000	28.40	$28,000	28.40	$29,000	29.41	$30,000	30.43	986,000
Winston Salem Journal Winston Salem, N.C. (Available daily)	$ 2,500	25.51	$ 3,300	33.67	$ 3,900	39.80	$ 4,525	46.17	98,000
The News Tribune Woodbridge, N.J. (No Sunday; rates are for Saturday and daily)		25.29		27.82		45.88		45.88	53,000

Source: Newspaper Preprint Corporation.

er. Here are some of the fascinating facts and figures about comics as an advertising medium.

Each week, usually on Sunday, 50.3 million color comics are distributed through 460 different newspapers. These comics literally saturate the major and secondary markets, providing 50 percent or better coverage in 278 of the 300 strategic metropolitan markets of the country. There are two major comic groups—Puck and Metro.

The Puck Group is available through two networks: the National Network and the American Network. The National Network, made up of newspapers that almost all have circulations of over 100,000, is distributed through 65 papers in 64 cities. The American Network, made up of newspapers with circulations of under 100,000, is distributed in 74 papers in 73 cities. Also available through Puck are four geographically concentrated editions: the Pacific Group, made up of 12 West Coast newspapers; the California/Nevada/Washington group, with 9 papers; the Texas Group of 11 papers; and the Ottaway Newspaper with 7 papers.

Metro Sunday comics are available on the basis of newspaper networks. There are two networks: a basic network of 71 newspapers, and a selective network of 25 newspapers. Total circulation is 34,315,019 for the two networks, comprising 96 newspapers. Standard Rate and Data Service also lists 15 other smaller comic groups, regionally oriented. The size of these groups ranges from the Texas Sunday Comic Section, with a circulation of 822,176 to the Wyoming Color Comic Group, with a circulation of 41,259. Combined, Metro and Puck have a total circulation of 52,465,019. Metro's cost per thousand for a four-color page is $7.46; Puck's is $13.45.

The demographic characteristics of comics readers are quite a surprise to most advertisers, who seem to have ill-conceived ideas about this type of reader. The median age of the adult comics reader is 40.3, slightly younger than the U.S. median age of 40.1.

**Table 7-2. Summary of Circulation and Rates for
Sunday Newspaper Supplements.**

Publication	Circulation	Four Color		Black-and-White	
		Page	CPM	Page	CPM
Sunday Mag/Net	22,723,339	$243,174	$10.70	$199,238	$8.77
Parade	22,163,416	205,975	9.28	167,835	7.57
Family Weekly	12,444,275	92,910	7.47	105,870	8.51
Totals	57,331,030	$542,059	$ 9.45	$472,943	$8.25

Source: Branham Newspapers, Inc. 1982

Exhibit 7-1. First Page of a Six-Page Newspaper Insert for Columbia House

Exhibit 7-2. Comic-Page Advertising

Calls attention to an envelope inserted loose in the newspaper.

One of the major misconceptions about comics readership is that the higher one's education, the less likely one is to read the comic pages. Statistics from *Simmons Total Audience Study,* as illustrated in Table 7-3, dispute this.

Finally, there is the misconception that the higher one's income, the less likely one is to read comics. Again, the figures refute this.

Among direct response advertisers, the largest users of comic-page advertising in the past have been photo finishers. Huge photo finishing businesses have been started from scratch using comics as a prime advertising medium. The availability of the ad-and-envelope technique in conjunction with comic-page advertising serves a genuine need of photo finishers because they are able to provide an envelope in which

Table 7-3. Demographic Characteristics of Readers of Comics Compared with U.S. Population.

Characteristic	Comics Readers	U.S. Population
Age		
18-24	18.1%	17.9%
25-34	23.4	23.1
35-44	16.3	16.1
45-64	28.4	27.6
65 and above	13.8	15.3
	100.0%	100.0%
Education		
Graduated from college	17.2%	15.5%
Attended college	19.8	16.8
Graduated from high school	39.0	38.4
Attended high school	13.5	14.8
Did not attend high school	10.5	14.5
	100.0%	100.0%
Income		
$25,000 and above	41.5%	37.2%
$15,000-24,999	26.5	12.5
$10,000-14,999	17.5	12.6
$8,000-9,999	5.3	19.6
$5,000-7,999	4.5	11.9
$4,999 and under	4.7	6.2
	100.0%	100.0%
Median income	$21,785	$19,856

the prospect can return completed film rolls. The standard charge for a free-standing envelope or for affixing a card or envelope to the ad averages about $15 per thousand, plus the cost of printing the response vehicle. With ad-and-envelope, the direct response advertiser provides the same impetus to response with a reply card or reply envelope.

Following the photo finishers with comic-page advertising have been insurance companies and land developers. Opportunities obviously are there for a host of other direct response advertisers seeking mass circulation at low cost. Comic-page advertising traditionally limits advertising to one advertiser per page. Thus full-page advertising is not essential to gain a dominant position. Comics, not unlike syndicated supplements, should be tested before one goes full run. You can test individual papers among the Metro Group, the Puck Group, and the independent groups.

ROP Advertising

We have been exploring formats carried by newspapers—preprints, syndicated supplements, and comics. Not to be overlooked, of course, is run-of-paper (ROP) advertising. Generally, direct response advertisers have failed to get the results with ROP advertising that they have obtained from newspaper preprints and syndicated newspaper supplements. One obvious reason is that four-color advertising is not generally available for ROP. Another is that ROP ads don't drop out for individual attention. But many successes can be cited for small-space ROP advertising, small-space ads that have run frequently year after year in hundreds of newspapers. When small-space ads are run over a long period of time with high frequency, the number of reader impressions multiplies rapidly in proportion to the cost.

Effect of Local News On Results

A major difference between newspaper advertising and all other print media is that the newspaper reader is more likely to be influenced by local news events. All newspaper advertising appears within the atmosphere of the local news for a given day. A major scandal in local politics or a catastrophe in a local area such as a tornado can have a devastating effect on the advertising appearing in a given issue. Magazines, on the other hand, do not tie in closely with local events. Magazines are normally put aside to read during hours not taken up by involvement in local events. Because local events have a strong effect on response, positively or negatively, markets with similar demographics don't always respond in the same manner. All newspaper advertising tends to be *local,* even though a schedule may be national.

Developing a Newspaper Test Program

When a direct response advertiser first considers testing newspapers as a medium, he has a myriad of decisions to make. Should he go ROP, the newspaper preprint route, local Sunday supplements, syndicated supplements, TV program supplements, comics? What papers should he test? Putting ad size and position aside for the moment, we have two initial considerations: the importance of advertising in a mail order climate and the demographics of markets selected as they relate to the product or service you are offering.

If you had one simple product, say a stamp dispenser, for instance, and a tiny budget, you might place one small ad in one publication. You could run the ad in the mail order section of the *New York Times Sunday Magazine.* Generally if you don't make it there, you won't make it anywhere. Running such an ad would give a "feel." If it works, it would be logical to test similar mail order sections in major cities such as Chicago, Detroit, and Los Angeles.

Simple items, which are suited to small-space advertising in mail order sections, greatly simplify the testing procedure. But, more often than not, multicity testing in larger space is required.

Prime direct response test markets in the United States include Atlanta, Buffalo, Cleveland, Dallas-Fort Worth, Denver, Des Moines, Indianapolis, Omaha, and Peoria. In the selection of test markets, you should analyze the newspaper to make certain it has advertising reach and coverage and offers demographics that are suitable to your product. If there are two newspapers in a market, it is worthwhile to evaluate both of them. Let us say that because of budget limitations advertising can be placed in only a limited number of markets. Such criteria as circulation, household penetration, women readers, and advertising linage relating to the product to be advertised should be measured.

A number of sources will provide the data necessary for evaluation. You would begin with SRDS's *Newspaper Rates and Data* for general cost and circulation information. *SRDS Circulation Analysis* would provide information about metro household penetration. *Simmons Total Audience Study* could then be used to isolate men or women readers of a particular age group. Other criteria to be measured include retail linage in various classifications and spendable income by metro area.

Demographics are a major consideration market by market whether you are going ROP, preprints, local supplements, syndicated supplements, or TV program supplements. Once an advertiser develops a test program that closely reflects the demographics for his product or service, expansion to like markets makes possible the rapid acceleration of a full-blown program. But selecting newspapers is tedious, because there are hundreds from which to choose as compared with a relative handful

Exhibit 7-3. Mail-Order Shopping Guide from the Chicago Tribune *Sunday Magazine*

of magazines whose demographics can be more closely related to the proposition. As an example, a test newspaper schedule could be placed in the following markets: Atlanta, preprint; Buffalo (*Courier Express*), *Parade* remnant; Cleveland, Metro comics; Dallas-Fort Worth, ROP; Denver, preprint; Des Moines, ROP; Indianapolis, preprint; Omaha, Metro comics; and Peoria, *Parade* remnant. If there is more than one newspaper in a test market, the paper with the most promising demographics should be selected.

A test schedule like this would be ambitious in terms of total dollars, but it would have the advantage of simultaneously testing markets and formats. Once a reading has been obtained from the markets and formats, the advertiser can rapidly expand to other markets and will have the advantage of using the most productive formats.

Advertising Seasons

As in direct mail and magazine direct response advertising, there are two major newspaper direct response advertising seasons. The fall mail order season begins roughly with August and runs through November. (A notable exception is a July insertion which is often useful especially when using a pretested piece.) The winter season begins with January and runs through March.

Exceptions to the two major direct response seasons occur in the sale of seasonal merchandise. Christmas items are usually promoted from September through the first week of December. A nursery, on the other hand, will start promoting in late December and early January, then again in the early fall. Many nurseries follow the practice of promoting by geographical regions, starting earlier in the south and working up to later promotion in the north.

Timing of Newspaper Insertions

Beyond the seasonal factor of direct response advertising in newspapers, timing is important as it relates to days of the week. According to the *E&P Yearbook, Bureau of Advertising Circulation Analysis,* the number of copies of a newspaper sold per day is remarkably constant month after month—despite such events as summer vacations and Christmas holidays. And people buy the newspaper to read not only the editorial matter but also the ads. According to an *Audits & Surveys Study,* the percentage of people opening an average ad page any weekday, Monday through Friday, varies less than 3 percent, with Tuesday ranking the highest at 88 percent.

There is no question that the local newspaper is an integral part of practically everyone's daily life. While magazines may be set aside for reading at a convenient time, newspapers are read the day they are delivered or purchased or are not read at all. Monday through Thursday are favorite choices of many direct response advertisers for their ROP advertising. Many direct response advertisers judiciously avoid the weekday issue containing grocery advertising.

As we have seen, more and more newspapers are accepting preprints for weekday insertions. This can be a major advantage considering the larger number of preprints appearing in most big Sunday newspapers.

Newspaper Response Patterns

Newspapers have the shortest time lapse from closing date to appearance date of all print media. In most cases, ads can appear in the newspaper within 72 hours after placement. Depending on the format used, up to 90 percent or more of responses will be reached for a typical direct response newspaper ad within these time frames: ROP, after the second week; preprints, after the third week; syndicated newspaper supplements, after the third week; and comics, after the second week.

Naturally, response patterns vary according to the proposition. Thus, it is important for each advertiser to develop his own response pattern. But the nature of newspaper advertising permits a quick turnaround. *Dow Theory Forecasts*, for instance, has run ads in hundreds of newspapers. Dow is able to project results, giving you the option of deciding whether to repeat an ad, within a week after the first orders are received.

Determining Proper Ad Size

In direct response newspaper advertising, as in retail or national newspaper ads, few people dispute the claim that the larger advertisement generally will get more attention than a smaller one. But whether the full-page ad gets twice the attention of the half-page ad or four times the attention of the quarter-page ad is debatable. It is cost per response that counts. Just as in magazine advertising, less space is usually indicated for inquiry advertising and more space is dictated for a direct order ad.

According to a study conducted by the Bureau of Advertising in 1971 relating to mail-back newspaper coupons, the size of the space seems to be a factor in reader response only to the extent that it is a factor in initial reader attention. In this study, 85 percent of newspaper inserts ran ads of 1,000 lines or more. Only half used fewer than 1,000 lines, with a minimum of 500 lines per ad.

A low-budget advertiser often must choose between a single full-page ad and several small ads over an extended time. The proper guide to follow in determining the initial size of ads is to base the size on the space required to tell the *complete story*.

Trying to sell membership in a record and tape club in a small space would be ludicrous. Experience shows that one must offer a wide selection of records in the ad to get memberships. The same is true for a book club. On the other hand, if you are selling a single item at a low price—say, a cigarette lighter for $4.95—the complete story can be told in a small space. Where small-space advertising can tell the whole story, consistency and repetition often prove to be keys to success.

Aside from the obvious requirement of using a full page or more for a proposition, constant testing of ad sizes will establish the proper size to produce the most efficient cost per inquiry or per order.

The Position Factor

Newspapers and magazines have many similarities in respect to the importance of position in direct response advertising. Research has demonstrated high readership of newspaper ads, whatever the position. However, direct response advertisers still prefer right-hand pages. Generally, such advertisers find that ads are more effective if they appear in the front of the newspaper than in the back. And placement of coupon ads in the gutter of any newspaper page is almost always avoided.

All newspapers are printed in sections. Special consideration should be given to the reading habits of men and women as they relate to specific sections of a newspaper. Three major sections of any given newspaper are sports, women's pages, and general news. Table 7-4 shows results of a study by *Million Market Newspapers* of 32,000 ads. What this study obviously shows is that any appeals to sports-minded men will get high readership on the sports pages. If you have a product that appeals to women, you will get high readership in the women's section. A product that appeals to both men and women calls for running the ad in the general news section.

Table 7-4. Newspaper Advertisements Featuring Products of Interest to Men or Women by Section Placement.

Section Placement	Median Performance	
	Men	Women
Sports............................	114	49
Women's......................	63	101
General news................	100	101

Source: "Million Market Newspapers," Starch studies of 32,000 ads (1961-63).

Color vs. Black and White

The possibilities of using color in newspaper advertising may be regarded as similar to those for magazine advertising with one major exception. If you plan to use one or more colors other than black in an ROP ad, you simply can't get the quality that you can in a color magazine ad. This does not mean the ROP color should not be tested. A majority of newspapers that offer color will allow A/B splits of color vs. black and white.

According to a December 1981 Bureau of Advertising Study (1981 cost figures), using the top 100 markets as a group, two-color ROP costs 21 percent more than the same full page in black and white. Four-color ROP costs 25 percent more than the same full page in black and white. In both cases, these comparisons are based on cost per thousand copies of the newspaper.

Studies have been made via split-runs and the recognition method to test the attention-getting power of both two-color and full-color ROP. Such studies have shown increases of 58 percent for two color and 78 percent for full color above the level of results for black-and-white versions of the same ads. Comparable cost differences are 21 percent and 25 percent.

When Starch "noting score" norms are used to estimate the same attention-getting differential, a different conclusion is reached. The differences are about 10 percent and about 30 percent (when size and product category are held constant). Using norms means comparing a black-and-white ad for one product in another city at another time. These variables inevitably blur the significance of comparisons.

For the direct response advertiser, these studies are interesting. However, you should remember that genuine controlled testing is the only way to get true figures.

Self-quiz

1. Name the two obvious advantages of preprints.

a. _____

b. _____

2. Which is the most popular format for a preprint?

☐ Card   ☐ Multipage

3. Name the three major syndicated newspaper supplements.

a. _____

b. _____

c. _____

4. Indicate major market penetration for each of the supplements.

Sunday Metro	Top 43 metros	_____
	C & D counties	_____
	Below top 150 metros	_____
Parade	Top 43 metros	_____
	C & D counties	_____
	Below top 150 metros	_____
Family Weekly	Top 43 metros	_____
	C & D counties	_____
	Below top 150 metros	_____

5. Define a Dutch Door.

_____

_____

_____

_____

6. What is remnant space?

_____

_____

_____

_____

7. What are the names of the two major comic groups?

a. _____

b. _____

8. The higher one's education, the less likely one will read the comic pages.   ☐ True   ☐ False

9. The higher one's income, the less likely one will read the comic pages.   ☐ True   ☐ False

10. What is the advantage of the ad-and-card and ad-and-envelope for comic page advertisers?

_____

_____

_____

11. How many advertisers will comics groups allow per page?

_____

12. What major advantage to direct response advertisers is offered by preprints and supplements over ROP advertising?

_____

_____

_____

13. What is the major difference between newspaper advertising and all other print advertising as related to potential results?

_____

_____

_____

14. What are the two initial considerations in the development of a newspaper test program?

a. _____

b. _____

15. If you have a single item that is suitable for advertising in a small space and a limited budget for testing, which publication would you test first?

_____

16. Name nine prime test markets for newspaper direct response advertising:

a. _____   f. _____

b. _____   g. _____

c. _____   h. _____

d. _____   i. _____

e. _____

17. What are the two main seasons for newspaper direct response advertising?

a. _____

b. _____

18. Give the preferred weekdays for ROP advertising:

_____

_____

19. Depending on the format used, up to 90 percent or more of responses will be reached for a typical direct response newspaper ad within these time frames:

ROP .... after _____ week(s)

Preprints .... after _____ week(s)

Supplements .... after _____ week(s)

Comics .... after _____ week(s)

20. The size of newspaper space seems to be a factor in reader response only to the extent it is a factor in:

_____

_____

21. When running ROP, direct response advertisers should specify:

☐ Left-hand page   ☐ Right-hand page

22. What is the major disadvantage of running color ROP?

_____

_____

_____

_____

Pilot project

You are the advertising manager of a mail order operation selling collectibles. You have been successful in magazines offering a series of historic plates. You have never used newspapers, but now you have a $75,000 budget to test the medium.

Outline a newspaper test plan.

1. Select your test cities.
2. Will your tests run in the Sunday edition or the weekday edition, or both?
3. What formats will you test—preprints, supplements, comics, local TV books, ROP?
4. What size preprints or ads will you test?
5. At what time of the year will you run your tests?

Note: Remember that if you use preprints, your total space budget should cover printing costs.

Chapter Eight

Electronic Media

There is a new wave sweeping through direct marketing. It is an electronic wave. Revolution or evolution, its impact on direct marketing is significant. It has even given birth to a new term: *directronic marketing.*
Electronic media may be divided into three broad categories.

- One-way media, including broadcast television, radio, and one-way cable systems
- Two-way media, including two-way cable television systems, interactive Videotex (or Viewdata), and computer information systems
- Stand-alone media including video disc, video cassettes, and self-contained computers

It is possible to identify certain characteristics that differentiate electronic direct response media from the more traditional print and mail media. They have one or more of the following qualities:

- Moving visuals
- Sound effects, music, or the spoken word
- A limited time length for the message
- Information on demand
- Instant interactive capability

Uses of Electronic Media

Electronic media can be used by direct marketers for any of the classic direct response purposes: direct sale, lead generation, support of other media, and key outlet marketing.

Lead generation usually is employed for items or services that either have a high selling price or must be tailored to an individual customer's unique needs. In either case, a followup with more extensive information via mail or a personal sales call are required to close the sale.

Exhibit 8-1. Storyboard for Columbia Record Club

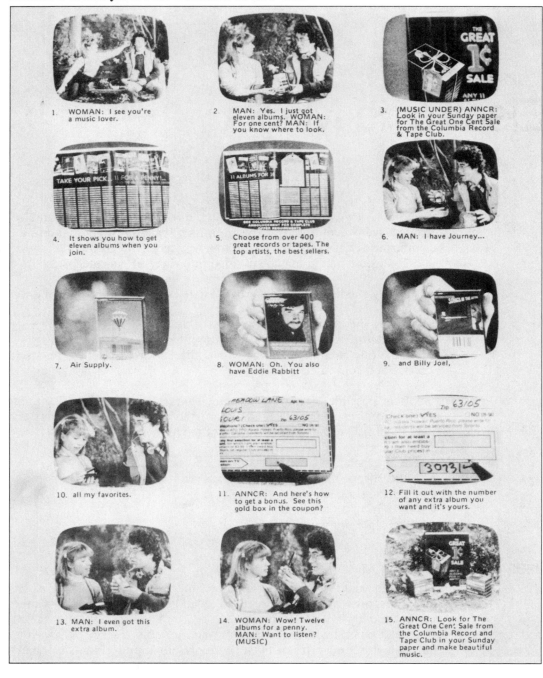

Support TV is directed at the mass audience. Viewers are asked to look for an ad or insert in a certain publication or for a mail package addressed to them. The intent is to generate awareness of, and interest in, the more detailed communication in the other medium.

A further wrinkle on support media was invented by the Wunderman, Ricotta and Kline agency when they developed a method of tracking the effect of support television on a print effort for the Columbia Record Club. Their invention was labeled the "gold box." Viewers were told about a record offer as it was appearing in a corresponding magazine insert. They were then told—in a manner suggesting they were getting "inside" information—to look for the "gold box" in the insert. By filling the box with the number of an extra album in addition to the set included in the printed offer, they would also receive that album as a free bonus. Not only was it possible to see the effect of the television commercial on the insert response, it also was clear that the tracking device actually increased overall response to the offer, often by 50 percent or more.

A growing application of electronic media to the direct marketing process is commonly called key outlet marketing. Under this application an item is offered only through key retail stores or chains. In a variation, called a dealer locator program, the customer is asked to call a toll-free telephone number to determine the name and address of the nearest dealer. The telephone message, which may be prerecorded, can be used to give more selling information, plus directing the customer to the most convenient dealer.

Broadcast TV

Broadcast TV is that friendly and familiar medium we all know from its regular intrusion into our homes. In fact, intrusiveness is one of its major characteristics. It is highly visible to a mass audience: 81.5 million American homes receive television and the average household watches it for 6.5 hours per day.

Especially at the network level, TV can be very costly. On highly rated shows, often not the best places for direct response advertising to appear, the cost of a single national 30-second announcement can run as high as $400,000. Longer time periods are proportionately more expensive while lower rated day-parts are less expensive.

Ratings

It is important to keep in mind that the cost of a commercial time period is based on its "rating." This is a measure of its share of the total TV households viewing the show. The more highly rated the show, the higher the cost. One rating point equals one percent of the total households in the market. A show with a 20 rating is being watched by 20 percent of television households.

When the total ratings of all the time periods in a schedule are combined, the result is called gross rating points (or GRPs). Simply stated, if a television schedule has 100 GRPs per week, it is reaching the equivalent of 100 percent of TV households in the market in that week. Obviously, this is a statistical reach with varying degrees of duplication. It does not guarantee 100 percent of the individual homes will be reached.

Commercial Lengths

While 30 seconds is the most common time length for general or image advertising, direct marketers seldom find that adequate to tell their selling story in a persuasive way. Ninety to 120 seconds is usually required for a direct sale commercial, while 60 to 90 seconds are usually required for lead generation commercials. On the other hand, support commercials with sufficient GRPs prove effective with a combination of 10-second and 30-second commercials. But key outlet marketing usually requires longer lengths.

Of course, with the popularity of 30-second announcements and the premium broadcasters can get for them, it is not always possible to clear longer length commercials, particularly during periods of high demand.

Reach and Frequency

Television advertisers use two terms in measuring the effectiveness of their television schedules. *Reach* refers to the number of *different* homes exposed to the message within a given time segment. *Frequency* is a measure of how many times the average viewer will see the message over a given number of weeks. Frequency also can be measured against viewer quintiles (eg. heaviest viewers, lightest viewers, etc.)

The combination of reach and frequency will tell you what percentage of the audience you are reaching and how often on average they will see your message. Television schedules often are purchased against reach and frequency goals and actual performance measured in postanalysis.

For most direct marketers, reach and frequency are not as important as actual response rates, which represent a true return on the media dollar. But a knowledge of what reach and frequency are is critical when television is used in a supporting role.

Buying Time

Buying time for very specific time periods is the most expensive way to purchase it. You pay a higher price to guarantee your message will run at a precise time within a predetermined program environment. Television time also can be bought less expensively. Stations will sell ROS (run-of-station) time, time available during periods the station has been unable to sell at regular rates. This is particularly true with independent (non-network) stations, which often have sizable inventories of unsold time. If the station, however, subsequently sells the time to a specific buyer, your commercial will be pre-empted.

Pre-emptible time can be an excellent buy for direct response advertisers because of the combination of lower cost and quite respectable response rates. When buying pre-emptible time, it also is possible to specify the day-parts (daytime, early fringe, late fringe, etc.) for slightly more than straight ROS rates. This can be important for the direct marketer with a specific target audience for his product. Such spots still may be pre-empted at any time, however.

Television time also may be purchased on the basis of payment per inquiry (or PI) and bonus-to-pay-out. PI allows the station to run as many commercials as it wishes, whenever it wishes. There is no charge for the time, but the station receives a predetermined sum for every inquiry or sale the advertisement generates for the advertiser. The advertiser is not committed to pay for a spot until it delivers an inquiry or sale and then only in relation to responses.

But there are disadvantages. It is almost impossible to plan methodically for fulfillment. Such programs cannot be coordinated reliably with other efforts or promotion timetables. And, since the station will run the commercials that it feels will perform best for it, your spot may never run and you may not know it until it has jeopardized your entire selling program.

Bonus-to-pay-out involves a special arrangement with the station to deliver a certain number of responses. A schedule is negotiated with the station to guarantee a certain minimum schedule. If, at the end of the schedule, the response goal has not been reached, the station must continue to run the commercial until it is reached. This method provides a better planning base for the direct marketer.

With television time in high demand, such opportunities are not as available as they once were. But, if they can be located, they can be a superb vehicle for direct marketers.

TV Schedules

What kind of broadcast television schedule is most productive and/or efficient for the direct marketer? It depends on the objective. For direct sale or lead generation commercials, which require the viewer to get up and take some action within minutes, certain criteria apply. For example, the television viewing day is divided into various *day-parts*. There is weekday daytime, early evening or fringe, prime time, late night or fringe, and weekend. Each day-part tends to reach one group or combination of viewers better than the others.

It is important to know your primary target group so you can select the most appropriate day-part. Prime time is so called because it reaches the largest audience with the most exciting shows. It is also the most expensive. The more attentive viewers are to the show, the less likely they are to respond immediately. Therefore, times of lower viewer involvement and attentiveness are better and less expensive for the advertiser who expects a direct response. Reruns, talk shows, old movies, and the like often are the best vehicles for direct response advertisers. These tend to run predominantly in daytime, fringe, and late night time slots. (See Table 8-1.)

Similarly, because independent stations tend to run a higher percentage of syndicated reruns and movies, their viewers tend to have a lower level of attentiveness to the programming. But even on independent stations, avoid news shows and other high-interest programming. Check the ratings. They are a good guide.

Seasonality is another factor in direct response TV. The first quarter and third quarters respectively are the best seasons for television response, just as they are for print and mail. Moreover, television time pricing is related to viewing levels, which are seasonal and vary month to month as well as by day-part. (See Table 8-2.)

Table 8-1. Viewer Attention Levels by Program Type
Percent at Full Attention

	Adults	Men Total Audience	Women Total Audience
Weekday daytime			
"Today Show"	43	50	38
Serials	64	61	64
Quiz/Game shows	66	76	61
Situation comedies	57	60	56
Early evening			
Situation comedies	64	64	63
Action/adventure	69	69	69
Talk shows	68	76	67
News	68	77	65
Prime time			
Movies	77	76	77
Variety	70	74	68
Drama	72	74	70
Situation comedies	66	67	64
Sports	62	65	52
Late night			
News	70	71	67
Talk shows	66	66	67
Movies	76	75	77

Source: Simmons 1981.

**Market
Performance**

Some geographic locations are good for certain products or offers. Others are simply not receptive. It pays to know ahead of time what a market's propensity is. Previous experience with mail or print can be a reasonably reliable guide.

In any event, it is not necessary to jump in up to your neck. Start with a handful of markets, two to five, say, and test the waters. Try a one- or two-week schedule. As few as 10 commercials per week can give you a reading. Monitor your telephone response daily. You'll know within two or three days if it's bust or boom. After a week or so you'll have an even more precise fix on how well your commercial is doing. If it holds up, stay with it—until it starts to taper off. Then stop. Don't try to milk a stone.

Meanwhile, move on to other markets in the same methodical and measured way. You always can return to your most successful markets later in the marketing year after your commercial has had a rest. Or come back with a new offer.

Radio

Radio, too, is a mass medium. But it is possible to buy radio on a more selective basis than broadcast television. There are many more radio stations than television stations, and each has its own personality, which

**Table 8-2. Index of Seasonality of Viewing, By Daypart
(Annual Average = 100).**

	Day	Early Evening	Prime	Late Evening	Sat. & Sun. Morning
Households					
January-March	108	**112**	**113**	105	**111**
April-June	92	91	98	99	93
July-September	98	82	83	98	81
October-December ...	102	**115**	107	97	**115**
Men					
January-March	**113**	**115**	**113**	109	104
April-June	89	87	96	101	85
July-September	90	77	80	91	74
October-December ...	107	**120**	**111**	98	**132**
Women					
January-March	106	107	**113**	105	103
April-June	96	93	96	99	86
July-September	91	82	80	98	86
October-December ...	105	**118**	**111**	98	**122**

Source: A. C. Nielsen Audience Demographic Report, 1974.

Note: Levels in bold-face type are 10 percent or more above the average viewing index.

is reflected in its programming. Some stations feature rock and roll music, some classical music, some are "talk" or "all news" stations. Each selects its audience (or vice versa) by its programming format. And, of course, radio costs less to use—both in media charges and production.

With radio as a direct response or support medium, audience selection is important. Radio measurement, unlike television, is not based on households, but on individual listeners. This is a testimony to the individual way that radio is listened to and to the fact that the average home has 5.5 radios in it, often one or more per person or room.

While radio ratings can tell you the demographics of a station's audience, station formats give you some idea of the psychographics of that audience. So if you know who your target customers are, you can determine what station or stations to use to reach them. (See Table 8-3.)

Day-parts are as important in radio as they are in television. Certain times of day have larger audiences. And listenership varies by age throughout the day. With most radio formats, the audience peaks at "drive times." These are in the morning (6 to 10 A.M.) and evening (3 to 7 P.M.). These are the most expensive times to buy on radio, but they usually are not the best times for direct response advertisers. The person behind a wheel cannot run to the phone, or even get a pencil to write a number down.

Radio is inherently a low-reach, high-frequency medium. People tend to listen regularly to the same station, with little switching, and many different stations divide up the total radio audience. Maximum reach potential is about 60 percent and only when several stations are bought. Reach builds slowly while frequency increases quickly: 50 GRPs in one week of daytime television will achieve 30 percent reach at a frequency of 1.7. Those same 50 GRPs in radio will take four weeks to reach 31 percent, but the frequency level will be 6.5.

When buying radio for direct marketing purposes, be sure to consider your communications objective and the reach and frequency of various station ratings and formats by day-part. If radio is being used for direct response, its frequency and targetability provide plenty of opportunity to achieve good response rates at low cost. If it is being used for support, several stations will have to be purchased across all day-parts to obtain the desired reach. Radio also can be used to support TV, adding frequency to television's reach.

Time lengths for messages on radio are fairly standardized at 60 seconds. This is the most economical unit. Thirty-second spots cost proportionately more (75 percent of the 60-second rate).

One advantage of radio for the direct marketer is its combination of low cost and quick turnaround time, making it easy and economical to experiment. You can be extremely topical or exploit fast-breaking events. A thoroughly respectable radio commercial can be on the air within 24 hours of a decision to use it.

Cable TV

Cable TV *looks* like broadcast TV, but it is different in many ways. First, the cable TV audience is highly defined. The cable operator knows who is tied into his system—he sends them a bill every month. This demographic information, and some psychographic information, is available to the advertiser.

Table 8-3. Radio Listening By Station Format

	Age Groups					
	18-24	25-34	35-44	45-54	55-64	65+
MEN						
Adult Contemporary......................	225	128	53	36	82	26
All News.............................	32	76	111	166	119	123
Beautiful Music...........................	44	39	165	123	175	100
Black	207	141	120	51	2	9
Classical/Semi-Classical	40	53	105	256	133	40
Country................................	65	102	174	93	116	47
Golden Oldies...........................	327	73	87	12	17	29
Middle of the Road......................	63	121	142	124	66	70
Progressive.............................	190	227	26	11	47	8
Soft Contemporary	235	157	50	43	68	11
Standard................................	69	57	145	141	105	109
Talk	41	51	83	172	178	124
Top 40	205	149	69	44	33	40
WOMEN						
Adult Contemporary......................	199	151	82	65	22	42
All News.............................	41	52	48	136	167	184
Beautiful Music...........................	18	100	130	169	126	76
Black	199	139	118	85	19	7
Classical/Semi-Classical	60	61	262	171	36	34
Country................................	63	90	181	111	107	63
Golden Oldies...........................	195	221	61	30	25	2
Middle of the Road......................	97	137	95	126	87	46
Progressive.............................	260	134	109	19	41	—
Soft Contemporary	235	157	50	43	68	11
Standard................................	30	68	126	157	139	106
Talk	15	24	96	170	137	198
Top 40	223	126	127	64	24	5

Source: RAB, Research Dept., 1980.

With roughly 60 percent of the country's homes passed by cable and about half of those subscribing (as of November, 1982) we already know the cable TV viewer tends to have a higher income, more education, and is younger than the broadcast television audience and appears to have above average mail and telephone ordering habits.

With many more channels available than are available on broadcast TV, there has been some evidence that cable will provide more special interest programming, suggesting cable TV may take on the audience selectivity traits of radio or special interest magazines. Also, because the audiences are smaller, investment in cable TV can be less than for broadcast TV.

Two-way Cable Systems

One variant on the "normal" cable system must be mentioned at this point: two-way cable. This is an intriguing variant because, while not yet broadly available, it promises a unique ability for the viewer to respond directly to the commercial message merely by pushing a button on a keypad connected to the channel. This allows instant ordering or additional information, or even actual goods, charged to a pre-authorized credit account. This will be discussed further under the subject of interactivity.

Buying Cable

Cable can be purchased in many ways. One way is to negotiate rates with independent cable system operators with local origination capability. Another is to buy cable via super-stations. These are broadcast television stations (WTBS-Atlanta, WOR-New York, WGN-Chicago) that make their signal available to cable operators via a satellite-based transponder. The cable operator collects the super-station signal off the satellite and uses it to provide additional programs on an empty channel. The advertiser buys the super-station as a local station, for example in Atlanta, and gets the cable circulation as a bonus. Obviously, there is a premium charge for the extra circulation.

There also are special interest networks (ESPN, SPN, TeleFrance, ARTS, etc.), which may be purchased through a single source. These provide an even more tailored audience design that can be related to the direct marketer's key prospect file.

At present, standard ratings customary for broadcast TV are not available for cable systems. Cable program ratings are being developed, however, and will be available to advertisers in the near future. Meanwhile, P.I. and bonus-to-pay-out schedules are fairly easy to negotiate on cable, due to the larger inventory of unused cable commercial time.

Advantages of
Cable

First, there is the opportunity to match a product, offer, or creative approach to a special audience through association with special-interest programming. The marketer of collectibles, for example, could tie in with a show on that subject. Such a show, with its narrow interest, would never be cost justified on broadcast TV.

With the lower cost and greater availability of commercial cable time, it is possible to create commercials to the longer length necessary to tell a complete story. This makes it possible to include information that adds value to the communication and builds a need for the product. Some cable channels already run entire shows that are made up of 5- to 10-minute "infomercials." These are low-pressure, low-budget discussions of products, their benefits and the quality of their manufacture.

As these new media opportunities expand, direct marketers will learn to use them increasingly well. And, at current prices, the cost of learning is not unreasonable.

Table 8-4. Cable Networks Accepting Advertising

Program Source	Number of Households (1,000)	%US	Format
Black Entertainment TV (BET)	2000	2.4	Black
Cable Health Network	5050	6.1	Health/Sci
Cable News Network (CNN)	16660	20.0	News
Cable News Network II (CNN II)	2100	2.5	News
CBN-Cable	18600	22.3	Various
ESPN	19294	23.2	Sports
Financial News Network (FNN)	5200	6.2	Financial News
Hearst/ABC-Arts	8200	9.8	Cultural
Hearst/ABC-Daytime	7200	8.6	Women
Modern Satellite Net.	6567	7.9	CNSMR INF/WM
Music Television	7800	9.4	Music
National Spanish Net.	N.A.	N.A.	Spanish
Satellite News Channel 1	3890	4.7	News
Satellite News Channel 11	N.A.	N.A.	News
Satellite Program Net. (SPN)	5700	6.8	Various
TeleFrance	7000	8.4	French
USA Network	13500	16.2	Various
Weather Channel	6000	7.2	Weather
WGN (Chicago)	9074	10.9	Various
WOR (New York)	15494	18.6	Various
WTBS (Atlanta)	24157	29.0	Various

Source: Leber Katz Partners, Nov. 1982.

It is possible also to totally integrate programming and commercial material in what might be called "commercialgrams." Video catalogs can informatively and entertainingly describe, demonstrate, and dramatize a selection of interrelated products. Intermittently, the viewer is given the telephone number to call to order. And, in the semi-interactive version of cable now being pioneered by Warner-Amex's QUBE, an order can be placed right through the cable system without stirring from the chair.

Computer Networks

Another electronic medium available to the direct marketer now, but not broadly used, is the computer network. There are today over six million personal computers in place in the U.S., most being purchased by business people who rationalize the cost as an extension of their business activities. Many are connected via telephone lines to central data bases such as the Source, and Dow Jones News Retrieval Service. In fact, the venerable *New York Times* now has its entire library available to computer owners and operators.

Most applications at the present time are essentially business-to-business, but this does not exclude opportunities for consumer products. One of the largest and most successful "programs" available to the computer networker is CompuServe's comparative shopping service. Various brands of merchandise offered for sale by various merchants can be called up from the data base. The user can make an item-by-item, feature-by-feature comparison, including price—all done with the calculating aid of the computer. The user can actually order the item he wants, via the return leg of his telephone line, for later delivery to his home or office. In this sense, we are dealing with an electronic sales directory or catalog. It differs from a printed catalog in that, for the most part, computer networks are limited to text-only displays.

Buying Time

Buying time or space (no one is quite sure which it is) on a computer network is more difficult than imagining ways to use it. There are no "ratings" since the selling messages are viewed on demand. There are only subscriber universes. For example, the Source has 24,854 qualified subscribers who pay to access the service. Dow Jones News Retrieval has 54,000. And CompuServe has 34,100.

Purchasing time/space on a computer network must be done through negotiation with individual network operators. Expect to pay a certain basic fee for storage of your data in the computer memory, plus a charge per access by users and extra charges for each time data must be entered or updated.

Obviously, the graphics limitations of the system probably will not be satisfactory for items whose benefits must be visualized to be understood or for items that require a strong emotional content in the selling message. But for goods that are familiar to the customer—such as brand name or business supplies—it should be a very effective and efficient way to sell direct.

Teletext and Videotex

Next, let's look at the latest additions to the electronic media menu: teletext and videotex (or viewdata). These two media appear to be similar. Both offer text and graphic presentations *on demand* from the viewer. But the similarity stops there.

Teletext is a system of transmitting frames of information via a regular TV broadcast signal. It is a one-way transmission via the vertical blanking interval—the interval when the television signal leaves the bottom of your screen and jumps back to the top to start scanning again. Since the amount of time available for transmission is so short, a very limited amount of information can be transmitted without requiring an unreasonably long wait between frames. Most experts feel 100 different frames is about the maximum.

The viewer plucks these frames off the air and makes them appear on the screen by pressing the appropriate code buttons on his teletext-modified television set. They appear on the screen either on a separate channel reserved for teletext frames or they may be super-imposed over the screen on which some action is appearing. For example, the viewer could select up-to-the-minute basketball scores while watching his favorite reruns of M*A*S*H. While there are few commercial teletext systems now operating in the U.S., there are numerous tests underway. One system that will be operating in selected markets is KeyFax provided by Centel and Field Enterprises.

Teletext is so new as to have no established procedures or techniques for purchasing it. Since there is no current way of identifying who or how many viewers are accessing what frames, it is most likely there will be opportunities to buy teletext time/space on a per inquiry basis. When future addressable decoders are developed for television sets, per access may become a common way to buy teletext time/space, with charges for storage and for updating each frame.

While it is difficult to project exactly what the most productive use of teletext will be, there is an opportunity for direct marketers to experiment at generally low cost. Sponsored information will be one way to gain the viewer's attention. Financial service firms, for example, may offer their products, in conjunction with a presentation of the latest financial news.

The limitations of teletext are in the volume of data (or number of frames) available and the requirement that ordering be accomplished via the traditional modes of mail or telephone.

Videotex, as it is called in the U.S.—or viewdata, as the Europeans call it—shares neither of these limitations. It ties an individual television set to a remote host computer via telephone line or coaxial cable. For practical purposes, it is unlimited in its capacity to store and deliver information. And it is completely interactive through the same telephone line or cable over which the data is received. The system is activated by a keyboard (just like a typewriter) or keypad (similar to a television tuner). The message, which the user requests through the activator, appears on the television screen in text and graphic form.

Interactivity gives videotex its transaction ability. It allows the user not only to get the product information he or she wants but also to actually order and pay for the merchandise right at the television set. While videotex images, unlike regular TV, are text and graphics only, they occasionally reach quite extraordinary dimensions, depending on the technology used to transmit the message. In fact, some videotex systems are experimenting with full photographic images.

Buying Videotex

Locating and buying videotex is mostly a matter of locating the various firms who are experimenting with the technology. These primarily are electronic, banking and communication companies. (See Table 8-5.) Eventually, the cost of videotex should be within reach of most direct marketers. To date, however, no standards have been established. The first "commercial" videotex service in the U.S. began in the fall of 1983. Prior to that, the only commercial experience has been in the U.K. and Germany, where a proven market for videotex has been established.

Of course, there will be no "ratings," only the total subscriber universe that can access an advertiser's information and proposition. Undoubtedly there will be charges to advertisers to store each frame of information, to enter or update a frame, and possibly a royalty payable to the system operator for each purchase made on the system. The latter will be a variant on the per inquiry pricing system.

It will be important to learn how to use various "navigation" systems to lead the prospect easily and quickly to your company and your product. It will be possible to cross-reference other products that a satisfied customer may want to purchase from the same reputable supplier. It will be possible to react to changes in market condition, stock status, size and color availability, and price with instantaneous changes in the data base. Lastly, it will be feasible to qualify prospects, to gain extensive knowledge about other products they have owned and recently purchased, their preferences across a wide range of products, and how they found their way to your "electronic store." The opportunities will be plentiful. There is no reason anything that can be sold by mail, newspaper, or telephone cannot also be sold via videotex.

Video Cassettes and Video Discs

Finally, some stand-alone media merit investigation, primarily video cassettes and video discs.

Video cassettes are pretaped television presentations packaged in a cassette that can be played at home by viewers at their convenience. They are similar to audio cassettes except that they deliver full-motion visuals, sound, and music—all in color. Similarly, video discs resemble phonograph records in appearance and function. Material is prerecorded for playback at the user's convenience.

There are differences besides physical appearance. Within the current technology the video disc has a much greater and more easily accessible storage capacity. The laser-based video disc can hold 54,000 separate frames of information on each side. Fractions of seconds are

Table 8-5. U.S. Videotex, Teletext, and Electronic Publishing Tests and Operations

CBS-AT&T Videotex (New Jersey)	100	(T)
CentelVision (Virginia)	100	(T)
Pronto (Chemical Bank, NY)	300	(C)
HomeBase (Citibank, NY)	100	(T)
Shawmut Bank of Boston	100	(T)
Chase Home Banking (Chase Manhattan Bank, NY)	100	(T)
MacroTel, Inc. (Empire Bank, Buffalo)	12	(T)
BankShare (Huntington Bank, Columbus)		
Day and Night Video Banking (First Interstate Bank, LA)	200	(T)
FirstHand (First Bank Systems, Minneapolis)	285	(T)
Bank-at-Home (Financial Interstate, Knoxville)	600	(C)
INDAX (Cox Cable)		
San Diego	500	(T)
Omaha	100	
Times Mirror Videotex (Palos Verdes & Mission Viejo, CA)	350	
StarText (Ft. Worth)	171	
Electronic Editions (Spokane, WA)	140	
Harris Electronic News (Hutchinson, KS)	58	
AgVision (ELANCO, Indianapolis)	850	
Louisville Courier Journal (Louisville)	45	
A-T Videotext (Tiffin Advertiser Tribune, Tiffin, OH)	30	
Time Video Information Services (San Diego and Orlando)	400	(T)

Source: Arlen Communications Inc., December 1982.

Note: (T) indicates a *test*, generally with no fee for users
     (C) indicates a *commercial* service

all that is required to locate the specific information the user wants. While cassettes also can store massive amounts of information, locating individual references is an inherently slow process. Both systems provide full-color video with sound.

The real future for video disc and video cassette media will be realized in the development of "hybrid" systems. In this scenario, the instant update and interactive capacity of videotex or computer networks is wedded, through digital electronics, to the vast permanent storage and full video presentation capability of video discs and cassettes.

It may behoove those who have a wide variety of products to offer to be first into the system and to underwrite not only the cost of distributing the video discs or cassettes, but also some of the cost of the playback equipment to build a sizable, technologically captive audience.

Creative Development for Electronic Media

The traditional approach to direct marketing copy, usually initiated by the copywriter who prepares a concept rough, will also work for electronic media. But it requires that the copywriter have an extensive working knowledge of the medium to match his or her experience in direct response copy. This is a rare commodity given the short history of these media for direct response purposes.

Moreover, as graphics have become increasingly important in all direct response media, a new approach to creating direct response messages has developed: the team approach. In this approach, the copywriter and art director receive the appropriate input together and work together to devise the best form for the message. Both build on the thoughts of the other to arrive at a combination of words, pictures, sound, music and action that reinforce one another and provide a clear, compelling exposition of the selling message.

Developing Creative Strategies

The starting point for this activity must be with the creative strategy. Since it is the copywriter/art director team who must execute the strategy, it is wise to have them involved in the development of the creative strategy. They bring to the task both an understanding of their prospect and knowledge of the executional limitations they will face.

As with any medium, the creative strategy for electronic media basically involves itself with three elements: the prospective consumer, the competition, and the message. Ask yourself three questions:

1. Who are my target customers?
2. What other products or services are currently meeting, or are capable of meeting, their needs?

3. What can I say to convince them the product or service I am offering is the best way to meet those needs?

Obviously, identifying some consumer need is a critical step in this process.

Identifying a consumer need leads to the establishment of an objective for the advertising. In direct response advertising, our objective almost always is to get the prospect to take some immediate step; e.g. to request further information, to visit a dealer, or to purchase the product or service. But the advertising objective should also include *why* the prospect should take this step—what benefit will accrue to him or her.

Following this, the creative strategy can be articulated. Describe the primary prospects, not just in demographic terms but also in terms of psychographics. What is known about their lifestyles, purchase behavior, attitudes, that can help to target the creative approach for maximum effect?

Next, describe the primary competition. Is it a competing brand in the same product category, or another product category that currently is being used to meet the prospect's need—however unsatisfactorily? Or is it an attitudinal set, other demands on discretionary spending, or some combination of all these?

Now we come to the last part of our strategy—the message. What will be our promise to our target prospect and why should it be believed?

You'll notice this strategy development process does not make provision for the offer, a critical element in direct response advertising. An offer adds value to the direct response transaction, and while it should take its direction from the strategy, it is not an inherent part of it.

After a strategy has been developed the next step is developing a concept.

Concept
Development

This is one of the most difficult processes to describe: a concept is an abstract entity that defies easy definition. At this point the art director and the copywriter put together all the pieces of the strategy and blend them synergistically to arrive at a positioning of the product/service and its benefits that is bigger, more involving, more important, more memorable and more compelling than the sum of the executional parts.

Following the identification of one or more concepts that will drive the advertising forward, and often be coincidental with it, the creative team will come up with various copy, art, or production techniques that wed with the concept and bring it to life. Often these techniques (eg. product demonstration, celebrity endorsement, slice-of-life dramatization, humor, animation, question and answer, etc.) are an integral part of the concept.

When preparing the direct response message for electronic media, it's important to know and abide by certain "keys" to success in all direct response advertising. One of those is to tell as much of the product story as you can within the allotted time and space available. Whereas general advertising can be content to leave the viewer or listener with an impression to be conjured up later, the direct response commercial must give the prospect as much information as necessary to close the sale or force the next step. In other words, "the more you tell, the more you sell."

And, of course, it is important to ask for the order. Let the viewer/ listener know exactly and clearly what he or she should do next and why. Don't be bashful. The prospect has stayed with you because he or she is interested in your message. Let them know how they can have the benefits for themselves.

Creating for Broadcast TV

In wrestling with concepts for television, remember it is a visual medium and an action medium. And you are using it in a time of great video literacy. Your concept must be sharp, crisp. It must be designed to jar a lethargic and jaded audience to rapt attention. So your concepts require the best and most knowledgeable of talent.

When you have arrived at your concept, it's time to write a script and do a storyboard. The script format is two adjacent columns, one for video descriptions and one for copy and audio directions. The two columns track together so that the appropriate words and sounds are shown opposite the pictures they will accompany. Video descriptions should make it possible to understand the general action in any given scene. It is not necessary at this point to spell out every detail.

The storyboard follows from and accompanies the script. It is a series of artist's drawings of the action and location of each scene. There should be enough individual pictures (called frames) to show the flow of the action and important visual information. Most concept storyboards run 8 to 16 frames, depending on the length of the commercial, the complexity of the action, and the need to show specific detail.

Novices make two important errors when doing television storyboards. One is a failure to synchronize the words and the pictures. At no point should the copy be talking about something different than what the picture is showing, nor should the picture be something that is unrelated to the words.

The second mistake is a failure to realize most people who evaluate a storyboard equate frames with the passage of time. Each frame in an eight frame storyboard will often be interpreted as 1/8th of commercial time. If some intricate action takes place over five seconds, it could take four or five frames to illustrate. Meanwhile, a simple scene that may run

10 seconds can often be illustrated with one or two frames. Imagine the confusion the reviewer of the storyboard faces. Make sure your storyboards show elapsed time. Often an elapsed time indicator next to the picture will do the trick.

Once you have developed a television storyboard you feel is a good representation of what you want to accomplish, it is possible to evaluate it in the following fashion.

The first thing to look for is AQRI (Acquire Quick Related Interest). You have five seconds or less to capture and hold your target prospect's attention. Have you used those five seconds well? The attention must be related to the subject of the commercial. An irrelevant attention-getting device will only lose the viewer after the proposition begins to develop. And you may miss the very people you want to interest. Get the viewer's attention. Do it quickly. But do it relevantly.

Next you can score your commercial from 1-5 (1 being poor, 5 being excellent) against these criteria.

- Is it simple, clear, easy to understand?
- Is it credible, believable?
- Is it original in its approach, commanding interest with its freshness?
- Is it relevant to the benefit of the product or service?
- Is it empathetic, giving your audience a good feeling about the product, the company, and the advertising as being appropriate to the way they live their lives?

If it can pass this quiz with a score of 25, you should have a winner. A score of 20 would pass, too. But can't you do better?

Of course, these are only guidelines. They are not rules. Even if they were, the essence of all great advertising, including direct response, is to break the rules to reach people in a way they haven't been reached before. But it is something quite different to violate *principles* that have been developed over years of observation. Do so only at your own peril.

There is a set of rules that relates to the law. Various industry self-regulatory bodies and instruments of the government watch over the airwaves. They require that advertising be truthful and not misleading. Don't say (or picture) anything in your commercial that you can't substantiate or replicate in person. And don't make promises your product or service can't deliver on.

As you design your direct response commercial, there are some important techniques to keep in mind. If at all possible, integrate your offer with the remainder of your commercial. It will make it easier for the viewer to comprehend and respond. And it will give your offer, and your product or service, the opportunity to reinforce each other in value and impression.

Also, if possible, integrate the 800 toll-free number into the commercial. You should plan to have the telephone number on the screen for at least 25 seconds, and more, depending on the length of the commercial. Try to find ways to make it "dance" on the screen. Bring it on visually as it is announced on the sound track. Highlight it with flairs or color or find some other way to make it an integral but highly visible part of the commercial and the offer. The following is a good example of a commercial designed to generate an immediate response.

Video	Audio
1. *Open on MCU of professional demonstrator in kitchen, hacking at wooden block.*	**Demonstrator:** I'm purposely chopping this hardwood block to smithereens to demonstrate an amazing new product: Miracle Mac Knives!
2. *Zoom to ECU of demonstrator still hacking at block. Super card 1 (flashing: warning).*	**Dem. (VO):** Ladies and gentlemen, please don't try this on the knives in your kitchen drawer. Miracle Mac Knives are the *only* knives in the world that can take this kind of punishment.
3. *Cut to demonstrator cutting paper into strips.*	and keep coming back for more!!
4. *Cut to ECU of demonstrator: gestures to blade.*	The secret is space-age, chrome molybdenum steel—the hardest steel ever made—that stays sharp, for *life,* without any grinding or sharpening tools!
5. *Hands demonstrate sharpening.*	Imagine! Just a simple pass over the back of a china plate restores the original cutting edge.
6. *Pull back for MCU of demonstrator.*	**Demonstrator:** Grab a pencil and paper folks because I want to send you a set of these amazing Mac Knives for 30 days *free!* But first, watch.
7. *Demonstrate tomato.*	**(VO):** You can cut a tomato paper-thin slice after slice, and never lose a drop of juice;
8. *Demonstrate roast.*	carve meat from the bone as clean as a whistle;
9. *Demonstrate radishes.*	decorate radishes like an expert;
10. *Demonstrate bread in mid-air.*	cut bread a sixteenth of an inch thin;
11. *Demonstrate turkey.*	carve a turkey clear down to the bone in seconds;
12. *Demonstrate potato.*	even take an eye out of a potato so easy you won't believe it!

Video	Audio
13. *Cut to ECU of hands demonstrating blade.*	And just look at this: Each knife is scientifically designed to keep your fingers away from the cutting board,
14. *Hands demonstrate tips.*	with safe rounded tips,
15. *Hands demonstrate hole.*	and handy hanging hole,
16. *Hands demonstrate handles.*	plus teak handles that are permanently bonded to the steel for super strength.
17. *Pull back to demonstrator who displays knives one at a time.*	**Demonstrator:** And now, during this special TV offer, you can own one, two, three, four Miracle Mac Knives for just $19.95.
18. *Dissolve to knives and box. Super card 2: 30-day free trial.*	**Dem (VO):** But first, try them at home for 30 days free! No need to send any money!
19. *Cut to knife rack demonstration. Super card 3: Free! When you send $19.95 plus one dollar shipping and handling.*	However, if you use your credit card or include payment with your order, we'll include this handsome hardwood knife rack at no extra cost! If not fully satisfied, return the knife set, keep the knife rack, and we'll refund your purchase price of $19.95.
20. *Demonstrator assembles sandwich and cuts it.*	Try the knives that are so hard, so sharp, they slice through a Dagwood sandwich in one stroke!
21. *Cut to slide of phone number and address. Super card 4: offer for cable TV viewers only.*	**Demonstrator:** Order your set today. Give the knives a real workout for 30 days. Here's how: Call 000-0000 right now or write Mac Knives, care of Station OOO, Charleston, West Virginia. Send only $19.95 plus one dollar shipping and handling. That's Mac Knives, care of Station OOO, Charleston, West Virginia, or call 000-0000 now.

A support television commercial differs from a straight response commercial in ways worthy of note. Since it seeks to reach the largest number of people, it usually runs in time periods when 30 seconds is the prevalent availability. It must have a greatly condensed message, placing a premium on simplicity. It almost must pay a larger than usual tribute to the image considerations of the client. As it seeks no immediate response, but directs the viewer elsewhere, memorability and a positive attitude about the advertiser become extremely important.

Contrast this 30-second support TV commercial with the preceding direct sale commercial (audio portion only):

Look for this brochure in Sunday's paper; because 9 out of 10 of these homes have no guarantee they'll be rebuilt if destroyed by fire. But with Allstate's new home replacement guarantee, your home will be rebuilt completely even if rebuilding costs more than you're covered for. Take the first important step to get Allstate's Home Replacement Guarantee. Look for this brochure in Sunday's paper because you never know when fire will strike.

Creating for Radio

In its early days, television was perceived by many copywriters as nothing more than illustrated radio. With evolution of the medium we learned how limited that vision was. Now, in this age of video, there is a tendency to think of radio as television without the pictures. That perception is equally wrong.

Radio is the "writer's medium" in its purest sense. Words, sounds, music, even silence are woven together by the writer to produce a moving tapestry of thought, image, and persuasion. Connection with the listener is direct, personal, emotional, primal. In fact, research by educational groups has found that information taken in through the ear is often remembered more readily and more vividly than that received visually.

In writing for radio, it is important to consider a station's format. The "country and western" station has a different listening audience from the "all-news" station. Different people listen to classical music vs. talk-back or rock programming. Tailor your message and its style to the format of the station it is running on. That doesn't necessarily mean make it sound exactly like the station's programming. Sometimes it makes sense to break the flow of programming to stand out as a special message, but only within the framework of the format that has attracted the station's listeners.

Remember also that radio is more personal than TV. Radios are carried with the listener, in a car, at the beach, at the office, in the bathroom, even joggers with their earphones are tuned into the radio cosmos. Moreover, because the radio listener can supply important elements in the message mosaic, the conclusion drawn from it is likely to be more firmly held than that which the individual has not participated in. Do not fill in all the blanks for your listeners. Let them provide some of the pieces. At the same time, be sure the words you use are clear in their meaning and emotional content. Be sure the sounds are clearly understandable and recognizable. If not, find some way to augment them with narrative or conversation that establishes a setting that is easy to visualize.

Use music whenever you can justify its cost and consumption of commercial time. Music is the emotional common denominator. Its expression of joy, sorrow, excitement, romance, action, etc., is as universally understood as any device available to you. When it comes time to consider music, contact a music production house. There usually are several in every major city. Los Angeles, New York and Chicago have scores of them. They usually will consult at no charge. Or consider library music that can be purchased outright at low cost. If you can live with its often undistinguished quality, it can be an excellent value.

Another aspect of radio is its casualness. Whereas television tends to command all of our attention and concentration, radio usually gets only a portion of it. It is important to keep radio commercials simple and stopping. Devices such as special sounds (or silence) can arrest your listener's attention. To hold it, the idea content must be cohesive and uncomplicated. Better to drive one point home than to flail away at many. If many points must be covered, they all should feed to a strong central premise. This advice is appropriate for all advertising. But for radio it is critical.

The length a radio commercial runs is usually 60 seconds. This not only should be adequate for most commercial messages but also is the time length listeners have become accustomed to. Thirty-second commercials are available but are not a good buy for direct response purposes.

One other thing that everyone who listens to radio will appreciate is that radio lends itself to humor. For some reason we have become used to hearing humor on radio, and we respond positively to it. The following radio commercial employs humor effectively to address small business owners, while talking to the public at large.

Husband:	How did we get into this anyway?
Wife:	Who knows, we tried to make it work.
Husband:	Well, I guess it's over.
Wife:	We better get on with it.
Husband:	Okay, you get the car.
Wife:	Right.
Husband:	I get the sofa bed. You get the fridge.
Wife:	Right.
Husband:	I get the Bell System Yellow Pages Directory. You get the——
Wife:	Hold on—that doesn't mean the Gold Pages Coupon Section does it?
Husband:	Why sure it does.

Wife:	I get the Gold Pages Coupons.
Husband:	Well come on—you're getting the bedroom set too.
Wife:	You can have the bedroom set. I want the Gold Pages Coupons good for discounts at local merchants.
Husband:	I'll tell you what.
Wife:	What?
Husband:	I'll throw in the oil painting and the end tables.
Wife:	I want the Gold Pages.
Husband:	Look you can have everything else. Just let me keep the Gold Pages Coupons.
Wife:	Get off your knees. You really want them that bad?
Husband:	I do absolutely.
Wife:	We could split them.
Husband:	You mean———tear them apart?
Wife:	You're right—it won't work.
Husband:	No. Neither will this.
Wife:	It won't work.
Husband:	You mean———
Wife:	We'll just have to stay together.
Husband:	Dolores—what a mistake we almost made.
Wife:	Lorraine!
Husband:	Lorraine—what a mistake we almost made.
Wife:	Who's Dolores?

Creating for Narrowcast/Cable

Much of what has been said about creating messages for broadcast TV applies to cable as well. But there are some differences. Time lengths are more flexible. Longer commercials to tell a more complete story are more affordable. Messages can be tailored to meet the needs or preconceived notions of a smaller universe of prospects than with broadcast. Cable programming generally is narrower in its interest, drawing viewers who have a special interest in sports (or a special kind of sport), the arts, news, public issues, etc.

Much as with radio, commercials can be shaped to correspond to special interest "formats." Commercials that are not compatible with programming of a given channel, while they may gain attention, probably will not gain as much favor or (positive) response.

Beyond standard broadcast-type commercials, two other basic types of direct response commercials have emerged as appropriate for cable. One is the so-called infomercial. Helpful information about a product, its use, and its benefits is offered as a service to the viewer at the same time an attempt is being made to sell the product. Recipes, tips for homemaking or auto care, how to use and maintain tools, how to care for garments, and financial planning information all fit into this category.

There have been a number of attempts to tie commercial messages into program formats. A home shopping show used an interview format with representatives of the manufacturers or retailers of products serving as guests. Each interview ran for about 10 minutes while a resident host and hostess asked questions about the product. The results were mixed, although mostly disappointing. An interview is only as interesting as the host, the interviewee, and the subject matter. Since the latter two elements were "locked in," most of the shows were predictably sleep-inducing.

A newer test, started in 1982 in Peabody, Massachusetts, is providing longer-length infomercials over a channel called CableShop. The viewer can telephone the cable operator and request a commercial be shown at a certain time. While not many people seem to be taking advantage of pre-ordering a commercial, there is evidence sponsors are getting a very satisfactory percentage of voluntary viewership. The formats for these infomercials vary by product and service, though they tend not to be interviews. Overall, they seem to be more helpful and interesting to watch than the interview format. The moral is, infomercial or not, you can't bore people into paying attention.

A second category of direct response advertising on cable is the video catalog. Similar to a printed catalog, it is a series of products presented photographically with appropriate descriptive copy and ordering information. But instead of being static, it is dynamic and sequential.

A video catalog requires the proper pacing. Too much time spent on an item will bore the viewer, especially if he or she is not inherently interested in the product. On the other hand, too little time will not provide enough opportunity to explore the item's use and appearance, either by demonstration or copy.

Entertainment value also should be included. Just as a printed catalog with good layout, good photography, and good copy attracts a larger audience, entertainment in a video catalog will draw more people whose interest can be moved towards purchase. To the degree good writing, good art direction, and good production values are compromised—and often they must be for economic reasons—recognize they not only will diminish the audience but also diminish the quality image of merchandise and merchant.

Other advice for the video cataloger includes respecting the customer's interest and building your format to honor it. The customer wants to see how the item looks, wants to know what kind of person would buy it. What colors, sizes, styles does it come in. Can you demonstrate how it works? Do it. Can you show how it's made; how to put it together or take it apart; some way it can be used that might not have been thought about? That's what interests the customer.

And lastly, the prospect must be led to your video catalog. There must be promotion and publicity. If it is organized by subject matter, tell them when each segment will run. And run it several times. The average prospect picks up a catalog several times before she or he is done with it.

Creating for Computer Networks

Computer networks are both a media frontier and a creative frontier. This is a rational medium for rational decisions, not emotional ones. This is an informational medium with little or no graphic capabilities, yet it reaches millions, often when their minds are on business. Products or services being promoted on this medium will have to concentrate on factual data with a minimum of "hype."

Items to be sold via computer networks will require carefully crafted copy. Given the nature of the medium, and of the customers when they are using it, copy that adroitly sells while it succinctly tells will be extremely important. In addition, direct response advertisers on computer networks should look for opportunities to cross-sell within the medium. The customer pleased with one item and the mode of purchase is a "best prospect" for another item in the same mode.

Creating for Teletext and Videotex

As we have done earlier, we will discuss these two media together because they share some similarities of form. Both are still largely experimental, but the technology for improved graphics, including the someday possibility of transmitting still photographic images, is moving forward rapidly.

For the present, however, graphic presentation is limited by the band-width available to transmit electronic impulses. These impulses fill the screen, which is divided into pixcels, with various colors and forms. Depending on the technology involved, they can range from looking like children's plastic interlocking blocks to looking very representational. The opportunities here for art directors and designers are exciting. Better and better visualizations of products and services must be created to accompany text just as current print advertising so effectively weds copy and picture.

Exhibit 8-2 shows a room setting with Viewtron equipment in place along with examples of advertising frames that can be called upon command.

Videotex, because it is an on-line interactive medium, is capable of some small degree of animation. A figure can appear to be walking, a light blinking, an object moving across the screen. This capability can be used to highlight relevant points from the textual material and maintain visual interest in the frame.

Exhibit 8-2. Viewtron: Advertising on Command

Exhibit 8-2. Viewtron: Advertising on Command

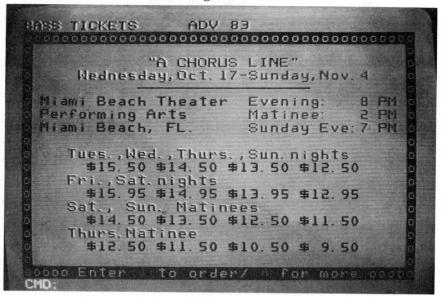

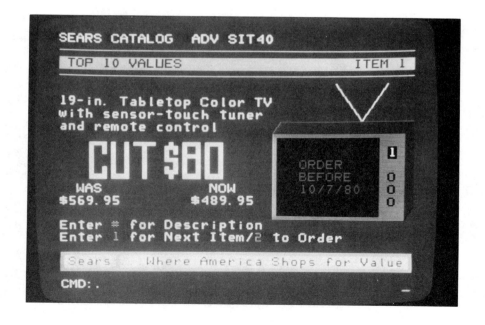

In both videotex and teletext, the frames can be thought of as electronic "pages" that must be "turned" by the viewer. Effective copy is critical not only to communicate benefits clearly and compellingly but also to carry reader interest over to the next frame.

One technique likely to find important use is quizzes or games. With the customer responding to probes, questions and other stimuli, he or she can be carried through an entire selling sequence while painlessly enjoying the game.

Getting the customer to act by calling up the order form and placing an electronic order requires skillful language and offers of the sort discussed elsewhere in this book. Furthermore, design of a simple, easy-to-understand, easy-to-complete order form enhances selling in videotex as it does in other direct response media.

Creating for Video Disc and Video Cassette

We include these two media apart from standard or cable TV because their unique reference-ability makes them immediately interactive with the customer in much the same way as a printed catalog. Video disc and video cassette systems offer the additional advantage of allowing products to be demonstrated. Movement through the material can be frozen, reversed, or rapidly advanced. When combined with the ability of videotex to provide constantly changing product and stock data, this will become a formidable tool for direct marketing and a welcome resource for the customer.

Maximizing its value, in either mode, will demand creative approaches that combine clarity of thought, simple presentation, ease of navigation through the system, excitement and drama, demonstration whenever possible, and a healthy respect for the informational needs of the customer. Offers and techniques will have to be developed within this framework. But the potential is gargantuan.

Research and Results Tracking

Research and results tracking are as important with electronic media as with all other media. An entire chapter has been written about the overall subject, with helpful reference to its use as a creative tool. (See Chapter 17.) In the form of attitude and usage studies, research can tell you what categories of prospects would be most interested in your product or service and why. On a more qualitative basis, research can tell you whether the advertising message ideas you have developed will be understood and if they will be important enough to the prospect to stimulate action. You can also learn if there are any hidden negatives in your approach.

Research has also been devised that can measure the memorability of a commercial message. Viewers are exposed to the commercial, contacted 24 hours later, and asked to play back anything they can recall about the commercial. Some general marketers have been using this testing technique for years and have norms based on hundreds of tests. But since there never has been a correlation between memorability and persuasion, much less sales, advertisers who rely exclusively on recall testing do so, in the words of David Ogilvy, as the drunk leans on the lightpost: more for support than illumination.

Finally, measurement of actual performance in electronic media is as critical as it is for mail or print. And the equation is much the same. The cost of your electronic program divided by the total number of inquiries or sales it generates will give you an actual cost per response or order. That number should not exceed the projected cost established at the outset of your plan.

Careful analysis of your results can tell you which stations pulled best, which time slots or program adjacencies worked best, and which products or creative approaches performed most efficiently. Discontinue those that did worse than your projections. Expand those that did better. And test new markets, stations, time slots, programs, approaches and products against the same standards.

Research in its many forms is a necessary ingredient in, and a powerful ally of, direct response advertising that works in the electronic media.

Self-quiz

1. Define a GRP (Gross Rating Point).

_____

_____

_____

2. Define these terms:

a. "P.I."

_____

b. "Bonus-to-payout"

_____

3. What are the three elements of creative strategy?

a. _____

b. _____

c. _____

4. How long a TV schedule and how many exposures are necessary to evaluate the potential of a direct response offer on television?

_____

_____

_____

5. Match the medium with the most appropriate characteristic:

a. Videotex   _____ Intrusiveness

b. Computer networks   _____ Personal use

c. Television   _____ Text and simple graphics only

d. Radio   _____ High interactivity

e. Teletext   _____ Extensive storage capacity

f. Video cassettes/discs _____ Limited number of frames

6. How does the target audience for support TV differ from the target audience for direct sale TV?

_____

_____

_____

7. Define the terms *reach* and *frequency.*

Reach _____

Frequency _____

8. What is the most common length for a radio commercial?

_____

9. Describe the relationship between a direct response offer and a creative strategy.

_____

_____

_____

10. What is the best time length for the following TV commercials:

Direct Sale: _____

Lead Generation: _____

Support: _____

11. What are the two most common errors encountered in a television storyboard?

a. _____

b. _____

12. What charges are likely to be incurred when purchasing time/space on a videotex system?

_____

_____

_____

13. Why isn't prime time the best time slot for a direct sell or lead generation TV commercial?

_____

_____

_____

Pilot Project

It is your assignment to sell an album of rock music by a "hot" group for $9.95. The medium you are to use is radio. Prepare a 60-second commercial for a rock station format.

Chapter Nine

Co-ops

Package goods firms, for the most part, disavow direct marketing as a part of their marketing mix. And yet, a direct marketing vehicle—the cents-off coupon—is integral to most of their marketing programs.

Cents-off coupons qualify as direct marketing, in my opinion, because they meet the three requirements of a direct response proposition: (1) a definite offer (a discount on a specified product); (2) all the information necessary to make a decision (all cents-off coupons contain complete information); (3) a response device (the coupon, when presented at the checkout counter, becomes the transaction device).

Promotions come and go. But cents-off coupons continue to grow. (See Table 9-1.)

When consumers are asked why they continue to redeem coupons, they give three major reasons:

1. Coupons save money.
2. Coupons inform consumers about old-line products and give encouragement to try new products.
3. Coupons reduce the cost of the products consumers buy.

Table 9-1. Growth of Coupon Distribution (excludes in-ad coupons).

Year	Number (Billions)
1975	35.7
1976	45.8
1977	62.2
1978	72.7
1979	81.2
1980	90.8

Marketers use coupons:
- To improve competitive penetration in a market
- To move out-of-balance inventories
- To stimulate product demand at the retail level as a means of obtaining retailer agreements to stock a product
- To accelerate the introduction and widespread use of a new product
- To get new users for an old product

Mass Market Penetration

The dominant force in cents-off coupon distribution is Donnelley Marketing, publisher of the Carol Wright mail co-op, distributed to more than 24 million selected households seven times a year.

While Carol Wright distribution is indeed huge, it is a carefully segmented distribution carved from Donnelley's 70 million household residential data base. Carol Wright gives the following demographics for the typical homemaker who receives their co-op:

> A married woman (76%) between 25 and 49 years old (68%) whose household income exceeds $15,000 (79%) and whose family size is three or more persons (61%). She is at least a high school graduate (86%, with 53% having attended college). Her children are under 18 years old (57%), she lives near one or more high-volume supermarkets (91%) and collects and uses cents-off coupons on a regular basis (95%).

Donnelley has identified the households they select as "heavy users." These "heavy users," surprisingly, skew to families with annual incomes over $15,000 rather than those of poverty income under $5,000. And, quoting from readership studies they have conducted, nearly all (95 percent) open and look through the Carol Wright ensemble. Each coupon is seen, on average, by more than two-thirds (71 percent) of the recipients. Better than a third (40 percent) indicate a positive brand message response. And of those who redeem the coupons, more than three quarters (78 percent) buy new brands or brands they do not regularly use, depending on product category.

Media and Redemption Rates

Mail distribution of cents-off coupons, while highly effective, is dwarfed by distribution in other media. Table 9-2 shows the latest distribution figures available in the DMA "Fact Book."

While direct mail coupon distribution is, by far, the most expensive distribution channel on a cost-per-thousand basis, this is compensated for by a much higher average redemption rate. (See latest DMA figures in Table 9-3.)

Traditional Co-ops

While the vast majority of participants in Carol Wright co-ops are package goods firms, some direct marketers include mail order offers in their co-ops. However, most direct marketers who use co-ops tend to use those that have a greater number of direct response offers. Types of direct response co-ops available break into the following categories.

1. *Mail order co-ops.* These are arranged by direct marketers who put their own co-ops together. They induce other direct marketers to join forces with them and make combined mailings to their buyer list. The income from other marketers naturally reduces mail circulation cost for the sponsor.

2. *In-house co-ops.* A variation of the commercial co-op is the in-house co-op. In this case the sponsor (marketer) co-ops only products or services that he sells. The advantage is that selling costs are spread over several offers, rather than one.

Table 9-2. Distribution of Coupons By Media.

Media	Percent
Newspapers	48.2
Magazines	13.3
Direct mail	3.4
In/on packs	7.7
Sunday supplements	9.0
Free-standing inserts	18.4

Table 9-3. Average Coupon Redemption Rates.

Medium	Average Redemption
Direct mail	11.6%
Magazines	2.9%
Newspapers ROP	3.1%
Sunday supplements solo	2.1%
Newspaper free-standing insert	5.1%
Newspaper comic section	1.5%

3. *Vertical co-ops.* Here we are talking about specific groups, such as business people, college students, new mothers, school teachers, accountants, lawyers, engineers, and so forth.

4. *Magazine co-ops.* Many magazines sponsor a co-op of their own, their circulation list serving as the channel of distribution. This service offers two major advantages to the sponsoring magazine: (1) a chance for additional revenue from regular magazine advertisers, (2) an inducement to prospective advertisers to test the responsiveness of the magazine's market.

Standard Rate & Data Service (SRDS) has an entire section devoted to co-op mailings in its periodic directory called *Direct Mail List Rates and Data.* The listings contain much valuable information.

Sales/Costs Ratios

Quoting averages is always dangerous, but as a rule-of-thumb response for individual pieces in a co-op is about one-fourth the response of a solo mailing. The cost, however, is likewise about one-fourth. Response

Exhibit 9-1. A Co-op Mailing

A Store Redemption Coupon and a direct response offer among 43 inserts in a typical Carol Wright co-op.

Exhibit 9-2. Three Examples of Participants in *Advertising Age's* Loose Pack Postcard Deck

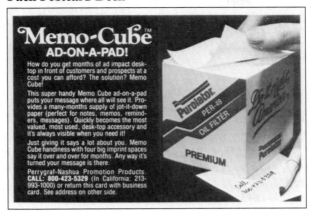

Memo-Cube™
AD-ON-A-PAD!

How do you get months of ad impact desktop in front of customers and prospects at a cost you can afford? The solution? Memo Cube!

This super handy Memo Cube ad-on-a-pad puts your message where all will see it. Provides a many-months supply of jot-it-down paper (perfect for notes, memos, reminders, messages). Quickly becomes the most valued, most used, desk-top accessory and it's always visible when you need it!

Just giving it says a lot about you. Memo Cube handiness with four big imprint spaces say it over and over for months. Any way it's turned your message is there.

Perrygraf-Nashua Promotion Products. **CALL: 800-423-5329** (In California: 213-993-1000) or return this card with business card. See address on other side.

ExpoSystems® –
Instant Versatility

Now you can create a modular display in minutes - with ExpoSystems! The possibilities are endless...add on, subtract or rearrange components to fit any show - large or small. Our Multiscreen® system is easy to assemble, portable, durable and immediately available for delivery! For complete kits, call toll-free:

(800) 237-4531
In Florida, call collect 813/623-2402.

ExpoSystems®
a Cllague company

Name _____
Title _____ Phone _____
Company _____
Address _____
City _____ State _____ Zip _____

The future belongs to Direct Response Advertising ... Learn How and Why It Will Affect You ...

RESPONSE TELEVISION: Combat Advertising of the 1980s
By John Witek

This book is the first and only book about TV direct marketing. Special attention is paid to the opportunities for direct marketing on cable television and through today's interactive systems such as QUBE and Prestel. This lively volume takes a look at direct response, support, and lead-generating commercials, showing how they work and can be made more effective through creative innovation.   **Hardcover $19.95**

Order now! Read FREE for 15 days. If not satisfied, return for full credit. PLEASE RUSH _____ copy(ies) of RESPONSE TELEVISION: Combat Advertising of the 1980s @ $19.95 per copy plus $1.25 for shipping and handling.

☐ Bill me later, including shipping and handling charges.
☐ Check enclosed for $ _____ (Illinois residents add 6% sales tax). Crain Books pays shipping and handling.

Name _____
Company _____
Address _____
City _____ State _____ Zip _____

rates do vary, of course. A 50 percent discount offer from *Time*—so well known that little explanation is necessary—is likely to pull much better than that for an unknown publication. Also a new product offer, because of restricted space in a co-op, is likely to pull far less than one-fourth of a solo mail effort.

Co-op Formats

Direct marketers have two basic formats available to them: postcard and "loose" inserts. Most postcard publications carry three postcards to the page, the reply card unit size measuring approximately 6″ x 3⅝″. An advertiser can purchase a single card or two or three adjacent cards.

Sponsors determine the size and weight limitations for loose inserts. Typically the weight limitation is one-quarter ounce, and the size limitation is 5″ x 8″. If the advertiser exceeds the weight limitation, he is usually subject to a surcharge.

Getting Co-ops Read

Participants in co-ops face fierce readership competition. You can greatly improve your chances for getting your piece read and acted on by knowing the behavior patterns of people who receive co-ops. Phil Dresden, an expert on co-ops, provides a valuable insight:

> I have witnessed a number of focus group research interview sessions through a one-way mirror. Different groups of housewives were brought in and handed co-op envelopes filled with coupons and offers. There was an amazingly consistent behavior pattern. The participants, without exception, sorted each envelope's contents into two piles. Later when they were asked what was the basis for the two piles, they answered: "Interesting-not interesting; like-dislike; value-no value." Your offer must find its way to the right pile during that initial sorting.
>
> The way to get into the first pile is to have a simple message clearly stated with effective graphics. The more alternatives you offer, the less your response will be. In a phrase, don't get sorted out; keep it simple. You only have a few seconds to make an impact. Inserts in direct mail co-ops are more like ads in a magazine than like regular direct mail. If the offer appears to be too much trouble, if it appears that the message is going to take some time and effort to get at, the housewife goes to the next offer.
>
> Before you release your final mechanical to the printer, write two questions down on a piece of paper and see if you can answer them honestly: (1) Have you given the potential respondent an opportunity for dialog with you? (2) What precisely are you asking the potential respondent to believe and to do?

Generally, in co-op direct marketing advertising the recipient sees little and remembers less. Any purchase is basically made on impulse, and response levels can be seriously impacted if the potential respondent does not act within a short time span. The products and services should fall into the pattern of something wanted or needed now.

Testing a Co-op

As Phil Dresden points out, testing co-ops is a tricky business. When you test an insert in a co-op, you are doing so with one group of partners; when you "roll out," you are likely to be participating with a different group of partners. So you must live with this variable. Here are a few simple rules for testing co-ops based on the Dresden experience:

1. Because testing is a trial for a subsequent major promotion, it is important to ensure conditions such that the major promotion will be as close to the original as possible.

2. Know what your break-even point is and test a sample large enough so your result can be acted upon.

3. Test the co-op first and leave the segments for later unless your product clearly suggests a particular segment. For example, if your product is aimed entirely at a female market, test only the female portion of a co-op mailing.

4. Test a cross section of the complete co-op list. If no "nth" sample is available, request distribution in several different markets—all widely dispersed.

5. Don't let too much time elapse between your test and your continuation, especially if the item you are testing is of a seasonal nature.

Package Inserts

The never-ending quest for reducing selling costs has led many major direct marketers to offer package insert programs to noncompeting advertisers. A sample array of package insert programs is shown in Exhibit 9-3.

Jack Oldstein, president of Dependable Lists, Inc., states, "Package inserts offer immediacy, guaranteed mail order buyers, with no waste circulation, the understood endorsement by the mailer of your product to his loyal customers, and the names used are fresher than the next update."

Virgil D. Angerman, formerly sales promotion manager of Boise Cascade Envelope Division, gives this sage advice about package insert programs. "The planning of a package insert program is much like planning a direct mail campaign. The advertiser should evaluate the type of person who will receive the package insert. The advertiser should ask if he or she is the logical prospect for a particular merchandise or service. The questions should be raised, will the insert do a thorough selling job? Is the offer attractive? Have you made it easy to send an inquiry or order?" Just as with mailing lists, best results are realized when you match your offer to the market. If you are selling insurance to older people, using package inserts with vitamin shipments makes sense. If you are selling sports apparel, using package inserts with shipments going to fishermen and hunters makes sense, and so forth.

Exhibit 9-3. Co-ops and "Piggybacks"

LIST TYPE, SOURCE, DESCRIPTION & SIZE	COST & MINIMUM	CONTACT YOUR BROKER OR	ENTER NUMBER ON INFO CARD
StarCrest Package Insert Program. Direct-response customers receptive to home-centered offers. Average unit of sale: $20. Sex: 93% female. Source: 100% direct mail. Four SMPs required. Total: **150,000-200,000 monthly.**	$40/M No Test	Woodruff-Stevens 40 East 34th Street New York, NY 10016 (213) 725-1555	177
Mail-Order Buyers Package Insert Program. Individuals have responded to package inserts, direct mail, and inserts in newspaper supplements. Items are moderately priced and cover a variety of interests. Sex: 70% female. Average unit of sale: $10. SMP required. Total: **65,000 per month**	$35/M Test 10,000	Nora Nelson Inc. 621 Avenue of the Americas New York, NY 10011 (212) 924-7551	178
Bank Systems & Equipment Action Reply Card Mailing. Fall mailing to top-qualified bank/thrift purchasing decision makers. October 1 deadline for Fall program. Mailing frequency: 2/year. Total: **35,025**	$33/M No Test	Gralla Publications 1515 Broadway New York, NY 10036 (212) 869-1300	179
Frederick's of Hollywood Package Insert Program. August mailing to women who are buyers of high style apparel, beauty and health aids, shoes, and jewelry. SMP required. Mailing frequency: 6/year. Total: **41,000 in August.**	$35/M Test 10,000	List Services Corp. P.O. Box 2014 Ridgefield, CN 06877 (203) 438-0327	180
Xerox Education Publications Package Insert Program. Inserts placed into the introductory packages of weekly reader books, including children's clubs and continuity buyers. Source: 100% direct response. SMP required. Total: **3,500,000**	$45/M Test 25,000	Qualified List Corp. 135 Bedford Road Armonk, NY 10504 (212) 324-8900	181
Alves Photo Service Package Inserts. Nationwide audience of mail-order buyers of film processing. Unit of sale: $5-$15. Source: 50% direct mail, 50% space ads. SMP required. Total: **10,000 weekly.**	$20/M Test 25,000	Leon Henry Inc. 455 Central Avenue Scarsdale, NY 10583 (914) 723-3176	205
Popular Club Package Insert Program. Credit-oriented homemakers buying a broad spectrum of products from a merchandise catalog. Unit of sale: $70. Sex: 98% female. Median age: 35. Average income: $15,000. Mailing frequency: 1/year. Total: **810,000**	$30/M Test 10,000	E.J. Krane Inc. P.O. Box 663 Princeton Junction, NJ 08550 (609) 452-2885	183
Sunset House Insert Program. Buyers of beauty products, jewelry, health aids, horticulture items, housewares and novelty items. Source: 90% direct mail. Average unit of order: $10-$13. Sex: 78% female. Total: **100,000**	$40/M Test 10,000	Woodruff-Stevens & Associates 40 East 34th Street New York, NY 10016 (212) 725-1555	217

Professional mailing list brokers will provide list cards of firms who accept package inserts just as they supply list cards of direct marketers who make their mailing lists available for rental.

Other Co-ops

While special interest, package insert, and newspaper co-ops offer mass distribution opportunities to direct marketers at low cost, there are also several off-beat co-ops available.

Many paperback book publishers make card inserts available to direct response advertisers. Circulation can run into the millions. Direct response advertisers can select distribution by title. Thus, the advertiser can fairly well estimate the demographic profile of readers by the type of book they are buying. *Gone with the Wind* would probably be a good distribution channel for an offer to women, *The Parsifal Mosaic* for an offer to men, and so forth.

One of the more recent developments is co-op distribution via grocery stores. Producers of grocery bags have devised manufacturing facilities whereby inserts can be pre-inserted in grocery bags. Thus, when the housewife empties her grocery bag, one or more direct response offers are included. Another medium available through retail grocery stores is what is commonly called the "supermarket rack." Shoppers are exposed to a variety of literature in racks adjacent to check-out counters.

Co-ops are a major tool for direct response advertisers when used correctly. They are not suitable for selling a $400 calculator, but are excellent for getting inquiries about a $400 calculator. Co-ops are highly preferred for in-store coupon redemptions and for scores of direct response offers requiring a minimum of information for a targeted audience.

Self-Quiz

1. Why do cents-off coupons qualify as direct marketing?

_____

_____

_____

2. Heavy users of cent-off coupons skew toward families with:

☐ Annual income under $5,000

☐ Annual income over $15,000

3. Which is the largest distribution channel for cents-off coupons?

☐ Newspapers   ☐ Magazines   ☐ Direct mail

4. Which medium shows the highest average redemption rate:

☐ Newspapers   ☐ Magazines   ☐ Direct mail

5. Name four types of traditional co-ops.

a. _____

b. _____

c. _____

d. _____

6. A co-op is likely to pull about one-fourth that of a solo mailing at about _____ the cost.

7. What is the difference between "loose" insert co-ops and postcard co-ops?

_____

_____

_____

8. Describe how housewives tend to sort out the contents of co-op envelopes.

_____

_____

_____

_____

9. What is the one variable you must live with in scheduling the continuation of a co-op you tested previously?

_____

_____

_____

_____

10. Name five advantages of package inserts.

a. _____

b. _____

c. _____

d. _____

e. _____

Pilot Project

You have become promotion director of the *Advertising Age* postcard program, which is distributed several times a year to its 70,000 plus subscribers.

As a prelude to developing your promotion program, it is your assignment to develop a list of prospects whose propositions you feel will appeal to advertising agency personnel, marketing executives, advertising managers, advertising research executives, and graphic arts personnel.

Please break your prospect categories into two segments: primary and secondary. Expand the list for each to 12, using the first three as starting points.

Primary	**Secondary**
1. Advertising and marketing books	1. Investment opportunities
2. Premiums	2. Office forms
3. TV production	3. Office equipment
4. _____	4. _____
5. _____	5. _____
6. _____	6. _____
7. _____	7. _____
8. _____	8. _____
9. _____	9. _____
10. _____	10. _____
11. _____	11. _____
12. _____	12. _____

Chapter Ten

Telemarketing

Telemarketing is an advertising medium. It, along with direct mail, print, broadcast, point-of-purchase, and other media can be made to work both synergistically and effectively within your total advertising plan.

But the key to properly utilizing telemarketing is, not unlike any advertising medium, to first understand and plan it properly. If you limit telephone to "boiler room" selling or "cold selling," you will not likely get the results you can expect from a planned telemarketing program.

What Is Telemarketing?

In its simplest definition, telemarketing is the planned, professional, and measured use of telecommunication in sales and marketing efforts. (The three key words in this definition are *planned, executed,* and *measured.*) To better understand this process, let's look at the telemarketing spectrum developed by AT&T, probably the nation's most sophisticated user of telemarketing. (See Exhibit 10-1.)

This chart illustrates the evolution of the telemarketing process, from its simplest form—order taking—to its most complex—full account management. Let's begin our look with a brief definition of each of these functions. It should be assumed that each level includes not only the steps in its definition but the functions preceding it as well.

1. *Order taking.* Long before sophisticated direct response programs were used to generate mass numbers of orders, a much more personalized method of communication was used to accept orders from customers—the telephone. Today, while volume and processes have changed, many companies still utilize telemarketing in this first stage. Multimedia campaigns are used to generate in-coming calls and the telemarketing center is used to "accept the orders."

2. *Customer service.* This level of telemarketing accomplishes two functions. (1) It addresses the "complaint handling" need through telecommunications (replacing the more costly personal function) and (2) it cross-sells and upgrades current customers after the service problem has been solved (the telephone application of "selling on the service call").

3. *Sales support.* While the two preceding levels are sales and service applications of telemarketing, this level tends to act as support to the sales force. This can come through scheduling sales calls, maintaining

Exhibit 10-1. Potential Applications of Telemarketing

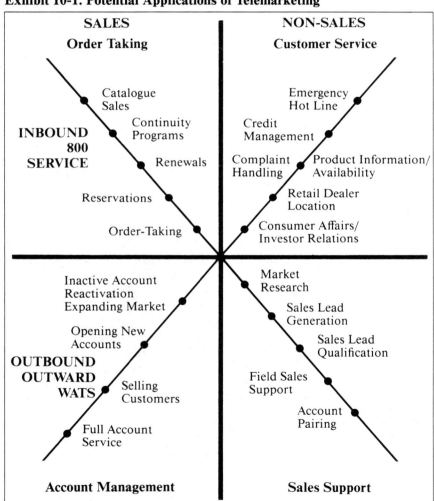

SALES | NON-SALES

Order Taking | **Customer Service**

INBOUND 800 SERVICE

Catalogue Sales
Continuity Programs
Renewals
Reservations
Order-Taking

Emergency Hot Line
Credit Management
Complaint Handling — Product Information/ Availability
Retail Dealer Location
Consumer Affairs/ Investor Relations

OUTBOUND OUTWARD WATS

Inactive Account Reactivation
Expanding Market
Opening New Accounts
Selling Customers
Full Account Service

Market Research
Sales Lead Generation
Sales Lead Qualification
Field Sales Support
Account Pairing

Account Management | **Sales Support**

supplies and vendors, followup on sales calls, credit management, or handling and selling to marginal accounts.

4. *Account management.* The highest form of telemarketing, account management, virtually replaces personal contact with customers. (Specifying which accounts should be handled by telephone can be determined in many ways: by size of firm, by sales volume, by location, etc.) Telephone account management requires a planned, predetermined ongoing relationship by qualified telemarketing sales specialists.

As you can imagine, there are numerous applications of each of these levels in the spectrum of telemarketing. No level will ever totally replace a salesforce. However, like lead generation (covered in Chapter 14), anything that can be used to bring down the cost of a personal sales call (currently averaging $203) will ultimately make your firm more efficient and profitable. The proper use of telemarketing can do this and more.

The Role of Telemarketing in the Total Promotion

Before we begin delving into specific applications of telemarketing, it is critical that we discuss the need to include this important advertising medium within the total marketing mix. Often times, telemarketing is viewed as simply a means of taking an order once the campaign is launched. It is far more than that.

The telemarketing portion of a campaign must be developed with the same care as all other portions. Here are some questions to be answered up-front when telemarketing is a part of the total marketing mix.

- What information does the telemarketing specialist need to know?
- Will the specialist have to consult, or simply sell?
- Does a script need to be developed? If so, will it reflect the "tone" of all other communications?
- Has the capacity of the telemarketing center been considered and planned for?
- Will these be leads or direct sales? If leads, will they be prequalified?
- Will there be a need for telephone followup after the initial contact?
- How will the orders be processed?
- How will data be captured for later use?

In order to answer these and other questions, let's begin by looking at some specific telemarketing applications that would be handled at a telemarketing center.

Telemarketing Contacts: Inbound and Outbound Sales Process

Telemarketing applications can basically be segmented into two broad categories: inbound and outbound. Inbound, calls that are stimulated through advertising or customer need, tend to be handled in a very different manner than outbound, calls that the telemarketing center initiates for a sales or service function.

Once a telemarketing program is under way, applications can and will cross over into both inbound and outbound calls. How a specific telemarketing application gets defined is very much dictated by the needs and objectives of your individual plan.

Inbound Process

Not surprisingly, the inbound applications tend to be a more common way to begin utilizing telemarketing. For one thing, most firms already have some sort of customer service need, which this addresses. More importantly, the calls generated from an advertising campaign will yield predisposed prospects with an interest in your product/service, either wanting more information or ready to purchase.

Typically, an 800 number is utilized with inbound advertising program campaigns. This benefit to the consumer (you're paying for the call) will increase response to your offer. This can be dramatic when you're making an offer across a broad geographic region.

Following are some examples of common inbound telemarketing applications. They tend to cluster at the beginning of the telemarketing spectrum.

1. *Lead handling.* When a lead generation campaign is launched, a fulfillment procedure must be developed. Almost always, a key factor will be telemarketing (see Chapter 14 for complete details on how to generate leads). When the leads flow into the telemarketing center, one or more of the following activities will occur:

- lead qualification—further qualifying the leads for followup either by a sales staff or telephone.
- fulfillment decision—discussing the interest of the caller to determine appropriate literature to be sent.
- consultative selling—moving the interested prospect into a discussion about items in your product line.
- closing the sale—actually convincing the prospect to purchase the product or service.

2. *Order taking.* When direct sales are practical (rather than a lead for followup, a telemarketing center can be used to write the order. In this case, the following activities might take place:

- product information—giving additional information such as color, sizes, quantity, prices, etc.
- payment information—method of payment, verification of credit, etc.
- delivery modes—shipping alternatives and time frames.

3. *Customer service/inquiry handling.* A well-organized telemarketing center should be able to handle all questions about a product line to the complete satisfaction of the customer. Inquiries from customers might require:

- immediate action—the specialist will discuss the problem thoroughly and take steps towards an immediate solution.
- information gathering—it is critical that information be captured and organized in a way that will facilitate appropriate response to the customer or prospect's need.
- followup—whether it be fulfillment material, resolution of a complaint, whatever, chances are that the telemarketing specialist will have to get back to the initial caller.

These customer service/inquiry handling applications are often treated with a special 800 number and a team to handle them. By centralizing this service, you help to eliminate potential problems. The sample call record in Exhibit 10-2 illustrates how to productively handle customer service inquiries. Ideally this application will turn a problem around and result in a sale.

Outbound Process

Moving further into the telemarketing spectrum, let's look at outbound applications. These are more complex and more difficult to manage. For one thing, a higher level of telemarketing specialist is required. These specialists initiate contacts. They are, in fact, salespeople rather than order takers. An essential part of any outbound telemarketing application is the data. The right target market selection (and subsequent list selection) will make or break an outbound promotion.

Often firms find it productive and profitable to utilize one or more WATS lines with outbound telemarketing applications. While your individual situation will determine the appropriateness to your needs, a commitment to this type of program will almost always be more efficient with WATS. Quite simply, it gives you the advantage of wholesale rates, which decrease on a cost-per-contact basis as your usage increases.

With these thoughts in mind, let's look at some common outbound telemarketing applications.

1. *Opening new accounts.* With the high cost of sending a salesperson out to call on "cold" prospects, many firms use carefully screened lists to open new accounts through telemarketing. The following actions may occur from this type of application.

- penetrating the decision maker—a major part of this application is not simply targeting to the right firms, but also reaching the decision makers. Getting past the secretary in itself is a careful process that requires a planning effort.
- scheduling appointments for salespeople—sometimes, a personal sales call may have to follow telephone contact. When this is required, this will have become a predisposed prospect, making the likelihood of a sale greater.
- consultative selling—when a sale is to be completed by telephone, the specialist must have full knowledge of the product line as well as the prospects' individual needs in order to optimize the likelihood of a sale.

2. *Sales support/time management.* There are several functions that a telemarketing center can accomplish to aid the sales force in servicing existing accounts. The following types of actions will occur:

Exhibit 10-2. Telemarketing Call Record

TELEMARKETING CALL RECORD

Customer _____ Title _____

FOLLOW-UP TO INITIAL CONTACT
1) ☐ Salesperson to visit

Company Name _____

Date: _____ Time: _____ ☐ AM ☐ PM

Address _____

2) ☐ Literature to be sent

City _____ State _____ Zip _____

Type of Literature: _____

3) ☐ Follow up telephone call to be made

Telephone _____ (area code)

Date: _____ Time: _____ ☐ AM ☐ PM

Type of business _____

Customer Service Specialist: _____ Total Time: _____

CALL DATE	CALL INFORMATION COMMENTS	SERVICES/PRODUCTS SOLD	CALL RESULT/SALE				
			Promotional Sale	Upgrade/Cross Sale	Item	Value $	Next Contact Date

- scheduling—time and territory management can be effectively accomplished through a telemarketing center. The results will yield better control of both expenses and productivity of your sales force by having a resource committed to effective scheduling.
- selling marginal accounts—for those existing accounts that require some or no personal calling, the telemarketing specialist can take orders, maintain contact, and answer questions in conjunction with or without the sales force.
- inventory control—maintaining supplier relationship and inventory controls can be accomplished through telemarketing.

3. *Account management.* This application is full management of appropriate accounts through telemarketing. It is most effective when data, including all customer records, are available (preferably on computer) with access through the telemarketing center. When properly utilized, this application will allow cycling through customers on a regular basis to accomplish the following:

- cross-selling new products
- reactivating inactive accounts
- replenishing materials supply
- notification of special promotions, sales, volume discounts, etc.
- maintaining dialogue with key customers

Account management is a very proactive application and represents telemarketing in its most sophisticated form. To accomplish it, special consultants should be assigned, each managing his or her own segment of the customer file. As is the case with other telemarketing applications, those accounts deemed appropriate to manage this way is up to the criteria set by your own company.

Obviously, no telemarketing application will be clear cut. That is, the lines between application definitions will change as your telemarketing efforts mature and the needs of your market are identified. However, when developing an application, clear objectives should be set along with careful measurement criteria (covered later in this chapter). This will ensure that your telemarketing efforts are tracking along a planned and measured course.

Telemarketing Decisions: "In-House" Center or Commercial Telemarketing Services

Once you've decided how telemarketing fits into your marketing mix, the next question is how to implement the program. Aside from the promotional decisions, comes a decision of whether to fulfill "in house" or to use an outside service. Many companies of all sizes have successfully implemented their own telemarketing centers. This requires a commitment in terms of people and dollars, albeit initially a small dollar commitment can be made during the trial period. Oftentimes, companies will first try one or more telemarketing applications through a commercial service before bringing the applications in house. Let's look at the implications of both inside and outside telemarketing resources.

The In-House Telemarketing Center: An Ongoing Process

The single most important factor in establishing a telemarketing center is management commitment. Without an identified need and a commitment to meet this need, a telemarketing effort will surely fail. Organization and proper staffing of the center are essential to success.

Organization and Staffing

The people who run your telemarketing center are the key elements to its success. How effectively they function individually will have a direct bearing on the productivity and cost efficiency of the telemarketing program. For this reason, whether you hire new people or transfer present employees to staff the center, you should select them with care. The first qualities to look for are a pleasant voice and a helpful, personal-interest attitude. While you can provide training to fill in many gaps in an individual's knowledge, enthusiasm cannot be learned. And because telemarketing is a vehicle for selling, it is essential to seek people who demonstrate a natural sales ability and feel comfortable, act naturally, and speak articulately in a sales situation.

All members of your telemarketing staff should receive basic training in the methods and procedures to be used in operating the center as well as information about your company and its products or services. Your training program might include:

- Printed materials about the company and its history
- Brochures, pamphlets or catalogs about the company's products and their general history
- A tour of the plant, offices or showroom
- A demonstration of the product(s) or service(s), with explanation of main selling points, benefits, and features
- Meeting field sales and service people, if appropriate
- Visiting the shipping department
- Information about price lists, warranties, local, and national dealers

After the basic training program, a staff member may require additional instruction related to specific telemarketing functions to which he or she has been assigned, such as screening incoming calls, handling inquiries and service requests, taking orders, and managing credit.

The manager of the telemarketing center should above all be a person with sales and management abilities. This manager will be responsible not only for a sales force, but will also perform the role of coordinating all efforts with the advertising promotion department. The feedback from the telemarketing center to advertising will be a key factor in determining future promotional efforts for both inbound and outbound programs.

How to Set up Your Telemarketing Center

In setting up a productive telemarketing center your first consideration must be space. It is necessary to designate a specific area for the center within your office facilities that is used only for telemarketing activities. Specifying a particular area for the telemarketing center helps create a more organized and efficient work atmosphere. It reduces the problems of unnecessary noise, interruption, and distraction that can undermine the efforts of your telemarketing staff. Furthermore, the psychological effect of giving the staff their own area enhances their sense of professionalism.

The telemarketing center can be located in part of a general office, if space is limited. But when facilities permit, a separate office should be allocated for the center. It can be furnished with individual communicating booths for the telemarketing staff. Such booths, lined with acoustical tile and separated by glass upper-partitions, will provide a quiet working area and a sense of privacy without isolation.

It is essential for each member of the telemarketing staff to have an individual working area, equipped with:

- A desk and chair
- Adequate file space
- Sufficient lighting
- Basic telephone equipment, such as local telephone, an 800 line, RCF (Remote Call Forwarding) line, and/or WATS line.

There also must be enough space for the information and materials used in telemarketing activities. The staff should have convenient access to catalogs, price sheets, estimating guides, production schedules, and other related product or service data, as well as sales records, prospect and customer information, and a supply of record-keeping forms. If your systems are computerized, each member of the staff should have access to a terminal to provide timely data and transmission during calls.

An efficient way to deal with calls coming into and going out of your telemarketing center is to handle them according to function.

**Exhibit 10-3. Typical Telemarketing Center
Functional Organization Plan**

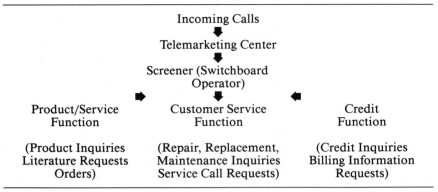

Individuals could be given responsibility for handling different types of incoming calls: product or service inquiries, customer assistance requests, or credit-related calls. With a smaller telemarketing staff, individuals can handle several tasks, coordinating the taking and placing of calls to make the most of slow periods and down-time. Make sure your telemarketing staff knows the procedure for dealing with each type of call.

Capacity Planning

The productivity of your telemarketing center will, to a large degree, rest on how you plan and manage the inbound and outbound contacts that add up to capacity. As the chart in Exhibit 10-4 demonstrates, once you have determined your monthly capacity, you must then decide how the telemarketing specialists will spend their time to accomplish the number and type of telemarketing contacts you have determined.

In Exhibit 10-4, the capacity stated for June was 6,000 contacts. It was assumed that 1,000 contacts would consist of customer service and scheduling sales appointments. An additional 2,000 contacts could be made to open new accounts in the target market. Because of an advertising campaign, 2,000 in-coming contacts were projected for order taking, and 1,000 for lead handling. While these capacity figures will fluctuate and must be monitored for efficiency, it is important that a careful plan be developed so the center can be managed in a productive manner.

Once the capacity has been planned, the telemarketing specialists' time should be scheduled accordingly. In this example, we have 6,000 total contacts. If we assume, for example, that each specialist can handle 25 contacts per day, Table 10-1 illustrates distribution of time.

Table 10-1. Capacity Analysis: June

# of Specialists	# of Business Days	# of Contacts per Day per Specialist	Total Capacity
10	24	25	6,000

Although it requires a commitment and expense, the many benefits a telemarketing center can bring to your business include:

• Increased sales, profits and market share, usually directly measurable
• Decreased cost of doing business, also directly measurable
• Improved customer service, the cost of which may be displaced through reductions of service visits and correspondence, fewer product returns, increased sales of collateral products and services
• Enhanced public image
• Increased management efficiency, as improved feedback results in more timely, better targeted marketing

Let's look at how some companies have instituted their own telemarketing programs.

American Express Catalog Sales handles about 1.5 million orders a year. Fifty percent of those are received by phone. The merchandise ranges from plain high-ticket items to fancy high-tech products. Five

Exhibit 10-4. Telemarketing Capacity Planning Chart

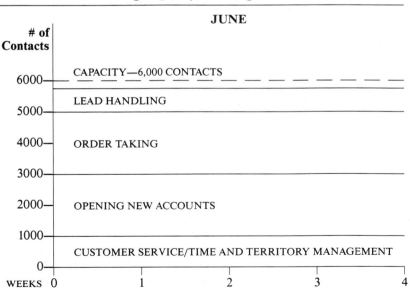

years after the telemarketing program began, American Express had increased sales from $29 million to more than $115 million.

B. F. Goodrich uses telemarketing to help establish itself as a leader in the chemical industry because of its product differentiation and top-quality service. Its telemarketing program has helped to reduce the size of its field sales force by 25 percent and has cut its sales/ordering costs by roughly $250,000 in one year.

J. C. Penney Life Insurance has an "800" number to answer inquiries about Penney's insurance programs in general or personal policies in particular. Not only has the company enjoyed major sales increases through telemarketing, but this program reinforces the credibility of their direct mail orders. Customer service representatives handle about 14,000 of these calls each week.

Olan Mills, a family owned chain of photography studios, uses telemarketing to set up appointments for sittings. Years ago, it replaced its door-to-door salesmen with a phone operation. Prior to the switch-over, the company had 30 studios. Today it has 550 with sales of over $100 million a year.

Montgomery Ward Insurance Group has an outbound telephone selling program that brings in about $150 million worth of life insurance sales a year. In addition, its "800" number is featured in all advertising and policyholder communications. In one year, more than 360,000 calls were received.

Whirlpool puts an 800 number on every appliance, warranty, use and care guide, and in all its sales literature. Customers are encouraged to call with questions or problems. The company estimates that it saved its customers about a half million dollars on repair and service calls. And the company itself saved nearly $200,000 on unnecessary visits to customers who were still under warranty.

Digital Equipment Corporation uses telemarketing for order processing. Its catalogs generate about 14,000 calls a month for computer accessories and supplies. The company claims that its market is expanding so rapidly that, without telemarketing, it would not be able to keep up with that expansion.

Great North American Stationers Inc. uses telemarketing to sell desk-top supplies, via an inside sales force. In less than 10 years, the company has grown from $25,000 to $14 million in sales.

Hickory Farms markets corporate gift packs using direct mail and followup phone calls. During the Christmas selling season sales increased by 47 percent. One in every seven letters resulted in a sale—a rousing response rate of more than 14 percent.

IBM employs telemarketing to sell office equipment and supplies. Its sophisticated telemarketing center performs several functions: order processing, lead qualification, outbound followup to unclosed sales, marginal account handling. Results? Increased sales force productivity and reduced selling costs.

The Commercial Telemarketing Service

Many marketers find the services of professional telephone sales agencies preferable to internal operations. The professional telephone marketer can help implement a campaign and assist in structuring initial goals in the same way an advertising agency applies its experience to guide a client.

An outside telephone sales operation should be examined in the same manner you would consider the services of the advertising agency, direct mail supplier, or media consultant. Ask the same questions and set the same standards for that company's personnel as you would apply to your own people.

Has the company shown a creative talent and expertise in telephone selling? How much help are they willing to give? Will they merely pick up the phone and say what you tell them to say? Or will they come up with worthwhile suggestions for a return on investment?

A list of past clients is always a good indication of just how effective any telephone marketing agency will be. Is their experience broad-based? Have they completed projects for well-known, reputable clients? Do they know your business and how best to reach your audience?

What are the limitations of their calling capacity? Will the company be able to meet time, location, and volume requirements? And, does the service this agency offers meet your needs effectively and at a cost-effective level? Many professional telephone marketing companies utilize a network of home workers, and other part-time personnel who make calls from their home phones. While this type of call operation can be less expensive, fully staffed central workshops with local WATS lines often produce higher response rates that offset incremental costs.

Some of the benefits of using a commercial service include:

- Flexibility in changing capacity, since most such firms have access to additional lines
- Less expense for setup of equipment, since it is already in place
- Inexpensive trial applications can be tested prior to full-scale setup
- Immediate telemarketing expertise available

One of the leading telephone sales agencies in the U.S. is CCI (Campaign Communications Institute). Their chairman, Murray Roman, pioneered commercial telemarketing. Among the many innovations Roman developed was the taped message. Here is the technique. The live communicator makes a brief introduction and gives a statement as to the reason for the call. He then tells the prospect that a prominent, authoritative, or notable person—whose name, of course, is clearly mentioned—has prepared a special taped message. The caller emphasizes that the taped message will take no more than two minutes to play.

In this approach, the call is being taken out of the level of a salesperson approach. The prospect personally is asked to listen. He then gives permission to hear someone he has heard of, relates to, perhaps respects or even idolizes. Many notable persons have made such tapes in support of business interests or to help nonprofit, philanthropic organizations raise funds. The list of those whose tapes have helped in selling is long. It includes, to name but a few, movie star Charlton Heston, editor Norman Cousins, civic leader Bess Myerson, broadcaster Betty Furness, investment counselor Gustave Levy, President Richard Cremer of the Montgomery Ward Auto Club, Vice-President Robert Meyers of American Express, and Dr. Jerry Caulder for Monsanto.

On a business-to-business sales level, the effect of the personal call plus the taped message can be maximized when it is made by a national sales manager, a board chairman, or an industry-recognized consultant.

This peer relationship between a calling executive and a called decision maker, gives the prospect a feeling that he is talking with a knowledgeable authority rather than simply with an order taker. The technique serves also to function like the printed or broadcast endorsement, even when the tape maker simply talks about the virtue of the product, service, or cause without specifically saying, "I use it."

Here is an actual example of a script that has been used successfully. It opens with the communicator's introduction, followed by the taped message, and closes with the communicator's return to the line for the purpose of obtaining the order:

Hello. This is David Jones, of the Bell & Howell Business Equipment Group. I'm using this special telephone message approach because I'd like to bring to your attention, as directly as I can, an important new breakthrough in automated banking systems.

Over the years, we at Bell & Howell have been concerned with the needs of many banks that cannot justify the cost of large and elaborate equipment to handle statement rendering and mailing efficiently, accurately, and economically. I believe, based on our sales to banks of smaller or similar size, that our new Matchmaker 2, specially designed to handle your volume of demand deposit accounts, can provide just this type of streamlined statement handling at a cost that may well be significantly lower than what you can incur in your present manual system. Here's how it works:

The new Matchmaker 2 and one operator are all that you need to automate your statement rendering and mailing system. In a fraction of the time that the costly hand method takes, the Matchmaker 2 automatically counts the number of transactions and matches checks, deposit slips, statements, and special inserts, then stuffs and seals envelopes, ready for mailing. Designed to handle an average of three to four hundred statements per hour, the Matchmaker 2 gets statements in the mail on time every month. And because it's from Bell & Howell, any user is assured of continuous, efficient performance and dependable service.

So that you may judge its value and application for your bank's special requirements, our telephone communicator will be happy to arrange to have one of our representatives call on you at a time that is convenient. I hope you'll take this opportunity to consider the new Matchmaker 2 but, in any case, thank you for taking the time to listen.

The use of standardized, quality-controlled tape represents something more than just a technique suitable for use via telephone. It epitomizes the entire concept of the vital distinction between modern telemarketing and mere "selling over the telephone."

Measurement and Analysis of Results

In the past, the telephone has been viewed as an overhead expense to be reduced, rather than a revenue-generating tool. This makes the need to track and report the results of your telemarketing efforts as important as any other sales or promotional process. Further, telemarketing, like any direct response medium, can and should be measured to ensure that the effort is being managed efficiently.

A record-keeping procedure is perhaps the most important element of your telemarketing center's operating system. In order to monitor and evaluate your telemarketing efforts, it is first necessary to record the information related to each customer call. A customer call record, such as the one shown earlier in this chapter, will simplify this job and ensure that all necessary data is recorded. In many cases, it is helpful to use carboned, triplicate forms. This allows the telemarketing staff member to place the original in a master file of all customers contacted, and retain one copy for reference when recontacting the customer in the future. The third copy is then used as the basis of an evaluation system for your telemarketing program. The data contained in your customer call records provides you with concrete evidence of just how productively and cost efficiently you are selling your existing customers.

To be of real value, customer call records must be kept accurately and maintained for every customer contacted, regardless of whether or not the call resulted in a sale. Otherwise, it is impossible to measure with precision the profitability of these calls.

There are two broad areas that must be measured and evaluated to ensure the success of the telemarketing effort. Those are quantitative and qualitative.

Quantitative Measurement

Quantitative factors are the directly measurable variables that result from the promotion and sales processes of a telemarketing campaign. Examples of these would be:

- Number of calls generated from a campaign
- Number of calls handled by the telemarketing center
- Number of calls handled by each telemarketing specialist
- Number of sales and dollar volume of sales
- Average revenue per sale
- Distribution of sales, product line analysis
- Sales conversion rate for lead generation programs
- Revenue to expense ratios

The quantitative data captured from your telemarketing effort will be the basis of reports to management on how the program is performing. The specific data captured and reported must be a reflection of your program's goals.

Qualitative Measurement

Qualitative factors are indirectly measurable through both analysis of quantitative variables and observations of the center's day-to-day performance. Rather than measuring the performance of the specific numbers, these factors will measure the productivity of the center's operation and the promotion's effectiveness. Examples of these variables would be:

- Ability of individual telemarketing specialists to consult or cross-sell
- Efficiency of management of telemarketing center's capacity
- Productivity of center and staff
- Appropriateness of critical elements of promotional message
- Efficiency of inbound and outbound calling plan
- Effectiveness of target market selection

The qualitative factors are every bit as important as the quantitative ones. If they are not met, poor performance of the directly measurable factors (the quantitative factors) will surely result.

Telemarketing is a sophisticated, efficient medium that can dramatically optimize your bottom line profit goals. The key to the success of a telemarketing program is careful *planning, execution,* and *measurement.*

Self-Quiz

1. Define telemarketing.

_____

_____

_____

2. What are the four functions of telemarketing?

a. _____   c. _____

b. _____   d. _____

3. The more common way to launch telemarketing is by utilizing the
☐ Inbound Process   ☐ Outbound Process.

4. Give three examples of common inbound telemarketing applications.

a. _____

b. _____

c. _____

5. Give three examples of common outbound telemarketing applications.

a. _____

b. _____

c. _____

6. What is meant by capacity planning?

_____

_____

_____

_____

7. Name at least three things that should be asked of a commercial telemarketing service before hiring them.

a. _____

b. _____

c. _____

8. What is the theory behind the taped telephone message?

_____

_____

_____

9. Name at least five quantitative factors that should be measured in a telemarketing campaign.

a. _____

b. _____

c. _____

d. _____

e. _____

10. Name at least five qualitative factors that should be analyzed as a result of a telemarketing program.

a. _____

b. _____

c. _____

d. _____

e. _____

Pilot Project

You are the marketing director of an envelope company. You have a customer base of 100,000 small business firms, all secured by direct mail. You have decided to test the efficiency of telemarketing.

Your assignment is to develop a telemarketing test plan. In developing the plan, please answer the following questions.

1. Will you use a commercial organization to structure your test, or will you structure the test in-house? And why?

2. What data, or measures will you use to estimate when inventories might be depleted for each customer?

3. What information might you request from each customer in the process of your calls?

4. What special offers might you make in an effort to get repeat business by telephone?

Section III
Creating and Producing
Direct Marketing

Chapter Eleven

Techniques of Creating Direct Mail Packages

Direct mail is an expensive advertising medium. It costs you 15 to 20 times as much to reach a person with a direct mail package as it does to reach him with a 30-second TV commercial or a full-page ad in a newspaper. But direct mail has certain unique advantages that more than compensate for its higher cost. If you understand what these advantages are and use them properly, you will be able to bring in orders or responses at a cost equal to or below that of space or broadcast. And, as a general rule, customers acquired by direct mail are usually better customers in terms of repeat business than those acquired by space or broadcast advertising.

Selectivity

Through careful list selections and segmentation, direct mail can give you pinpoint selectivity unmatched by any other advertising medium. You can literally pick out households one by one, mailing only to those that are the best prospects for your offer. The fundamentals of list selection and segmentation are discussed in Chapter 5. Review these carefully.

Virtually Unlimited Choice of Formats

In direct mail, you are not restricted to 30 seconds of time or a 7 x 10 page. You can use large, lavishly illustrated brochures. You can have any number of inserts. You can use pop-ups, fold-outs, swatches—even enclose a phonograph record. What you can do is limited only by your imagination and budget constraints. For example, one enterprising mailer used a unique response device: he mailed a carrier pigeon to each prospect. The respondent taped his reply to the pigeon's leg and released the pigeon. The mailer didn't even have to pay a return postage charge!

Personal Character

Even though you mail in the millions, you are still mailing individual pieces to individually addressed human beings. Every recipient knows that an ad or TV commercial was not created specifically for him, but for a mass audience. Direct mail approaches the prospect on a personal level that, with personalized letters, even extends to a greeting by name. As any salesperson will agree, you can sell much better when you are talking to an individual rather than to people en masse.

No Competition

In most advertising media, the advertising is an adjunct, not the main reason the person is watching the TV channel or reading the magazine. In direct mail, advertising arrives all by itself to be opened and read at the recipient's leisure. When it is read, there is nothing to compete with it for your prospect's attention.

Most Testable Medium

With direct mail you can virtually simulate laboratory conditions for testing. You control exactly when the mail is dropped; you control exactly who gets which test package. Many magazines and newspapers can give you an A/B split; direct mail will give you as many "splits" as you care to have.

Unique Capability to Involve the Recipient

Direct mail offers a wide choice of devices that involve the recipient, such as tokens, stamps, questionnaires, and quizzes. And with direct mail, you can literally get the recipient to "talk back" to you—to open a dialogue—by asking him questions and giving him space to respond on the reply device.

Selecting the Format

Because direct mail offers an unlimited choice of format, a good place to start is deciding which basic format you wish to use. There are three basic formats to choose from:

The *classic format* utilizes a separate outer or mailing envelope. The size of that envelope, the material from which it is made (paper, plastic, foil), and the number of colors in which it is printed can vary widely. And what goes inside that envelope can vary even more widely. Classic formats range from simple, dignified, businesslike letters (Exhib-

it 11-1) to lavish packages stuffed with brochures, inserts, gift circulars—
even pop-ups and phonograph records (Exhibit 11-2). The classic format
is the most personal of the direct mail formats. For this reason, it almost
always includes a separate letter, either preprinted or personalized.

The *self-mailer* does not have an outer envelope. These mailers
vary from a single sheet of paper folded once for mailing to wonderfully
complex pieces with multiple sheets and preformed reply envelopes
(Exhibit 11-3). Generally, a self-mailer comes off the press complete,
ready to address and mail. As a rule, self-mailers are less expensive than
classic mailing packages. There is only one component to produce and
no inserting needed since the piece is completed on press.

Exhibit 11-1. A Classic Direct Mail Format

*The "classic
format" in direct
mail uses a
separate outer or
carrier envelope.
It can be quite
simple and
businesslike.*

Exbibit 11-2. Expanded Classic Direct Mail Format

The "classic format" can also be lavish, exciting, and packed with different pieces, as illustrated by this mailing by American Family Publishers.

Exbibit 11-2. Expanded Classic Direct Mail Format

Exhibit 11-3. Self-Mailer

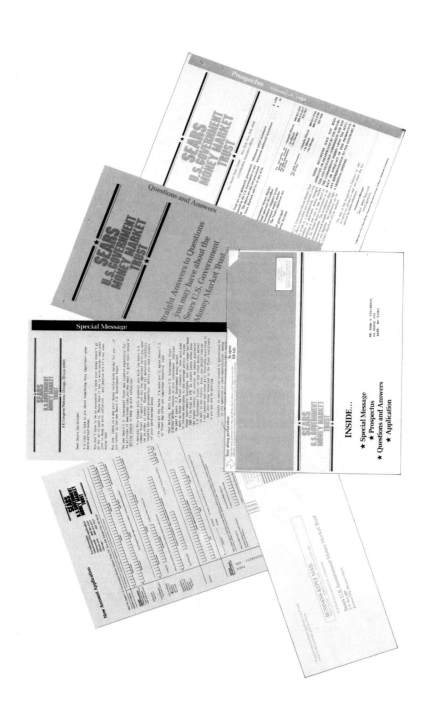

Shown here, a self-mailer, produced on one pass through the press. When opened, it "breaks apart" into a letter, question-and-answer sheet, prospectus, application, and even a pre-formed reply envelope.

The *catalog* is literally a magazine, with up to many hundreds of pages, stitched, glued, or perfect-bound. Catalogs require a highly specialized format, and their use is subject to many important guidelines. Catalogs are discussed in detail in Chapter 12.

No discussion of direct mail formats would be complete without mentioning some of the specialized devices that are used regularly in direct mail.

Involvement devices include stamps, tokens, rub-offs, sealed envelopes—one company even used a jigsaw puzzle that the recipient had to put together. Regardless of the format you use, reader involvement can make it dramatically more effective. If you get the reader involved with your offer and message, you're well on your way to a sale (Exhibit 11-4). A most effective way to get the reader involved is to include a product sample or swatch in the mailing. Obviously this device is not suitable for all types of merchandise, but nothing beats letting somebody touch, feel, and try what you're selling.

Specialized devices include die-cut shapes, tip-ons, and pop-ups. These can be great attention-getters. But be careful: you don't want to let the "gimmick" take the reader's attention from your basic sales message. One company tested an elaborate (and expensive) pop-up device and found that the mailing actually pulled better without it! The pop-up was stealing attention from the mailer's message.

In connection with formats, there are several tried-and-true variations you should consider for your mailing package.

The *second letter,* or "publisher's letter" (Exhibit 11-5), has become almost a "must" in direct mail today. Repeated testing indicates that such a letter boosts response 10 percent or more. This is either a folded letter or a letter in a separate sealed envelope that warns sternly: "Open this letter *only* if you have decided not to respond to this offer." Of course everybody opens it immediately. This gives you the chance to do a little extra selling, primarily in reassuring the prospect that he really has nothing to lose and everything to gain in accepting your offer.

The *closed-face envelope* (Exhibit 11-6) has the name and address of the recipient "typed" right on the envelope; there is no window or "slot" through which the name shows. Inside there are two or three other pieces (letters, applications) on which the recipient's name, address, and other information are also "typed." The mailing looks like a secretary typed it individually, but not so: these ingenious mailings are run on computer, then the outer envelope is literally folded around the pieces inside. Because they look so personal, closed-face packages are rarely discarded without opening.

Invitation formats have been around for a long time (see Exhibit 11-7). But they are very effective, especially for publishers, club memberships, and credit card solicitations. The format simulates a formal invitation ("You are invited to accept . . ."). The outside of the invitation usually carries a letter explaining the offer. Naturally, an RSVP—a call to action—is included in the mailing.

The *simulated telegram* is less formal but carries a lot of urgency (see Exhibit 11-8). It's popular as a followup mailing or part of a renewal series and has worked well for credit card solicitation, insurance, and loans-by-mail offers. The simulated telegram is usually printed on yellow stock and, more often than not, is computer-filled. (Caution: the basic telegram format is copyrighted by Western Union. You are not allowed to "lift" it.)

Exhibit 11-4. Involvement Device

A typical involvement device: the reader is asked to lift the simulated credit card from the top of the application and place it on the lower part to "validate" the application.

Exhibit 11-5. The Publisher's Letter

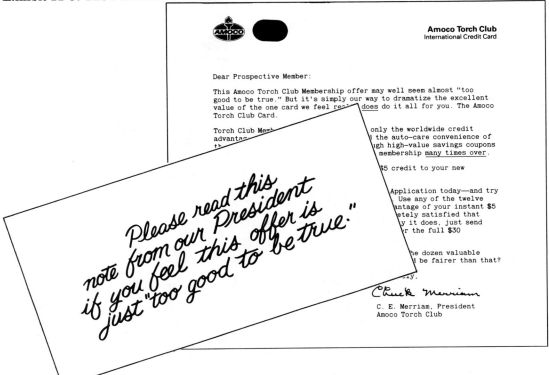

The "publisher's letter" or "second letter" has become a proven results booster in direct mail today.

Exhibit 11-6. Closed-Face Envelope

The "closed-face" envelope has no slot or window through which the recipient's name shows. It looks like it was personally typed, but it's actually a computer letter with the envelope "folded" around the contents.

Exhibit 11-7. The Invitation Format

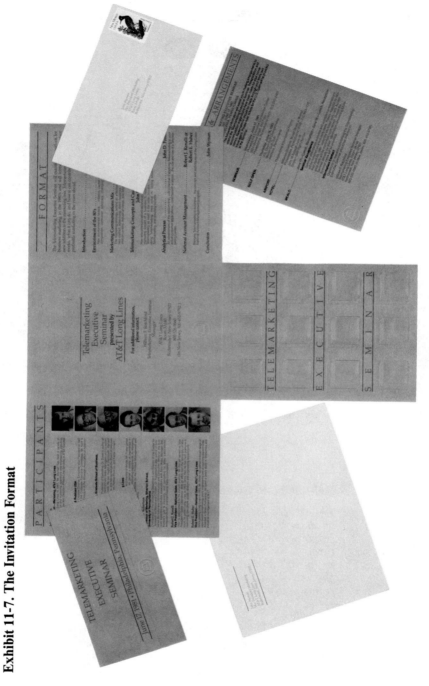

Invitation formats remain an effective technique. After all, who can turn down an invitation?

Exhibit 11-8. The Simulated Telegram

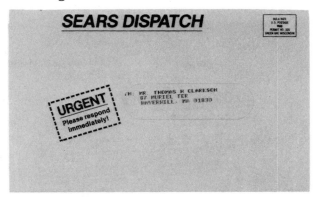

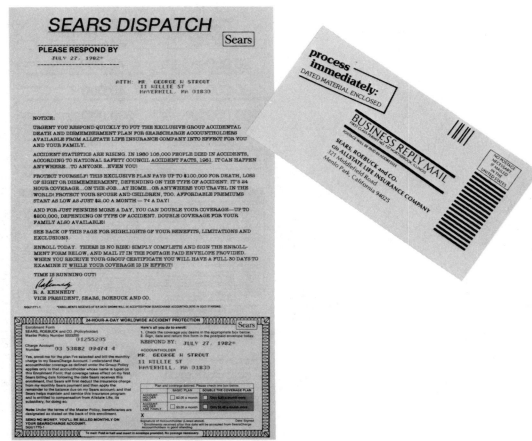

The "simulated telegram" mailing copies the look and urgency of a telegram.

Exhibit 11-9. Personalized Letters

Personalized letters appear to be individually typed. New personalization techniques can vary the size and face of the type, and "laser" personalization permits economical small-run personalization.

Personalization is common today regardless of what format you use. Personalization is done by computer, by ink-jet imaging or by laser printing (Exhibit 11-9). Each method has its advantages and its particular requirements. Each method requires specific preparation of materials, so you would be well advised to seek professional production help if you are planning a personalized mailing.

When you run into somebody who tells you that personalized letters "always" outpull nonpersonalized ones, be skeptical. In my experience, personalized letters *usually* outpull nonpersonalized ones, but not always. Also, they have to outpull by enough to pay for the extra cost of personalization. When you use personalization, use all the information you can. But don't scatter the person's name indiscriminately throughout the letter. A good rule to follow is to write a personalized letter as you would write a letter to any person you know fairly well.

Which format for your mailing piece? That depends. It depends on your budget. It depends on whom you're trying to reach. Do you want a package that will stand out on the businessman's desk? Or is it something designed for leisurely reading by the consumer at home? If you're not sure, you should use the classic format with a separate outer envelope and a separate letter. The great preponderance of direct mail today uses this format, and while it is more expensive than a self-mailer, it will usually pull better.

One further caution on formats: postal regulations, which govern the mailability of any given piece, change regularly. You are well advised to check the layout of your mailing piece with your local post office before you produce it. There are few things in life more disheartening than a phone call that begins: "This is the post office, and we're holding your mail because . . . ."

The Creative Process

Now that we have the product or service, our offer (proposition) and our format, we're ready to create the mailing piece. Right? Wrong. And therein lies a basic failing in a lot of direct mail produced today. The writer is too anxious to dash to his typewriter, and the artist is too anxious to get to his drawing board. Why does this occur? Marketing is "work," but creative effort is *fun,* and we all tend to do what we like to do. But unless the creative work is grounded in good, solid marketing, it is not going to work—or at least, not as well as it should.

The key word is *discipline.* Creative work must be disciplined, or it ends up trying to be all things to all people and, in reality, becomes nothing to anybody.

How do creative people gain this discipline? With hard work—work that is done before one word of copy is written or one piece of the mailing is designed. Listen to Gene Schwartz, a professional direct response writer, as he describes how he "listens first with my ears, and then with my eyes":

> "Listen with your ears . . . and your eyes"
>
> 1. Sit down with the owner of the product—the man who's hiring you—and pump hell out of him. Put it on a tape recorder and have him talk for three or four hours.
>
> Ask him where the product comes from, what it does, what are its problems and how he's tried to cure them, why it's better than its competitors, who likes it, who doesn't like it, what proof he's got that it works, what strange uses people have got out of it, what funny stories he has accumulated in regard to its manufacture or use, what problems he was trying to solve when he created it, how he would improve it if he had unlimited money, what causes most of his refunds, who works for him to help him make it, how it is made, how he keeps up the quality, who writes him what about it, etc.
>
> 2. Talk to his customers. Do it in person, or on paper. See if they agree with him. If they don't, find out why.
>
> 3. Listen to his competitors. They often tell you more about the opportunities they're missing in their ads than the opportunities they're seeing and therefore seizing. Let them write a possible head or two for you—out of the body copy of their ads.
>
> 4. Then put all the material down, in one big pile, and underline it. Start blending it together, like you'd make a cake. Give first priority to your head and subheads, then the body claims. And then type it up, preferably adding little of yourself except as selector and condenser.
>
> Direct response creative pros use a variety of techniques for approaching the moment of truth. But they all have one thing in common: They dig, dig, dig. The hack, on the other hand, just sits down to write. Miracle performances don't happen by accident—they're created.

The Copywriter as Salesperson Listen to Don Kanter, long-time vice president of Stone & Adler, who has a unique way of describing some copywriters. "The trouble with many copywriters," he says, "is that they think their job is to write copy." Kanter quickly explains this by adding, "That is equivalent to a salesperson saying, 'My job is to talk.' The job is not to 'talk.' For a writer, the job is not to 'write.' For both, the job is to *sell*. Selling is the end result; writing is merely the means a copywriter uses to reach that end. This is true of all advertising copywriting; it is especially true of direct response copywriting because the writer is usually the only salesperson with whom the prospect will ever come in contact. If he or she doesn't make the sale, there is nobody else to do it."

The Benefit/ Price/Value Equation

To sell effectively, the direct response writer must know why people buy. They buy, essentially, when they consider something to have value. This is often expressed in a simple equation: benefit divided by price equals value. In other words, every time a person is confronted with a buying decision, he subconsciously assigns a worth to the benefits he perceives. At the same time, he assigns a worth to the price he must pay. And subjectively, very subconsciously, he divides one into the other to reach his buying decision. If, in his mind, the benefits outweigh the price, he will buy. If the price outweighs the benefits, he will not buy.

What is Price?

To most people, *price* is the monetary amount asked for the goods or services being sold: the $29.95, or $39.95, or $5.00 per month, or whatever. But there is more to price than that. There's time. We are asking the customer to wait before he or she can enjoy the benefits of what he or she buys. There's the factor of buying the product sight unseen (unlike retail purchasing, where you can see, touch, and often try what you are buying). There's a factor of buying from a company the customer may not know. There's the risk that the product or service may not deliver the benefits that have been promised. In direct marketing, all of these are part of the price that must be paid. While we may not be able to do much about the actual price (the $29.95, or $39.95, or $5.00 a month), we can (and we must) do everything possible to reduce the other factors of price to the minimum.

How? By using the proven techniques that direct marketing has pioneered:

- Testimonials
- Guarantees
- Free trial offers or cancellation privileges
- Reassurance about the stature and reliability of the selling company

What is a Benefit?

Let's assume we are selling a stereo system. This system has two three-way speakers, each with a big "woofer" and "tweeter" and a mid-range. That's a benefit. Right? Wrong. That's a selling point or product feature. It's a distinction that every writer must recognize and keep in mind. A benefit is something that affects the customer personally. It exists apart from the merchandise or service itself. A selling point or product feature is something in the product or service that makes possible and supports the benefit. Our stereo system with two three-way speaker systems is a selling point. It is a quality in the product itself. That I can enjoy lifelike, three-dimensional sound is the benefit. It is this benefit that affects me personally. This benefit is made possible by the fact that this stereo system has two three-way speakers. Remember, it is the benefit that the customer really wants to have. It is the selling point that proves to him that he can really have it.

Translate Selling Points into Benefits

Before you write any copy, therefore, it is very important to dig out every selling point you can and translate each selling point into a customer benefit. The more benefits the customer perceives (i.e., the more benefits you can point out to him), the more likely he will buy. Here's an example. Suppose you're writing copy to sell a portable counter-top dishwasher. These are some of the selling points in this merchandise. And alongside each is the benefit which that selling point makes possible:

Selling Point	Benefit
1. Has a 10-minute operating cycle.	1. Does a load of dishes in 10 minutes; gets you out of the kitchen faster.
2. Measures 18 inches in diameter.	2. Small enough to fit on a counter-top; doesn't take up valuable floor space.
3. Transparent plastic top.	3. Lets you watch the washing cycle; you know when the dishes are done.
4. Has universal hose coupling.	4. Fits any standard kitchen faucet; attaches and detaches in seconds.

Copy Strategy and Basic Human Wants

With your benefits down on paper, you now have to decide on the copy strategy or the appeals that will do the best selling job. Creative people refer to this in different ways. Some talk about how you "position" the product in the prospect's mind. Others refer to "coming up with the big idea" behind the copy. What is it about your offer and benefit story that is most appealing? When you stop to think about it, people respond to any given proposition for one of two reasons: to gain something they do not have or to avoid losing something they now possess. As you can see from the accompanying chart, basic human wants can be divided into these two categories. The professional copywriter carefully sifts and weighs the list of basic human wants to determine the main appeal of his proposition. (In Chapter 13 you'll see how the same product can be slanted to employ many different appeals just by changing your headline.):

The desire to gain:	The desire to avoid loss:
To make money	To avoid cricitism
To save time	To keep possessions
To avoid effort	To avoid physical pain
To achieve comfort	To avoid loss of reputation
To have health	To avoid loss of money
To be popular	To avoid trouble
To enjoy pleasure	
To be clean	
To be praised	
To be in style	
To gratify curiosity	
To satisfy an appetite	
To have beautiful possessions	
To attract the opposite sex	
To be an individual	
To emulate others	
To take advantage of opportunities	

Eleven Guidelines to Good Copy

Does your proposition offer the promise of saving time and avoiding hard or disagreeable work? Most people like to avoid work. Saving time is almost a fetish of the American people. Appeal to this basic want, if you can.

Does your proposition help people feel important? People like to keep up with the Joneses. People like to be made to feel that they are part of a select group. A tremendous number of people are susceptible to snob appeal. Perhaps you can offer a terrific bargain by mail and capitalize on the appeal of saving money. The desire to "get it wholesale" is very strong.

Don Kanter uses these guidelines as checkpoints for good, professional copy:

1. Does the writer know his product? Has he or she dug out every selling point and benefit?

2. Does the writer know his market? Is he or she aiming the copy at the most likely prospects rather than at the world in general?

3. Is the writer talking to the prospect in language that the prospect will understand?

4. Does the writer make a promise to the prospect, then prove that he or she can deliver what was promised?

5. Does the writer get to the point at once? Does he or she make that all-important promise right away?

6. Is the copy, especially the headlines and lead paragraphs, germane and specific to the selling proposition?

7. Is the copy concise? There is a great temptation to overwrite, especially in direct mail.

8. Is the copy logical and clear? Does it "flow" from point to point?

9. Is the copy enthusiastic? Does the writer obviously believe in what he or she is selling?

10. Is the copy complete? Are all the questions answered, especially obvious ones like size and color?

11. Is the copy designed to sell? Or is it designed to impress the reader with the writer's ability? If somebody says "that's a great mailing," you've got the wrong reaction. What you want to hear is, "That's a great product (or service). I'd love to have it."

Finally, you might consider this outline for a creative strategy, which organizes the information about the product or service into a *disciplined* format. Remember: to be useful, this outline must be *written*.

Outline for a Creative Strategy

- *The product.* What it is, what it does, how it works, what it costs, what its features are, what its *benefits* are, what makes it different, what makes it better—even what its weaknesses are.
- *Competitive products.* How they compare with ours in terms of features, benefits, and price.
- *The market.* How big is it and what share of it do we have? Who buys the product today and why? Who else *should* buy it and why? Who are our present customers and future prospects in terms of demographic characteristics, such as age, sex, marital status, income, and education. Who are they in psychographic terms? Are they liberal or conservative, avante garde or traditional?
- *The media.* What's going to carry our message? If space or broadcast media are to be used, which ones, how often, and in what space or time units? If direct mail is the only medium, what lists will we be using—specifically or in general? What do we know or assume about quantities, formats, colors?
- *The budget.* What limitations should govern our creative thinking in terms of creative staff time, layout costs, photography, illustrations, production costs?
- *Objectives.* As specifically as possible, what are we trying to *do,* in terms of overall goals and specific goals, in accordance with the total program, and in line with specific components within the program? Among all possible goals, what are our priorities? Which ones are primary and vital; which are secondary and merely desirable; which are nice but expendable?
- *Creative implementation.* How do we propose to organize what we know or assume about the product, the competition, and the market

to achieve our stated objectives? How will we position the product? What relative emphasis will we give to product features and product benefits? What do we anticipate as our central copy theme? How will it be executed visually? And how will it be orchestrated among various elements of the program? Most important of all from a response standpoint, what will our offer be and how will it be dramatized?

How your creative strategy document addresses these questions, the order in which you address them, and the format in which you cast them are all minor matters. They can be varied according to circumstances. When the creative strategy is thoroughly digested by both the writer and the artist, they both have a good idea of what the mailing package should accomplish, how, and why.

The Interdependence of Copy and Art

The copywriter has traditionally played the basic role in creating direct mail advertising. But thankfully, this is changing, and in more and more shops the art director is assuming his rightful place as co-creator, with the writer, of direct mail advertising. It is the art director who brings concepts to life. It is the art director who devises graphics that command the reader's attention. It is the art director who leads the reader through the various pieces of the mailing package so that the copywriter's words will have the greatest possible impact.

The direct marketing art director is different from those found in general advertising. Like the direct marketing writer, the direct marketing art director knows that the purpose of the work he designs is to *sell,* and his professional efforts are pointed to that end. For example, his choice of typography is *not* based on what typeface is "hot" at the Art Director's Club this month. It is based on what personality the typefaces must express—whether they must shout or whisper; whether they are hard-edged or soft, bold or refined. Likewise his use of color, photography, and illustration.

Creating the Classic Mailing Package

Now that we've looked at formats and discussed copy, let's turn to the individual pieces in a so-called classic mailing package.

The Outer Envelope

The outer envelope, or carrier envelope (Exhibit 11-10), has one job: to get itself opened. To accomplish this, the envelope can use many techniques:

- It can dazzle the reader with color, with graphics—and with promises of important benefits (including wealth, in the case of sweepstakes offers) if the reader will only open it.

- It can impress the reader with its simplicity and lead him to believe that the contents must be very important.
- It can tease the reader and so excite his curiosity that he simply must open it.

To help accomplish its purpose, the envelope can be the traditional paper envelope (perhaps with extra cut-outs or "windows"), or it can be made of transparent polyethelene or foil. Whatever it's made of, and whatever it says, the outer envelope sets the tone of your mailing. It must harmonize with the materials inside.

The Brochure

As noted, most mailing packages require a good brochure or circular in addition to a letter. It can be a small, two-color affair or a beautiful, giant circular that's almost as big as a tablecloth. But the job it has to do is the same, and it deserves your best creative effort.

One way or another your circular has to do a complete selling job. To give yourself every chance for success, review the appearance, content, and preparation of your circular. The following is a handy checklist for this purpose.

Appearance
1. Is the circular designed for the market you are trying to reach?
2. Is the presentation suited to the product or service you are offering?
3. Is the circular consistent with the rest of the mailing package?

Content
4. Is there a big idea behind your circular?
5. Do your headlines stick to the key offer?
6. Is your product or service dramatized to its best advantage by format and/or presentation?
7. Do you show broadly adaptable examples of your product or service in use?
8. Does your entire presentation follow a logical sequence and tell a complete story—including price, offer, and guarantee?

Preparation
9. Can the circular be cut out of regular size paper stock?
10. Is the quality of paper stock in keeping with the presentation?
11. Is color employed judiciously to show the product or service in its best light?

The Order Form

If Ernest Hemingway had been a direct response writer, he probably would have dubbed the order form "the moment of truth." Many prospects make a final decision on whether to respond after reading it. Some even read the order form before anything else in the envelope because they know it's the easiest way to find out what's being offered at what price. The best advice I can offer on order forms comes from

Exhibit 11-10. Various Envelope Formats

The outer envelope can be vibrant and exciting . . .

dignified and businesslike . . .

or it can tease the reader.

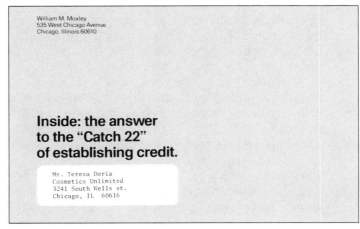

Henry Cowen, a direct marketing specialist. He says, "There are direct mail manuals around that recommend simple, easy-to-read order forms, but my experience indicates the mailer is far better off with a busy, rather jumbled appearance and plenty of copy. Formal and legal-looking forms that appear valuable, too valuable to throw away, are good." The key words in Cowen's statement are "too valuable to throw away." The order form or reply form that appears valuable induces readership. It impels the reader to do something with it, to take advantage of the offer. High on the list of devices and techniques that make order forms look valuable are certificate borders, safety paper backgrounds, simulated rubber stamps, eagles, blue handwriting, seals, serial numbers, receipt stubs, and so on. And sheer size alone can greatly add to the valuable appearance of a response form (Exhibit 11-11). (You've seen examples of many of these techniques on the order forms shown in Chapter 3.)

By all means, don't call your reply device an order form. Call it a Reservation Certificate, Free Gift Check, Trial Membership Application, or some other benefit heading. It automatically seems more valuable to the reader.

Getting back more inquiry and order forms starts with making them appear too valuable to throw away. But to put frosting on the cake, add the dimension of personal involvement. Give the reader something to do with the order form. Ask him to put a token in a "yes" or "no" slot. Get him to affix a gummed stamp. Have him tear off a stub that has your guarantee on it. Once you have prodded the prospect into action, there is a good chance you will receive an order.

Finally, the order form should restate your offer and benefits. If a prospect loses the letter or circular, a good order form should be able to stand alone and do a complete selling job. And if it's designed to be mailed back on its own (without an envelope), it's usually worthwhile to prepay the postage.

Gift Slips and Other Enclosures

In addition to the letter, brochure, and order form, one of the most common enclosures is a free gift slip. If you have a free gift offer, you'll normally get much better results by putting that offer on a separate slip rather than building it into your circular (Exhibit 11-12).

If you insert an extra enclosure, make sure it stands out from the rest of the mailing and gets attention. You can often accomplish this by printing the enclosure on a colored stock and making it a different size from the other mailing components. Most free gifts, for example, can be adequately played up on a small slip that's 3½ x 8½ or 5½ x 8½.

Another enclosure that's often used is a business reply envelope. This isn't essential if the order form can be designed as a self-mailer. But, if you have an offer that the reader might consider to be of a private nature, an envelope is usually better. Buying a self-improvement book,

Exhibit 11-11. Order Forms

The order form (which should never be called an order form) is the moment of truth in a direct mail package. It must look too valuable to throw away.

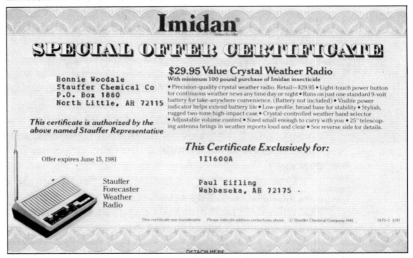

for example. Or applying for an insurance policy, where the application asks some personal questions. Also, the extra expense of a reply envelope is often justified if you want to encourage more cash-with-order replies.

The Letter—The "Key Ingredient" of Direct Mail

If any one piece in a direct mail package is key, that piece is the letter. One of the prime advantages of direct mail is its capacity for personal, one-on-one communication, and the letter provides that personal communication. It's no wonder, then, that more has been written about how to create a good direct mail letter than any other part of the direct mail package.

One of those who has written cogently on the direct mail letter is Mal Decker, a highly respected direct marketing creative consultant. Mal calls it "The Almighty Letter," and offers these insights into what a good direct mail letter should be:

Exhibit 11-12. Free Gift Offers

If you have a free gift with your offer, you'll get better results by highlighting it with a separate slip.

"The Almighty Letter"

1. It is a salesperson talking to his prospect. If he's a Tiffany salesman he writes in one style and if he's a grapefruit or pecan farmer or a beef grower he writes differently. ('Cause he tawks diffrunt.)
2. It is one individual unique salesperson "talking" to one individual prospect; that is, one particular person who has written a letter to one individual who (the writer prays) *represents* most or at least a good share of the prospects.
3. It is a salesperson doing the job he or she obviously loves and is good at—not because he puts himself up and the prospect down or vice versa—because he knows his product inside and out and is totally confident in and at ease with it and its values and benefits—even its inconsequential shortcomings—and wants to get his prospect in on a good thing.
4. It is a salesperson with a sense of rhythm, timing, dramatic effect, and possibly even humor—gaining the attention, piquing the curiosity, holding the interest, engaging the rationality, anticipating and assuaging the doubts, and winning the confidence (and the signature) of the prospect.
5. It is the most highly personal, intimate form of commercial writing; therefore

   - It is *not* a monolithic corporation addressing a computer-generated market profile; it is not impersonal in tone, from our content;
   - It is *not* one or more pieces of paper 8½" x 11" with a letterhead on top and a signature on the bottom and the most cherished sales pitch of the V.P. Marketing sandwiched in between.
   - It is *not* set in standard type, is *not* illustrated with photographs, is *not* printed in four color process, does *not* have a bang-tail or envelope-pocket or other devices attached.
   - Briefly, it is as close as possible to what you can do with your own typewriter.

6. It has a style, tone, and personality of its own:

   - It *can* have an "eyebrow" above the salutation to tease, tantalize, or help the reader pre-view the letter, especially if it is four or more pages.
   - It *can* have handwritten notations in the margins, a scrawled P.S., or underlining for emphasis in a second color of the same hue and hand as the signature.

- It *can* be printed on two sides (as long as the stock is opaque) on a wide variety of papers as long as they resemble correspondence papers.

7. It is addressed personally for maximum response—especially to hot prospects—with a personal salutation if you know the prospect's name. Of course, a customer should always be addressed by name unless you want to turn a current customer into a former customer.

8. It is quickly scannable; that is, a reader should get the gist of the proposition simply by reading the (1) eyebrow, (2) lead paragraph, (3) cross-heads, (4) wrap-up, and (5) P.S. If not, send it back to surgery, because without a strongly integrated skeleton, the body of the argument will slump.

9. It is easy on the eye, open, inviting, and varying in its "texture"—with normal margins;—individual paragraphs with a line space between;—at least one cross-head per page (two per page for long letters);—occasional variation in paragraph width;—a quotation, underlined sentence or phrase, numbers or bullets to list benefits, and/or other bits of "color" to maintain reader interest by promoting visual variety. The longer the letter, the more important these techniques. (We frequently re-edit and re-type final finished letter copy five and six times to achieve the right "texture" and "color".)

10. Once the reader's *attention* is gained, his *curiosity* aroused and his *interest* developed through an artful eyebrow and/or lead paragraph, the writer's job is to *maintain* interest while *building* confidence and credibility, and *closing* the sale. It is much like fly-fishing with a barbless hook: once the trout strikes, the line must be kept taut until the quarry is securely in the net. Let the least little bit of slack develop and the trout will spit out the fly—and he won't come back.

For an illustration of Decker's philosophy at work, see Exhibit 11-13.

Seven-Step Formula

Here's a letter-writing formula that has served me well. I believe it follows a more detailed route than most formulas. And, used wisely, it should not stifle your creativity.

Promise a benefit in your headline or first paragraph—your most important benefit. You simply can't go wrong by leading off with the most important benefit to the reader. Some writers believe in the slow buildup. But most experienced writers I know favor making the important point first.

Immediately enlarge on your most important benefit. This step is crucial. Many writers come up with a great lead, then fail to follow through. Or they catch attention with their heading, but then take two or three paragraphs to warm up to their subject. The reader's attention is gone! Try hard to elaborate on your most important benefit right away, and you'll build up interest fast.

Tell the reader specifically what he or she is going to get. It's amazing how many letters lack details on such basic product features as size, color, weight, and sales terms. Perhaps the writer is so close to his proposition he assumes the reader knows all about it. A dangerous assumption! And when you tell the reader what he or she's going to get, don't overlook the intangibles that go along with your product or service. For example, he's getting smart appearance in addition to a pair of slacks, knowledge in addition to a 340-page book.

Back up your statements with proof and endorsements. Most prospects are somewhat skeptical about advertising. They know it sometimes gets a little overenthusiastic about a product. So they accept it only with a grain of salt. If you can back up your own statements with third-party testimonials or a list of satisfied users, everything you say becomes more believable.

Tell the reader what she might lose if she doesn't act. As noted, people respond affirmatively either to gain something they do not possess or to avoid losing something they already have. Here's a good spot in your letter to overcome human inertia—imply what may be lost if action is postponed. People don't like to be left out. A skillful writer can use this human trait as a powerful influence in his or her message.

Rephrase your prominent benefits in your closing offer. As a good salesperson does, sum up the benefits to the prospect in your closing offer. This is the proper prelude to asking for action. This is where you can intensify the prospect's desire to have the product. The stronger the benefits you can persuade the reader to recall, the easier it will be for him or her to justify an affirmative decision.

Incite action, Now. This is the spot where you win or lose the battle with inertia. Experienced advertisers know once a letter is put aside or tossed into that file, you're out of luck. So wind up with a call for action and a logical reason for acting now. Too many letters close with a statement like "supplies are limited." That argument lacks credibility. Today's consumer knows you probably have a warehouse full of merchandise. So make your reason a believable one. For example, "It may be many months before we go back to press on this book." Or "Orders are shipped on a first-come basis. The sooner yours is received, the sooner you can be enjoying your new widget."

Exhibit 11-13. The Almighty Letter

> This letter may be very important to you.
>
> It brings news of an intriguing new philatelic collectible combining precious 23K gold with a very limited stamp issue.
>
> Beyond its bright prospects as a collectors item, this extraordinary issue commemorates some of the most brilliant art ever created in gold!

Dear Friend,

The weight of Tutankhamun's coffin puzzled the diggers who discovered the boy-king's tomb in 1922. Was it fashioned from some strange leaden substance not known to modern man?

The coffin, carved of wood in the shape of a mummy, then gilded, was opened -- only to reveal a second similar coffin. It was decorated with gold leaf and inlaid with a mosaic of multi-colored glass. But neither one of these coffins, if emptied, could weigh more than a hundred pounds.

The secret had to lie inside the second coffin. It was opened and within it was a third coffin, much different from the other two: it was solid gold! It weighed 2,448 pounds and two ounces -- a metal value of almost $12,500,000 based on $425 per ounce!

Within this gold coffin lay the mummy of Tutankhamun -- masked in solid gold!

Nearby were four more solid gold coffins, nearly exact replicas of the third coffin -- in miniature! They held the king's viscera.

No, the archeologists reflected, the material that added such weight to the wooden coffin was not strange. It was, in fact, familiar. Gold was man's first metal, older than Egypt itself. The puzzlement was the extravagant use of gold -- unknown and unimaginable, even to learned men!

The experience of a lifetime

The solid gold mask and miniature gold coffin are just two of the fifty-five treasures in the Tutankhamun Exhibition -- probably the most brilliant art ever created in gold -- that millions of Americans were privileged to see. The sheer amount of gold in this dazzling display is extremely impressive: it is unlikely that many Americans other than the guards at Fort Knox will ever see as much

West Redding, Connecticut 06896

A letter which illustrates the principles of a winning letter.

Exhibit 11-13. The Almighty Letter (continued)

gold again in their lifetimes! And the artistic, historic, and cultural values far exceed any measurement.

Gold has been called the royal metal: the king of metals and the metal of kings. Primitive man found it in the form of nuggets and fashioned it into ornaments. Modern man uses it in the critical electrical terminals of spacecraft because it is impervious to attack by anything known in space.

Yes, gold is imperishable and forever.

Perhaps that explains Tutankhamun's lavish use of the yellow metal. The Egyptians believed that an essential business of life -- although a pleasurable pursuit for a favored few -- was to prepare for the life beyond death. It was of cardinal importance that the most critical accountrements placed in the tomb survive the endlessness of eternity. Gold would endure.

Of all the splendors of Tutankhamun's 3300-year-old treasures, only gold has emerged as perfect as the day it was entombed. The Great Sphinx, the Temples of the Gods, and even the pyramids are disintegrating. Yet even today, there is no material that could survive another 3300 years more handsomely than gold.

An appropriate commemoration

The discovery of the tomb of Tutankhamun on November 26, 1922, still stands as one of the greatest archeological finds of all time. The significance of the discovery went far beyond the incredible wealth uncovered, for it revealed an entire way of life of one of the greatest of all civilizations.

The momentous American tour of the Tutankhamun Exhibition provided a firsthand inspection of those exquisite works of art by eight million Americans. Fifty million more saw these treasures on television. Never before in history had so many Americans seen such a sumptuous collection of art.

The Tutankhamun Exhibition is an event in the annals of art and history that we will not be likely to see again in our lifetimes. It richly deserves to be commemorated. What better way to celebrate the triumphant exhibition than with gold itself! And of all the possible forms, none seemed as appropriate as the 23K bas-relief stamps which made the British island of Staffa famous in the world of stamp collecting.

America's finest designers

Thirty-eight objects and motifs from Tutankhamun's tomb were selected by Walter Brooks, a distinguished artist who has won seven different design commissions from the United States Postal Service. Each one of the thirty-eight subjects was then commemorated in a stamp design reviewed by a committee including Leonard Everett Fisher and Robert Hallock who have also received many design commissions for American stamps. Finally, each design was

Exhibit 11-13. The Almighty Letter (continued)

reviewed and approved by Dr. V. L. Davis, noted Egyptologist, and only then was it given over to a team of master engravers that must be considered among the finest in the world!

The thirty-eight stamps which comprise the Tutankhamun Exhibition Issue, "Treasures of Tutankhamun," tell the fascinating story of the boy-king's eighteen years of life in the Egypt of the XVIII dynasty, and his anticipation of life as a god in the next world, as it was meant to be told -- in gold.

<u>Priceless art -- commemorated in 23K gold!</u>

The high relief and intricate detail of these stamps is made possible through the use of highly malleable 23K gold -- 95.8% pure -- as pure as the priceless art it commemorates.

A sheet of 23K gold -- backed by the sheerest tissue coated with a special adhesive and a protective covering -- is placed over each engraving. (The adhesive is of prime importance to collectors in order that this issue -- a British private local stamp -- function as valid postage which can be applied to mail, whether or not anyone would ever use 23K gold so extravagantly!) A soft blanket is placed over each sheet. Then the full weight of the seven-ton press is released. The results are breathtaking! The great pressure forces the soft gold into every hairline of the engraving to produce an incredibly detailed bas-relief sculpture against a gleaming background of gold.

The same exacting process is repeated for each of the thirty-eight engraved designs until the issue is completed.

A custom-designed collectors album is provided to you at no additional cost with your first stamp. The rich black cover of the album is luxuriously decorated with the hieroglyphic cartouches of Tutankhamun's names -- in gold.

Each stamp is elaborately protected and securely sealed in a transparent sleeve with a complete description of the subject commemorated. The stamp will remain in mint condition indefinitely as long as the seal is kept intact.

The price of each stamp is only $20 plus shipping and handling, and this price will be maintained for the entire series. And if you should ever decide to cancel your subscription, for any reason, you need only send a written request to my attention and your subscription will be terminated upon receipt of your request.

<u>The characteristics of an heirloom</u>

The history of stamp collecting has proved over and over again that the best designed, most artistic stamps are generally the most highly valued.

If these stamps are from an especially small issue, their value is further enhanced.

Exhibit 11-13. The Almighty Letter (continued)

And if, instead of paper, these stamps are made of ageless gold, they take on the characteristics of an heirloom.

Of course, some astute collectors will ferret out Gerald Rosen's 1979 <u>Catalogue of British Local Stamps</u> and discover that the first two gold Staffa series now catalogue at double their original selling price. "The 13 Original Colonies" and "The Twenty-Three Gold Producing Nations of the World" have gone from $20 to $45. (You will find a full discussion of catalogue listings and their significance in the accompanying folder.) It is quite possible that the Tutankhamun Exhibition Issue will also be catalogued at increasingly higher values as the issue gains the recognition it so richly deserves. But regardless of its catalogue value, "Treasures of Tutankhamun" will remain one of the unique collectibles of our time -- a true philatelic heirloom.

The worldwide Tutankhamun Exhibition Issue is strictly limited to 55,000, and each subscription will be registered and numbered in order of receipt. Of this total, <u>only 25,000 sets are allocated to all of North America</u>.

The first set now rests securely in the Cairo Museum, home of the treasures of Tutankhamun, and the last set will be sealed in the archives of the Postal Agent of Staffa, Scotland. All others will be open to subscription.

However, as it is our aim to achieve the most widespread owner-ship of the "Treasures of Tutankhamun" within this small issue, we will accept no more than two subscriptions per individual.

If you find this opportunity of interest and wish to be assured of early acceptance, we earnestly suggest you place your order promptly. Please use the Subscription Application enclosed.

I hope to have the pleasure of serving you.

Sincerely,

George Worthington

George Worthington

P.S. If you ever decide to sell your complete collection of stamps, The Gold Collection Limited respectfully requests that you give it first opportunity to meet your price.

G.W.

Writing a Winning Letter

Choosing the
Lead

Whatever formula or philosophy you adopt, the first task is to decide on the lead for the letter. Nothing is more important. Numerous tests have shown that one lead in a letter can pull substantially better than another. Let's look at six of the most common types of leads used in sales letters. To help you compare them, let's take a sample product and write six different leads for that product. The product we'll use is a businessman's self-improvement book, which includes biographical sketches of a dozen prominent business leaders.

1. *News.* If you have a product that is really news, you have the makings of an effective lead. There is nothing more effective than news. If you have a product or service that's been around a while, perhaps you can zero in on one aspect of it that's timely or newsworthy.

Example: Now you can discover the same success secrets that helped a dozen famous business leaders reach the top!

2. *How/what/why.* Any beginning newspaper reporter is taught that a good story should start out by answering the main questions that go through a reader's mind—who, what, when, where, why, and how. You can build an effective lead by promising to answer one of these questions and then immediately enlarging on it in your opening paragraphs.

Examples: How successful people really get ahead;
[or]

What it takes to survive in the executive jungle;
[or]

Why some people always get singled out for promotions and salary increases.

3. *Numbered ways.* This is often an effective lead because it sets the stage for an organized selling story. If you use a specific number, it will attract curiosity and usually make the reader want to find out what they are.

Example: Seventeen little-known ways to improve your on-the-job performance—and one big way to make it pay off!

4. *Command.* If you can use a lead which will command with authority and without offense, you have taken a big step toward getting the reader to do what you want.

Example: Don't let the lack of education hold you back any longer!

5. *Narrative.* This is one of the most difficult types of leads to write, but it can prove to be one of the most effective. It capitalizes on people's interest in stories. To be effective, a narrative lead must lead into the sales story in a natural way and still hold the reader's interest. Ideally, the lead should also give the reader some clue to where the story is going or why he or she should be interested.

Example: When he started in the stock room at IBM, nobody ever thought Tom Watson would some day be president of this multibillion dollar corporation.

6. *Question.* If you start with the right type of question, you can immediately put your reader in the proper frame of mind for your message. But be sure the question is provocative. Make it a specific question, promising benefits—one that's sure to be answered in the affirmative.

Example: If I can show you a proven way to get a better job, without any obligation on your part—will you give me a few minutes of your time?

It is impossible to put too much emphasis on the importance of working on your leads. The lead is the first thing your reader sees. Usually he or she makes a decision to read or not read at this point. I always write out at least three or four different leads, then choose the one I think will do the best job of appealing to the reader's basic wants.

Make a Letter Look Inviting

Here's a final, very important tip from top professional writers. They try to make their letters look attractive, inviting, and easy to read. (See Exhibit 11-14.) The pros keep paragraphs down to six or seven lines. They use subheads and indented paragraphs to break up long copy. They emphasize pertinent thoughts, knowing that many readers will scan indented paragraphs before they decide whether to read a letter clear through. They use underscoring, CAPITAL LETTERS, and a second ink color to make key words and sentences stand out. And they skillfully use leader dots and dashes to break up long sentences.

Scan the two versions of the Wards letter in Exhibit 11-15. Notice how much more inviting the letter on the left is compared to the original typewritten version. Same copy, but one letter encourages reading and the other doesn't.

Letter Length and the Postscript

"Do people read long copy?" The answer is Yes! People will read something for as long as it interests them. An uninteresting one-page letter can be too long. A skillfully woven four-pager can hold the reader until the end. Thus, a letter should be long enough to cover the subject adequately and short enough to retain interest. Don't be afraid of long copy. If you have something to say and can say it well, it will probably

Exhibit 11-14. The Kiplinger Letter

STANLEY R. MAYES *ASSISTANT TO THE PRESIDENT*

THE KIPLINGER WASHINGTON EDITORS, INC.

1729 H STREET, NORTHWEST, WASHINGTON, D. C. 20006   TELEPHONE: 887-6400

THE KIPLINGER WASHINGTON LETTER   THE KIPLINGER TAX LETTER
THE KIPLINGER AGRICULTURAL LETTER   THE KIPLINGER FLORIDA LETTER
THE KIPLINGER CALIFORNIA LETTER   THE KIPLINGER TEXAS LETTER
CHANGING TIMES MAGAZINE

<u>More Growth and Inflation Ahead...</u>
<u>and what YOU can do about it.</u>

The next few years will see business climb to the highest
level this country has ever known. And with it...inflation.

This combination may be hard for you to accept under today's
conditions. But the fact remains that those who do prepare for both
inflation AND growth ahead will reap big dividends for their foresight,
and avoid the blunders others will make.

You'll get the information you need for this type
of planning in the Kiplinger Washington Letter...
and the enclosed form will bring you the next 26
issues of this helpful service on a "Try-out" basis.
The fee: Less than 81¢ per week...<u>only $21 for the</u>
<u>6 months just ahead</u>...and tax deductible for business
or investment purposes.

During the depression, in 1935, the Kiplinger Letter warned
of inflation and told what to do about it. Those who heeded its advice
were ready when prices began to rise.

Again, in January of 1946, the Letter renounced the widely-
held view that a severe post-war depression was inevitable. Instead
it predicted shortages, rising wages and prices, a high level of
business. And again, those who heeded its advice were able to avoid
losses, to cash in on the surging economy of the late '40s, early '50s
and mid '60s. It then kept its clients prepared for the swings of the
'70s, keeping them a step ahead each time.

Now Kiplinger not only foresees expansion ahead, but also
continuing inflation, and in his weekly Letter to clients he points
out profit opportunities in the future...and also dangers.

The Kiplinger Letter not only keeps you informed of present
trends and developments, but also gives you advance notice on the
short & long-range business outlook...inflation forecasts...energy
predictions...housing...federal legislative prospects...politics...
investment trends & pointers...tax outlook & advice...labor, wage
settlement prospects...upcoming gov't rules & regulations...ANYTHING
that will have an effect on you, your business, your personal finances,
your family.

To take advantage of this opportunity to try the Letter and
benefit from its keen judgments and helpful advice during the fast-

(Over, please)

One of the most famous letters in direct mail, the Kiplinger letter. With minor changes it has been running

changing months ahead...fill in and return the enclosed form along
with your $21 payment. And do it with this guarantee: That you may
cancel the service and get a prompt refund of the unused part of
your payment any time you feel it is not worth far more to you than
it costs.

I'll start your service as soon as I hear from you, and
you'll have each weekly issue on your desk every Monday morning
thereafter.

Sincerely,

Stanley Mayes
Assistant to the President

SAM:kga

P. S.   More than half of all new subscribers sign up for a full year
at $42. In appreciation, we'll send you FREE five special Kiplinger
Reports on receipt of your payment when you take a full year's service,
too. Details are spelled out on the enclosed slip. Same money-back
guarantee and tax deductibility apply.

(and working) for 35 years! Notice how it follows the "seven-step formula" for writing sales letters.

Exhibit 11-15. Effective Letter Design

This November, you're invited to take an exciting look at what computers can do for you...

...at the landmark course that will give you--as it's given thousands of executives--the confidence and know-how you need to:

* Clear up the mystery and confusion of data processing!
* Make your computer work harder for you!
* Tell your systems people what <u>you</u> want--instead of the other way around!
* Make computers your partner in management

Dear Executive:

If you're baffled by computers...baffaloed when systems people use words like "byte" and "nanosecond"...if you're tired of the data processing department telling <u>you</u> what can be done, because you don't know enough to give the orders...

...it's time you took the American Management Associations' course that's cured thousands of "computer phobia"...

FUNDAMENTALS OF DATA PROCESSING FOR THE NON-DATA PROCESSING EXECUTIVE

Not for programmers or DP professionals...this 3-day course is one of the few computer seminars just for you, the data processing <u>user</u>! One at which you'll take a fascinating look at what computers can do for you...and learn how to utilize them to become a more effective manager...

...And this November, you can attend any of 12 sessions in 10 major cities across the country--<u>including a city near you!</u>

Thousands of managers and executives have attended this landmark course and, without hesitation, many have called it "the best course they've ever taken." <u>Here's what just a few of the recent attendees had to say:</u>

"I got terrific ideas and concepts that I can implement and

(inside...)

American Management Associations · 135 West 50th Street · New York, N.Y. 10020 · (212)586-8100

Notice how much more inviting the letter on the right is, even though the letters have identical copy.

```
* * * * * * * * * * * * * * * * * * * * * * * * * * * * * * * * * * * *
*                                                                     *
*          This November, you're invited to take an exciting look    *
*                   at what computers can do for you...              *
*                                                                     *
*   ...at the landmark course that will give you--as it's given      *
*  thousands of executives--the confidence and know-how you need to: *
*                                                                     *
*     * Clear up the mystery and confusion of data processing!       *
*     * Make your computer work harder for you!                      *
*     * Tell your systems people what you want--instead of the       *
*       other way around!                                            *
*     * Make computers your partner in management                    *
*                                                                     *
* * * * * * * * * * * * * * * * * * * * * * * * * * * * * * * * * * * *
```

Dear Executive:

   If you're baffled by computers...buffaloed when systems people
use words like "byte" and "nanosecond"...if you're tired of the data
processing department telling you what can be done, because you
don't know enough to give the orders...

   ...it's time you took the American Management Associations' course
that's cured thousands of "computer phobia"...

                    FUNDAMENTALS OF DATA PROCESSING
                 FOR THE NON-DATA PROCESSING EXECUTIVE

          Not for programmers or DP professionals...
          this 3-day course is one of the few computer
          seminars just for you, the data processing
          user! One at which you'll take a fascinating
          look at what computers can do for you...and
          learn how to utilize them to become a more
          effective manager...

          ...And this November, you can attend any of
          12 sessions in 10 major cities across the
          country--including a city near you!

   Thousands of managers and executives have attended this landmark
course and, without hesitation, many have called it "the best course
they've ever taken." Here's what just a few of the recent attendees
had to say:

      "I got terrific ideas and concepts that I can implement and

                                          (inside...)
```

American Management Associations · 135 West 50th Street · New York, N.Y. 10020 · (212) 586-8100
```

do better than short copy. After all, the longer you hold a prospect's interest, the more sales points you can get across and the more likely you are to win an order.

Regardless of letter length, however, it usually pays to tack on a postscript. The P.S. is one of the most effective parts of any letter. Many prospects will glance through a letter. The eye will pick up an indented paragraph here, stop on an underlined statement there, and finally come to rest on the P.S. If you can express an important idea in the P.S., the reader may go back and read the whole letter. This makes the P.S. worthy of your best efforts. Use it to restate a key benefit. Or to offer an added inducement, like a free gift. Even when somebody has read the rest of the letter, the P.S. can make the difference between whether the prospect places an order. Use the P.S. to close on a strong note, to sign off with the strongest appeal you have.

The Value of Versioned Copy

Suppose, just suppose, that instead of sending exactly the same letter to all your prospects, you could create a number of versions for each major segment of your market. And rather than talking about all the advantages and benefits of the product, you could simply zero in on those that fit each market segment. Sounds like a logical idea that should increase response, doesn't it?

Yet my own experience with versioned or segmented copy has been mixed. Sometimes I've seen this technique work very effectively; other times it's a bomb. So I suggest that you test it for yourself. If your product story should be substantially different for certain audience segments—and you can identify and select them on the lists you're using—develop special versions of your regular copy and give the technique a try.

One type of versioned copy that generally does pay off is special copy slanted to your *previous* buyers. Customers like to think a firm remembers them and will give them special treatment. In going back to your satisfied buyers, there's less need to resell your company. You can concentrate on the product or the service being offered.

How to Improve a Good Mailing Package

So far we've been talking about how to create a new mailing package. Let's suppose you've done that, and you want to make it better. Or you've got a successful mailing package you've been using for a couple of years (your control) and you want to beat it. How do you go about it? One of the best ways I know is to come up with an entirely different appeal for your letter. For instance, suppose you're selling an income tax guide and your present letter is built around saving money. That's probably a tough appeal to beat. But to develop a new approach you might write a letter around a negative appeal, something people want to avoid. Experience with many propositions has proved that a negative appeal is often stronger than a positive one. Yet it's frequently overlooked by copywriters. An appropriate negative copy appeal for our example might be something like, "How to avoid costly mistakes that can get you in trouble with the Internal Revenue Service." Or, "Are you taking advantage of these six commonly overlooked tax deductions?"

Another good technique is to change the type of lead on your letter. Review the examples of six common types of leads given earlier. If you're using a news lead, try one built around the narrative approach. Or develop a provocative question as the lead. Usually a new lead will require you to rewrite the first few paragraphs of copy to fit the lead, but then you can often pick up the balance of the letter from your control copy. A top creative man who has a well-organized approach for coming up with new ideas is Sol Blumenfeld, a veteran direct mail professional. Here are some of the approaches Blumenfeld uses:

The Additive Approach

This means adding something to a control package that can increase its efficiency in such a way as to justify the extra cost involved. Usually, this entails using inserts. Inserts that can be used to heighten response include testimonial slips, extra discounts, a free gift for cash with order, and a news flash or bulletin. Other additive ideas include building stamps or tokens into the response device. And, if you have logical reason to justify it, add an expiration date to your offer.

The Extractive Approach

This copy exercise requires a careful review of your existing mailing package copy. You often can find a potential winning lead buried somewhere in the body copy.

The Innovative Approach

Unlike the extractive approach, this is designed to produce completely new ideas. If you are testing three or four new copy approaches, at least one of them should represent a potential breakthrough, something that's highly original, perhaps even a little wild. I encourage writers to let themselves go, because we've seen them produce real breakthroughs this way—dramatic new formats, exciting copy approaches, and offers that have really shellacked the old control!

Some Final Tips

When you create your own direct mail, you might check it against the following list of pointers. Remember that these are *guidelines,* not rigid rules, and that when I say "X will usually outpull Y," that means every so often X will not outpull Y.

With that caution in mind, here are the guidelines:

Mailing format	• The letter ranks first in importance. • The most effective mailing package consists of outside envelope, letter, circular, response form, and business reply envelope.
Letters	• Form letters using indented paragraphs will usually outpull those in which paragraphs are not indented. • Underlining important phrases and sentences usually increases results slightly. • A separate letter with a separate circular will generally do better than a combination letter and circular. • A form letter with an effective running headline will ordinarily do as well as a filled-in letter. • Authentic testimonials in a sales letter ordinarily increase the pull. • A two-page letter ordinarily outpulls a one-page letter.
Circulars	• A circular that deals specifically with the proposition presented in the letter will be more effective than a circular of an institutional character. • A combination of art and photography will usually produce a better circular than one employing either art or photography alone. • A circular usually proves to be ineffective in selling news magazines and news services. • In selling big-ticket products, deluxe large-size, color circulars virtually always warrant the extra cost over circulars 11 x 17 or smaller.
Outside Envelopes	• Illustrated envelopes increase response if their message is tied into the offer. • Variety in types and sizes of envelopes pays, especially in a series of mailings.
Reply forms	• Reply cards with receipt stubs will usually increase response over cards with no stub. • "Busy" order or request forms that look important will usually produce a larger response than neat, clean-looking forms. • Postage-free business reply cards will generally bring more responses than those to which the respondent must affix postage.
Reply envelopes	• A reply envelope increases cash-with-order response. • A reply envelope increases responses to collection letters.

Color

- Two-color letters usually outpull one-color letters.
- An order or reply form printed in colored ink or on colored stock usually outpulls one printed in black ink on white stock.
- A two-color circular generally proves to be more effective than a one-color circular.
- Full color is warranted in the promotion of such items as food items, apparel, furniture, and other merchandise if the fidelity of color reproduction is good.

Postage

- Third-class mail ordinarily pulls as well as first-class mail.
- Postage-metered envelopes usually pull better than affixing postage stamps (and you can meter third-class postage).
- A "designed" printed permit on the envelope usually does as well as postage metered mail.

Self-quiz

1. What unique advantages permit direct mail to do a better selling job than any other advertising medium?

a. _____

b. _____

c. _____

d. _____

e. _____

2. What are the three basic formats of direct mail?

a. _____

b. _____

c. _____

3. Complete the following true-false quiz:

a. Personalized letters will always outpull non-personalized ones. _____

b. A "publisher's letter" will usually boost response 10 percent or more. _____

c. A pop-up device is a sure-fire way to increase response. _____

d. Simulated telegrams are "passé." _____

4. Complete this equation for making a sale:

Benefit *divided by* _____ *equals* _____.

5. What is the difference between a benefit and a selling point?

_____

_____

_____

_____

6. What are some of the basic wants inherent in most people?

a. _____   f. _____

b. _____   g. _____

c. _____   h. _____

d. _____   i. _____

e. _____   j. _____

7. What do most people desire to avoid?

a. _____   d. _____

b. _____   e. _____

c. _____   f. _____

8. Name 11 guidelines to good direct mail copy.

a. _____   g. _____

b. _____   h. _____

c. _____   i. _____

d. _____   j. _____

e. _____   k. _____

f. _____

9. What is the key objective in preparing an order form? Make order forms look _____

_____

10. Name four typical involvement devices.

a. _____

b. _____

c. _____

d. _____

11. Name the six most common types of leads used in sales letters.

a. _____   d. _____

b. _____   e. _____

c. _____   f. _____

12. List the points in the seven-step letter writing formula in sequence:

a. _____   e. _____

b. _____   f. _____

c. _____   g. _____

d. _____

13. What are the two best applications of a P.S.?

a. To restate _____

b. To offer an added _____

14. Define each of these approaches for improving a good mailing package:

a. The additive approach _____

_____

_____

b. The extractive approach _____

_____

_____

c. The innovative approach _____

_____

_____

Pilot Project

You are the advertising manager of a major national chain store group (e.g., Sears, Wards, J.C. Penney, etc.). Your company wants to get more of its credit cards in the hands of qualified persons. Your assignment: prepare a direct mail package to "sell" your store's credit card.

Assumptions:

- The credit card is free; there is no yearly charge or fee to have one.
- It is honored in your company's stores from coast to coast for anything sold in those stores.
- In addition to your company's own credit card, your company's stores also accept the two bank credit cards (VISA and MasterCard).

The objective of your direct mail package is to get creditworthy persons to fill out an application for the card. They will be credit-checked, and a certain number of persons will be turned down. Another obvious objective is that, when a person has applied and been approved for the card, you want him or her to *use* it.

There are some steps to guide you through the decisions you will have to make:

1. Write a creative strategy. Pay particular attention to *competitive products, market* and *creative implementation.*

2. Which format would you select: classic or self-mailer. Why?

3. Here are some selling points (or product features) of the card. Below each one, list the *customer benefit* made possible by that selling point. (To get you started, the first one is filled in.) Note: more than one benefit can usually be derived from a single selling point.

    a. Lets you charge purchases.
       You don't need to carry cash. _____

    b. Card is good nationwide.

       _____

    c. Card is good for anything sold at our stores.

       _____

4. What is the "big idea" behind your mailing package? How will you implement this theme in the letter? Circular? Outer envelope? Order form (application)?

5. Are you going to use any additional pieces, such as gift slips or a publisher's letter?

6. Write your sales letter. Pay particular attention to the "seven-step formula."

7. How could you use versioned copy in your letter?

Chapter Twelve

Techniques of Creating and Marketing Catalogs

America's long-standing love affair with the catalog has intensified over the past decade. The consumer—the employed female in particular—has turned to the catalog as a way to save shopping time. Business firms, engaged in the sale of equipment and supplies to other businesses, have turned to the catalog as a means of reducing the high cost of person-to-person selling.

With the expansion of catalog marketing more sophisticated marketing methods are being applied. Mailings to direct response lists—primarily buyers from other catalogs—have long been the major mode of circulation for consumer catalog marketers. Catalog marketers in the business-to-business field have used a mix of direct response lists and compiled lists. But some of the major consumer catalog marketers have also established their own catalog stores in high density shopping areas. Sears, the grand-daddy of catalog store operations, has approximately 950 such units.

What may be a new trend in catalog marketing is exemplified by a firm in Tuxedo Park, New York, called Catalogia, Inc. *DM News* reported in their September 15, 1982, issue that their retail stores offer shoppers more than 350 catalogs from which to select merchandise. The story in *DM News* explains how the system works:

> The customer does not have to request any given catalog. A selection can be made by requesting customer service personnel to access the computer file for catalogs which carry certain items.

293

The computer program is designed to lead the customer to the specific catalogs and page numbers for the merchandise requested. A list of selected catalogs and page numbers is produced for each item the customer desires.

The customer is then given the catalogs listed. Each bound catalog contains order forms, note paper and a pen.

The shopper selects merchandise directly from the catalogs, not from the computer screen. Payment can be by cash, credit card or approved check.

Credit cards honored are American Express, Master Card and Visa.

A receipt for the order is given to the customer, with an individual order number.

A Catalogia Suggestion Program assists customers by supplying gift items for undecided shoppers. By activating a special computer program, the store clerk asks the shopper a series of questions to develop the character of the individual or situation. When the details are fed into the computer, it searches a series of categories:

Exhibit 12-1. Catalog Stores

sports, hobbies, travel, birds, smoking articles and many others. A range of gifts is then suggested to the shopper.

There is no direct contact by an individual store with a catalog firm. Orders go into a central computer controlled by Catalogia. Each day's orders are batched by catalog house and transmitted each evening from the computer to a teletype terminal at each catalog order center. The teletypes are tied to the Catalogia computer by acoustic coupling.

By handling the payment at the store, Catalogia is able to take its fees and any other charges "off the top" when remitting money to each catalog organization. There is no extra charge to the customer.

Among the catalogs currently at Catalogia stores are: Horchow's Trifles, Eddie Bauer, Camp Beverly Hills, Furniture Craft, Green Mountain Company, Sharper Image, Lillian Vernon, Wine Spectator, Scully & Scully, Victoria's Secret, Williams-Sonoma, Shapler's House of Almonds, Jennifer House, Sportpages, Eastern Mountain Sports and Chicago Art Institute.

Updating of catalogs is brought about by the catalog firm notifying its Catalogia account executive at headquarters. Then each Catalogia store is notified through the computer.

How Consumers Perceive Successful Catalogs

Catalog circulation is, of course, the final act in the catalog process. There's got to be a reason for being for every catalog, a niche to fill. And merchandise selection and position, creative concepts, copy and graphics are all critical to the total catalog process. In the final analysis your catalog must be *perceived* as worthy to browse and act upon .

Dick Hodgson, a noted direct marketing consultant and catalog specialist, points out that there are four key perceptions that must be held by the consumer in order for the catalog operation to be successful.

1. Perceived Availability.

Mr. Hodgson points out that while the product or service being sold may be available from a neighborhood merchant, this becomes a major competitive issue only if the potential buyer is aware of this fact and thus determines it would be easier to purchase from a nearby source.

The Brookstone Company offers a catalog that carries the slogan: "Hard To Find Tools." Actually, many of the tools Brookstone sells—or similar tools that will do the same jobs—are available through local hardware merchants. But they're the type of articles merchants keep in those bins under their counters or in the stockroom, "just in case somebody asks for them." Thus, the reader of a Brookstone catalog perceives such tools to be truly "hard to find." Brookstone has had steady and profitable growth serving buyers who have come to depend on its catalog rather than the local merchants as a source for tools and, as Brookstone puts it, "Other Fine Things."

Direct marketers have developed many special techniques to encourage their customers to perceive their products or services as being unique and thus not easily available elsewhere. Marketers emphasize their exclusive colors, designs, and packaging; special combinations of products; attractive and easily understood credit plans; early introductions of new or improved products; and a variety of other effective techniques that traditional retailers have been reluctant to adopt.

2. Perceived Authority.

The second of Dick Hodgson's benchmarks for a successful catalog is *perceived authority.* Successful catalog operations, Dick points out, either trade on an area of established authority or go to great lengths to build a base of authority from which to sell. Take, for example, those successful airline seatback catalogs. Note how much space they devote to luggage and other travel-related items. With their years of experience in handling luggage, airlines are perceived by the consumer as having clearly established themselves as authorities on the durability of luggage. And when the airline says a bag is durable, the consumer has got to believe it knows what it is talking about.

One sometimes wonders why so many catalogs seem to waste so much space on seemingly ego-centered editorial material about the facilities and the people of the companies behind them. It's not just an ego trip in most cases, but rather it's a carefully calculated effort to build authority in the minds of customers and prospects to encourage buying with confidence. And such space is far from wasted when it eliminates the need for a lot of back-up copy for each item in the book.

3. Perceived Value.

The third of Dick Hodgson's points is perceived value. Suppose that you are a consumer interested in a jade necklace. You go to the leading department store in your city and look at a small assortment of jade necklaces. Then you "shop" the Gump's catalog, which is produced twice a year by the famous Gump's store in San Francisco. You know the reputation of Gump's for its precious items from the Far East, including jade. If you are typical, your perception of value would be heavily swayed toward Gump's because of its "authority" with respect to jade.

4. Perceived Satisfaction.

As previously mentioned, a guarantee of satisfaction is a key in mail order. The American consumer has been trained in the perception that if he is unhappy with his purchase he can return it for replacement, full credit, or full refund.

The customer's perceived satisfaction doesn't start and end with the guarantee. Smart direct marketers are very selective in the merchandise they offer to forestall potential fears customers might have about dissatisfaction. In fashions, for example, direct marketers often purposely select styles that don't involve critical fits. They select colors that reproduce well and are easily visualized from printed illustrations. And they prepare copy which not only romances the product, but carefully spells out details which, if misunderstood, could result in dissatisfaction.

Four Types of Catalogs

The function of catalogs can be better understood by categorizing the types of catalogs and examining the characteristics of each. There are four general types of catalogs: retail catalogs, full-line catalogs, business-to-business catalogs, and consumer specialty catalogs. Each type bears special considerations.

Retail Catalogs   A recent phenomenon on the marketing scene has been the interest in catalogs by retailers. Some stores, most notably Neiman-Marcus, have been famous for their catalogs for decades. For most stores, the principal objective has been to build in-store traffic. Now, however, emphasis is shifting to other objectives. A major new goal is generation of mail and phone orders from customers outside the retailers' trading area.

So the objectives of the retailer are not necessarily similar to those of the mail order catalog entrepreneur who does not have a retail store. The retailer usually wants store traffic inside his trading area and mail order sales outside it. Also, the retailer can opt for a catalog largely underwritten by vendor money, vendors considering such funds to be "advertising allowances." But the store pays a price when the vendor pays to "advertise" an item in the store's catalog.

The vendor catalog. Some time ago, someone got the idea that the "smart" way for a retail catalog operation to go was to sell "advertising" in the catalog to vendors, with vendors underwriting all, or most, of the cost. You can't argue with the arithmetic. But with each "ad" a retailer accepts, he compromises mail order principles. Vendors dictate the catalog makeup. Retailers don't.

A giant step closer to a true mail order catalog is the well-executed "store traffic" catalog. Many stores produce such catalogs and mail them to charge customers in their trading areas. The prime objective is to produce mail order sales.

This creates a dilemma. For example, a store might be a leader in the sale of sterling silver in its trading area so it features sterling silver in its catalog. The result might be big in-store sales, but zero mail order sales. For another example, a department store that is a leader in "high fashion" apparel finds that only staple apparel sells in its catalog. Dilemma: Should it leave "high fashion" out of its catalog and risk losing some of its big in-store sales?

The problem isn't severe if the retailer restricts distribution to his trading area with building store traffic being the prime objective. But suppose the retailer decides to mail the catalog outside his trading area, soliciting "pure" mail orders? His mail order sales are certain to be diluted to the extent he has violated sound mail order principles.

The extent to which retailers build healthy mail order operations in the future will be dependent upon two basics: the application of sound mail order principles and long-term commitment.

Full-line Merchandise Catalogs

In the purest sense there are only a handful of full-line merchandise catalogs in this country, catalogs that, in effect, are complete department stores. Among these are Sears, Ward, Spiegel, and J. C. Penney. Among the subcategories of full-line merchandise catalogs is the "wholesale" catalog, which features selections of merchandise such as appliances, electronics, and jewelry. Most such catalogs are backed by vendor money, the vendors paying all or a portion of the cost for running catalog pages featuring their merchandise.

Business-to-Business Catalogs

A real phenomenon of the past decade has been the growth of business catalogs through which business sells to business. But in spite of phenomenal growth during the past decade, the potential in this area has hardly been scratched.

It might be said that the growth of the business catalog has been in close ratio to the ever-ascending cost of the industrial salesperson's call. Because it costs so much for a company to maintain a salesperson on the road, he must necessarily limit his calls to prospects with the greatest sales potential. Consequently, salespeople must purposely pass up many prospects simply because they can't afford the cost of the call. This leaves a tremendous void to be filled by the business catalog.

Consider the Fortune 500 company that learned through research that salespeople couldn't afford to call on any customer who purchased less than $200 in supplies a year. This giant corporation had several hundred thousand prospects who failed to meet the minimum annual purchase requirement. To overcome the problem this corporation developed a full-scale selling catalog to use in conjunction with a telephone program. The results were remarkable. Fourteen percent of all prospects contacted by mail and phone placed orders, orders that the sales force could not afford to take in person.

The business catalog has proved to be the ideal vehicle for servicing the aftermarket for companies that sell capital goods equipment through sales forces. Consider the visual products division of a major corporation like Minnesota Mining and Manufacturing. Its salespeople in one division derive a major share of their income from the sale of overhead projectors. The aftermarket for these products consists of transparencies and other supplies. It is worthwhile for the salesperson to sell the overhead projector, but in most cases he can't afford to go back to sell $25 to $35 worth of supplies. The supplier catalog performs this function.

The business specialty catalog is not limited to aftermarkets, of course. There are scores of operations that use catalogs as their sole marketing vehicle to businesses. Witness this success story.

In 1956, Jack Miller started selling pencils, paper and a few other office supplies, using the telephone in the rear of his father's poultry store near Wrigley Field in Chicago. He was newly married and his venture as a minority owner in a small briefcase sales operation had just failed. He found an office products wholesaler who agreed to do business with him, borrowed $2,000 from his family to start his inventory, and began knocking on doors.

"While my father wrapped chickens, I wrapped my orders," Miller recalls. When Miller's business started growing, his wife's uncle let him store his stock in the basement of the uncle's nearby two-flat apartment building, where Miller had to shovel several thousand pounds of coal out of a bin to make room for an office.

His first mailing was on postcards, to 150 customers, advertising five sale-priced items.

"There was practically no one in the mail order office supply field," he says. "There were mail order operations selling industrial equipment or office furniture, but not supplies." But his idea to become the Sears, Roebuck of the office products field caught on, and Miller was joined in the business by his brothers, Harvey and Arnold. The growing discount catalogue operation kept moving into larger and larger warehouses.

Quill Corp., now one of the largest office supply houses in the country, is sending out 23 million catalogues a year and doing more than $50 million in sales.

Consumer Specialty Catalogs

The most dramatic growth over the past decade has occurred in the area of consumer specialty catalogs—catalogs that fill special needs or cater to identifiable lifestyles. The great Sears, Roebuck and Company, for example, in addition to its basic full-line merchandise catalog now publishes some 20 special-interest catalogs offering auto parts, western apparel, tall men's clothing, winter sporting goods, convalescent products, and similar groups of products for market segments.

A true mail order phenomenon in the consumer specialty catalog field is Hanover House of Hanover, Pennsylvania. Harold Schwartz, their dynamic entrepreneurial president, has brought a new concept to catalog marketing. Instead of living or dying with one book, Harold spreads his marketing over 17 catalogs. Each book is different. Each appeals to different markets.

When one book is down, or expected to be down, another one is usually up. For a down book, circulation will be cut. For an up book, circulation will be expanded. Based on the economic cycle a book is in, pricing strategy will be changed to encourage ordering, to boost average order, to keep the Hanover multimillion customer list churning at maximum performance. A list of the 17 catalogs and the markets they cater to follows:

- "First Editions": For the fashion-conscious woman with an active life who has little time for shopping and values the opportunity to shop by mail at her convenience.
- "Synchronics": A compendium of electronic equipment, incorporating the latest in technology for home consumption.
- "The Chelsea Collection": Hanover's quality fashion catalog, targeted at a more affluent and fashion-aware customer.
- "Cosmopedics": A catalog of women's and men's shoes at extremely low prices.
- "Pennsylvania Station": A fascinating selection of gifts, home decor accents and fashions for a sophisticated customer who is aware of the latest trends in all aspects of life.
- "Mature Wisdom": A full-color catalog, utilizing large, bold type for easy reading, and featuring products designed to be appealing and useful to people over 55 years of age.
- "Hampton Farms": A gourmet food shop in a catalog, targeted to corporate and individual gift shoppers.
- "Hanover Collection": Drawing upon merchandise that has appeared in Hanover's larger catalogs, it re-exposes highly successful items with a broad-based appeal.
- "New Hampton General Store": A fascinating mix of home accents, unique gifts, old-fashioned collectibles, along with a selection of country store fare.
- "Old Village Shop": A large and varied collection of out of the ordinary gifts, fashions, and home decorating ideas from all over the world.
- "Lakeland Nurseries Sales": A unique gardening catalog with every home gardening need from rare, hard-to-find exotic plants to all the old garden favorites, to a vast selection of fruit and nut trees, groundcovers, flowering shrubs, and the latest horticultural developments.
- "Adam York": A prestige gift catalog, offering upscale gifts, and fashions targeted primarily to male shoppers with a great deal of discretionary income.
- "Fashion Galaxy": A fashion catalog designed to capture the market slightly below markets targeted for other fashion offerings.
- "Rainbow Gifts": An array of unique collectibles, decorating accessories, gourmet culinary tools, plus unusual items for tots to teens.

- "Unique Collection": Features only best sellers from larger catalogs.
- "Hanover House": Its theme is "New Ideas for Better Living." The book appeals to the budget-conscious and features gifts, gadgets, personal items, health and beauty aids, and needs for the car, garden and pets.
- "Night 'n Day Intimates": Presents intimate apparel in an elegant and tasteful context. Targeted primarily to women, the catalog is also mailed to men with gift-giving suggestions.

Proof of the soundness of Harold Schwartz's multicatalog concept—specific catalogs for specific market segments—is confirmed by Hanover's last reported sales and profit figures. Sales for the current 12 months were $105 million, compared to $74 million the previous 12 months—a 37 percent increase. Profits went from $4.8 million to $8.7 million.

Catalog Creativity

The tremendous growth in catalog sales, both in the business market and the consumer market, has brought unprecedented competition. This has created a paradox: unprecedented growth accompanied by unprecedented failure.

Reasons for failure are many, with shortage of capital being high on the list. But even an abundance of capital does not assure success. The X factor, the one distinguishing mark that makes one catalog stand out from all others in its class, is *creative execution*, without doubt.

And if I were asked to identify the one person who has done the most to raise the level of catalog creativity, I would say without a moment's hesitation, "She is Ms. Jo-Von Tucker, president of Jo-Von Tucker & Associates of Dallas, Texas." Jo-Von has created more upscale catalogs than anyone. The pages that follow capture her incisive thinking about catalog creativity.

Before a graphic marketing solution can be found for a catalog, a certain amount of "homework" should be done. A thorough understanding of the specific market is as important as knowing the product or service line well. Any available research regarding the lifestyle of the prospective customer should be considered as valuable marketing input. By learning up-front about habits and leisure activities we simultaneously gain access to needs and requirements of the consumer.

Vignette of the Upscale Market

Market research data gives us a profile of an affluent mail order customer. As high as 85 percent of upscale catalog buyers are female. The national work force in America currently reflects that in excess of 55 percent are women.

In order to define "upscale," one must look beyond Webster's contribution and resort to demographic monetary measures of income. By today's inflationary standards, a single income of $35,000 annually qualifies, as does a two-income annual total of $50,000. The key to consider (and the most difficult to track) is discretionary income. A family that earns $50,000 annually but has living commitments of $45,000 does not necessarily reflect a $5,000 discretionary income, because of unscheduled commitments or other unplanned living expenses.

Discretionary income can be tracked by numbers of mail order purchases and projected by average dollar order of each purchase. A mail order company can program its computers to track buying behavior of its own customers, but must rely on conjecture or sharing of information to expand the portrait beyond their area of control.

Assuming from industry statistics that 50 percent of mail order customers are married and that they have an average of 1.5 children per household, we know that the prospects have *needs* for their children as well as for themselves. During the course of a year they will purchase

The Quality-, Style-Conscious Upscale Buyer

Photo: Courtesy of The Photographers, Inc.

clothing, sports equipment, toys, learning supplies and gifts—some via the mail. Time is a priority to this customer because with today's active lifestyle there exists less leisure time than in our recent history. People choose to do other things with available leisure time than traditional retail shopping. Many opt for the convenience of mail order as an alternate shopping style.

An ideal prequalification consideration for customer acquisition is one of having bought through the mail previously, either from competition or from a similar offering. An established inclination to purchase quality products from catalogs gives us insight into how this customer responds, both to merchandise categories and to graphic selling techniques.

A complete study of an upscale mail order customer should be used to fill in a canvas for a portrait, each bit of data completing another segment of the sketch. The types of stores at which consumers hold charge cards will help identify "quality of lifestyle"; active sports participation, home entertaining. Knowledge about civic and/or political activities, charity involvement, travel frequency and many other factors can be used to fill in the blanks—to educate direct marketers to their customers' needs.

The Competitive Mailbox

With the recent deluge of mail order catalogs comes a challenge to the producers of such marketing tools: to be better, more unique, slicker, and more credible than the catalog that arrives in the prospect's hands at the same time as yours. Catalogs have evolved to a high level of sophistication during the past 10 years, and the customer has been educated through multiple exposures to expect this kind of presentation. Clean, contemporary graphics combined with dramatic photography and understated copy, all wrapped up in shiny high-gloss printing on quality paper. The look of today's catalogs—a creatively produced marketing vehicle designed to present, excite, motivate and, ultimately, to sell.

The importance of establishing both an image and credibility for a catalog cannot be emphasized too strongly. On any given day, three or more catalogs may arrive simultaneously. There's no likelihood a prospect will order from all catalogs received on a given day: more likely a single catalog will capture attention and interest. In order for the chosen catalog to be yours, the most creative marketing decisions must have been made at each step of production, culminating in an outstanding catalog presentation.

To put your catalog to the supreme test, conduct your own private survey. Select three or four competitive catalogs and lay them out next to your most recent issue. Try to be objective, and put yourself in the customer's frame of mind as you glance at each catalog. Which one do you reach for first, and why? Does your catalog make a definitive statement about your company and about what's inside the pages? Does it entice you to open it and to scan through? When you pick it up, does it give you a tangible impression of quality?

Now here is the crucial test: open your catalog and that of a competitor to any spread. Compare the two presentations. Do they look alike? Could your two-page spread be pulled from your catalog and dropped into the competitive book and still blend in? If so, you've got a problem! You have produced a "me too" book, and the customer will know it.

Filling A Niche

"Me too" books are all too common in the industry. And what a waste, considering the cost of catalog production today!

To establish a niche in an overcrowded marketplace, you must have a "raison d'être," a reason for being. It should begin with the selection and editing of merchandise, and conclude with the physical presentation. Additionally, a niche is enhanced by special techniques in fulfillment and customer service. Set yourself apart from your competition by continually seeking new items (even more reason for merchandise exclusivity and product development) and by refinement of your catalog creative efforts.

The Bon Appetit *appeal to the good life.*

Photo: Courtesy of Bon Appétit and Knapp Communications

Think of the mailbox as a crowded marketplace where many vendors are milling around, setting up displays of their wares. To simply spread a blanket on the ground and dump your products in a heap is not enough. Instead, use each spread within your catalog as a window display. It is, of course, your decision whether to opt for a Neiman-Marcus-type presentation or that of a variety store. I firmly believe (based on 20 years' experience in cataloging) that quality sells better! It does not matter whether you are selling caviar or pots and pans, *tasteful graphics are more successful* because the prospective customer is receptive to them.

The Paper Store

Catalogs are effective for a variety of reasons. First, they provide a convenient way of shopping. Second, they are capable of provoking an emotional response. Third, due to around-the-clock, toll-free telephone numbers and available order forms, there is no time limit for the customer. Fourth, an edited selection can be presented. And, fifth, a catalog can be ultimately considerate.

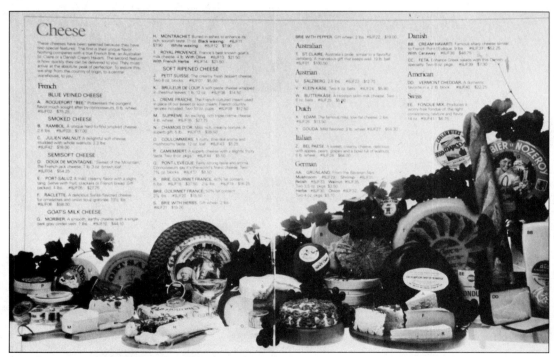

The Bon Appétit *appeal to the good life. Photo: Courtesy of Bon Appétit and Knapp Communications*

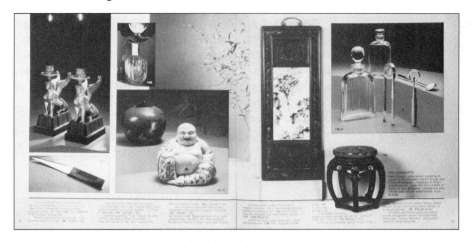

The Paper Store: Convenience and Multiple Appeals.

Photos: Courtesy Creme de la Creme (top), Gucci (middle), American Express (bottom).

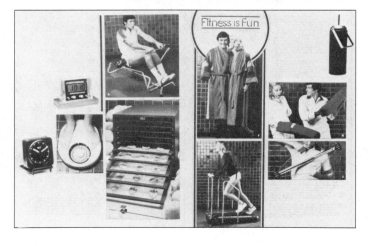

In relation to the fifth point, the catalog medium has an inherent advantage. It will never be rude, and it is always accessible when the customer is ready to buy. As a sales force it can be totally controlled to reflect company policy and image, as opposed to the retail store personnel situation. Mail order has an opportunity to be a thoughtful selling process because of editing. The customer is not asked to go through racks and racks of clothing items or to peruse hundreds of shelves of decorator items. Instead, an experienced, knowing merchant has done the editing for her, eliminating duplicates and offering a narrow array of products that are tastefully designed and quality produced.

In fact, we have learned a valuable lesson about the importance of editing mail order merchandise; customers have shown us that too many choices of a product category tend to confuse a prospective buyer. Many times a prospect will decide not to buy at all, rather than make a choice from too many similar items.

Catalog Psychology

The application of psychology to catalog marketing is an important element in being considerate of the customer and in motivating a decision to buy. It is understood by very few cataloguers and actually applied by even fewer.

Consideration involves showing the merchandise most effectively—scaling it with a simple prop or accessory so that the customer immediately understands the size of the item; showing it in use, so its benefits are readily grasped; answering any possible questions about the product in the copy, succinctly, so as not to take advantage of the prospect's time; controlling the reproductions in separations and printing, so that the item is shown in the actual color that the customer will receive. The design and graphics of the catalog are clean, with ample white space for framing the photography and providing relief for the prospect's eyes. The type is also clean, with limited reverse copy used, and no reverses out of busy photographic backgrounds.

The use of color is another application of catalog psychology. Research tests have proved that people respond predictably and emotionally to colors. Certain colors, such as warm earth tones, are comfortably perceived and provide pleasurable backgrounds for merchandise. And there are some colors that work negatively, provoking an unpleasant reaction from a viewer. Bright pinks and orchids are such colors and should be avoided for photographic backdrops.

Nature's colors and tints seem to be the most acceptable to the eye. The human eye functions much like a camera lens, seeing all colors made up of a combination of red, yellow, blue and black. A mechanical tint is less believable to the eye than a photographic one, which has shades from light to dark, and all four colors from the spectrum as opposed to a screen combination of one or two colors. Using mechanical tints cheapens a catalog and costs credibility.

Conceptualizing A Catalog

If a catalog is to qualify as being convenient, unique and considerate, it must be well thought out. An effective catalog does not begin at the drawing board with pen on layout paper, but much in advance of that. It begins with conceptualizing.

Each of the key people involved in the production of a catalog must allocate adequate thinking time. The merchant must think about the products; the art director must plan the creative approach; print production must think about the preparation of specifications and the desired end result of reproduction. But the head of direct marketing is usually the one responsible for the up-front conceptualizing called "direction" or "point of view."

Point-of-view conceptualizing involves finite review of the target audience, the kind of merchandise to be offered, the image desired, the concept of graphics and format, the degree of credibility and quality reproduction, and many other determining factors. Communication of these weighed decisions is imperative to each of the members of the production team, so that directions can be followed and conceptualizing achieved.

I find it most helpful to make notes as I begin to seek a concept for a catalog. The notes help to move thoughts to paper and to hold them as they are refined and polished. From the notes I begin to make thumbnail sketches, again to help crystallize thoughts into a less fleeting form. The sketches needn't be works of art; they are there to help communicate thoughts. Neither should they be inflexible. Improvement will naturally come in the progression of the development and as other people are brought into the thinking process.

As conceptual thinking brings direction, it should be equally applied to merchandising, format, and reproduction. A catalog can present a schizophrenic image if one area is well thought out and others are simply thrown together without the proper conceptual foundation. Conceptualizing is a technique of *theorizing* a catalog. From theory you must move to reality, or the *realization* of the book.

To Theme Or Not To Theme

Part of the conceptualizing process is deciding whether or not your catalog will be presented in a theme mode. There are endless subjects for theming, from seasons to lifestyle, from needs to special interests. Themes provide you with a logical format for presentation. (Some catalog marketers opt for no-theme presentation, a potpourri mixing of merchandise lending interest to the book.)

A catalog does not have to be strictly themed. A combination presentation can be equally effective, using themes for special sections or spreads. Or, in reverse, a themed catalog can present one spread of merchandise in potpourri fashion, breaking the pacing of the book and making it more interesting for the customer.

If a theme is used, it should be carried out subtly as a cohesive element. Using a seasonal theme, like springtime, fresh spring flowers can be used as props (never to detract from the merchandise) and pastel spring colors can be selected as backgrounds for shots. Birds, bird nests, robins' eggs, green leaves, rain drops, clouds: nature's props are infinite in variety, but don't cheat! Fake flowers will look exactly like what they are. Use the real thing, or forget it. Otherwise, you will destroy the credibility that you are working so hard to achieve.

The Cover Story

A catalog cover must work harder than any other ingredient in the medium. It must instantaneously make a statement of believability and credibility for the company, as well as entice the prospective customer to open the pages of the catalog.

Approximately three seconds is the amount of time each catalog cover is given by the recipient. That translates to an equivalent of $1\frac{1}{2}$ seconds to establish credibility and $1\frac{1}{2}$ seconds to intrigue the customer with a promise of what is inside the catalog. An incredible selling job must be accomplished in a short span of time.

Because the allotted interest time is small, it generally pays off for a catalog company to establish a recognizable format for their covers. If your catalog is instantly recognizable by its cover, more of the customer's attention can be called to the promise of exciting merchandise offerings inside the book. Formats can be developed that say, at a glance, this is the new American Express Catalog or the Holiday Issue of Bachrachs.

A cover format need not be inflexible; it is entirely possible to design a cover concept that will allow variations within a general framework. Subject matter may vary, while type style and placement of the logo remain the same with each issue.

Covers may be editorial or merchandised, depending on your point of view. Most cataloguers currently produce merchandised covers because of the value of the front cover selling space potential. It is difficult to give up what usually proves to be the number one selling space in the catalog just to make an editorial statement.

A combination cover can also be used. An item of merchandise can be selected for the cover and shown somewhat esoterically, which results in an editorial look. American Express samples shown here demonstrate a continuity of look or image, with merchandise shown editorially. In addition, the American Express card (even more recognizable than the logo) is worked into the cover each time.

Successful Covers

*Combination
Look.
Photos: Courtesy
of American
Express.*

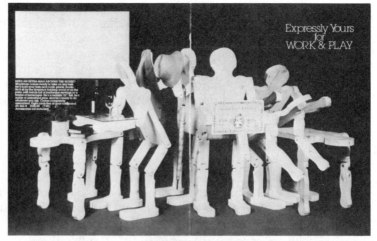

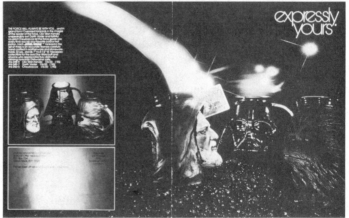

Bachrachs covers are merchandised, with the selling copy shown on the back cover and referenced again on the inside front cover. Since Bachrachs is a man's specialty clothing catalog, men's wear is shown on the front cover, usually treated seasonally in background and atmosphere.

It is a good idea to date your covers for identification purposes. Holiday 1984 or Summer 1984 will do for the wording, or you can be very specific if you produce seven or eight books a year, and label each issue with date of publication.

Very little space is devoted here to editorial covers because I would rather promote the sale of merchandise for any catalog. Additionally, I feel that it is more considerate of the customer to give an indication of what kind of items are inside the book. Editorial treatment of merchandise accomplishes both goals; i.e. to make a statement for the company image-wise and to let the customer know what to expect. And, it sells merchandise.

Selection of an item for the cover should be done carefully. Some generic guidelines are:

1. The item under consideration should be unusual, not generally found in other catalogs or stores. (Exclusive is even better.)
2. It should be deemed photographable by the creative staff.
3. It should be representative of the line of products offered inside the book.
4. It should be understandable, requiring only one depiction to show its features.

Creative Cover Techniques

The main ingredient that should be sought for a cover depiction is that of *drama*. A dramatic portrayal of a product lends impact to your cover efforts and will work harder for you than a pedestrian version. Williams-Sonoma chooses items that are representative, yet newsworthy, and features them dramatically with a Chuck Williams-prepared dish.

Drama can be obtained through lighting and composition of photography. Communicate to your creative director and photographer precisely what you are trying to achieve with your cover portrayal. And then allow them some creative license to bring back an outstanding cover shot. When composing the photograph they might discover a better angle that will enhance and further dramatize the product.

Good photography is your key to the finest reproduction. Be sure that you capture in photography the essence and quality of your point-of-view statement. Don't expect the separator, regardless of how accomplished he may be, to build something into the shot that is missing.

The Japanese have a phrase that relates to image and perception; they put great value in "presenting face." A catalog cover does exactly

Dramatic Covers: A Key Ingredient

Photos: Courtesy of American Express.

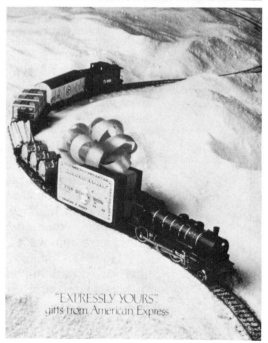

that to your customers. Although it requires weeks to create and is only recognized for a few brief seconds, the face that is presented has a lasting impression. It is important to present face by producing a unique, dramatic, quality-oriented cover. It is your official invitation to the customer to browse the pages of your paper store.

Graphic design is another important element. It can make the difference between a tasteful cover and a distasteful one. No matter how effective your cover photograph is, without good graphic treatment it will be wasted. Graphic format can vary from bold to subtle and understated and can change your statement from a shout to a whisper. Both kinds of statements can be successful, but rarely should you bounce from one to the other. Select your statement by knowing your customer, and sticking with the appropriate one. Refine it as you go along; each cover that you do should be better than the one preceding.

Catalog Design Techniques

A catalog is perceived by spreads, two facing pages. Customers do not see single pages one at a time, but rather the two facing pages as a visual element. Layout of pages should always be done bearing this in mind. The two-page spread should be worked as a unit, not individual pages as stand-alones.

If you imagine the spread as a blank canvas, then your mind (not your pencil) automatically begins to compose the white space as a physical frame for the items to be shown. Treatment of products does not have to be democratic. Drama in page layout is best achieved by varying the sizes of the depictions, so that at least one item on the spread is shown quite large and treated as important. Varying the size of the photographs also provides relief for the prospect's eyes, eliminating the monotony of a "comic book format" where all of the photographic boxes are the same size.

A layout format should blend from spread to spread, although it is not wise to repeat the exact same layout all the way through the book. Grid system layout is an easy way out—too easy! In fact, it reflects laziness or lack of creativity on the part of the designer. If you opt for grid system layout, you needn't pay the price of an accomplished catalog designer; a draftsman can do a grid system well.

The placement and arrangement of the elements should be done pleasingly and should help direct the eye to encompass the entire spread. This technique is called eye movement direction. The shape of the articles within the photographic boxes may have direction itself and should be used to subtly direct the eye at all times around or back into the spread. Even the gaze direction of the models can help to lead the prospect to the next depiction, which will lead to the next, etc., until every item on the spread has been perceived. A designer should not be

Effective Catalog Layout and Design

Photos: Courtesy of Artisans of China/Fingerhut Corporation (top), Nieman-Marcus (middle), and C&P Telephone (bottom).

a slave to eye movement direction, but should maintain an awareness of the power of being able to gently direct a prospect's attention.

Use of White Space

Unused white space can be the cleanest, most effective frame to set off the photography in a catalog. Type reads best when printed in black on white paper, and four-color photography stands out most dramatically when framed with white space. Use it effectively, and do not feel that because the white paper is there, it must be filled with another product. The proper allotment of space is just as important to the visual impact of a spread as the use of typography and photography.

Pacing and Pagination

The speed at which a prospect thumbs through a catalog is called pacing. Designers and planners of catalogs can, to a degree, control that page-turning speed. By placing some full-page impact shots spaced throughout the book you can gain the reader's attention for long spans of time. Additionally, the use of color can achieve the same thing; i.e., a reverse black spread sandwiched between several light, white spreads. A book that is all white tends to be perceived much like a long piece of staccato music. Varying the presentation gets better receptivity from the customer.

Pagination, or the assignment of items to a spread, helps to pace the catalog. An intriguing special interest spread, or grouping of items by theme, will capture attention and make the book more interesting. Sometimes the color of merchandise itself will suggest a theme, like primary colors, or natural earth tones. An entire spread of items can be put together for a patio party, including buffet servers, patio or garden candles, informal napkins, invitations, patio dresses, etc. Or how about a spread of products to make communicating easier? You could offer personalized stationery (formal and informal), electronic items like a telephone answering machine, a personal desk journal with appointment calendar, etc. And then accessory items for your at-home desk, like picture frames, small calculators, covered coffee mug, letter opener, and so on. Prospects accept pagination when it is done logically.

Copy as a Supportive Element

Without denigrating the role of copy, I must state for the record that catalogs are primarily a photographic medium. The pictures must first capture the prospect's attention. The copy should never detract from the graphic presentation but should be used subliminally to inform and enhance. Columnar copy, if keyed properly to the photography, is accepted as easily understandable and less distracting than cut copy, or copy that appears in individual blocks directly under the item. Cut copy tends to give a catalog a "chopped up" look.

Typography should be clean and well planned and used supportively as a graphic element. Type size should be readable, preferably 9 point with pleasing leading. Limit the number of type faces used to a bare

Dramatic Product Shots Through Lighting and Props

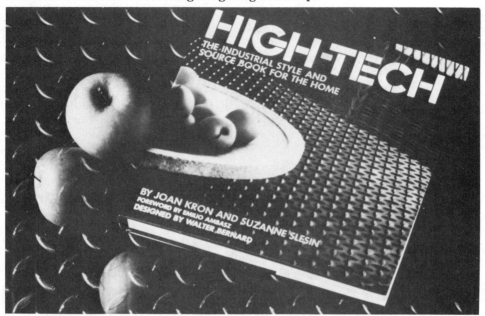

Photos: Courtesy of Edmund Scientific

Photo: Courtesy Gucci

Dramatic Product Shots Through Lighting and Props

*Photos: Courtesy
of The
Photographers*

minimum. If headlines are used, they should either explain or entertain. Usually a themed spread should be identified as such by a headline. Don't ask the prospect to guess why you grouped certain items together.

The content of catalog copy should be succinct, informative, descriptive, and, above all, accurate. In directing the writing of copy for catalogs, one usually must remind the copywriter of the need for discipline. It is more difficult to use fewer words to describe an item than it is to use more words. It is also important to develop an acceptable format for the listing and sequence of the item name, s.k.u. (stock keeping unit) number, price, and postage and handling charge.

Design Innovation

The preceding observations on catalog design are not to be considered iron-clad or self-sustaining. They are intended as guidelines and generic directions, possibly even as a foundation for your own individual style. There are endless ways to design a catalog, and each catalog deserves its own graphic identity. Don't be a look-alike, and don't rely on someone else's creative thinking for your catalog image. Formulate your own success story with innovation and refinement. Let others copy you, and feel good about it.

But if you are already an established leader in the field, do not be complacent about your standing. Continue to seek new solutions. Don't be afraid to experiment. Polish your presentation so that each catalog is better. And concentrate on customer consideration—not for the sake of graphic awards, but to help the merchandise sell better!

Keep your knowledge up to date on state-of-the-art technology. Advancements in reproduction are being made daily and are opening new doors to design techniques.

Photography Techniques For Catalog Marketing

Photography for catalogs should be used as a sculptor uses clay—a vital ingredient in the make-up of a marketing tool. It can be expressive and is definitely motivational. Densities and composition may be molded and formed to give life-like quality to inanimate objects, while shots involving models may be softly persuasive, yet show stunning clarity of detail.

Dramatization

As in cover photography, all of the product shots inside a catalog must sell one-to-one, and drama can be your best ally in accomplishing this. Emphasis on an item can be gained by lighting—special lighting that can spotlight, halo, or sculpt with dimension. Flat, overall lighting is not as effective for catalog work. Instead, get the maximum dramatic impact for each item by lighting to pick up details and shadows. Aim for crisp, clean highlights, but be careful not to drop the important middle tones!

The product should determine the lighting technique to be used. Different approaches are required to light a piece of crystal and a leather book. Keep your backgrounds as consistent across a spread as possible, and adjust the lights to best enhance the item being shot. Whether it is a table top shot on a small sweep or a location shot involving models, think the entire spread through before photography begins. That way you can communicate with the photographer to make your wishes known. Guesswork is costly and frustrating to everyone involved.

The Subtle Use of Props

Props should be used in photography to scale an item for size or to help explain its use. In a major setup shot that has plenty of room it's alright to use props in the background or foreground just to make the shot more interesting, as long as the props don't overpower the merchandise. When selecting a prop for scale, choose something that is easily understood at a glance. Commonly used props for scaling are flowers, fruit, and hands. You can also select stamps, coins, jelly beans, paper clips, or popcorn. Avoid using something that could be a variety of sizes, like books, candles, leaves, handbags, and ashtrays.

There is danger of overpropping at all times, and it is advisable to use props only when necessary and then prudently and tastefully. If the props overpower, the product gets lost. The example shown in Exhibit 12-22 of the glass bowl demonstrates overpropping. We had lots of requests for the recipe, but we sold very few glass bowls!

Maximizing Location Shootings

Location shootings for showing fashion items are effective in catalogs because: (a) They allow us to utilize nature's perfect lighting (which we cannot totally simulate in a studio); and (b) their background subject matter adds the element of entertainment for our prospects.

Whether you are shooting at the local park or halfway around the world, the rules should be the same. Don't crop out all of the background! If you have that in mind to start with (and most merchants do) save wear and tear on the shooting crew and stay in the studio. Location shots are difficult to plan and execute because of logistics, obtaining shooting permission, and moving merchandise, crew, equipment, and models around. Remember that the model needn't be centered in every shot. Allow some room for interesting composition, and don't tight-crop out all of the atmosphere. I once had a client who dragged me, merchandise, crew, models, and photographic equipment all over the world to shoot. And then insisted on cropping out all backgrounds. The books easily could have been shot in my backyard instead of in a foreign country!

Basics for Success

Catalog creativity has been emphasized in this section of the chapter. But this should not diminish in any way the vital ingredients of marketing, research, merchandising, list selection, print production, mailing, order forms, computers, toll free numbers, customer service, and fulfillment. Each has a priority role in the production and distribution of a successful catalog.

But catalog creativity seems to be the most misused and the most misunderstood of the necessary elements. By dissecting some of the major areas of creativity, perhaps we can eliminate some of the mystique and replace it with a more professional application of common sense rules. Although there is nothing common about creativity, neither is there anything sacred about it. It requires intense effort to crystallize an idea into a sound marketing piece. And not only is the marketplace ever changing, but so are the opportunities for presentation.

Creativity, as Jo-Von Tucker has so capably expressed, is the X factor necessary for leadership in a catalog category. Creative execution transcends the basics of a successful catalog operation. There are 10 basics important to success.

Photo: Courtesy of Neiman-Marcus.

1. *Right market positioning.* Every catalog must have a reason for being, must fill an identifiable, a reachable niche in the marketplace.

2. *Right merchandise selection.* Merchandise selection must fit the profile of the identified market. (Exclusive products, in particular, build customer loyalty.)

3. *Right positioning and grouping of merchandise.* Most professionals have found the best way to position merchandise is by popularity of categories, the most popular categories appearing up front in the book. Merchandise grouping should be arranged to achieve related buying opportunities and to maintain reader interest throughout the book.

4. *Right graphics.* To quote Jo-Von Tucker, "Catalogs are primarily a photographic medium." The graphics you use express the degree of authority you bring to the specific market you choose to serve.

5. *Right use of color.* Colors should provide pleasurable backgrounds for merchandise. Nature's colors and tints are considered to be the most acceptable to the eye.

6. *Right size.* Business-to-business catalogs should most always be $8\frac{1}{2}''$ x 11" in size for convenience in placing in industrial catalog reference files. The most popular consumer catalog size is $8\frac{1}{2}''$ x 11"—32 pages. However, a smaller page size, such as $5\frac{1}{2}''$ x $8\frac{1}{2},''$ should be considered if an $8\frac{1}{2}''$ x 11" page size would come in at less than 24 pages ("Heft"— thickness—denotes authority and encourages browsing.)

7. *Right copy.* Copy is subordinate to photography in catalog marketing, but it is vital. Copy must be disciplined, but it must include the basics: sizes, colors, materials, weight—if a factor, price. And, in a minimum of words, copy must appeal to the emotions for consumer catalogs and to rationalization for business catalogs.

8. *Right sales stimulators.* It can't be said too often: A catalog must sell on its own. Many catalogs just arrive and lie there. Other catalogs are live, vibrant, exciting—truly creative. Adroit sales stimulation, appropriate to the targeted market, is often the ingredient that pushes response beyond the norm.

The six sales stimulators in wide use by catalog marketers are: (1) the *Overwrap:* a sheet wrapped around the front and back cover, allowing extra space to encourage browsing and to stimulate ordering by offering incentives. (2) *Early order stimulators:* free gifts for ordering by a specific date, or an extra sweepstakes incentive for ordering by a specific date. (3) *Toll-free phone orders:* a convenient and cost-free incentive to order. (4) *Charge privileges:* an encouragement to buy without cash through use of bank cards and travel-and-entertainment cards. (5) *Free trial periods:* an incentive to examine and try merchandise with privilege to return. (6) *Free gifts, or discounts tied to size of order:* a stimulant to larger average orders.

9. *Right order forms.* Experience has proved that a bound-in order form with return envelope stimulates more orders than an on-page order form.

10. *Right sales analysis.* It's sad but true—the most beautiful, most imaginative catalog ever conceived turns downright "ugly" if sales don't meet projections. Every catalog should and *must* be analyzed page by page to avoid future failures, to build upon successes.

How to Analyze Results

The catalog sales manager looks at item exposure in a catalog the same way an advertising manager looks at space advertising in print media. Every inch of space you use in a catalog costs a certain amount of money. The cost of space is charged to the item being advertised.

Table 12-1 illustrates the importance of analyzing by item and by page. Let's examine these pages, starting with page 23. Note that three items are offered, one getting a space allocation of a half page and the other two each getting one-fourth page. Note the half-page allocation has an advertising cost of $968 as compared to an advertising cost of $484 for the quarter-page units.

Table 12-1. Analysis of Sales Results for Selected Pages From a Typical Catalog.

Page Number	Item Number	Space Allocation	Dollar Volume	Advert. Cost	Product Cost	Total of Costs	Item Profit	Item Loss	Page Profit (Loss)
23	1618	½ page	$6,699	$ 968	$1,608	$2,576	$4,123		
	1619	¼ page	556	484	133	617		$ 61	
	1620	¼ page	1,004	484	241	725	279		
Totals for page			$8,259	$1,936	$1,982	$3,918	$4,402	$ 61	$4,341
47	2612	⅔ page	$8,592	$1,291	$3,007	$4,298	$4,294		
	2613	⅙ page	386	323	135	458		72	
	2614	⅙ page	193	323	68	391		198	
Totals for page			$9,171	$1,937	$3,210	$5,147	$4,294	$ 270	$4,024
67	3499	½ page	$ 817	$ 968	$ 531	$1,499		$ 682	
	3500	¼ page	925	484	426	910	$ 15		
	3501	¼ page	316	484	205	689		373	
Totals for page			$2,058	$1,936	$1,162	$3,098	$ 15	$1,055	($1,040)
69	4621	¾ page	$3,226	$1,452	$1,484	$2,936	$290		
	4622	¼ page	1,689	484	777	1,261	428		
Totals for page			$4,915	$1,936	$2,261	$4,197	$ 718		$ 718

Source: Stone & Adler

It is significant that item #1618, with a space allocation of one-half page, did $6,699 in sales, over 80 percent of the total sales for the page. Item #1619 lost a small amount of money. Item #1620 made a minimum profit. If profits were calculated for the total page, ignoring the contribution of each item, then item #1619 would not show up as a loser and item #1620 would not show up as a minimum profit item.

Page 47 is also a profit maker. But note that only item #2612 shows a profit, whereas the other two items are losers.

Page 67 is a bad page. Two of the items lost money and the other just broke even. Total loss for the page was $1,040.

Finally let's look at page 69. Both items were profitable. But take careful note that the item allocated three-fourths of a page produced $290 in profit, whereas item #4622, which was allocated only one-fourth of a page, produced $428 in profit.

Let's take a closer look at these figures through the eyes of the catalog sales manager. The first thing he will do is to look at his big winners. From the four pages he has two big winners: items #1618 and #2612. He allocated one-half page to item #1618. For the next edition of his catalog, he well may consider increasing the space to three-fourths of a page or even a full page. He allocated two-thirds of a page to item #2612. For the next edition, he may consider going to one full page.

Now let's look at the losers. Item #1619 was a small loser. He may consider dropping this to one-sixth of a page or eliminating it entirely. On page 47 he had two losers: items #2613 and #2614. Since he allocated only the minimum one-sixth of a page, he can go one of two ways: either eliminate the items entirely or give them more space with the hope that additional space will put them in the profit column.

On page 67 he also had two losers: items #3499 and #3501. He gave one-half page to item #3499. Now he must decide whether it should be eliminated entirely. Since he gave only one-fourth page to item #3501, it is a moot question whether he can put it in the profit column by reducing the space further. These are difficult decisions to make.

One factor that will influence a catalog sales manager's decision is whether the catalog features full-line selection or not. The general merchandise house with full-time selections often must live with losers, whereas the specialty merchandise house (like Miles Kimball, Foster & Gallagher, and Hanover House) is rarely confronted with the problem.

The sophisticated catalog sales manager sees things in numerical results that the neophyte rarely sees. For the sake of illustration, let's assume item #1618, a big winner, was a sport sweater. The catalog sales manager asks himself, "If sport sweaters sell so well, why shouldn't we test sport jackets, sweatshirts, and jacket emblems?" Thus he builds on a winner. Superb creativity and marketing know-how: these are the foundations of successful catalog operations.

Self-quiz

1. What is the concept behind the *Catalogia* retail store?

_____

_____

_____

2. What are the four key perceptions that must be held by the consumer in order for a catalog operation to be successful?

a. Perceived _____   c. Perceived _____

b. Perceived _____   d. Perceived _____

3. What are the four general types of catalogs?

a. _____

b. _____

c. _____

d. _____

4. What is the X factor—the one distinguishing mark—that makes one catalog stand out from all others in its class?

_____

5. As high as _____ percent upscale catalog buyers are female.

6. To establish a niche in an overcrowded marketplace, you must have

_____.

7. Bright pinks and orchids work ☐ positively ☐ negatively for photographic backdrops.

8. What is meant by conceptualizing?

_____

_____

_____

9. A catalog cover must instantaneously make a statement of _____

_____ and _____

for the company.

10. The main ingredient that should be sought for a cover depiction is

_____.

11. A catalog is perceived by _____.

12. Define these two terms:

Pacing: _____

Pagination: _____

13. Catalogs are primarily a(n) _____medium.

14. Props should be used in photography to _____

_____, or to _____.

15. Location shootings are particularly effective for fashion items. Why?

_____

_____

_____

Pilot Project

You have a favorable connection with a leisure apparel manufacturer who has agreed to make available his line of leisure apparel and to also develop some exclusive fashions for you if you can find a niche for a catalog operation.

You have done some basic research and believe there is a niche for you among people who jog, particularly singles in the $35,000 and above income bracket and marrieds in the $50,000 and above income bracket.

Realizing there are just so many jogging outfits you can offer for various ages, male and female, you determine you should also offer other leisure apparel that might appeal to those whose lifestyle includes jogging.

With this as background develop a marketing plan that will include the following:

1. An appropriate name for the catalog.
2. A list of 20 leisure apparel items other than jogging outfits that might appeal to joggers.
3. What publications you might use to get catalog requests.
4. What mailing lists you might test.
5. Whether you would opt for location photography and, if so, where?

Chapter Thirteen

Techniques of Creating Print Advertising

Many of the creative techniques needed for creating a successful direct mail package (Chapter 11) are also necessary in creating productive direct response ads in magazines and newspapers. But the space available for words and pictures is much more severely limited, and most of the gimmicks, gadgets, showmanship, and personal tone of direct mail do not apply here. This throws a heavy load of responsibility for the success of the ad on a carefully worded headline, a compelling opening, tightly structured copy, and appropriate visual emphasis.

Before the actual work of creating an ad begins, two important questions should be answered: Who is the prospect? and What are the outstanding product advantages or customer benefits?

Often there is no single clear answer but, rather, several distinct possibilities. Then the profitable course of action is to prepare ads embodying all your most promising hypotheses and split-test as many of them as your budget permits.

Visualizing the Prospect

Every good mail order or direct mail piece should attract the most attention from the likeliest prospects, and every good creator of direct response advertising visualizes his prospect with varying degrees of precision when he sits down at his typewriter or drawing board.

Good direct response advertising makes its strongest appeal to its best prospects and then gathers in as many additional prospects as possible.

And who are the prospects? They are the ones with the strongest desire for what you're selling. You must look for the common denominators.

For instance, let's say you are selling a book on the American Revolution. Here are some of the relevant common denominators that would be shared by many people in your total audience.

1. An interest in the American Revolution in particular
2. An interest in American history in general
3. A patriotic interest in America
4. An interest in history
5. An interest in big, beautiful coffee table books
6. An interest in impressing friends with historical lore
7. A love of bargains
8. An interest in seeing children in the family become adults with high achievement

Now, out of the total audience of 1,000, some readers would possess all eight denominators, some would possess some combination of six, some a different combination of six, some just one of the eight, and so on.

If you could know the secret hearts of all 1,000 people and rank them on a scale of relative desire to buy, you would place at the very top of the list those who possessed all eight denominators, then just below them those who possessed just seven, and so on down to the bottom of the scale, where you would place people who possessed none.

Obviously, you should make as many sales as possible among your hottest prospects first, for that is where your sales will be easiest. Then you want to reach down the scale to sell as many of the others as you can. By the time you get down to the people possessing only one of the denominators, you will probably find interest so faint that it would almost be impossible to make your sales effort pay unless it were fantastically appealing.

Obvious? Yes, to mail order professionals who learned the hard way. But to the tenderfoot, it is not so obvious. In his eagerness to sell everybody, he may muff his easiest sales by using a curiosity-only appeal that conceals what is really being offered.

On the other hand, the veteran but uninspired pro may gather up all the easy sales lying on the surface but, through lack of creative imagination, fail to reach deeper into the market. For instance, let's say that of 1,000 readers, 50 possess all eight denominators. A crude omnibus appeal that could scoop up many of them would be something like, "At last—for every liberty-loving American family, especially those with children, whose friends are amazed by their understanding of American history, here is a big, beautiful book about the American Revolution you will display with pride—yours for only one-fifth of what you'd expect to pay!" A terrible headline, but at least one that those possessing the eight denominators of interest would stop to look at and consider. You may get only 5 percent readership, but it will be the right 5 percent.

Now, on the other hand, suppose you want to do something terribly creative to reach a wider market. So you do a beautiful advertising message headed "The Impossible Dream," in which you somehow work your way from that starting point to what it is you're selling. Again, you may get only 5 percent readership, but these readers will be scattered along the entire length of your scale of interest. Of the 50 people who stopped to read your message, only two or three may be prime prospects possessing all eight denominators. Many people really interested in books on the American Revolution, in inspiring their children with patriotic sentiments, and in acquiring big impressive books at big savings will have hurried past unaware.

The point: don't let prime prospects get away. In mail order you can't afford to. Some people out there don't have to be sold; they already want what you have, and if you tell them that you have it, they will buy it. Alone they may not constitute enough of a market to make your selling effort pay, but without them you haven't got a chance. So, through your clarity and directness, you gather in these prime prospects; then through your creative imagination you reach beyond them to awaken and excite mild prospects as well.

Once the prospect is clearly visualized, a good headline almost writes itself. For example, here is an effective and successful headline from an ad by Quadrangle/The New York Times Book Company. It simply defines the prospect so clearly and accurately that the interested reader feels an instant tug:

> For people who are almost (but not quite) satisfied with their house plants . . . and can't figure out what they're doing wrong

A very successful ad for Washington School of Art, offering a correspondence course, resulted from our bringing the psychographic profile of our prime prospect into sharp focus. We began to confront the fact that the prospect was someone who had been drawing pictures better than the rest of us since the first grade. Such people are filled with a rare combination of pride in their talent and shame at their lack of perfection. And their goal is not necessarily fame or fortune, but simply to become a "real artist," a phrase that has different meanings to different people. So the winning headline simply reached out to the right people and offered them the right benefit:

If you can draw fairly well (but still not good enough) we'll turn you into a real artist

Of course, a good headline does not necessarily present an explicit definition of the prospect, but it is always implied. Here are some classic headlines and the prospects whom the writer undoubtedly visualized:

Can a man or woman my age become a hotel executive?

The prospect is—probably—a middle-aged man or woman who needs, for whatever reason, an interesting, pleasant, not too technically demanding occupational skill such as hotel management, and is eager for reassurance that you *can* teach an old dog new tricks. Note, however, how wide the net is cast. No one is excluded. Even a person fearing he may be too young to be a hotel executive can theoretically read himself into this headline:

Don't envy the plumber—be one

The prospect is a poorly paid worker, probably blue-collar, who is looking for a way to improve his lot and who has looked with both indignation and envy at the plumber, who appears not much more skilled but earns several times as much per hour.

How to stumble upon a fortune in gems

The prospect is everybody, all of us, who all our lives have day-dreamed of gaining sudden wealth without extreme sacrifice.

Is your home picture-poor?

The prospect is someone, probably a woman, with a home, who has a number of bare or inadequately decorated walls, and who feels not only a personal lack but also, perhaps more important, a vague under-lying sense of social shame at this conspicuous cultural "poverty." Whether she appreciates it or not, she recognizes that art, books, and music are regarded as part of the "good life" and are supposed to add a certain richness to life.

Be a "non-degree" engineer

This is really a modern version of "don't envy the plumber." The prospect is an unskilled or semiskilled factory worker who looks with a mixture of resentment and grudging envy on the aristocracy in his midst, the fair-haired boys who earn much more, dress better, and enjoy special privileges because they are graduate engineers. The prospect would like to enjoy at least some of their job status but is unwilling or unable to go to college and get an engineering degree.

Are you tired of cooking with odds and ends?

The prospect is Everywoman who has accumulated over the years an enameled pan here, an aluminum pot there, an iron skillet elsewhere, and to whom a matched set of anything represents neatness, order, and elegance.

Can you call a man a failure at 30?

The prospect is a young white-collar worker between 25 and 32 who is deeply concerned that life isn't turning out the way he dreamed and that he is on the verge of failing to "make it"—permanently.

Selecting Advantages and Benefits

Advantages belong to the product. Benefits belong to the consumer. If the product or service is unique or unfamiliar to the prospect, stressing benefits is important. But if it is simply a new, improved model in a highly competitive field where there already exists an established demand, the product advantage or advantages become important.

Thus, when pocket electronic calculators were first introduced, such benefits as *pride, power,* and *profit* were important attributes. But, as the market became flooded with competing types and brands, product advantages such as the floating decimal became more important.

There are two kinds of benefits, the immediate or obvious benefit and the not-so-obvious ultimate benefit—the real potential meaning for the customer's life of the product or service being sold. The ultimate benefit often proves to have a greater effect, for it reaches deeper into the prospect's feelings.

For a girl who is a prospect for a course in Speedwriting shorthand, the obvious benefit is "a good job with more pay." But a strong possible ultimate benefit was expressed in the headline:

Catch yourself a new boss, etc.

Needless to say, the "etc." could easily be interpreted to mean "husband."

Victor Schwab, one of the great mail order pioneers, was fond of quoting Dr. Samuel Johnson's approach to auctioning off the contents

Exhibit 13-1. Classic Direct Response Ad

*"Can he really play?" a girl whispered.
"Heavens no!" Arthur exclaimed. "He
never played a note in his life."*

They Laughed When I Sat Down At the Piano But When I Started to Play!~

ARTHUR had just played "The Rosary." The room rang with applause. I decided that this would be a dramatic moment for me to make my debut. To the amazement of all my friends, I strode confidently over to the piano and sat down.

"Jack is up to his old tricks," somebody chuckled. The crowd laughed. They were all certain that I couldn't play a single note.

"Can he really play?" I heard a girl whisper to Arthur.

"Heavens, no!" Arthur exclaimed. "He never played a note in all his life. . . But just you watch him. This is going to be good."

I decided to make the most of the situation. With mock dignity I drew out a silk handkerchief and lightly dusted off the piano keys. Then I rose and gave the revolving piano stool a quarter of a turn, just as I had seen an imitator of Paderewski do in a vaudeville sketch.

"What do you think of his execution?" called a voice from the rear.

"We're in favor of it!" came back the answer, and the crowd rocked with laughter.

Then I Started to Play

Instantly a tense silence fell on the guests. The laughter died on their lips as if by magic. I played through the first few bars of Beethoven's immortal Moonlight Sonata. I heard gasps of amazement. My friends sat breathless — spellbound!

I played on and as I played I forgot the people around me. I forgot the hour, the place, the breathless listeners. The little world I lived in seemed to fade — seemed to grow dim—unreal. Only the music was real. Only the music and visions it brought me. Visions as beautiful and as changing as the wind blown clouds and drifting moonlight that long ago inspired the master composer. It seemed as if the master

Pick Your Instrument

Piano
Organ
Violin
Drums and Traps
Banjo
Tenor Banjo
Mandolin
Clarinet
Flute
Saxophone

*Cello
Harmony and Composition
Sight Singing
Ukulele
Guitar
Hawaiian Steel Guitar
Harp
Cornet
Piccolo
Trombone
Voice and Speech Culture
Automatic Finger Control
Piano Accordion

musician himself were speaking to me—speaking through the medium of music—not in words but in chords. Not in sentences but in exquisite melodies!

A Complete Triumph!

As the last notes of the Moonlight Sonata died away, the room resounded with a sudden roar of applause. I found myself surrounded by excited faces. How my friends carried on! Men shook my hand — wildly congratulated me— pounded me on the back in their enthusiasm! Everybody was exclaiming with delight—plying me with rapid questions. . . . "Jack! Why didn't you tell us you could play like that?". . . "Where did you learn?"—"How long have you studied?"—"Who was your teacher?"

"I have never even seen my teacher," I replied. "And just a short while ago I couldn't play a note.'.

"Quit your kidding," laughed Arthur, himself an accomplished pianist. "You've been studying for years. I can tell."

"I have been studying only a short while," I insisted. "I decided to keep it a secret so that I could surprise all you folks."

Then I told them the whole story.

"Have you ever heard of the U. S. School of Music?" I asked.

A few of my friends nodded. "That's a correspondence school, isn't it?" they exclaimed.

"Exactly," I replied. "They have a new simplified method that can teach you to play any instrument by mail in just a few months."

How I Learned to Play Without a Teacher

And then I explained how for years I had longed to play the piano.

"A few months ago," I continued, "I saw an interesting ad for the U. S. School of Music—a new method of learning to play which only cost a few cents a day! The ad told how a woman had mastered the piano in her spare time at home—and without a teacher! Best of all, the wonderful new method she used, required no laborious scales— no heartless exercises — no tiresome practising. It sounded so convincing that I filled out the coupon requesting the Free Demonstration Lesson.

"The free book arrived promptly and I started in that very night to study the Demonstration Lesson. I was amazed to see how easy it was to play this new way. Then I sent for the course.

"When the course arrived I found it was just as the ad said — as easy as A.B.C! And, as

the lessons continued they got easier and easier. Before I knew it I was playing all the pieces I liked best. Nothing stopped me. I could play ballads or classical numbers or jazz, all with equal ease! And I never did have any special talent for music!"

• • • • •

Play Any Instrument

You too, can now teach yourself to be an accomplished musician—right at home—in half the usual time. You can't go wrong with this simple new method which has already shown 350,000 people how to play their favorite instruments. Forget that old-fashioned idea that you need special "talent." Just read the list of instruments in the panel, decide which one you want to play and the U. S. School will do the rest. And bear in mind no matter which instrument you choose, the cost in each case will be the same—just a few cents a day. No matter whether you are a mere beginner or already a good performer, you will be interested in learning about this new and wonderful method.

Send for Our Free Booklet and Demonstration Lesson

Thousands of successful students never dreamed they possessed musical ability until it was revealed to them by a remarkable "Musical Ability Test" which we send entirely without cost with our interesting free booklet.

If you are in earnest about wanting to play your favorite instrument—if you really want to gain happiness and increase your popularity—send at once for the free booklet and Demonstration Lesson. No cost — no obligation. Right now we are making a Special offer for a limited number of new students. Sign and send the convenient coupon now — before it's too late to gain the benefits of this offer. Instruments supplied when needed, cash or credit. U. S. School of Music, 1831 Brunswick Bldg., New York City.

U. S. School of Music,
1831 Brunswick Bldg., New York City.

Please send me your free book, "Music Lessons in Your Own Home", with introduction by Dr. Frank Crane, Demonstration Lesson and particulars of your Special Offer. I am interested in the following course:

....

Have you above instrument?...............

Name...
(Please write plainly)

Address...

City.................... State...........

This ad, written by John Caples, a member of the Direct Marketing Hall of Fame, is considered one of the classics of direct response writing.

of a brewery: "We are not here to sell boilers and vats, but the potentiality of growing rich beyond the dreams of avarice."

It pays to ask yourself over and over again, "What am I selling? Yes, I know it's a book or a steak knife, or a home study course in upholstering—but what am I *really* selling? What human values are at stake?"

For example, suppose you have the job of selling a correspondence course in advertising. Here is a list of ultimate benefits and the way they may be expressed in headlines for the course. Some of the headlines are patently absurd, but they illustrate the mind-stretching process involved in looking for the ultimate benefit in your product or service.

- *Health:* "Successful ad men are healthier and happier than you think—and now you can be one of them."
- *Money:* "What's your best chance of earning $50,000 a year by the time you are 30?"
- *Security:* "You are always in demand when you can write advertising that sells."
- *Pride:* "Imagine your pride when you can coin a slogan repeated by 50 million people."
- *Approval:* "Did you write that ad? Why I've seen it everywhere."
- *Enjoyment:* "Get more fun out of your daily job. Become a successful ad writer!"
- *Excitement:* "Imagine working until 4:00 a.m.—and loving every minute of it!"
- *Power:* "The heads of giant corporations will listen to your advice—when you've mastered the secrets of advertising that works." (Just a wee bit of exaggeration there, perhaps.)
- *Fulfillment:* "Are you wasting a natural talent for advertising?"
- *Freedom:* "People who can get million dollar advertising ideas don't have to worry about punching a time clock."
- *Identity:* "Join the top advertising professionals who keep the wheels of our economy turning."
- *Relaxation:* "How some people succeed in advertising without getting ulcers."
- *Escape:* "Hate going to work in the morning? Get a job you'll love—in advertising!"
- *Curiosity:* "Now go behind the scenes of America's top advertising agencies—and find out how multimillion dollar campaigns are born!"
- *Possessions:* "I took your course five years ago—today I own two homes, two cars, and a Chris-Craft."
- *Sex:* "Join the guys and gals who've made good in the swinging advertising scene."
- *Hunger:* "A really good ad man always knows where his next meal is coming from."

Harnessing the Powers of Semantics

A single word is a whole bundle—a nucleus, you might say—of thoughts and feelings. And when different nuclei are joined together, the result is nuclear fusion, generating enough power to move the earth.

A whole new semi-science, semantics, has been founded on this unique property of words. The newspaper columnist, Sydney Harris, has popularized it with his occasional feature, "Antics with Semantics." A typical antic goes something like this: "I am sensible in the face of danger. You are a bit overcautious. He is a coward." The factual content may be the same, but the semantic implications vary widely.

Semantics is the hydrogen bomb of persuasion. In politics, for example, entire election campaigns sometimes hinge on the single word "boss." If one side manages to convince the public that the other side is controlled by a boss or bosses, but that the first side has only "party leaders," it will probably win the election.

In direct marketing, clear understanding and skillful use of semantics can make a powerful contribution to ad headlines. Here are a few examples.

What do you think when you read the word "Europe"? Perhaps there are certain negative connotations—constant military squabbles, lack of Yankee know-how, and so on. But far more important in the psyche of most Americans are the romantic implications—castles, colorful peasants, awesome relics of the past, charming sidewalk cafes, all merging into the lifelong dream of making the Grand Tour of Europe.

Another semantically rich word is "shoestring." A man is a fool to start a business of his own with inadequate capital. But if he succeeds, he is a "wizard," and his inadequate capital is seen in retrospect as a "shoestring." Harian Publications got the idea of linking these two words with a couple of modest connectives and achieved verbal nuclear fusion that sold thousands of books on low-cost travel: *Europe on a Shoestring.*

Because there is no copyright on semantic discoveries, Simon and Schuster could capitalize on Harian's discovery and publish their *$1 Complete Guide to Florida.* In fact, they were so successful they broke the mail order "rule" that a product selling for only $1.00 cannot be profitably sold in print ads.

For the word "Europe" they simply substituted another semantically rich word, "Florida," and came up with another powerful winner. A one-inch advertisement using this headline drew thousands of responses at a profitable cost per order, even when this tiny ad appeared to be completely lost on a 2,400-line page filled with larger ads screaming for attention.

Exhibit 13-2. The Power of a Strong Headline

At 4½ she's reading 3rd grade books

a child prodigy? not at all! your child, too can be reading one, two or three years beyond his present age level...even if he's a "poor" reader now

Prove it to yourself...with this 10 day free trial!

Reading is fun for Sarah—as it *should be* for every child. At age four and a half, she's already choosing her own books at the San Diego, Cal. library.

She reads books many third graders find "hard going." Yet she won't enter first grade for another year.

Sarah is typical of thousands of children who learned to read with "Listen and Learn with Phonics"—a reading kit that actually makes reading fun.

"Listen and Learn with Phonics" was developed by a reading expert. It has been endorsed, after extensive testing by teachers, schools, and educators.

This practical (and inexpensive) home-learning kit *fascinates* eager young minds from three to ten. The child *hears* the letters or sounds on the phonograph record, *sees* them in his book and repeats them himself. This makes an absorbing *game* of better reading—with amazing results!

FOR EXAMPLE:

- Slow or average readers show sudden, often spectacular improvement in reading, in spelling, in understanding.

- Older children often advance their reading skills several years beyond their age levels.

- Young "pre-schoolers" actually *teach themselves to read* by this simple but startlingly effective phonics method of words, pictures, and records.

6 TEACHING GAMES INCLUDED FREE
Set includes six separate "word building" games. All six are sent with your Listen and Learn Phonics Set FREE of charge!

TEACHERS & PARENTS ACCLAIM RESULTS
"I received your Combination Teaching Set and am positively delighted with it! . . . your marvelous approach to reading is just what we need."
Mrs. Rogavin, Central High School, Snyder, N.Y.

"We purchased 'Listen and Learn With Phonics' . . . for our nine year old son . . . within two weeks his reading had improved 100%."
Mrs. Gregory Knight, San Leandro, Cal.

4-MONTH UNCONDITIONAL GUARANTEE
If not delighted with the progress shown by your child—just return the set for complete refund.

These "Learning Tools" Simple to Use!
You don't need special teaching skills to use this program. Nor do you need any special knowledge of phonics.

In fact, your child needs no special supervision on your part. This set is so simple, so fascinating, he can learn "on his own" *without help.*

10-DAY FREE TRIAL—PLUS 4-MONTH MONEY-BACK GUARANTEE!
Results are so dramatic, the publishers will make the complete kit available to your child with an equally dramatic FREE trial and guarantee.

Under the terms of this unusual offer you can test the kit free of charge for ten days. Moreover you may use the kit for four months and then return it for *full refund* if you're not completely satisfied with your child's progress!

See for yourself how fast your child can learn to read. Just fill out and mail the coupon below. There's no obligation, and six teaching games are included free—yours to keep whether you buy or not. Americana Interstate, a division of Grolier, Inc., publishers of Book of Knowledge, Mundelein, Ill.

THE RED WORD BOX

THREE UNBREAKABLE 33⅓ RPM RECORDS

LETTER AND WORD STRIPS

FOUR ILLUSTRATED WORD BOOKS

TURN-A-WORD GAME

Good Housekeeping

- - MAIL COUPON FOR 10-DAY FREE TRIAL! - -

CAREER INSTITUTE, MUNDELEIN, ILL. 60060 P2-593

Send me for Free Examination, complete Listen and Learn with Phonics plus Free Educational Games. If not satisfied at the end of 10 days, I may return the $19.95 set and owe nothing. Otherwise, I'll send a first payment of $5.90 and then 3 monthly payments of $5 each which includes shipping and handling.

Name _____

Address _____

City _____ State _____ Zip _____

Child's Grade Level _____ Your Phone No. _____

☐ SAVE! Enclose check or money order for $19.95 and we pay shipping and handling. Same free trial privilege with full immediate refund guaranteed. (Illinois residents add $1.00 Sales Tax.)
This offer available in Canada. Canadian residents mail coupon to Illinois address. Shipment of books and all services will be handled within Canada.

This classic ad, appearing in scores of publications over a period of years, consistently outpulled all ads tested against it. Its success may well be attributed to the major headline's strong appeal to parental pride.

The fascinating thing about this kind of verbal nuclear fusion is that once it has been achieved it can be repeated almost endlessly—not only in the same form but in other forms as well.

For example, a real breakthrough in selling *Motor's Auto Repair Manual* was achieved many years ago with the headline, "Now You Can Lick Any Auto Repair Job." Every single word made a contribution to the power of the headline, as indeed each word always does in an effective headline. "Now" made the ad a news event, even after it had been running for years. "You," perhaps the sweetest word ever sounded to the ears, made it clear that the benefit included the reader and not just professional auto mechanics. "Can," another great word, promises power, achievement. "Lick" promises not only sure mastery but sweet triumph. Notice how much richer it is than "do." "Any" increases the breadth of the promise to the outermost limit. "Auto" selects the prospect and defines the field of interest. "Repair" defines the proposition, and "Job" emphasizes the completeness of its scope.

Once this breakthrough had been achieved, it was possible to make the same statement in many different ways with equal success. "Now Any Auto Repair Job Can Be 'Duck Soup' for You," "Now Any Auto Repair Job Can Be Your 'Meat,' " and so on.

"Engineer" is a rich, many-faceted word. To an artist or a writer, the word may connote a literal-minded square. To an engineer's prospective mother-in-law, it may connote a good provider. To an engineer, it means a degree in engineering and professional standing earned by hard study at college.

But to the manual and semiskilled workers in an electronics plant, our agency reasoned, in developing appeals for the Cleveland Institute of Electronics, the word "engineer" suggests the college-educated wise guy who is the fair-haired boy in the plant—an object both of envy on the part of the worker and of secret derision born of envy. We couldn't promise "You too can be an engineer," because "engineer" by itself is taken to mean a graduate engineer, and completion of CIE courses doesn't provide college credits or a college degree. However, many of the job titles in our promotion, such as "broadcast engineer," "field engineer," or "sales engineer," have the word "engineer" in them without requiring a college degree. So we were legitimately able to promise prospective enrollees the prestige and other rewards of being an engineer in an ad headed, "Be a Non-Degree Engineer." (See Exhibit 13-3.)

Semantic considerations like these cause mail order people to spend hours discussing and tinkering with a single headline or even a single word in the headline. It will pay you to study the mail order headlines you see used over and over again and try to analyze and apply the semantic secret of their success.

Exhibit 13-3. The Power of Semantics

How to Become a "Non-Degree" Engineer in the Booming World of Electronics

Thousands of real engineering jobs are being filled by men without engineering degrees. The pay is good, the future bright. Here's how to qualify...

By G. O. ALLEN

President, Cleveland Institute of Electronics

THE BIG BOOM IN ELECTRONICS—and the resulting shortage of graduate engineers—has created a new breed of professional man: the "non-degree" engineer. He has an income and prestige few men achieve without going to college. Depending on the branch of electronics he's in, he may "ride herd" over a flock of computers, run a powerful TV transmitter, supervise a service department, or work side by side with distinguished scientists designing and testing new electronic miracles.

According to one recent survey, in military-connected work alone 80% of the civilian field engineers are not college graduates. Yet they enjoy officer status and get generous *per diem* allowances in addition to their excellent salaries.

In TV and radio, you qualify for the key job of Broadcast Engineer if you have an FCC License, whether you've gone to college or not.

Now You Can Learn at Home

To qualify, however, you do need to know more than soldering, testing circuits, and replacing components. You need to really know your electronics theory—and to prove it by getting an FCC Commercial License.

Now you can master electronics theory at home, in your spare time. Over the last 30 years, here at Cleveland Institute of Electronics, we've perfected AUTO-PROGRAMMED™ lessons that make learning at home easy, even if you once had trouble studying. To help you even more, your instructor gives the homework you send in his undivided personal attention—it's like being the only student in his "class." He even mails back his corrections and comments the same day he gets your work, so you hear from him while everything is still fresh in your mind.

Does it work? I'll say! Better than 9 out of 10 CIE men who take the U.S. Government's tough FCC licensing exam *pass it on their very first try.* (Among non-CIE men, 2 out of 3 who take the exam *fail.*) That's why we can promise in writing to refund your tuition in full if you complete one of our FCC courses and fail to pass the licensing exam.

Students who have taken other courses often comment on how much more they learn from us. Says Mark E. Newland of Santa Maria, Calif.:

"Of 11 different correspondence courses I've taken, CIE's was the best prepared, most interesting, and easiest to understand. I passed my 1st Class FCC exam after completing my course, and have increased my earnings by $120 a month."

Mail Coupon for 2 Free Books

Thousands of today's "non-degree" engineers started by reading our 2 free books: (1) Our school catalog "How to Succeed in Electronics," describing opportunities in electronics, our teaching methods, and our courses, and (2) our special booklet, "How to Get a Commercial FCC License." To receive both without cost or obligation, mail coupon below.

CiE **Cleveland Institute of Electronics**
1776 E. 17th St. Dept. PS-6, Cleveland, Ohio 44114

Cleveland Institute of Electronics
1776 East 17th Street, Dept. PS-6, Cleveland, Ohio 44114

Please send me without cost or obligation:

1. Your 40-page booklet describing the job opportunities in Electronics today, how your courses can prepare me for them, your methods of instruction, and your special student services.
2. Your booklet on "How to Get a Commercial FCC License."

I am especially interested in:

☐ **Electronics Technology**   ☐ **Electronic Communications**
☐ **First Class FCC License**   ☐ **Industrial Electronics**
☐ **Broadcast Engineering**   ☐ **Advanced Engineering**

Name .... Age ......
(Please print)

Address..

City ....State..........Zip.......

Present Job Title ....

☐ Accredited Member National Home Study Council
A Leader in Electronics Training...Since 1934

The power of semantics is shown in this strong headline. It incorporates many favorable connotations in the promise to become a "Non-Degree Engineer."

Building in the "Hook"

A successful direct marketing ad must compete fiercely for the reader's time and attention. No matter how great the copy is, it will be wasted if the headline does not compel reading. So most successful headlines have a "hook" to catch the reader and pull him in. The most common hooks are such words as *why, how, new, now, this, what*. They make the reader want to know the answer. *Why* it is? *How* does it? *What* is it?

Consider the flat statement:

Increasing your vocabulary can help you get ahead in life

This is merely an argumentative, pontifical claim. It doesn't lead anywhere. But notice how the addition of just one word changes the whole meaning and the mood;

How increasing your vocabulary can help you get ahead in life.

This unstylish, uncreative headline, and the copy that followed sold hundreds of thousands of copies of a vocabulary book. It selected the prospect (people who were interested in larger vocabularies), it promised an ultimate benefit (*success*), and it built in a hook (*how*).

Of course, the hook can be merely implied. There is no hook word in the headline, "Be a Non-Degree Engineer." But there is a clear implication that the copy is going to tell you how to achieve this.

Writing the Lead

Perhaps the most troublesome and important part of any piece of mail order copy is the lead, or opening. A lead that "grabs" the reader doesn't guarantee that he will read the rest of the copy. But one that fails to grab him does practically guarantee that he *won't* read the rest.

Always remember in writing or judging a lead that your reader has better things to do than sit around and read your advertising. He doesn't really want to read your copy—until you make him want to. And your lead has got to make him want to.

A common error in writing leads is failure to get to the point immediately—or at least to *point* to the point. Haven't you had the experience of listening to a friend or associate or public speaker who is trying to tell you something but not able to get to the point? Remember how impatient you felt as you fumed inwardly, "Get to the point!" Your readers feel that same way about copy—and can very easily yawn and turn away. A good roundabout lead is not impossible, but it takes a brilliant writer.

A good principle to follow is that the copy should proceed from the headline. That is, if your headline announces what you are there to talk about, then you should get down to business and talk about it. Although it is true that some successful advertising merely *continues* the message started by the headline or display copy, there is far less danger of confusion if the copy *repeats* and *expands* the headline message, exactly the way a good news item does.

Notice how marvelously these leads from the *Wall Street Journal* news columns form a bridge between the headlines and the rest of the stories:

New postage-stamp ink to speed mail processing

NEW YORK—U.S. postage stamps will soon be tagged with a special luminescent ink that will permit automatic locating and cancelling of the stamps to speed processing of the mail.

Affluent Americans awash in documents snap up home safes

NEW YORK—There's a popular new home appliance that won't wash a dish, dry a diaper, or keep a steak on ice. It's a safe. And it's being propelled into prominence by a paper work explosion.

Notice, too, that although the lead restates the thought of the headline, it does it in a different way, recapping the thought but also advancing the story.

Classic Copy Structure

In a classic mail order copy argument, a good lead should be visualized as the first step in a straight path of feeling and logic from the headline or display theme to the concluding call for action. In that all-important first step, the reader should be able to see clearly where the path is taking him. Otherwise he may not want to go. (This is the huge error of ads that seek to pique your curiosity with something irrelevant and then make a tie-in to the real point. Who's got time for satisfying that much curiosity these days?)

The sections of a classic copy argument may be labeled *problem, promise of solution, explanation of promise, proof, call to action.* However, if you're going to start with the problem, it seems like a good idea at least to hint right away at the forthcoming solution. Then the reader won't mind your not getting to the point right away, as long as he knows where you're going. A generation ago, when the pace of life was slower, a brilliant copywriter could get away with spending the first third of his copy leisurely outlining the problem before finally getting around to the solution. But in today's more hectic times, it's riskier.

Here is an ad seeking Duraclean dealers in which the problem lead contains the promise of solution.

I found the easy way to escape from being a "wage slave"

I kept my job while my customer list grew ... then found myself in a high-profit business. Five years ago, I wouldn't have believed that I could be where I am today.

I was deeply in debt. My self-confidence had been shaken by a disastrous business setback. Having nobody behind me, I had floundered and failed for lack of experience, help, and guidance.

Now the copy could have simply started out, "Five years ago, I was deeply in debt," and so on. But the promise of happier days to come provides a carrot on a stick, drawing us down the garden path. You could argue that the headline had already announced the promise. But in most cases, good copy should be able to stand alone and make a complete argument even if all the display type were removed.

Here, from an ad for isometric exercises, is an example of the flashback technique referred to above:

[Starts with the promise]

Imagine a 6-second exercise that helps you keep fit better than 24 push-ups. Or another that's capable of doubling muscular strength in 3 weeks!

Both of these "quickie" exercises are part of a fantastically simple body-building method developed by Donald J. Salls, Alabama Doctor of Education, fitness expert and coach. His own trim physique, his family's vigorous health and the nail-hard brawn of his teams are dramatic proof of the results he gets—not to mention the steady stream of reports from housewives, athletes, even school children who have discovered Dr. Salls' remarkable exercises.

[Flashback to problem]

Most Americans find exercise a tedious chore. Yet we all recognize the urgent personal and social needs for keeping our bodies strong, shapely, and healthy. What man wouldn't take secret pride in displaying a more muscular figure?

What woman doesn't long for a slimmer, more attractive figure? The endless time and trouble required to get such results has been a major, if not impossible hurdle for so many of us. But now [return to the promise] doctors, trainers, and physical educators are beginning to recommend the easy new approach to body fitness and contour control that Dr. Salls has distilled down to his wonderfully simple set of 10 exercises.

Of course a really strong, exciting promise doesn't necessarily need a statement of the problem at all. If you're selling a "New Tree that

Grows a Foot a Month," it could be argued that you don't actually have to spell out how frustrating it is to spend years waiting for ordinary trees to grow; this is well known and implied.

Other Ways to Structure Copy

There are as many different ways to structure a piece of advertising copy as there are to build a house.

But response advertising, whether in publication or direct mail, has special requirements. The general advertiser is satisfied with making an impression, but the response advertiser must stimulate immediate action. Your copy must pile up in your reader's mind argument after argument, sales point after sales point, until his resistance collapses under the sheer weight of your persuasiveness, and he does what you ask.

One of the greatest faults in the copy of writers who are not wise in the ways of response is failure to apply this steadily increasing pressure. This may sound like old-fashioned "hard sell," but, ideally, the impression your copy makes should be just the opposite. The best copy, like the best salesperson, does not appear to be selling at all, but simply to be sharing information or proposals of mutual benefit to the buyer and seller.

Of course, in selling certain kinds of staple merchandise, copy structuring may not be important. There the advertising may be compared to a painting in that the aim is to convey as much as possible at first glance and then convey more and more with each repeated look. You wouldn't sell a 35-piece electric drill set with a 1,000-word essay but, rather, by spreading out the set in glowing full-color illustrations richly studded with "feature call-outs."

But where you are engaged in selling intangibles, an idea or ideas instead of familiar merchandise, the way you structure your copy can be vitally important.

In addition to the classic form mentioned above, here are some other ways to structure copy.

With the "cluster-of-diamonds" technique, you assemble a great many precious details of what you are selling and present them to the reader in an appropriate setting. A good example is the "67 Reasons Why" subscription advertising of *U.S. News & World Report,* listing 67 capsule descriptions of typical recent news articles in the magazine. The "setting"—the surrounding copy containing general information and argumentation—is as important as the specific jewels in the cluster. Neither would be sufficiently attractive without the other technique.

The "string-of-pearls" technique is similar but not quite the same. Each "pearl" is a complete little gem of selling, and a number of them are simply strung together in almost any sequence to make a chain.

David Ogilvy's "Surprising Amsterdam" series of ads is like this. Each surprising fact about Amsterdam is like a small-space ad for the city, but only when all these little ads are strung together do you feel compelled to get up from your easy chair and send for those KLM brochures. This technique is especially useful, by the way, when you have a vast subject like an encyclopedia to discuss. You have not one but many stories to tell. And, if you simply ramble on and on, most readers won't stay with you. So make a little list of stories you want to tell, write a tight little one-paragraph essay on each point, announce the subject of each essay in a boldface subhead, and then string them all together like pearls, with an appropriate beginning and ending.

The "fan dancers" technique is like a line of chorus girls equipped with Sally Rand fans. The dancers are always about to reveal their secret charms, but they never quite do. You've seen this kind of copy many times. One of the best examples is the circular received in answer to an irresistible classified ad in *Popular Mechanics*. The ad simply said "505 odd, successful enterprises. Expect something odd." The circular described the entire contents of a book of money-making ideas in maddening fashion. Something like: "No. 24. Here's an idea that requires nothing but old coat hangers. A retired couple on a Kansas farm nets $240 weekly with this one." "No. 25. All you need is a telephone—and you don't call them, they call you to give their orders. A bedridden woman in Montpelier nets $70.00 a week this way." And so on.

With the "machine gun" technique, you simply spray facts and arguments in the general direction of the reader, in the hope that at least some of them will hit. This may be called the no-structure structure, and it is the first refuge of the amateur. If you have a great product and manage to convey your enthusiasm for it through the sheer exuberance of your copy, you will succeed, not because of your technique, but despite it. And the higher the levels of taste and education of your readers, the less chance you will have.

Establishing the Uniqueness of Your Product or Service

What is the unique claim to fame of the product or service you are selling? This could be one of your strongest selling points. The word "only" is one of the greatest advertising words. If what you offer is "better" or "best," this is merely a claim in support of your argument that the reader *should* come to you for the product or services offered. But, if what you are offering is the "only" one of its kind, then the reader *must* come to you if he or she wants the benefits that only you can offer.

Here are some ways in which you may be able to stake out a unique position in the marketplace for the product or service you are selling:

"We're the largest." People respect bigness in a company or a sales total—they reason that, if a product leads the others in its field, it must be good. Thus "No. 1 Best-Seller" is always a potent phrase, for it is not just an airy claim but a hard fact that proves some kind of merit.

But what if you're *not* the largest? Perhaps you can still establish a unique position. . . . "We're the largest of our kind." By simply defining your identity more sharply, you may still be able to claim some kind of size superiority. For example, there was the Trenton merchant who used to boast that he had "the largest clothing store in the world in a garage!"

A mail order photo finisher decided that one benefit it had to sell was the sheer bigness of its operation. It wasn't the biggest—that distinction belonged, of course, to Eastman Kodak. But it was second. And Eastman Kodak was involved in selling a lot of other things too, such as film and cameras and chemicals. Their photo finishing service was only one of many divisions. So the advertiser was able to fashion a unique claim: "America's Largest *Independent* Photo Finisher."

"We're the fastest-growing." If you're on the way to *becoming* the largest, that's about as impressive a proof of merit as being the largest—in fact, it may be even *more* impressive, because it adds the excitement of the underdog coming up fast. *U.S. News & World Report* used this to good effect during the 1950s while its circulation was growing from approximately 400,000 to about three times that figure: "America's Fastest-Growing Newsmagazine." Later, the same claim was used effectively for Capitol Record Club, "America's Fastest-Growing Record Club."

"We offer a unique combination of advantages." It may be that no one claim you can make is unique, but that none of your competitors is able to equal your claim that you have *all* of a certain number of advantages.

In the early 1960s, the Literary Guild began to compete in earnest with the Book-of-the-Month Club. They started offering books that compared very favorably with those offered by BOMC. But the latter had a couple of unique claims that the Guild couldn't match—BOMC's distinguished board of judges and its book-dividend system, with a history of having distributed $375 million worth of books to members.

How to compete? The Guild couldn't claim the greatest savings; one of Doubleday's other clubs actually saved the subscriber more off the publisher's price. It couldn't claim that it had books offered by no other club; some of Doubleday's other clubs were offering some of the same books, and even BOMC would sometimes make special arrangements to offer a book being featured by the Guild.

But the Guild was able to feature a unique *set* of advantages that undoubtedly played a part in the success it has enjoyed: "Only the

Exhibit 13-4. A/B Copy Test

The makers of Wynn's Friction Proofing Oil wanted to test two different sales appeals: (1) Get more power with less gas; (2) save one gallon of gas in every ten. These two "reader ads" were written to test the appeals. The second appeal brought twice as many sample requests as the first one.

ADD THIS PRODUCT TO ANY MOTOR OIL FOR MORE POWER WITH LESS GAS

Sluggish motors get a new lease on life with Wynn's Friction Proofing Oil. This new chemical compound added to your present brand of motor oil every 1000 miles, bonds a super-slick surface to engine parts. This virtually eliminates the friction drag that wastes up to half your car's power, and gives you so much extra mileage from gasoline that it's like getting one gallon free with every ten you buy. Besides paying for itself in gasoline savings, Wynn's cuts carbon and sludge, frees sticky valves, reduces wear and repairs. Try Wynn's for new pep, power, economy from your car. We're so sure you'll continue to use it that we make this special introductory offer of a regular 1000-mile size 95¢ can of Wynn's for only 10¢. Just send your name and address, enclosing 10¢ in coin or stamps. By return mail you'll get a certificate entitling you to a 95¢ can of Wynn's without additional charge at any Wynn dealer. Limit one. Offer expires April 30. Write today—Wynn Oil Company, Dept. A-4, Azusa California.

AT SERVICE STATIONS, GARAGES, NEW CAR DEALERS

CAR OWNERS! SAVE ONE GALLON OF GAS IN EVERY TEN

Sluggish motors get a new lease on life with Wynn's Friction Proofing Oil. This new chemical compound added to your present brand of motor oil every 1000 miles, bonds a super-slick surface to engine parts. This virtually eliminates the friction drag that wastes up to half your car's power, and gives you so much extra mileage from gasoline that it's like getting one gallon free with every ten you buy. Besides paying for itself in gasoline savings, Wynn's cuts carbon and sludge, frees sticky valves, reduces wear and repairs. Try Wynn's for new pep, power, economy from your car. We're so sure you'll continue to use it that we make this special introductory offer of a regular 1000-mile size 95¢ can of Wynn's for only 10¢. Just send your name and address, enclosing 10¢ in coin or stamps. By return mail you'll get a certificate entitling you to a 95¢ can of Wynn's without additional charge at any Wynn dealer. Limit one. Offer expires April 30. Write today—Wynn Oil Company, Dept. C-12, Azusa, California.

AT SERVICE STATIONS, GARAGES, NEW CAR DEALERS

Literary Guild saves you 40 percent to 60 percent on books like these as soon as they are published." Other clubs could make either of these two claims, but only the Guild could claim both.

"We have a uniquely advantageous location." A classic of this was James Webb Young's great ad for "Old Jim Young's Mountain Grown Apples—Every Bite Crackles, and the Juice Runs Down Your Lips." In it Jim Young, trader, tells how the natives snickered when his pappy bought himself an abandoned homestead in a little valley high up in the Jemes Mountains. But "Pappy" Young, one of the slickest farmers ever to come out of Madison Avenue, knew that "this little mountain valley is just a natural apple spot—as they say some hillsides are in France for certain wine grapes. The summer sun beats down into this valley all day, to color and ripen apples perfectly; but the cold mountain air drains down through it at night to make them crisp and firm. Then it turns out that the soil there is full of volcanic ash, and for some reason that seems to produce apples with a flavor that is really something."

Haband Ties used to make a big thing out of being located in Paterson, New Jersey, the silk center of the nation. Even though most of the company's ties and other apparel were made of synthetic fibers, somehow the idea of buying ties from the silk center made the reader feel he was buying ties at the very source. In the same way, maple syrup from Vermont should be a lot easier to sell than maple syrup from Arizona.

Finally, suppose you believe that you have something unique to sell, but you hesitate to start an argument with your competitors by making a flat claim that they may challenge. In that case you can *imply your uniqueness* by the way in which you word the claim. "Here's one mouthwash that keeps your mouth sweet and fresh all day long" doesn't flatly claim that it's the only one. It simply says, "at least *we've* got this desirable quality, whether any other product does or not." *Newsweek* identified itself as "the news magazine that separates fact from opinion"—a powerful use of that innocent word "the" which devastates the competition.

Effective Use of Testimonials

If you have a great product or service, you have an almost inexhaustible source of great copy practically free—written by your own customers. They will come up with selling phrases straight from the heart that no copywriter, no matter how brilliant, would ever think of. They will write with a depth of conviction that the best copywriters will find hard to equal.

The value of testimonials in mail order advertising has been recognized for nearly 100 years, is generally taken for granted, and nonetheless is frequently overlooked. If a survey were conducted of companies dependent on responses by mail the survey would undoubtedly reveal that a shockingly high percentage of those companies have no regular, methodical system of soliciting, filing, and using good testimonials. Yet a direct marketing enterprise may often stand or fall on whether it makes good use of testimonials.

Many years ago the Merlite Company was founded to sell the Presto midget fire extinguisher, entirely through agents. The advertising job was to pull inquiries from prospective agents, who were then converted to active salespeople by the followup direct mail package. One of the first efforts for Merlite was the creation of a testimonial-soliciting letter. From this letter, which was mailed to a fair number of their best agents, came the story which formed the basis for a successful small space ad which ran for years and resulted in the sale of thousands of units. The headline: "I'm Making $1,000 a Month—and Haven't Touched Bottom Yet!" In those days, $1,000 a month was big money—it represented just about the top limit of the wildest dreams of people of modest means. If the ad had claimed, "Make $1,000 a month selling this amazing little device," it would have sounded like a hard-to-believe get-rich-quick scheme. But the fact that an actual agent said it (his name and picture appeared in every ad) made the possibility a fact, not a claim. And the "haven't touched bottom yet" was a homey additional promise that probably no city slicker copywriter would have thought of if he were creating a fictional testimonial.

Many U.S. School of Music ads in the past were built around testimonials. Being able to play a musical instrument has a deep meaning for people that could best be expressed by the students themselves. One ad bore a headline extracted from an ecstatic student's comments: "I Can't Believe My Ears—I'm Playing Music! My friends all think it's me, but I keep telling them it's your wonderful course."

One of the most appealing and effective stories used in art school advertising was that of a Florida mother who enrolled in the course and became one of the state's best-known painters. Her story was filled with more joy of fulfillment, credible praise for the course, and identification for other women than could be used in the ad. For instance, the day her textbooks arrived, she felt like a "child with a new toy." Her instructors were "just wonderful. I actually came to feel they were my friends." But what if you're a homemaker tied down with housework and babies? Isn't it hard to find time to paint? "It's not as hard as it sounds. When you have something exciting to look forward to, the housework flies. It's like when you're expecting a guest. You seem to get through the chores easily because you're looking forward to the visit." But won't hubby and kids be resentful if Mom spends a lot of time painting? Not her family. "They're so enthusiastic. Everytime I complete a painting, it's like a wonderful family party at our home." Isn't this reassuring? Isn't this what every creative woman would enjoy? And doesn't she make it all sound wonderfully possible and attainable?

You may have received some unsolicited testimonials that you have gotten permission to use and are already using. But, if you expand this by setting up a methodical testimonial-soliciting program, you can increase tenfold your effective use of testimonials. Because the quality and usefulness of testimonials vary widely, the more testimonials you pull in, the more pure gold you should be able to pan from the ore. Of course, it's important to get the testimonial donor's signature on some kind of release giving you permission to use his comments, name, and photo, if any. The wording of the releases varies. Some companies are content with a very simple "You have my permission" sentence; others use a more elaborately foolproof legal form. You should consult your attorney about the kind you choose to use.

Your testimonial-soliciting letter should drop a few gentle hints about your interest in hearing of actual benefits and improvements from your product. Otherwise you'll get too many customers writing similar lines of empty praise such as "it's the greatest" and "it's the finest."

Justify the Price

"Why Such a Bargain? The Answer Is Simple." These eight magic words constitute one of the most important building blocks in the mail order sale. They have been expressed hundreds of different ways in the past, and will appear in hundreds of new forms in the future. But whether in the mail order ads of magazines and direct mail yesterday and today, or the televised home-printed facsimile transmission of tomorrow, the *price justification argument* will always be with us. It does an important job of making the low price seem believable and the high price not really so high.

Here are a number of examples of price justification from the past. As you read through them, ask yourself if it isn't likely that similar arguments will still be used in the year 2000.

Doubleday Subscription Service: "How can the Doubleday Subscription Service offer these extremely low prices? The answer is really quite simple. Not everyone wants the same magazines. By getting all the publishers to allow us to make their offers in one mailing, each subscriber has a chance to pick and choose; each magazine gets its most interested readers at the lowest possible cost. The savings are passed on to you in the lowest possible prices for new, introductory subscriptions."

Reader's Digest (Music of the World's Great Composers): "How is this low price possible? Without the great resources of RCA and the large 'audience' of *Reader's Digest*, such a collection would have to cost about $60.00. This sum would be needed to cover royalties to musicians, the cost of recording, transferring sound from tape to records, manufacturing and packaging. But because a single large pressing of records brings down the cost of manufacturing, and because the entire edition is reserved in advance for *Digest* subscribers, you can have these luxury-class records now at a fraction of the usual price for records of such outstanding quality!"

Singer (socket wrench and tool set): "This set is not available in stores—but sets like these sell regularly in stores at a much higher price. You save the difference because—unlike the usual store which sells just a few sets at a time, we sell many hundreds, thus enabling us to purchase large quantities at big savings which we pass on to you."

American Heritage (History of the Civil War): "The post-publication price of the standard edition will be $19.95; it can be kept down to this level because of the exceptionally large first printing. But if you reserve a copy before publication (a great help with shipping, storage, inventory, etc.) we shall be glad to reduce the $19.95 price by 25 percent." (Notice the double whammy here. First, the value of the post-publication edition is justified, and then the even greater value of the pre-publication edition is justified.)

Book-of-the-Month Club (Pre-Publication Society): "Like the 'limited edition'—a very old custom in publishing—'pre-publication' offerings are designed to help *underwrite* the costs of any publishing project where there is an exceptionally high risk and heavy investment. Under modern printing conditions, if a publisher can be assured of a relatively large edition, the per-copy cost is reduced with almost every extra thousand copies printed. In recent years the usual procedure has been for the publisher, himself, to print an elaborate circular announcing the 'pre-publication offer' (similar to the one enclosed) and to permit booksellers, at a slight cost, to mail these announcements to select good customers. Rarely, however, do more than a few hundred booksellers over the country participate in this kind of promotion, with the result that comparatively few book lovers ever learn of it, and usually only in large cities. The efforts of the Pre-Publication Society will be far more thorough and widespread."

Visual Reinforcement of Words and Ideas

All our powers of comprehension are built on our earliest sensations and associations. First comes touch, but that won't be much held to advertising until Aldous Huxley's "Feelyvision" is invented. Next, when we are several months old, comes image, as we learn to associate Mama's smiling face with getting fed, burped, and changed. Then comes the spoken word, when we learn to call Mama by name. This early experience with the image and the spoken word is what makes television such a potent advertising force.

Our earliest experience with the printed word is usually in our heavily illustrated first reader (or preschool picture book). It is printed in large clear serif type, in lowercase—which is why serif body types seem more readable than sans serif, and lowercase more comfortable than upper. And when the book says, "Oh! See the boy!" sure enough, there is usually a picture of a boy. This makes it less likely that we would stand up in class and read aloud, "Oh! See the doy!"

Advertising has seized on this fact of human development and developed it into an astonishingly effective tool of communication. It has learned, probably far more than ever before in human history, to team words and pictures for greater impact than either alone can achieve. Sometimes it's a *rebus*, in which a picture is substituted for some of the words. For instance, instead of saying *"(a summons, a will, a deed, a mortgage, a lease) are a few of the reasons why every family should have a lawyer,"* an ad for New York Life Insurance Company substituted a picture of such documents as a will and a mortgage, for the words in parentheses.

Sometimes, it's a *pantomime,* with the words providing only the necessary minimum of explanation. An Itkin Brothers office furniture ad showed in four pictures what the subhead promised: "In less than 45 minutes you can have four new offices without changing your address, increasing rent, or interrupting work." The pictures were the headline, and the four captions under the photos of the partitions being installed simply read: "8:45 . . . 8:50 . . . 9:15 . . . and 9:25."

Sometimes it's a *visual literalism*. For instance, our small-space ad for U.S. School of Music, headed "Are You Missing Half the Fun of Playing the Guitar?" showed only half a guitar. The instrument was literally sawed in half.

Sometimes it's an *abstract picture*. How the devil can you picture the abstract concept "two," for instance? Avis made it literal with a photo of two fingers.

Also, the overall appearance of the ad provides visual reinforcement. Even if there are no illustrations, which is often true, the typography and design can convey a great deal about what kind of company is behind the advertising. For decades most mail order advertising was notorious for being less attractive than general advertising; much of it still is. Whether this helps or hurts results is hotly debated. It may be that a certain homey or buckeye look adds an air of unsophisticated honesty and sincerity. But for any company involved in starting an *ongoing relationship with a customer,* the appearance of its direct marketing advertising should convey that it is a responsible, tasteful, and orderly company with which to do business.

The Response Device

Most direct response ads carry a reply coupon or card for ease of responding. The significant exception is small-space ads. A two-inch ad would have to be about twice as big to accommodate a coupon. Many advertisers find that it does not produce twice as many results.

A black-and-white page with an insert card (a postpaid reply post card inserted next to the ad) costs about two and a half times more than a black-and-white page alone but usually pulls at least four times as much as a page with coupon. (Advantages of insert cards were explored in Chapter 6).

There are many variations of the postpaid reply envelope, depending on cost and publication policy: oversize card insert, full-page insert with detachable card, four-page card stock insert with detachable card, eight-page newspaper advertising supplement with bound-in or stuck-on card or envelope, loose envelope (such as for film processing) inserted in Sunday newspapers, and so on.

The creative problem in preparing coupon or card copy is to summarize the message from the advertiser to the prospect as clearly, succinctly, and attractively as possible. Many readers tear out a card or coupon and leave it in a pocket or drawer for days or even weeks before deciding to send it in. At that point, the reader wants to know what this minicontract entails. It is important to provide as much resell and reassurance as possible.

If the advertiser is a club, the coupon copy should clearly spell out terms of membership.

Check boxes, numbers to be circled, and other aids to make completing the form easy should be provided wherever possible.

Any money-back guarantee, whether already mentioned in the adjoining copy or not, should be clearly stated.

"Telescopic" Testing

Standard practice in direct mail for many years is to test simultaneously as many as five or six or even ten or twelve different copy appeals, formats, or offers. Giving each package equal exposure over a representative variety of lists is probably the most scientifically precise research method in advertising. But this practice has *not* been so common in publication advertising. There, for a long time, advertisers were limited to the simple *A/B split-run* test, in which every other copy of a given issue of a publication would contain ad A and every other copy ad B (separately keyed, of course). This, too, is very precise. The main thing is to make sure that the circulation purchased is large enough to provide a statistically significant variation in results between the two ads. But for testing your way to a breakthrough, it can be *slow*.

If you test two ads, wait for the results; then test two more, and so on. A year or so may pass before you discover the "hot button." On the other hand, if you test the control against one ad in publication A and another in publication B (we often do), it is useful, but it does introduce *another variable,* the difference in the two publications. And a truly scientific test has only one variable.

All our experience and common sense tell us that six or eight tests are far more likely to produce a hit than only two. To solve this problem, direct marketing advertisers are turning increasingly to multiple ad testing. We call it "telescopic" testing, because it permits the advertiser to telescope a year's testing experience into a single insertion. Telescopic testing simply applies the direct mail principle of multiple testing to publication advertising. But it requires publications or formats with the *mechanical capability* of running such tests. Perhaps the first magazine to offer this capability was *TV Guide.* Because television programs are different in each region, *TV Guide* publishes 84 different regional editions. Theoretically, you could do *84 different split-runs,* one in each regional edition, in a single week. (But you wouldn't, because the circulation for each test would be too small.) By testing ad A vs. ad B in the first region, ad A vs. ad C in the next region, and so on, it is possible to test as many as 10 or 15 different ads or ad variations simultaneously. By assigning to Ad A results the numerical value of 100, we can give the other ad results proportionate numerical values and rank them accordingly.

An easier way to do multiple testing is by intermixed card stock inserts bound into a magazine so that Ad A appears in copy No. 1, Ad B in copy No. 2, Ad C in copy No. 3, and so on.

Advertisers began testing new appeals and offers by doing A/B regional splits of *black-and-white pages* and even *half-pages* in the local program section of *TV Guide.* The following examples illustrate what can be done:

- A book series achieved a 252 percent improvement.
- A correspondence course inquiry ad was improved 209 percent.
- A name-getting giveaway program brought its advertising cost per coupon down to 19 cents!

The technique of applying telescopic testing is discussed in Chapter 16. Today there are three basic methods of running multiple tests:

1. *Simultaneous split-runs in regional editions* of a magazine that offers such a service, with one ad used as a control in all the splits.
2. *Free-standing stuffers* or loose newspaper preprints, intermixed at the printing plant before being supplied to the publication.
3. *Full-page card inserts in magazines,* intermixed at the printing plant.

It's a rather expensive game to play, but major direct marketers today are playing for multimillion dollar stakes. And all it takes is one breakthrough to pay for all the necessary research in a very short time.

A dramatic example of the application of telescopic testing is provided by a series of six ads created for *Consumer Reports* and tested simultaneously against the control ad via intermixed bound-in inserts in *TV Guide*. Shown in Exhibits 13-5 through 13-11 is the first page of each of the seven insert tests. Study each carefully and see if you can give ratings for Ads A through G.

Have you rated the ads? Okay, let's review the actual results by coupon count. Ranking Ad A—the control ad—as 100, here is the relative pull of each ad, courtesy of Joel Feldman, Director of Marketing/Circulation for the magazine.

- Ad A—100 (control)
- Ad B—107
- Ad C—101
- Ad D—82
- Ad E—65
- Ad F—61
- Ad G—33

While the 7 percent gain scored by the winner, Ad B, may not seem like a startling improvement, it is important to keep in mind that this 7 percent was on top of the impressive gains scored by Ad A, the winner in previous tests. And the circulation of 500,000 given to each ad resulted in a sufficiently large number of responses to make the results highly significant statistically. So thanks to this test, the client could be confident that future publication advertising would be 7 percent more efficient—a substantial gain when applied to millions of dollars worth of advertising.

Exhibit 13-5. Control Ad A in Insert Test

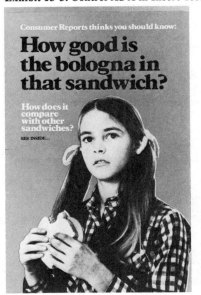

Exhibit 13-6. Ad B in Insert Test

Exhibit 13-7. Ad C in Insert Test

Exhibit 13-8. Ad D in Insert Test

Exhibit 13-9. Ad E in Insert Test

Exhibit 13-10. Ad F in Insert Test

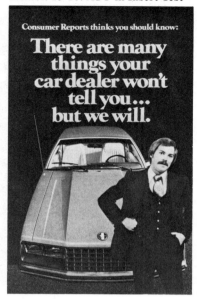

Exhibit 13-11. Ad G in Insert Test

Self-quiz

1. Good direct response advertising should make its strongest appeal to

_____

_____

2. Who are the best prospects?

_____

_____

_____

3. Advantages belong to the _____

_____

Benefits belong to the _____

_____

4. When are benefits more important?

_____

_____

5. When are advantages more important?

_____

_____

6. Fill in this list of ultimate benefits.

a. _____   j. _____
b. _____   k. _____
c. _____   l. _____
d. _____   m. _____
e. _____   n. _____
f. _____   o. _____
g. _____   p. _____
h. _____   q. _____
i. _____

7. Semantics is the hydrogen bomb of _____

8. Most successful headlines have a "hook" to catch the reader and pull him or her in. The most common hooks are such words as:

a. _____   d. _____

b. _____   e. _____

c. _____   f. _____

9. A common error in writing leads is that the writer _____

_____

10. A good writing principle is that body copy should _____

_____

11. What labels may be applied to the section of a classic copy argument?

a. _____

b. _____

c. _____

d. _____

e. _____

12. Name four other ways to structure copy.

a. _____

b. _____

c. _____

d. _____

13. What four-letter word is one of the greatest advertising words?

_____

14. Name five unique claims to fame that may prove to be the strongest selling points for a product or service.

a. _____

b. _____

c. _____

d. _____

e. _____

15. What is the major advantage of using testimonials in direct response advertising?

_____

_____

_____

_____

16. Name one of the most important building blocks in the mail order sale.

_____

_____

_____

_____

17. Name four ways you can give visual reinforcement to words and ideas.

a. _____

b. _____

c. _____

d. _____

18. When is a coupon not indicated for a direct response ad?

_____

_____

_____

_____

19. What is the definition of "telescopic" testing?

_____

_____

_____

_____

20. What are the three basic methods of running multiple tests?

a. _____

b. _____

c. _____

Pilot Project

You are a copywriter by profession. You have just been employed by a direct response advertising agency. The agency has been appointed by a home study school offering a course in _accounting_. Your copy supervisor has asked you to come up with headlines designed to get inquiries. Develop one headline for each of these ultimate benefits:

Health: _____

_____

Money: _____

_____

Security: _____

_____

Pride: _____

_____

Approval: _____

_____

Enjoyment: _____

_____

Excitement: _____

_____

Power: _____

_____

Fulfillment: _____

_____

Freedom: _____

_____

Identity: _____

_____

Relaxation: _____

_____

Escape: _____

_____

Curiosity: _____

_____

Possessions: _____

_____

Sex: _____

_____

Hunger: _____

_____

Section IV
Managing Your Direct
Marketing Operation

Chapter Fourteen

Managing A Lead Generation Program

Many products and services cannot be sold cost effectively through a one-step sales effort. A two-step, or multistep, program is usually necessary when a significant customer investment is required, or when personal interaction is necessary to complete a transaction. The two major uses of a lead generation program are:

1. Identifying prospect/customer interest or potential prior to committing to the cost of a face to face sales visit
2. Generating interest and stimulating traffic into a local retail outlet

The first instance is *lead qualification* and the second is lead (or traffic) generation. If your needs can be met by either of these activities, you need a lead generation program.

Types of Lead Generation Programs

There are three overall types of lead generation programs. While the principles that govern are the same, the needs that dictate the programs differ.

Business-to-Business

The primary objective in business-to-business lead generation is to get qualified leads from prospects who, in effect, raise their hands and say, "I'd like more information about your proposition." The thrust of the promotion can be as simple as encouraging prospects to request literature with an inducement to order by mail. Telephone followups of those who request literature is often an integral part of the lead generation program. For more complex propositions, requiring interaction with a live salesperson, the objective is to get a request for a salesperson to call. However, the cost of an industrial sales call being what it is today—McGraw-Hill estimates in excess of $200—mail and phone followup is more and more becoming the norm, rather than the exception.

A recent development, in the office equipment field in particular, is the establishment of office equipment stores. In this case manufacturers like IBM and Xerox use direct marketing methods to induce qualified prospects to visit their stores to discuss their needs and to see live demonstrations.

Business to Consumer

The feasibility of lead generation programs for consumer products is most always dictated by price point and available channels of distribution. The unit of sale inherent in package goods, for example, obviates the practicality of a lead generation program except in the case of a cents-off coupon co-op. (See Chapter 9—Co-ops.)

However, lead generation programs do make eminent sense for the likes of a lawn care service, where the annual expenditure is in the area of $100. Or for electronic equipment like Betamax. Or for refrigerators, or air conditioning, or freezers, or insulation—each a considered purchase of magnitude for the consumer.

Some manufacturers sell major equipment directly to the consumer. Most sell through traditional retail channels. In the former, the objective is to get qualified leads and to complete the transaction by mail and/or telephone followup. In the latter, the objective is to drive a qualified prospect into a retail outlet.

Public Relations

A third type of lead generation program uses public relations as the medium for getting leads. Done right, PR is an extremely effective method of producing leads in both the consumer and business field.

As a matter of fact, more often than not, editorial mention of a free booklet offer or a new product is likely to produce more leads than a space ad. The theory is that the reader puts more stock in editorial mentions than in ads. The other side of the coin is that conversions to orders are more likely from space ads than from editorial mentions.

The policies of publishers vary when it comes to giving free editorial mention. Some publishers give editorial mention only if an ad is placed; others give editorial mention irrespective of space advertising. Many firms prepare and distribute their own news releases to likely publications. However, there is no substitute for a good public relations agency in getting news releases placed.

Planning and Implementing a Lead Generation Program

There are four basic tasks that must be managed up front before any lead generation program is introduced.

1. Gathering Input from the Sales Force.

When planning a promotion, marketers often overlook the most valuable tie to their customer base—the sales force. No source will be able to relate to the specific needs and product application for a market as well as the sales force. They are on the "firing line." They know what is going on out in the territory, who their competition is, the spheres of influence among their prospects. Even the message in your communications can be influenced in both tone and content by the sales force.

2. Setting the Objectives of the Program.

The special need for objectives in a lead generation program relates to the quality of leads. An abundance of leads can be meaningless if an insufficient number convert to sales. The key question is, What ratio of sales to inquiries do we need to make this program profitable? This must be spelled out when setting objectives.

3. Determining the Promotion Strategy.

Strategies should identify the steps required for accomplishing the program's objectives. They are the road map for getting from where you are to where you want to be. In addition, they should mesh with the strategies being applied by the sales force and other distribution channels. For example, if the sales force's strategy is soliciting the legal profession to sell word processors, then the promotion's strategy may be to develop a direct mail/lead generation campaign directed at the legal profession. This, in turn, would provide qualified leads from the legal profession for the sales force to convert into sales.

4. Planning the Implementation Stage of the Lead Generation Program.

Once objectives and strategies are established, the time to implement the program—make it come alive—arrives. Implementation involves consideration of the following areas:

- *Sales Force Involvement.* Any sales force can make or break a lead generation program. Front-end involvement, as stated, is essential. So is foreknowledge of the full promotional effort, including media selection, samples of ads and/or mailing packages and detailed explanations of any offers or incentives. Finally, a feedback loop should be established for a qualitative assessment of positive and negative results of the promotion.
- *Capacity and Lead Flow Planning.* Lead flow is not a faucet that can be turned on or off at will. Lead flow must be planned so that leads come in at a rate equal to the sales force's capacity to handle. While there will be more on this subject later in this chapter, the key point to remember is that either too few leads or too many leads will work to the detriment of the program.
- *Creative Strategy.* Creative strategy for a lead generation program should reflect the creative strategies applied for other advertising efforts, including general advertising, but the look and feel of the

communication should be consistent with the overall image of the company to get the full benefits of an integrated campaign.

- *Media Strategy.* The key question is, given the target market and the product offering, what media will most effectively accomplish the task? Whether it be mail, print, broadcast, cable—whatever the medium—key considerations such as penetration, key prospects reached, number of contacts etc., must be considered.

- *Fulfillment Strategy.* As simple as it sounds, one must know exactly what will happen to a lead, once it's received. If there is to be a brochure, for example, ample quantities must be in stock before the initial communication occurs. Measurement systems must be in place (covered later in this chapter). Systems must be in place for scheduling sales calls, referring leads to the field, call-back programs, etc. Failure to be ready to fulfill promptly can kill the best of promotions.

You've informed your sales force, planned capacity, made your offer, and the leads start coming in. How do you manage this process to ensure the maximum effectiveness and efficiency for the entire program?

Capacity Planning

Let's begin by taking a closer look at capacity planning. We said that it was a critical component of the up-front planning process, but it is also key to managing on an ongoing basis. No matter how carefully planned, a program can change because of internal and external variables.

For instance, postal deliveries might be slower or faster than anticipated, a computerized customer file might malfunction, a new product could take twice as much time to sell to a lead than anticipated. The possibilities are endless, but the point is simple: Plan your capacity to be flexible to change.

Let's look at a typical capacity planning chart that indicates an optimum lead flow. (See Table 14-1.) Assuming a salesperson can average one cold prospect call a day, Table 14-1 shows how many calls each office can make in a working month of 20 days (20 calls per person). This information determines what quantity of mail is required at a 5 percent return to furnish leads for these calls, given that probably 20 percent of them will be qualified calls and the rest will be screened out prior to a sales call.

Thus, control can be exercised over mailings so that the two salespersons in Denver, for example, will not be suddenly swamped by scores of sales leads. In their district, 4,000 mailing pieces would be needed to furnish them with 40 qualified leads, as many as the two salespersons can follow up in one month. ZIP code selectivity helps to target mailings within a district.

To keep a constant flow of leads moving to the field at an average of 3,500 a month would require 70,000 mailing pieces per month. A year's campaign (12 months multiplied by 70,000) requires 840,000 mailing pieces.

Of course, all of this up-front planning and development is directed towards providing the sales center with an even flow of qualified leads. In simple terms, the sales center is a centralized location that houses your telemarketing sales force. This subject will be covered in detail throughout the telemarketing section of this book.

Table 14-2 illustrates a sales center with a need for about 450 leads per week. Direct mail, television, radio, and print are all being utilized.

Table 14-1. Capacity Planning Chart

District Offices	Number of Salespeople In Each	Total Qualified Calls Needed Each Month	Total Leads Required (at 20% Qualified)	Mailings Required (at 5% Return)
Indiana	10	200	1,000	20,000
Tennessee	14	280	1,400	28,000
Virginia	10	200	1,000	20,000
Michigan	10	200	1,000	20,000
Illinois	16	320	1,600	32,000
West Virginia	13	260	1,300	26,000
New Jersey	5	100	500	10,000
San Francisco	8	160	800	16,000
Maine	9	180	900	18,000
Seattle	9	180	900	18,000
New York City	10	200	1,000	20,000
Ohio	10	200	1,000	20,000
Texas	7	140	700	14,000
Utah	3	60	300	6,000
Connecticut	6	120	600	12,000
Pittsburgh	9	180	900	18,000
Philadelphia	11	220	1,100	22,000
Miami	3	60	300	6,000
Des Moines	7	140	700	14,000
Los Angeles	2	40	200	4,000
Denver	2	40	200	4,000
Atlanta	3	60	300	6,000
Totals	175	3,540	17,700	354,000

Table 14-2. Lead Flow Report

	Program Code	DMap	Post Class	Drop Date	Resp. %	Drop Quant.	Resp. Quant.	1/02	1/09	1/16	1/23	1/30	2/06	2/13	2/20	2/27	3/06	3/13	3/20	3/27
Payroll-Control Pkg.	CB-85555-001	1	1	1/02	3.00	35000	1050		74	179	273	263	53	53	53	53	32	21		
Payroll-Test Pkg.	CB-85556-T01	1	1	1/02	2.00	10000	200		14	34	52	50	10	10	10	10	6	4		
	CB-85556-T02	1	1	1/02	2.00	10000	200		14	34	52	50	10	10	10	10	6	4		
Accounting-Control	CB-86666-002	2	1	2/06	1.50	50000	750							53	128	195	188	38	38	38
Accounting-Test	CB-86667-T03	2	1	2/06	1.00	10000	100							7	17	26	25	5	5	5
	CB-86667-T04	2	1	2/06	1.00	10000	100							7	17	26	25	5	5	5
	CB-86667-T05	2	1	2/06	1.00	10000	100							7	17	26	25	5	5	5
	CB-86667-T06	2	1	2/06	1.00	10000	100							7	17	26	25	5	5	5
Direct Resp. T.V.								275	200	125			225	225	100			190	225	225
Direct Resp. Radio								100	75				75				50	100	100	100
Direct Resp. Print								75	75	75	75	75	75	75	75	75	75	75	75	75
Lead Flow Totals								450	452	447	452	438	448	453	443	447	456	452	458	458

Note: This is a hypothetical case.

Lead Qualification

It is no secret that in any lead generation program lead quality varies a great deal. In fact, generally speaking, about 20 percent of total leads will result in about 80 percent of total sales revenue. Given this, it makes sense to optimize time and effort with a good lead qualification system. There are two good reasons for optimizing time and effort.

1. Time is money: Given the cost of an industrial sales call (over $200 by a McGraw-Hill estimate) it costs too much to have a salesperson call on unqualified prospects.

2. Good leads get "cold": While salespeople are pursuing low-quality leads, high-quality leads get "cold." Each day a lead is not acted upon makes the likelihood of sales conversion less likely.

How can leads be qualified? The best way is to build screening devices into the upfront media selection.

Lists in the business field, for example, can be selected by sales volume, number of employees, or net worth. It must be recognized, however, that while such selectivity can produce a better qualified lead, it can also reduce the number of leads, sometimes significantly. If a product or service tends to have more of a mass application, this may not be desirable.

There are a number of ways to handle lead qualification after leads are received. The following is a prototype of a telephone script for lead qualification. A well-structured telephone script can help a telemarketing specialist to immediately "weed out" low-potential prospects prior to initiating a sales call.

Sales Representative: Thank you for calling us, Mr. Johnson. My name is Valerie Gelb. How can I help you?

Prospect: Well, I saw your advertisement and I'm interested in your (product).

Sales Representative: I'm pleased to hear that, Mr. Johnson. You know we have several models. It would help me to recommend the most efficient one for your needs, if I knew a little more about your company.
Just what product or service do you offer?

CUSTOMER RESPONSE

Sales Representative: That's interesting. You know we have quite a few customers in the same business in (City) who find our (product) does an unusually good job for them.
Where are you located?

CUSTOMER RESPONSE

Sales Representative: Well, in a business like yours, with so many locations, you must have used products similar to ours before. *Just how did they work out for you?*

CUSTOMER RESPONSE

Sales Representative: *Did they do what you expected of them or did you have any particular problems?*

CUSTOMER RESPONSE

Well, I can assure you won't have those kinds of problems with our product. Especially since we can offer you a model more suited for the way your company uses it. *By the way, is there more than one division in your company that might be using (product)?*

CUSTOMER RESPONSE

Sales Representative: That means you will need a considerable quantity to begin with—and a continuing supply. *Just how many (products) do you regularly use each month?*

With this series of six simple questions, a sales representative can qualify a prospect's sales potential in three important categories: the appropriateness of the product for the prospect's needs, the potential sales volume the prospect represents, and the ability of the company to fulfill the sale and service the account.

This questionnaire approach can also be an excellent means of capturing marketing information about prospects and customers. Demographic and psychographic information can be part of the feedback loop to the media selection and targeting of the initial "up-front" communication.

Table 14-3. Lead Sorting Form

Code	Lead Disposition	Analysis	Followup Action	Result
A	High Potential	Refer to outside sales force		
B	Medium Potential	Sell by telephone		
C	Low Potential	Resurface at later date		
D	No Potential	No potential-information seekers		

The most efficient way to sort leads is by degrees of potential. Table 14-3 shows how one very successful advertiser sorts leads.

Lead Flow Monitoring

As mentioned earlier in this chapter, the more quickly a lead is acted upon, the higher the likelihood of conversion. The theory behind this is that the interest is highest when a prospect has first responded to an offer. The longer that lead sits, the "colder" the prospect becomes. (While it differs by offer, a rule of thumb is that a lead should be acted upon within 10 days *maximum*. Sooner, if possible.)

But, as anyone who has worked with a lead generation program will tell you, sometimes leads come in at a greater rate than anticipated, no matter how carefully planned. Or, sometimes less than anticipated. The latter will not cause "cold" leads, but they could have impact on sales personnel morale, overhead costs, etc. Whether too high or too low, it pays to have contingency systems in place.

Contingency Planning

Let's look at a typical lead flow planning model to see the normal distribution of leads into a sales center.

In the case of this illustration, we have learned over time that the response to mailings will almost always follow this response curve with 50 percent of total response in the first four weeks, the balance over the next six weeks.

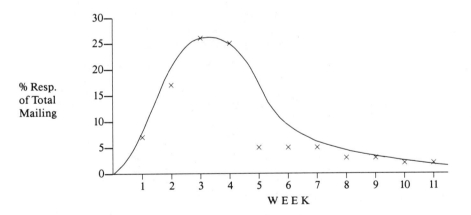

The next illustration is simply a series of these response "waves," each representing mailings. If print or broadcast were being used, a different formula for each would have to be developed.

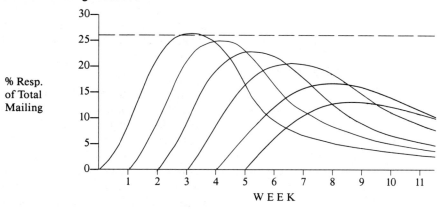

At best, our planning will keep us within 90 to 110 percent of the dotted line, our stated capacity. But what if some of the internal or external events mentioned earlier should change our response curve and create a shortfall? There are two basic systems that can be employed to effectively manage around this.

"In Que" or "Lead Bank" System

Many companies create a "lead bank" system, which is a purposeful manner of always being above capacity. When a lead enters the sales center, it first enters the lead bank before being dispatched for followup. If there is always an extra week's worth of leads, and they are handled first in, first out, no leads are penalized or allowed to get "cold." Naturally, the "lead bank" would be stocked with mail responses. You must handle telephone responses immediately.

If and when there is an underdelivery of leads the lead bank is drawn down until additional leads can be driven into the center. Or, the bank can be increased temporarily, when an overdelivery occurs until the up-front solicitation can be decreased.

Shelf Contingency

It is always wise to have additional up-front communications "on the shelf"—that is, produced and ready to go—in the event of an underdelivery. If the lead generation program is direct mail, for example, two weeks of additional mail packages in reserve will assure a timely response to an underdelivery problem. And, after normal capacity resumes, the lead bank can be replenished.

Tracking and Results Reporting

Tracking and results reporting are as important as management of leads in the sales center. These activities will result in quantification of the actual effort, relating the success of the program to its objectives, and, making management aware of the degree of efficiency, market penetration and revenue streams.

Tracking

Which information an advertiser decides to track is largely a function of individual needs. However, the following information data may be considered essential.

1. *Number of leads by effort.* Whether for a mailing, print ad, or broadcast spot, the number of leads responding to each effort should be captured. This is usually handled by a specific code for each.

For instance, a mailing with a split copy test is actually two mailings. Therefore, each response device should have a specific code, so when it's received at the sales center, the proper mailing can be credited. If telephone response is encouraged, as it should be, a specific phone extension code should be given for each mailing, thus making it possible to credit the proper promotion effort.

By capturing information by code, the winning test promotions will emerge.

2. *Quality of lead/conversion information.* The best pulling mailing or ad isn't always the most successful, for it is conversion to sales that is the true measure of success. The following comparison of two mailing packages illustrates the point.

	Number Mailed	Percent Response	Number Responses	Percent Conversion	# Sales
Package A	20,000	2.0	400	6	24
Package B	20,000	1.0	200	15	30

As you can see, package A would seemingly be the more successful package. But when conversion is factored in, the greatest number of sales actually came from package B. Other data captured might include: list utilization, demographic information, sales volume, number of employees, etc.

Once this data is captured, it is critical that it be maintained on a system. The critical element of this system is the customer file. This file should include all information captured from various offers, as well as follow-up information such as calls made, time between providing leads and sales calls, and cost per sale. The ideal is to be able to determine sales efficiency through cost per sale by office, individual salesperson, and by source of lead.

Results Reporting

There's little question that an efficient lead generation program will increase sales and cut sales costs. But it is essential that results be measured and reported. Documentation of results is essential for three basic reasons: (1) to measure against original objectives of the lead generation program, (2) to prove value to the sales force, and (3) to prove value to management.

Case Histories

Now let's take a look at how two companies approached lead generation programs as solutions to their specific marketing and sales needs.

1. AT&T Long Lines

One of AT&T Long Line's key marketing objectives is to encourage customers to use a broad spectrum of products and services where applicable. Telemarketing is an integral part of their lead generation program. And, in fact, the major products AT&T promotes to business are Outward WATS (wide area telephone service) and 800 (toll free) Service, both products being promoted as efficient sales and service tools.

AT&T preselects prospects by usage potential. Major prospects are assigned to national and local sales forces. This leaves a huge market of small to medium-size firms. And this is where a very effective direct mail lead generation program comes into play with the telephone as the followup sales instrument.

AT&T is committed to lead generation programs. A review of their 1981 program will exemplify their commitment.

First, a total revenue objective was set, based upon confidential, historical data, addressing such factors as quality of lead, conversion rates and revenue per sale by product. Based on an analysis of this data, they were able to establish their second objective—to generate 174,000 leads over 12 months. Since they knew they could achieve about a 1.5 percent response across the entire program, they concluded that about 11,600,000 mailing packages would be required.

Sounds pretty simple up to now, doesn't it? Well, let's briefly review some of the more "qualitative" factors that had to be managed into program strategies and implementation.

The first factor was program structure. AT&T had identified and developed several telemarketing applications. These telemarketing applications were methods for carrying out sales and management related functions most cost-effectively through the use of telecommunications. They had created applications for opening new accounts, collecting on overdue accounts, penetrating new markets, etc. Some were specifically for the smaller business market. Each of these had appeal to varying market segments and to varying functions within companies in their target market.

The solution? Significant testing was done to determine the best prospects for each program. Market segmentation analysis allowed roll-out to the market for each program on an appropriate and successful basis. Additionally, creative testing was done on an ongoing basis to measure such variables as format, message and graphics. All of this led to improved response and conversions.

Next, let's look at lead capacity. When mailings generate leads, both mail and telephone, they are received by the Bell System Sales Center (BSSC) in Kansas City, Missouri. It is the job of the consultants at the BSSC to convert leads into sales. The lead flow must be managed in a way that allows the consultants to handle a predetermined number of contacts per day.

The solution? A highly flexible computer model was developed to accommodate such variables as BSSC weekly capacity, number of mailing packages, response rates by program, mailing response curves, etc. The result was a predetermined number of leads delivered each week as dictated by revenue and capacity needs. Leads came within 10 percent of projections throughout the year.

Next, there was a very real concern about market saturation. Because of both market and corporate parameters, AT&T had a limited universe, approximately 1.5 million key firms in their house file. And yet their second objective—producing 174,000 leads—required mailing 11.6 million mailing pieces to this limited universe in order to achieve goal. As one can imagine, the possibility for market saturation was very real.

The solution? A decision was made to test a significant number of outside lists beyond their base list of 1.5 million business firms. This step increased their universe by 25 percent. Also, addressing to functional titles was tested. This expanded the universe because of contacting more than one prospect in a firm. For example, a credit management mailing might go to the V.P. of Accounting, while an opening new accounts mailing would be mailed to the V.P. of Sales, both in the same firm.

The next area was one everyone can all relate to—cost efficiencies. AT&T had set up-front parameters for the amount they were willing to spend for promotions as a ratio to income. And yet it was essential that creative execution be up to the standards of the AT&T image and that the program produce the desired number of high quality leads. The question was, "How do we keep on top of this objective?"

The solution? A system of quarterly management reviews. Each lead generation program was reviewed quarterly. Key questions were applied to each. Are we on quota? Can we effect production savings? What new mailing packages can we test that will improve the ratio of income to expense? As a result of close monitoring of new tests many new control packages emerged mid-stream in the total program. New cost efficiencies were the result.

Special mention should be made of the importance AT&T put to maintaining their corporate image. Not unlike most companies, AT&T wants all communications to relate to one another so they unmistakably come from the same company. This led to developing a creative product

Exhibit 14-1. Lead-Generating Letter

**Now your company can afford to add
Interstate Outward WATS service—the
minimum 10 hours usage requirement
has been eliminated!**

Bell System

2301 Main Street
P.O. Box 549
Kansas City, Missouri 64141

```
Mr Glenn
World Wide Health Svcs
328 Whiteworth Pike
Clementon, NJ  O8021


Dear Executive:

I'm sure you've considered using Outward WATS
before.  Perhaps you thought something like:
"A WATS line for our company?  It certainly
could help us control costs."

But you decided to wait.  Well, now there's no
longer any reason to delay implementing WATS
because...the rates for Interstate WATS have
changed dramatically.

    Now, you are no longer charged for
    10 hours minimum usage.  You pay only
    for the calls you actually complete.

What's more, WATS charges go down with increased
usage.

    Now, the more you use your WATS line,
    the less you pay on an hourly basis.

And, WATS gives your company the flexibility
of Evening, Night and Weekend Rate periods.

    Now, you can schedule your calls to take
    advantage of lower time charges and handle
    more business, much more cost-efficiently.

In addition to usage, your only other cost for
```

                           (over, please)

Get all the facts on how Outward WATS
can improve profitability.

Call Toll-Free 1 800 821-2121, ext. 722

or mail this request form today.

```
Mr Glenn
World Wide Health Svcs
328 Whiteworth Pike
Clementon, NJ  O8021

If address is incorrect, please make changes.


Telephone No. (_____)_____
                  Area Code
```

YES. I'd like to know more about how Outward
WATS can improve my company's profitability. The
majority of our customers are:

☐   ☐   ☐   ☐

Name _____ Title _____

Company _____

U22-073

Exhibit 14-1. Lead-Generating Letter

AT&T lead-generating letter seeking leads from chief executive officers of small to medium-size businesses.

WATS, after a one-time installation fee, is a monthly access charge of about $30 per line.

With the minimum usage charge no longer a factor, you need not wonder, "Can we afford Outward WATS?" Now, the question is, "Can we afford not to have WATS?"

The answer becomes clear when you think of WATS as:

> a management tool to improve your company's profitability.

Using Outward WATS, you can cost-efficiently implement Telemarketing programs, supplement face-to-face customer visits and perform many other sales-related functions. For example, with WATS you can:

- Prospect for new accounts, cost-efficiently.

- Keep in closer touch with field personnel and out-of-state branch offices.

- Service accounts, manage credit and deal with suppliers more effectively.

- Phone important messages to customers, suppliers and company personnel instead of using slower, less efficient mail service.

- Utilize sales people's time more productively by having them set up appointments and confirm them by telephone.

The Bell System's new Interstate WATS rate structure offers a tremendous advantage for many companies who were hesitant about implementing WATS. It is now easier to justify the modest cost of Interstate WATS for any company.

But don't take my word for it. Call our toll-free telephone number that appears on the front of this letter and get complete details for yourself. You'll talk with a Bell Business Consultant who specializes in the use of Telemarketing programs utilizing WATS service. Your Consultant will answer your questions and suggest ways your company can take advantage of Outward WATS to increase sales and improve profitability.

We look forward to hearing from you.

Cordially,

Ed Sellers

Ed Sellers,
Manager

The knowledge business

that closely tied in with their corporate advertising both from an image standpoint and as a way to transfer the benefits of their general advertising program to their direct mail program.

The solution to this concern was to design a creative approach that tied into, but did not copy, the overall corporate image of AT&T. This can be an especially difficult area because the creative guidelines for a direct mail package are significantly different than those of general or consumer advertising. They were able to accomplish this without sacrificing the performance of the mailings.

In total, the program exceeded its revenue objective for the year. This was the result of a well-planned, carefully executed program that identified and related to its objectives and strategies and that carefully tested and tracked results throughout the course of the year.

2. Wallace Business Forms

The second case history is that of the Wallace Business Forms lead generation program. Wallace Business Forms—one of the world's largest forms printers—is an outstanding example of a firm that has tied its lead-generating program to corporate objectives. The primary objective for the campaign was to increase market share of large users of forms in identifiable markets. The strategy was to use a dual media approach—direct mail and publication advertising—to reach the general computer market plus three vertical markets: banking, schools, and hospitals.

Full-page space ads addressed to the four markets, respectively, were placed in *Computerworld, Bank Systems & Equipment, School Product News,* and *Hospital Financial Management.* The copy positioned Wallace as a data processing problem solver, offering savings in time and money. Minor variations in the copy made each ad market-specific. A response coupon simply offered a free paper savings calculator. Besides attracting response, the ad fulfilled three other purposes: to expose the Wallace name and story, to allow Wallace to mail to the subscriber lists of the several publications, and to provide a "preprint" piece for inclusion in the direct mail package.

The direct mail package consisted of:

1. Outer envelope (Exhibit 14-2), printed on one side, with show-through premium, the paper savings calculator (Exhibit 14-3), plus the promise of a 25 percent savings on business forms cost.
2. The reply card (Exhibit 14-4) with a side flap graphically illustrating the premium, which shows through a die-cut window in the outer envelope.
3. An actual sample of a business form appropriate to the particular market (Exhibit 14-5).

Exhibit 14-2. Outer Envelope of Mailing Package

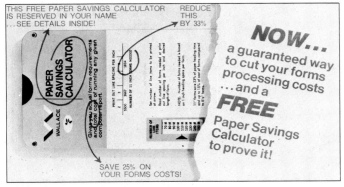

Exhibit 14-3. Free Premium—The Paper Savings Calculator

Exhibit 14-4. Reply Form Requesting a Premium

Exhibit 14-5. Sample Wallace Business Forms

4. A four-page letter personalized to that market (Exhibit 14-6), including an illustration of and benefit copy about the business form included in the mailing.

5. A preprint of the space ad for that market (Exhibit 14-7).

Total combined circulation for the four magazines in which the ad appeared was about 165,000, while 176,000 direct mail packages were sent out.

Almost 80 times as many leads resulted from the direct mail package as from the space ads. This was not surprising, since the ads were intended, as noted, to accomplish important ends other than simply attracting leads. From a standpoint of cost efficiency, the cost per inquiry for direct mail was a bit less than one-tenth that of space.

While space advertising can inform the market, expose the advertiser's name, contact prospects not reachable by direct mail, pave the way for salespeople, and capitalize on the prestige of an influential trade publication, it cannot equal direct mail for furnishing leads in the

Exhibit 14-6. First Page of Personalized Four-Page Letter

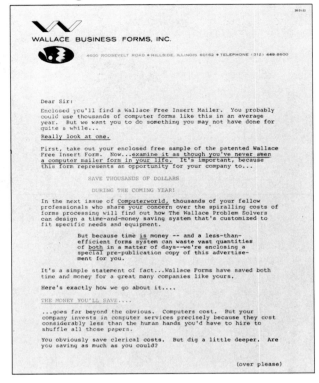

quantity needed and of the quality desired. Yet the most powerful strategy in lead generation is often the dual media approach, using space to enhance direct mail. This is especially true when advertising in a vertical market publication gives access to the publication's subscriber list.

Several factors are seen as contributing most strongly to the success of the mailings. The inclusion of an appropriate sample form offered dramatic, tangible proof of the quality of Wallace's product and its relevance to the recipient's own business. The copy was highly benefit oriented, with an emphasis on savings in the costs of forms. The premium chosen was valuable in itself because it would help the recipient realize the promised savings and also would qualify the lead by its very specific nature.

Drawing on the experience of this Wallace program and other successful lead generation efforts, let us present a checklist to which you might refer before settling on a strategy for your own programs:

Exhibit 14-7. Preprint of Space Ad

1. *Premiums.* Is it valuable or useful enough to improve response? Or is it so general in nature that it will attract too many nonprospects?

2. *Sample.* Is it possible to include a sample of my product in the mailing? If not, am I making it easy for the prospect to obtain a sample or see a demonstration?

3. *Format.* Does it attract immediate attention?

4. *Copy.* Does it stress benefits? Is it addressed specifically to the market it is intended to reach?

5. *Media.* How might a multimedia approach enhance my direct mail effort?

To which we can only add the three words by which all direct marketers live: test, test, and test.

Lead Followup Programs

The final area we'll discuss in this chapter is lead followup programs. A great deal of time and money is spent in generating leads, but only a relatively small portion actually convert to sales. The leads that are still

Table 14-4. Wallace Lead Program Cumulative Direct Mail Response

List Total Distribution	Computer World 28,417	Cum. %	School Product News 24,776	Cum. %	Hospital Finance 4,633	Cum. %	Bank Systems 10,421	Cum. %	Compiled List 99,809	Cum. %	Compiled List 8,068	Cum. %	Combined 175,924	Cum. %	Average C.P.I.
1st Week	97	.3	28	.1	12	.2			1,393	1.4	22	.2	1,552	.9	
2nd Week	1,325		351		104				2,656		128		4,564	2.5	
Cumulative	1,422	4.6	379	1.6	116	2.3			4,049	4.0	150	1.7	6,116	3.4	
3rd Week	809		238		81				587		92		1,807		
Cumulative	2,231	7.2	617	2.6	197	4.0			4,626	4.6	242	2.7	7,923	4.4	
4th Week	150		60		13		236				19		611		
Cumulative	2,384	8.4	677		210	4.5	236	2.3	4,729	4.8	261	3.2	8,534	4.9	
5th Week	89		16		9		200		98		8		420		
Cumulative	2,473	8.7	693	2.8	219	4.7	436	4.2	4,827	4.8	269	3.3	8,954	5.1	
C.P.I. (Gross)	$2.29		$7.15		$4.23		$4.78		$4.14		$5.95				$4.76
C.P.I. (Net)													6,000	3.41	$7.10

After Duplication and Pre-Screening Elimination

As a response record, this table cumulatively indicates responses by lists, quantity, percent, and time frame. The gross average cost per inquiry (CPI) as shown is $4.76. However, after duplications were eliminated and inquiries known to be unqualified were pre-screened, the result was a net CPI of $7.10. (Because list owners would not release names, a merge-purge process was not possible.)

deemed high to medium potential, but not converted to customers, should be maintained for later promotion. There can be scores of reasons why a prospect doesn't buy at a given point in time: a bad day, a bad month, a budget squeeze. A month later could be opportune. The fact that those who have not bought have previously shown an interest in a given product or service and have shown a predisposition to a product line or service gives just cause to continue to pursue. Even if the leads are not ultimately converted, you may learn valuable information about problems related to your product or promotion (i.e., marketing research).

The management of a successful lead generation program entails much more than simply dropping some mail or running an ad. It is the planned and efficient management of a series of activities, both front and back end, that will increase the overall efficiency and sales of a company's sales center.

Self-Quiz

1. What are the two questions you must ask to determine the need for a lead generation program?

a. _____

b. _____

2. What are the three overall types of lead generation programs?

a. _____

b. _____

c. _____

3. There are four basic tasks that must be managed upfront before any lead generation program is introduced. What are the four tasks?

a. _____

b. _____

c. _____

d. _____

4. What is the best way to make certain that the sales force isn't oversupplied or undersupplied with leads?

_____

_____

_____

_____

5. Usually about 20 percent of total leads will result in about

_____ percent of total sales revenue.

6. McGraw-Hill estimates the cost of an industrial sales call to be over

_____.

7. The most efficient way to sort leads is by degrees of potential. With high potential as the very best, name the three remaining degrees of potential.

a. High Potential   c. _____

b. _____   d. _____

8. A rule of thumb is that a lead should be acted upon within

_____ days maximum.

9. Most lead generation mailings will produce _____ percent of total response over the first four weeks.

10. What are the two best systems that can be used to manage around a shortfall in lead generation?

a. _____

b. _____

11. There are two ways that leads should be tracked. What are they?

a. _____

b. _____

12. There are three basic reasons why results of a lead generation program should be documented. What are the three basic reasons?

a. _____

b. _____

c. _____

Pilot Project

You work for a firm that manufactures central air conditioning systems for the home. Minimum sale comes to $5,000. All sales are handled through a sales force. The target market is home owners with a median income of $50,000 and over.

Your firm has decided to test the viability of a lead generation program and has selected Milwaukee, Wisconsin, as a test market. Your assignment is to develop a marketing plan for management review.

In preparation for actually writing the marketing plan, please answer the following questions.

1. What information will you need from the sales force?

Examples might be: (1) who is their major competitor? (2) who is the decision maker in the home? (3) what are the major objections the sales force has to overcome? What additional information will you need from the sales force?

2. What objectives will you set for the program?

For example, how many leads per day would you propose to furnish each salesperson? How would you propose to screen leads so you could classify between high potential and low potential? What other objectives would you set?

3. What would your strategies be for obtaining highly qualified leads?

One strategy, for example, might be an offer to conduct a free survey to determine the cost of central air conditioning in a home. Another strategy might be a special promotion to present customers in Milwaukee, asking them to provide names of friends whom they consider most likely to have an interest in central air conditioning. What other strategies might you employ?

4. How will you implement your lead generation program?

Here are some key questions you should answer in your marketing plan:

a. Will you ask your sales force to provide names of key prospects? How else will you involve the sales force?

b. What media strategies will you employ?

- Will you use compiled lists of homeowners? At what median income level?
- Will you use direct response lists? If you will—what kinds of direct response lists? (Lawn care subscribers, for example?)
- Will you use newspapers? Which ones?
- Will you use magazines? Which ones?
- Will you use radio? Which stations?
- Will you use TV? Which stations?
- Will you use Cable? Which station?

Chapter Fifteen

Mathematics of Direct Marketing

Outstanding creative work in direct marketing often brings recognition, awards and applause. Unfortunately good or even great creative work does not assure financial success. Analyses and accountability lie at the heart of successful direct marketing. Thus profitability can be measured each step of the way and programs can be expanded with predetermined financial risk.

Until 1967 there weren't many places to turn to for the development and application of advanced mathematical formulas to measure the many facets of direct marketing that go to make up its accountability and profitability. Indeed many of the most successful practitioners of the period, in spite of their seemingly satisfactory profitability, were using only the most rudimentary of mathematical principles.

It was typical to be able to state that promotion of a *total* customer file was profitable but to be unable to identify profitability by segments based upon various criteria, including frequency of purchase, recency of purchase, amount of purchase, and type of merchandise purchased.

Seeing this void in the direct marketing field, Robert Kestnbaum launched a unique management consulting firm not only to serve existing direct marketing operations but to provide feasibility studies for major corporations who wished to explore direct marketing. Since 1967, Bob Kestnbaum and his organization, Kestnbaum & Company, have served such distinguished firms as L. L. Bean, Sears Roebuck, American Express, IBM, Hewlett-Packard, Johnson & Johnson, Moore Business Forms, and AT&T. This chapter, a key chapter I might add, distills the mathematical formulas and principles developed by this unique management consulting firm.

Creativity in direct marketing brings recognition, awards, and applause. Unfortunately, profitability and success do not always accompany the recognition and the awards. Some of the attributes of direct marketing that appeal most to those who engage in it are the accuracy with which profitability can be evaluated and the careful way that a program can be expanded with predetermined financial risk. Accountability and analysis lie at the heart of successful direct marketing.

Profitability and Break Even

Establishing
Unit
Profitability

The most convenient starting point for establishing the profitability of an activity is to determine the contribution associated with each unit sold or with the average order handled. This process begins with separation of costs into variable and fixed.

For this purpose, variable costs are those which relate primarily to each order processed or each unit sold. They may be classified into merchandise costs which include everything related to making, delivering, and packaging the product and operating costs which include order processing, computer, warehousing, and shipping.

It is a good idea to use a worksheet to help identify all revenue and the variable and fixed cost items that come into play. Try to think of every possible cost that could be incurred and document the sources or components of each for future reference. Exhibit 15-1 illustrates a simple worksheet that can be prepared easily. Exhibit 15-2 illustrates a more detailed analysis that can be programmed on any size computer. It has the advantage of forcing attention on smaller units of activity and the frequency with which each kind of activity occurs.

Regardless of the form used, the output of the first part of the analysis (Exhibit 15-1 or 15-2) is the amount of money associated with each unit or each order that is available to pay for selling costs and other fixed costs. After the latter are recovered, the same amount of money becomes profit. This amount is labeled *order margin* by some people or *contribution* to selling cost, overhead, and profit by others. Regardless of the name used, note two things about its composition:

1. Some companies may include an allocation to cover overhead, thus making it a contribution to selling cost and profit only. This is the way the figures are treated in these exhibits.
2. No advertising or selling costs are included. The reasons are dealt with in the next section.

Selling Costs
and Overhead

In direct marketing the costs of placing advertisements, making mailings, or using the telephone should be considered as selling expense rather than advertising. The messages delivered by whatever media are chosen are the salespeople of direct marketing. As we will see in a minute, it is convenient to consider these selling costs as a special kind of semifixed expense in that a commitment is made to a given program before any sales are obtained.

When catalogs or other mailed materials are being used, it is customary to express selling costs on the basis of each thousand pieces mailed or otherwise distributed. When an advertisement is placed in a magazine or a broadcast medium, the cost of each advertising appearance or group of appearances is used.

Often it is advisable to test variations in advertisements and/or mailing packages. Because variations are tested in small quantities, inordinate costs occur for printing and extra creative efforts. It would be misleading to include these one-time costs as part of the regular profitability calculation. (An exception would be the development expense of a catalog to be used only during a single selling season.) It is generally preferable to consider the added costs of creative and small printing quantities as part of overhead expense. Evaluation of potential profitability of a total direct marketing effort should be computed on the basis of selling costs one expects to encounter in an on-going program of the size normally conducted for a roll-out.

Relationship Between Contribution per Order, Selling Cost, and Response Rate

Break-even and profitability are determined by the interrelationship between contribution to selling cost, overhead, and profit associated with an average order, the selling cost per thousand or per advertisement, and the response rate.

The total available contribution to selling cost, overhead, and profit may be viewed as a pie. Whatever portion of the pie is used to recover selling cost and overhead leaves the remainder for pre-tax profit. In the examples shown in Exhibits 15-1 and 15-2, an allocation to cover overhead has been included in the applicable costs. The contribution shown in lines 16 and 240, respectively, need to be applied only to selling cost and profit. If the available contribution equals 35 percent of net sales, as in this case, then that 35 percent must be divided between selling cost and profit. Thus a selling cost of 20 percent, or $8 per order, leaves 15 percent, or $6 per order, for profit. Conversely, a selling cost of 25 percent, or $10 per order, leaves a 10 percent pre-tax profit equal to $4 per order.

The relationship between selling cost and required response rate can be seen quickly. Assuming that we are satisfied with a 25 percent selling cost and 10 percent pre-tax profit, we have $10 per order to pay for whatever advertising medium is used. As is shown in the bottom portion of Exhibit 15-3, a statement insert costing $60 per thousand to print and place would produce the targeted profit if net sales equal six orders per thousand or 0.6 percent, while a catalog costing $400 per

text continued on page 398

Exhibit 15-1. Direct Mail Profitability Work Sheet

Promotion <u>Sample Catalog Test Mailing</u>

Line

Line			
1	Selling Price	$ 35.40	
2	Plus Service Charge	4.60	
3	Total Selling Price		$ 40.00
4		40.00	
5			
6	Merchandise Cost	13.05	
7	Drop Shipping & Delivery	2.30	
8	Goods Lost in Shipment	.13	
9	*Processing, Credit Check & Collection Cost	2.68	
10	*Cost of Returns	.06	
11	*Bad Debt	.31	
12	*Money Cost (Installment Receivable)	—	
13	Exchange Handling	.21	
14	Overhead & Inventory Carrying Cost	7.26	
15	Total Cost		26.00
16	Net Order Contribution		$ 14.00 (P)

Notes

Exhibit 15-1 is a simple worksheet that can be used to calculate the profitability of a direct mail promotion. There are four primary calculations involved:

1. *Contribution per net order to selling cost, overhead and profit (line 16).*

Total selling price including shipping and handling or service charge revenue is shown in line 3.

All order-related variable costs are itemized in lines 6 through 14 and summed in line 15. These costs are calculated on a *net order* basis. If certain overhead/fixed costs are estimated as a percent of sales, they can also be included as has been done here in line 14.

The second part of Exhibit 15-1 provides the detail calculations of those items marked with an asterisk. It appears on pages 380-81.

Order processing and collection costs are derived by multiplying the unit costs by the appropriate base assuming 100 gross orders. Order processing unit costs are multiplied by gross orders. Credit card discount costs are applied to net orders. The total is then divided by net orders to obtain the cost per net order.

Cost of returns are calculated in a similiar fashion. Unit costs are summed and multiplied by the return percentage. The result is then divided by the net orders expressed as a percentage of gross orders.

Bad debt is calculated by multiplying the estimated bad debt percent of sales by the total selling price.

Exhibit 15-1. Direct Mail Profitability Work Sheet (continued)

Circularization Costs per M

17 Circular $_____

18 Inserts   _____

19 _____   _____

20 _____   _____

21 Letters   _____

22 Order Forms   _____

23 Envelopes   _____

24 _____   _____

25 _____   _____

26 List Rental   _____

27 Inserting, Addressing, Mailing   _____

28 _____   _____

29 __Catalog Printing & Mailing__   ___291___

30 Postage   ___109___

31 _____   _____

32 Total Circularization Cost $___400.00___

33 Fixed Overhead per M   allocation incl. above

34 Total Circ. & Overhead $___400.00___(C)

35 Break-Even Net Sales per M (C) ÷ (P)   ___2.86%___   ___28.57___ orders

Notes Exhibit 15-1 (continued)

Contribution per net order (line 16) is derived by subtracting total variable cost (line 15) from the total selling price (line 3).

2. *Promotion and fixed overhead cost per thousand (line 34).* This involves a summing of the costs of all relevant promotional components and an estimate of the fixed overhead per thousand pieces mailed (line 17 through 33). Total cost per thousand is summed in line 34.

3. *Net orders per thousand required to break even (line 35).* This is calculated by dividing the promotion and overhead cost per thousand (line 34) by the net order contribution to selling cost, overhead and profit (line 16).

4. *Total profit at various levels of response* (top of page 380). Total profit at given response levels is calculated as follows:

Convert the response level to a projected net orders per thousand (line 37).

Subtract the orders required to break even (line 35) to obtain the unit sales per thousand earning full profit (line 39).

Multiply by net order contribution (line 16) to obtain net profit per thousand (line 41).

Multiply this figure by the total circulation quantity in thousands (line 42) to obtain total net profit (line 43).

Divide net pre-tax profit per M (line 41) by net sales per M (line 37) and multiply the quotient by 100 to obtain net pre-tax profit as a percent of sales (line 44).

Exhibit 15-1. Direct Mail Profitability Work Sheet (continued)

Total Profit at Various Levels of Net Pull

36 Projected Net Sales per M (dollars)	1,200.00	1,600.00	1,800.00
37 Projected Net Sales per M (units)	30.00	40.00	45.00
38 Less: Break-Even Net Sales (units) (Line 35)	28.57	28.57	28.57
39 Unit Sales per M Earning Full Profit	1.43	11.43	16.43
40 Net Order Contribution (Line 16)	× 14.00	14.00	14.00
41 Net Pretax Profit per M	$ 20.02	160.02	230.02
42 M Circulars Mailed	× 200.00	200.00	200.00
43 Total Net Profit	$ 4,004.00	32,004.00	46,004.00
44 Net Pretax Profit % to Sales	1.7%	10.0%	12.8%

Supporting Calculations and Assumptions

PROMOTION
TERMS
ASSUMPTIONS

Sample Catalog Test Mailing		
1. No. Pieces Mailed		200 M
2. Credit Check	Yes	X No
3. Gross Orders Rejected		0 %
4. Gross Shipments Returned		2.1 %
5. Net Sales Uncollectable		.78 %

*Order Processing and Collection Costs (Line 9)

a. Gross Orders	100 × $ 2.54	= $ 254	(a)
Less: Credit Rejects	__ × _____	= _____	
b. Gross Sales	__ × $_____	= $_____	
Less: Returns	__ × _____	= _____	
c. Net Sales	(A) 97.9 × $ .08	= $ 8	(b)
Total		$ 262	(B)
Cost Per Net Sale (B ÷ A)		$ 2.68	

(a)Includes mail order processing, phone order processing and order picking/packing.
(b)Credit card discount of 2 percent applied to.

Exhibit 15-1. Direct Mail Profitability Work Sheet (continued)

*Cost of Returns (Line 10)

Return Service Charge	$ .68
_____	_____
Drop Shipment Charge	_____
Shipping Out	_____
Shipping Back	2.25
Missing Items	_____
Total	$ 2.93 (A)
% Returns Projected	2.1 % (B)
Return Cost Per Net Sale (A×B) ÷ (100−B)	$ .06

*Bad Debts (Line 11)

Total Selling Price	$ 40.00 (A)
% Reserve for Bad Debts	.78 % (B)
Bad Debt Cost Per Net Sale (A × B)	$ .31

*Money Cost (Line 12)

Contract term plus _____ months _____(A)

Times Sales Decimal (if A is 12 or under divide by 12; if 13 to 24 divide
by 24; etc.) (A) ÷ _____ = _____(B)

Total Sales Price (Line 3) $_____(C)

Money Employed (B × C) $_____(D)

Effective Interest Rate _____%(E)

Money Cost (D × E) _____

Exhibit 15-2. Direct Marketing Profitability Analysis Average Contribution per Order

Line No		Base Cost 1	Factor % 2	Weighted Cost/Unit 3[a]	Net Cost Per Unit 4[b]
201.0	Selling Price	35.40	100.00	35.40	35.40
202.0	Installment Price	—	—	—	—
203.0	Shipping & Handling Revenue	4.60	100.00	4.60	4.60
204.0	Additional Options & Accessories	—	—	—	—
205.0	Total Average Sale	—	—	40.00	40.00
206.0					
207.0	Merchandise Cost	13.05	100.00	13.05	13.05
208.0	Premium for Purchase	—	—	—	—
209.0	Options or Accessories	—	—	—	—
210.0	Credit Card Discount	0.80	10.00	0.08	0.08
212.0	Sales Tax Not Collected	—	—	—	—
213.0	Bad Debt	40.00	0.78	0.31	0.31
214.0	Subtotal	—	—	13.44	13.44
215.0					
216.0	Order Card Postage	—	—	—	—
217.0	Order Processing	0.68	95.00	0.65	0.66
218.0	Order Picking/Packing	1.80	100.00	1.80	1.84
219.0	Shipping Cost	2.25	100.00	2.25	2.30
220.0	Premium for Examination	—	—	—	—
221.0	Credit Check	—	—	—	—
222.0	Return Handling	0.68	2.10	0.01	0.01
223.0	Return Refurbishing	—	2.10	—	—
224.0	Shipping Exchanges	4.73	3.00	0.14	0.14
225.0	Postage Refund, Return & Exchange	2.25	5.10	0.11	0.12
226.0	Goods Lost In Shipment	13.05	1.00	0.13	0.13
227.0	Telephone Order Processing	1.75	5.00	0.09	0.09
228.0	Subtotal	—	—	5.18	5.30
229.0					
230.0	Total Direct Costs	—	—	18.63	18.74
231.0					

Notes

Exhibit 15-2 is part of the output of a computer-programmed profitability analysis which is a more sophisticated counterpart to the worksheet in Exhibit 15-1. It involves much greater detail on the individual cost components and the frequency with which they occur.

Revenue components are itemized in lines 201 through 205, while direct costs are itemized in line 207 through 230.

Lines 232 through 238 detail the overhead and indirect costs. Contribution per order is derived in lines 240 and 242, while lines 243 and 244 calculate different combinations of selling cost and pre-tax profit which correspond to the 35% contribution to selling cost and profit (line 240).

Column 1 lists the base cost for each component.

Column 2 displays the weighting factor which is applied to the base cost. This factor is expressed either in terms of:

Exhibit 15-2. Direct Marketing Profitability Analysis (continued)

Line No		Base Cost 1	Rate % 2	Weighted Cost/Unit 3[a]	Net Cost Per Unit 4[b]
232.0	Cost of Money—Installment Receivables	—	12.00	—	—
233.0	Cost of Money—Receivables	—	12.00	—	—
234.0	Product Inventory	2.17	12.00	0.26	0.26
235.0	Overhead—Departmental	40.00	—	—	—
236.0	Overhead—Corporate	40.00	17.50	7.00	7.00
237.0	Subtotal	—	—	7.26	7.26
237.5					
238.0	Total Cost	—	—	25.89	26.00
239.0					
240.0	Contribution To Selling Cost & Profit	—	35.00	14.11	14.00
241.0					
242.0	Contrib. To Selling Cost, OH & Profit	—	53.15	21.37	21.26
243.0	Selling Cost if Pretax Profit Target is	10.00	25.00	—	10.00
244.0	Pre-tax Profit if Selling Cost Target is	20.00	15.00	—	6.00

a. Column 1 × Column 2.   b. Based on returns of 2.1%.

Line No	Supporting Calculations and Assumptions	Constant Assumptions
11.0	Selling Price	$35.40
13.0	Installment Terms: No. of Payments	—
14.0	Installment Terms: Amount of Payment	—
15.0	Total Installment Price	—
15.1	Implied Interest Charges	—
15.2	Simple Interest Rate "Reg Z"	—
16.0	Shipping & Handling Charge	$4.60
17.0	Additional Price of Option or Accessory	—
21.0	Merchandise Cost	$13.05
22.0	Cost of Premium, Free With Purchase	—
23.0	Cost of Option or Accessory	—
24.0	Cost of Premium, Free for Examination	—
25.0	Average Inventory Value	$2.17
31.0	Order Card Postage	—
32.0	Order Processing	$0.68
33.0	Order Picking/Packing	$1.80
34.0	Shipping Cost	$2.25
36.0	Telephone Order Processing	$1.75
41.0	Return Handling	$0.68
42.0	Return Refurbishing	—
43.0	Postage Refund on Returns & Exchanges	$2.25

Notes Exhibit 15-2 (continued)

Frequency of occurrence expressed as a percentage as in lines 201 through 230, or

An interest rate as in lines 232 through 234, or

A percentage of sales, as in lines 235 through 244.

Column 3 contains the weighted cost per gross unit obtained by multiplying column 1 by column 2.

Column 4 derives the cost per net unit by adjusting the values in column 3 by the return rate factor.

Exhibit 15-2. Direct Marketing Profitability Analysis (continued)

Line No		% Freq/% Rate 1	Discount /Uncollect 2
51.0	Cash With Order	90.00	0.87
52.0	Net 30 Days	—	—
61.0	Charge to American Express	—	4.10
62.0	Charge to Diners Club	—	—
63.0	Charge to Mastercard	5.00	2.00
64.0	Charge to Visa	5.00	2.00
65.0	Charge to Other Cards	—	—
67.0	Total Charge Cards	10.00	2.00
71.0	Installment Receivables	—	—
73.0	Sales Tax—Not Collected	—	—
81.0	Percent Purchased w/Option or Accessory	—	—
82.0	Percent Lost in Shipment	1.00	
83.0	Percent Returned Goods	2.10	
84.0	Percent Exchanges	3.00	
85.0	Percent Paying Shipping & Handling	100.00	
86.0	Percent Order Card Postage	—	
87.0	Percent Postage Refunds	100.00	
88.0	Percent Telephone Orders	5.00	
89.0	Percent Interest Paid	12.00	
91.0	Percent Corporate Overhead	17.50	
92.0	Percent Departmental Overhead	—	
92.5	OVHD=(0)%(Avg. Price+S&H) or (1)%Price	—	
93.0	Percent Selling Cost Target	20.00	
94.0	Percent Pre-tax Profit Target	10.00	

Notes Exhibit 15-2 (continued)

The second part of Exhibit 15-2 lists the input assumptions used to derive the profitability analysis report.

Lines 11 through 43 list the unit costs associated with each order, return and exchange.

The first column of lines 51 through 94 contains the weighting factors used in the profitability calculations:

Frequency of occurrence, in lines 51 through 88.

Interest rate, in line 89.

Percent of sales, in lines 91 through 94.

The second column contains the bad debt rate and credit card discount rates which are applied to each applicable transaction (lines 51 to 73).

Exhibit 15-3. Break-Even and Profitability Analysis

Average Order		$40.00
Contribution	35%	$14.00

	Statement Insert	Catalog
Promotion Cost Per 1000	$60.00	$400.00
Net Orders Per 1000 Required to Break Even	4.30	28.60
Net Response %	.43%	2.86%
Net Sales Per 1000	$172.00	$1,144.00

	Case A		Case B	
Target Profit	15%	$ 6.00	10%	$ 4.00
Promotion Cost Target	20%	$ 8.00	25%	$10.00

	Statement Insert	Catalog	Statement Insert	Catalog
Net Orders Per 1000 Required to Make Target Profit	7.50	50.0	6.0	40.0
	.75%	5.0%	.6%	4.0%
Net Sales Per 1000	$ 300	$2,000	$ 240	$1,600

Break-even orders = Promotion cost per thousand ÷ contribution per order.
Net orders per 1000 required to reach selling cost target = promotion cost per 1000 ÷ promotion cost target per order.
Net sales per 1000 = orders × $40.

Notes

Exhibit 15-3 displays the calculation of the response required either to break even or to meet certain profitability targets.

The first part of the exhibit displays the contribution per net order, both as a percent of sales and as a dollar figure. This figure was calculated in line 16 of Exhibit 15-1 and in line 240 column 4 of Exhibit 15-2.

The second part of the exhibit shows break-even calculations for two media: a statement insert and a catalog. For each medium:

The promotion cost per thousand is divided by the dollar contribution per order to obtain the net orders per thousand required to break even.

Response percent is simply orders per thousand divided by 10.

Net sales per thousand are calculated by multiplying net orders per thousand by the average order size, which in this case is $40.

The third part of the exhibit presents similar calculations for response required to meet different profitability targets.

Targeted profit per order is first established. For example, when the average order is $40 and targeted pre-tax profit is 15%, then $6 per order must be set aside as profit.

Allowable promotion cost equals total contribution per order less the targeted profit per order.

The promotion cost per thousand is divided by this new allowable promotion cost per order to obtain net orders per thousand required, to achieve the targeted profit.

Net sales per thousand are obtained by multiplying the required net orders by the $40 average order size.

thousand in the mail would require net sales of 40 orders per thousand or 4 percent.

Note that these calculations are based on *net sales.* If returns are 2.1 percent, then six net orders per thousand will require 6.1 gross orders or 0.61 percent response and 40 net orders per thousand will require 40.9 gross orders or 4.09 percent.

Profitability of a Continuity Program

The same calculation can be applied to determine the profitability of a continuity program. Suppose, for example, that a set of five $40 items is being sold, each successive item being shipped only when the preceding one is paid for. Exhibit 15-4 summarizes the figures for each shipment in the program individually as well as for the total program. Revenue and expenses are calculated for each shipment in exactly the same way as was illustrated in Exhibits 15-1 and 15-2, except that return and bad debt rates are much higher for the continuity.

Results for the total program are the sum of transactions made to the average customer starting in the program. Total net sales per starter are $124.74 and, after applicable expenses, contribution to selling cost and profit per starter is $29.51. Again, the marketer in this example can target how much of this contribution he wants to devote to acquiring a starter and how much he wants to leave as pre-tax profit. Since the total value of the sale is higher, the *absolute* amount that can be spent to acquire a starter and the *absolute dollar profit* per starter are greater.

The Arithmetic of Two-Step or Inquiry-Conversion Promotions

Up to this point, we have assumed that the seller uses an individual mailing or ad to produce sales. Very often it is more profitable to generate inquiries with various low-cost methods and then convert those inquiries into sales by using special mailings, by telemarketing (Chapter 10), or by a combination of these methods. In the example of the continuity offer, an average sale of $124.74 opens the possibility of using an inquiry-conversion approach.

Inquiries can be generated through any of the media available to the direct marketer. For example, if an advertisement costing $2,000 placed in a magazine produces 1,000 inquiries, the cost per inquiry would be $2. In addition, there will be a cost of perhaps $30 or $40 per thousand to process inquiries into a usable mailing list. As shown in the top portion of Exhibit 15-5 the seller must convert 14.4 percent of inquiries costing $2 each in order to generate a 10 percent pre-tax profit on sales.

Varying the media, kinds of advertisements, appeals, and offers will affect the cost of generating inquiries. Typically, the more highly qualified an inquiry, the more costly it will be to generate, but the higher the conversion rate will be. The thoughtful direct marketer will experiment continuously with various ways of producing inquiries and various means of converting them in order to fine-tune a program and to maximize profits.

Most companies find that an inquiry list will support repeated conversion mailings. There is likely to be a fall-off in response to each successive effort, but it is profitable to continue making conversion mailings until the incremental cost of the last mailing is greater than the contribution it generates.

The bottom portion of Exhibit 15-5 illustrates the results of a series of conversion mailings costing $225 per thousand to execute. Given the 10 percent objective for pre-tax profit, $17.04 is available from each order to pay for the order acquisition cost. This means in order to maximize short-term profit, a conversion series can be continued until the last mailing pulls 13.2 net orders or 14.3 gross orders per thousand or 1.4 percent, assuming returns of 7.4 percent. Short-term profit is maximized after the third conversion mailing since the actual selling cost for the fourth mailing exceeds the allowable cost. However, the total program would exceed the profit target until a fifth conversion mailing.

| Improving the Figures | To improve the bottom line, the direct marketer must focus on at least one and preferably on all of the three factors affecting profitability: unit contribution, selling cost, and response rate. Unit contribution can be improved by raising the gross margin, perhaps by upgrading the product or offering sets or combinations of items. Opportunities for cost reduction in every aspect of the business should be explored continuously. Chapter 3 deals with the importance of testing alternative advertisements, packages, appeals, and offers in order to improve response and performance. |

A special kind of analysis can be applied by catalog marketers. Not only can overall results be analyzed, but each item or category of products can be subjected to the same type of profitability analysis as well. When sales and profitability of items in a category or in a price range are aggregated, the performance of that group of items can be determined. Unprofitable individual items or categories of items can be eliminated, remerchandised, or given different amounts of space in order to improve their performance.

Return on Investment

So far, we have looked at direct marketing programs as though they occur at one point in time. Actually, of course, the events associated with the program take place over a period of several months or even years. When we consider the timing of revenues and costs, we can begin to obtain a picture of cash flows that are vital to the health of any business, as well as of return on investment, which may well be the best indicator of long-term business success.

Compared to other businesses, direct marketers do not have large investments in buildings and equipment. Often the most important considerations for direct marketers are the expenditure for inventory and the commitment that must be made to advertisements, catalogs, or other selling materials before any sales are received. For these reasons, several different ways of thinking about return on investment have been advanced. The more important ones will be reviewed here.

Return on Selling and Inventory Investment

For a company that is already in business, the major decisions that must be made in advance of each season or selling period are the size of the selling campaign to be undertaken and the amount of inventory to be purchased. Consider the case of a catalog marketer whose average order value is $40 including shipping and handling revenue and whose profitability is identical to that shown in Exhibits 15-1 and 15-2. Assume this company has two selling seasons a year and that it turns its inventory six times each year or three times each season. Its catalogs cost $400 per thousand, for which the bills are paid 30 days after mailing and from which most orders are received within 90 days of mailing.

Exhibit 15-6 shows a simplified profit and loss statement for 1,000 catalogs. The company is investing $400 for its catalogs, plus one-third of the $510 cost of goods, or a total of $570. Within a 90-day period it receives back this entire amount plus $148 in pre-tax profit. Some people calculate the return on the investment in inventory and selling cost as $148÷$570 or 26 percent. However, this return is actually received within 90 days, and theoretically the investment could be rolled over four times each year. The actual return is closer to four times 26 percent, or 104 percent. While this calculation has the advantage of being quick and easy to make, it is not only imprecise, but erroneous.

A better way to consider the mathematics of direct marketing and return on investment is to try to simulate revenues and expenses month-by-month as they are expected to occur. Exhibit 15-7 presents a simple financial model for the same catalog effort. Revenues flow in according to the historic response pattern that this cataloger has experienced. One-third of the needed inventory is purchased each month beginning one month in advance of mail date and catalogs are paid for 30 days after mail date. The total sales, costs, and pre-tax profit for the nine months involved are the same as in Exhibit 15-6. This analysis identifies a maximum monthly cash drain of $221 per thousand catalogs in month three and a cumulative cash drain that peaks in the first and again in the third months. Cash flow will be an important consideration to the

text continued on page 404

**Exhibit 15-4. Direct Marketing Continuity Program Profitability Worksheet
Average Contribution to Selling Cost and Profit per 100 Starters**[a]

Line No		Shipment Number					
		1	2	3	4	5	Total
1	Starters/Gross Shipments	100.00	76.50	61.93	52.39	45.79	336.61
2	Returns %	10%	8%	6%	5%	5%	7.40%
3	Net Shipments	90.00	70.38	58.21	49.77	43.50	311.86
4	Bad Debt %	15%	12%	10%	8%	8%	11.30%
5	Units Bad Debt	13.50	8.45	5.82	3.98	3.48	35.23
6	Net Sales	$3,600	$2,815	$2,328	$1,991	$1,740	$12,474
7	Merch Cost	1,175	918	760	650	568	4,070
8	Operating Costs	1,052	738	564	442	387	3,183
9	Fixed Costs	655	512	424	362	317	2,270
10	Contrib to Selling Cost & Profit	$ 718	$ 646	$ 581	$ 537	$ 469	$2,951
11	Cum Net Sales Per Starter	36.00	64.15	87.43	107.34	124.74	
12	Cum Contrib Per Starter	$ 7.18	$13.63	$19.44	$24.81	$29.51	

[a]Columns and rows may not foot exactly due to rounding.

Notes

Exhibit 15-4 calculates the cumulative profit per starter for a five-ship continuity program by tracing all activity associated with 100 starters and calculating a mini P&L for each shipment.

Line 1 contains the gross shipments for each item in the series. For each shipment after the first, the gross shipments equal the gross shipments for the previous item less returns and bad debt (lines 2 through 5). In a typical continuity program there would also be voluntary cancellations which would reduce subsequent shipments. These have been ignored here to simplify the example.

Line 6 contains net sales which are calculated by multiplying the net shipments by the $40 average order size.

Costs for each shipment are summarized in lines 7 through 9. Operating costs include bad debt. These costs are developed using the same cost factors illustrated in Exhibits 15-1 and 15-2. For example, fixed costs are calculated as 18.2 percent of net sales.

Contribution to selling cost and profit (line 10) is obtained by subtracting operating and fixed costs from net sales.

Cumulative net sales and profit are calculated in lines 11 and 12, respectively.

When the figures, other than percentages, in the total column are divided by 100, the value per starter is obtained. Thus there are 3.37 gross shipments per starter, $124.74 net sales per starter, and $29.51 contribution per starter.

Exhibit 15-5. Inquiry Conversion Profitability

A. REQUIRED RESPONSE RATE FOR ONE FOLLOW-UP MAILING

	$/Order	%
Net Sales	$124.74	100.0%
Contribution to Selling Cost and Profit	29.51	23.7
Pre-tax Profit at 10%	12.47	10.0
Allowable Selling Cost at 10% Profit	$ 17.04	13.7%

	Cost per 1,000 Inquires
Advertising Cost at $2.00 per inquiry	$2,000
Processing Cost	40
Total Acquisition Cost	2,040
First Follow-up Mailing	225
Total Initial Investment	$2,265

Net orders required to generate 10% Profit = $2,265÷$17.04 = 132.9 or 13.3%

Gross orders required assuming 7.4% returns = 132.9÷92.6% = 143.5 or 14.4%

Notes

Exhibit 15-5 highlights the profitability calculations for inquiry conversion programs. It uses the net sales per starter and contribution per starter derived in Exhibit 15-4.

Part A displays the calculation of the required response rate for a single follow-up mailing to an inquiry generation effort. The allowable selling cost at a 10% profit is calculated by subtracting the allocation for profit from the contribution to selling cost and profit per order. The initial investment per thousand inquiries is calculated by summing the:

Advertising cost.

Inquiry processing cost.

Cost of the first follow-up mailing.

Net orders required to generate the targeted profit are calculated by dividing the initial investment per thousand by the allowable selling cost per order.

Gross orders required per thousand are calculated by factoring up the net orders by a return rate assumption.

Exhibit 15-5. Inquiry Conversion Profitability (continued)

B. CONVERSION SERIES PROFITABILITY FOR 1,000 INQUIRIES

	Acquisition	Conversion Mailings #1	#2	#3	#4	#5
Quantity Mailed		1,000	880	838	822	815
Response Percent		12.0%	4.8%	1.9%	.8%	.3%
Orders		120	42	16	7	2
Less Returns		9	3	1	0	0
Net Orders		111	39	15	7	2
Cumulative Net Orders		111	150	165	172	174
Allowable Selling Cost at $17.04		$1,891	665	256	119	34
Cumulative Allowable Selling Cost		$1,891	2,556	2,812	2,931	2,965
Actual Selling Cost	$2,040	225	198	189	185	183
Cumulative Actual Selling Cost	2,040	2,265	2,463	2,652	2,837	3,020
Cum Balance Available For Selling Cost	($2,040)	($ 374)	$ 93	$ 160	$ 94	($ 55)

Notes Exhibit 15-5 (continued)

Part B outlines the profitability calculation for a series of five conversion mailings subsequent to the inquiry generation effort.

The quantity mailed on each subsequent mailing is equivalent to the previous quantity mailed less orders produced from the previous mailing. Often it is not practical to extract buyers and most of the conversion series is mailed to all inquirers.

Net orders are derived by subtracting returns. The 7.4% return rate was calculated in line 2 of Exhibit 15-4.

Allowable selling cost is calculated by multiplying the net orders by the allowable selling cost per order at a 10% profit, i.e. $17.04.

Actual selling cost includes the acquisition cost and the cost of each conversion mailing.

The cumulative balance available to spend on conversion mailings, taking into account the 10% profit target, is shown in the last row. A negative balance after the fifth conversion effort indicates that selling cost exceeds the allowable 13.7% by $55. Since total selling costs will equal $3,019.88 (total acquisition cost plus $225/M for conversion mailings), and total net sales are $21,704.76 (174 net orders x $124.74), the overall selling cost would be 13.9% if the last conversion effort were retained. Those last two orders, however, would cost $91.50 each to obtain ($183÷2) and would be very unprofitable.

management of this company. The internal rate of return[1] on these cash flows is 303.6 percent, which is a much more accurate way of stating return on this company's investment and is very different from the 104 percent calculated by the simple method in the preceding paragraph.

Long-Term or Lifetime Value of a Customer

Most direct marketing businesses are based on the proposition that it may be worthwhile to spend money to acquire a new customer because that customer will buy again from the company at which time a profit will be generated. Since different customers will make repeat purchases at different times and different rates, how can we determine the long-term value of a customer or a group of buyers?

One could approach this problem historically. Supposing that a catalog marketer were able to track all activity from 1,000 customers who were acquired at the same time in January, five years ago. During the five-year period examined, the company did not change its distribution policy. Catalogs were sent to all customers who had purchased within three years. While this simple catalog circulation policy has been used by many direct marketers, it is by no means recommended as the best or even as a desirable approach. (See Chapter 5 for a discussion of direct marketing data bases and segmentation.)

The same technique illustrated in Exhibit 15-7 is applied to each individual catalog mailing. All the revenues, costs, and cash flows associated with this group of 1,000 customers is analyzed month-by-month for 120 months until there are so few active customers left from the original 1,000 that their additional purchases would have negligible impact.

While this model is created on a monthly basis using a computer, Exhibit 15-8 summarizes the results for each year. Let us say that the owners of this company have targeted a long-term return on their investment of at least 25 percent per year. If we discount the annual pre-tax profit shown in this schedule at a 25 percent rate, then the value in that first January of all future profits in excess of a 25 percent per year return is $2,848 per thousand customers or $2.85 per customer. This means that, given the company's historic catalog circulation policy and actual sales results, the company could afford to have spent $2.85 in that first January to acquire each customer with the expectation of earning a 25 percent per year return on all such customers acquired.

Most companies are not in a position to track all of the sales and costs associated with each customer over an extended period of time. Moreover, companies change their policies with respect to the number and content of mailings sent and the rules used to determine who will

---

1. Internal rate of return is the single rate at which the discounted value of all cash flows is zero. It is a good measure of the true rate of return on cash flows.

receive each mailing. The sophisticated direct marketer today can build computer models that calculate the statistical probability of purchases in each season by customers having different profiles, can estimate the results of changing the nature, number, and effectiveness of mailings or other contacts, and can incorporate assumptions as to changes in order size, margins, and costs.

Such computer models can then be used to simulate the consequences of changes in strategy or policy. Exhibit 15-9 illustrates the impact on return on investment of the pursuit of three different strategies to build a catalog mail order business. The model assumes that the same amount of money is invested in each strategy. The strategies are to:

1. Mail more catalogs to rented lists to acquire more customers.
2. Expand the catalog by adding more products and increasing the number of pages.
3. Create an extra catalog to be mailed to better customers during the fall season.

The chart in Exhibit 15-9 illustrates that over the five-year horizon for which results are simulated, the company in question would invest most advantageously in expanding its product line. You will notice, however, that the customer acquisition strategy appears to be closing the gap quickly at the end of the period and might be expected to outperform the product line expansion strategy in the sixth or seventh year. Further study might indicate that this particular company could blend the two approaches by expanding the size of some of its catalogs and also enlarging its customer acquisition activities.

Measurements and Analysis

Calculating profitability. Determining lifetime value of customers. Developing long-range strategies for building businesses. Building models. These are the instruments sophisticated direct marketers use. But only well-planned and -executed campaigns produce the desired results.

The direct marketer builds on the strongest foundation if he plans each campaign around efforts that have been tested previously. (See Chapter 16 for more discussion of the statistics and strategy of testing.) Of course, a company launching a new business has no prior testing experience to use as the basis for its planning. Such a company must proceed cautiously, placing relatively few ads or mailing only the number of pieces required to determine whether a package, or an offer, or a list is successful.

Established direct marketers, however, plan their campaigns to achieve a predetermined balance between contacting former customers who would be expected to purchase at a high rate and seeking to acquire

text continued on page 409

Exhibit 15-6. Income and Expense Statement for 1,000 Catalogs

40 Orders at $40 per Order
(including shipping and handling revenue)

		Percent
Gross Sales	$1,600	
Returns	34	
Net Sales	1,566	100.0%
Merchandise Cost	510	32.6
Operating Cost	223	14.2
Fixed Cost	285	18.2
Contribution to Selling Cost & Profit	548	35.0
Selling Cost	400	25.5
Pre-tax Profit	$ 148	9.5%

Notes

Exhibit 15-6 illustrates a mini P&L for 1,000 catalogs mailed, assuming:
40 *gross* orders at $40 per order.
Returns at 2.1% of gross.
Cost factors identical to those shown in Exhibits 15-1 or 15-2.

Exhibit 15-7. Financial Model for 1000 Catalogs

	Month									
	1	**2**	**3**	**4**	**5**	**6**	**7**	**8**	**9**	**Total**[a]
Gross Sales	—	$608	$528	$208	$ 96	$ 80	$ 48	$ 16	$ 16	$1,600
Returns	—	13	11	4	2	2	1	0	0	34
Net Sales	—	595	517	204	94	78	47	16	16	1,566
Merchandise Cost	170	170	170	—	—	—	—	—	—	510
Operating Cost	—	85	74	29	13	11	7	2	2	223
Fixed Cost	—	108	94	37	17	14	9	3	3	285
Contribution to Selling Cost & Profit	(170)	232	179	138	64	53	32	11	11	548
Selling Cost	—	—	400	—	—	—	—	—	—	400
Cash Flow	($170)	$232	($221)	$138	$ 64	$ 53	$ 32	$ 11	$ 11	$ 148

Monthly internal rate of return (IRR) = 25.3%   Annualized IRR = 303.7%
a. Columns may not total exactly due to rounding.

Notes

Exhibit 15-7 displays a simplified financial model corresponding to the situation shown in Exhibit 15-6. The difference is that this model displays the timing of the revenues, costs and cash flows as they occur over nine months.

The monthly internal rate of return is the monthly rate at which the present value of the cash flows equates to zero.

The annualized internal rate of return is the monthly rate multiplied by 12.

Exhibit 15-8. Lifetime Value of 1000 New Buyers

	Yr 1	Yr 2	Yr 3	Yr 4	Yr 5
Gross Sales	$11,086	$7,505	$6,173	$2,830	$1,739
Returns	233	158	130	59	37
Net Sales	10,854	7,348	6,044	2,770	1,703
Merchandise Cost	3,538	2,395	1,970	903	555
Operating Costs	1,541	1,043	858	393	242
Fixed Costs	1,975	1,337	1,100	504	310
Contribution to Selling Cost & Profit	3,799	2,572	2,115	970	596
Selling Cost	1,600	1,600	1,600	625	408
Cash Flow	2,199	972	515	345	188
Discounted at 25%	1,759	622	264	141	62
Present Value	2,848	—	—	—	—
Lifetime Value per Customer	2.85	—	—	—	—

Notes

Exhibit 15-8 summarizes the long-term revenues, costs and cash flows associated with a group of 1,000 new buyers to a catalog operation similar to that displayed in Exhibit 15-7. These values were derived using a financial model like that shown in Exhibit 15-7 with the following significant differences:

It is assumed that there are four catalog mailings each year to this group of 1,000 customers.

Response rates to the catalog mailings vary by the recency of purchase starting with 9% for customers who purchased in the most current six-month season down to 3% for customers who have not purchased for 3 years.

The exhibit displays the annual totals resulting from the financial modeling technique applied to each catalog mailing.

The allowable investment to acquire a customer is derived by:

Discounting each year's cash flow at 25% to obtain a present value for the 5-year stream of cash flows.

Dividing the present value by 1,000 to obtain a lifetime value per customer.

The average order and cost structure of the catalog mailings is identical to that displayed in Exhibit 15-7.

Exhibit 15-9. Return on Investment

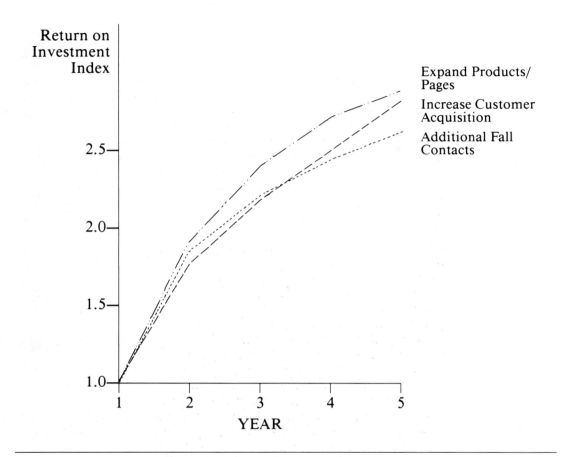

Return on
Investment
Index

Expand Products/
Pages

Increase Customer
Acquisition

Additional Fall
Contacts

YEAR

Notes

Exhibit 15-9 displays the performance of three alternative growth strategies, as measured by return on investment.

The three strategies are:

Expand products or pages for each catalog.

Increase customer acquisition efforts by mailing to more rented lists and expanding the space advertising budget.

Introduce an additional fall catalog each year.

The actual return on investment has been indexed to the return in the first year to disguise the actual figures.

new customers. The balance that each company strikes is dependent on the relative profitability of each type of effort and its long-range growth strategy.

Exhibit 15-10 illustrates a mail plan for the same catalog marketer we have used as an example throughout this chapter. The total mail plan calls for sending one million catalogs which produce a 4.63 percent gross response overall and an average order of $41. Prior experience with the company's own list of customers and rented lists range widely, as shown. Several new lists are included as tests. In order to keep expanding the business, it is wise for most direct marketers to utilize 10 percent to 15 percent of each campaign to test new lists, or packages, or offers.

Some aspects of this mail plan are worth pointing out. House lists totaling 200,000 former buyers are expected to produce approximately $3,200 sales per thousand. With an average order of $45, they are expected to produce a 7.25 percent gross response and 24.5 percent pre-tax profit. In contrast, mailings to proven rented lists are expected to show an average order size of $38 to $42 and response rates of 3.73 percent to 4.45 percent and 10 percent pre-tax profit. Test mailings of 5,000 to each of 20 new lists are expected to break even.

Using the same profitability calculation as is shown in Exhibits 15-1 and 15-2, the individual profitability of the mailing to each list is estimated. This is easy to do, since we know the selling cost associated with each list, namely catalog, postage, and mailing expense plus list rental where applicable. And we are estimating the response rate and average order size based on experience.

What is the actual profitability of this mailing? Exhibit 15-11 shows the actual results as of the report date and projected results at the end of the season. The company has been very careful to code its order forms to indicate the list to which each catalog was sent and has asked those customers placing their order by phone to look at the mailing label on the catalog and provide the list code shown thereon. By dint of these efforts, 80 percent of the orders received can be attributed to a specific list. The remaining 20 percent of orders that could not be coded by list must be allocated in the same proportion as attributed orders. This step is extremely important since one would otherwise underestimate the response from each list mailed and might be tempted to stop mailing lists that would then appear marginal.

Since this analysis is being prepared at a time when historic order response patterns indicate that the catalog is 80 percent done or that orders received to date represent 80 percent of all orders that will be received, the actual results for each list after allocation of uncoded orders are divided by 0.8 to produce projected results at the end of the

Exhibit 15-10. Mail Plan

1 Code	2 List Description	3 Mail Qty	4 Avg Order	5 Resp %	Catalog #101 Mail Plan 6 Gross Sales/M	7 Gross Sales	8 Net Sales/M	9 Selling Cost[a]	10 Sell Cost%[a]	11 Pre Tax Profit	12 Profit per M	13 Profit %[b]
1000	House List	200000	$45.00	7.25	$3262	$652400	$3193	$67000	10.49	$156544	$782	24.51
2010	Rollout List 1	70000	40.00	4.36	1744	122080	1707	28000	23.43	13830	197	11.57
2020	Rollout List 2	70000	40.00	4.27	1708	119560	1672	28000	23.92	12967	185	11.08
2030	Rollout List 3	70000	40.00	3.73	1492	104440	1460	28000	27.38	7786	111	7.61
2040	Rollout List 4	70000	42.00	4.09	1717	120190	1680	28000	23.80	13183	188	11.20
2050	Rollout List 5	70000	40.00	4.18	1672	117040	1636	28000	24.44	12103	172	10.56
2060	Rollout List 6	70000	38.00	4.09	1554	108780	1521	28000	26.29	9273	132	8.71
2070	Rollout List 7	70000	40.00	4.45	1780	124600	1742	28000	22.95	14694	209	12.05
2080	Rollout List 8	70000	40.00	3.82	1528	106960	1495	28000	26.74	8649	123	8.26
2090	Rollout List 9	70000	40.00	4.00	1600	112000	1566	28000	25.54	10376	148	9.46
2100	Rollout List 10	70000	40.00	3.91	1564	109480	1531	28000	26.12	9513	135	8.88
20	Subtotal	700,000	40.00	4.09	1636	1,145,130	1602	280,000	25.00	112,374	161	10.02
3001	Test List 1	5000	37.00	3.25	1202	6010	1176	2000	34.00	59	11	1.00
3002	Test List 2	5000	37.00	3.07	1135	5675	1111	2000	36.00	−55	−11	−0.99
3003	Test List 3	5000	40.00	3.16	1264	6320	1237	2000	32.33	165	33	2.67
3004	Test List 4	5000	34.00	3.16	1074	5370	1051	2000	38.04	−160	−32	−3.04
3005	Test List 5	5000	37.00	3.16	1169	5845	1144	2000	34.95	2	0	0.03
3006	Test List 6	5000	37.00	3.16	1169	5845	1144	2000	34.95	2	0	0.03
3007	Test List 7	5000	37.00	3.21	1187	5935	1162	2000	34.42	33	6	0.57
3008	Test List 8	5000	37.00	3.11	1150	5750	1125	2000	35.53	−29	−5	−0.52
3009	Test List 9	5000	37.00	3.16	1169	5845	1144	2000	34.95	2	0	0.03
3010	Test List 10	5000	37.00	3.16	1169	5845	1144	2000	34.95	2	0	0.03
3011	Test List 11	5000	38.00	3.16	1200	6000	1174	2000	34.05	55	11	0.94
3012	Test List 12	5000	37.00	3.16	1169	5845	1144	2000	34.95	2	0	0.03
3013	Test List 13	5000	36.00	3.16	1137	5685	1113	2000	35.94	−52	−10	−0.93
3014	Test List 14	5000	37.00	3.16	1169	5845	1144	2000	34.95	2	0	0.03
3015	Test List 15	5000	37.00	3.26	1206	6030	1180	2000	33.88	66	13	1.12
3016	Test List 16	5000	37.00	3.06	1132	5660	1108	2000	36.09	−60	−12	−1.08
3017	Test List 17	5000	42.00	3.16	1327	6635	1299	2000	30.79	273	54	4.20
3018	Test List 18	5000	32.00	3.16	1011	5055	989	2000	40.42	−268	−53	−5.42
3019	Test List 19	5000	37.00	3.16	1169	5845	1144	2000	34.95	2	0	0.03
3020	Test List 20	5000	37.00	3.16	1169	5845	1144	2000	34.95	2	0	0.03
30	Subtotal	100,000	37.00	3.16	1169	116,885	1144	40,000	34.96	43	0	0.04
	Total/Average	1,000,000	$41.36	4.63	$1915	$1,914,415	$1874	$387,000	20.65	$268,961	$269	14.35%

[a]Assumes rollout catalog cost of $335/M and list rental cost of $65/M.
[b]Percent of net sales assuming 2.1% returns.

Exhibit 15-11. Mail Report

Catalog No: 101
Week Ending: xx/xx/xx

Mail Date: xx/xx/xx
Percent Done: 80%

Code	List Description	Mail Qty	Cum Orders	Cum Sales	Avg Order	Adj Sales	Adj Sales/M	Sales	Sales/M	Resp%	Projected Sell Cost%[a]	Profit	Proj Prof/M	Prob of 10% Profit[a]
1000	House List	200000	8500	$385000	$45.29	$481249	$2406	$601561	$3007	6.64	11.38	$139124	695	100.00%
2010	Rollout List 1	70000	1899	74665	39.32	93331	1333	116663	1666	4.24	24.52	11974	171	83.12
2020	Rollout List 2	70000	2272	80000	35.21	100000	1428	125000	1785	5.07	22.89	14831	211	99.99
2030	Rollout List 3	70000	1735	73632	42.44	92040	1314	115050	1643	3.87	24.87	11421	163	57.69
2040	Rollout List 4	70000	2048	99225	48.45	124031	1771	155038	2214	4.57	18.45	25123	358	100.00
2050	Rollout List 5	70000	2028	70400	34.71	88000	1257	110000	1571	4.53	26.01	9691	138	5.27
2060	Rollout List 6	70000	2240	90880	40.57	113600	1622	142000	2028	5.00	20.15	20656	295	100.00
2070	Rollout List 7	70000	1822	85360	46.85	106700	1524	133375	1905	4.07	21.45	17700	252	100.00
2080	Rollout List 8	70000	1830	84825	46.35	106031	1514	132538	1893	4.08	21.58	17414	248	100.00
2090	Rollout List 9	70000	2311	87440	37.84	109300	1561	136625	1951	5.16	20.94	18814	268	100.00
2100	Rollout List 10	70000	2112	84748	40.13	105935	1513	132418	1891	4.71	21.61	17373	248	100.00
3001	Test List 1	5000	120	5500	45.83	6875	1375	8593	1718	3.75	23.78	944	188	74.13
3002	Test List 2	5000	80	3175	39.69	3968	793	4960	992	2.50	41.19	-300	-60	0.00
3003	Test List 3	5000	125	5550	44.40	6937	1387	8671	1734	3.90	23.56	971	194	78.12
3004	Test List 4	5000	96	3596	37.46	4495	899	5618	1123	3.00	36.38	-74	-14	0.00
3005	Test List 5	5010	140	4925	35.18	6156	1228	7695	1535	4.37	26.62	632	126	25.07
3006	Test List 6	5000	98	3877	39.56	4846	969	6057	1211	3.05	33.74	75	15	0.00
3007	Test List 7	5000	90	5575	61.94	6968	1393	8710	1742	2.80	23.45	984	196	74.62
3008	Test List 8	5000	79	3549	44.92	4436	887	5545	1109	2.45	36.84	-100	-20	0.00
3009	Test List 9	5015	130	4890	37.62	6112	1218	7640	1523	4.04	26.83	611	121	14.90
3010	Test List 10	5000	88	3765	42.78	4706	941	5882	1176	2.75	34.74	15	3	0.00
3011	Test List 11	5000	100	5590	55.90	6987	1397	8733	1746	3.13	23.40	992	198	79.50
3012	Test List 12	5000	89	3699	41.56	4623	924	5778	1155	2.77	35.37	-20	-4	0.00
3013	Test List 13	5000	150	6200	41.33	7750	1550	9687	1937	4.67	21.09	1319	263	99.01
3014	Test List 14	5000	134	5235	39.07	6543	1308	8178	1635	4.17	24.99	802	160	48.64
3015	Test List 15	5002	130	4325	33.27	5406	1080	6757	1350	4.05	30.27	314	62	0.15
3016	Test List 16	5000	135	4375	32.41	5468	1093	6835	1367	4.20	29.89	342	68	0.21
3017	Test List 17	5008	135	5440	40.30	6800	1357	8500	1697	4.19	24.08	909	181	67.12
3018	Test List 18	5000	98	3997	40.79	4996	999	6245	1249	3.05	32.71	139	27	0.01
3019	Test List 19	5000	155	6015	38.81	7518	1503	9397	1879	4.82	21.74	1219	243	97.41
3020	Test List 20	5000	85	5255	61.82	6568	1313	8210	1642	2.65	24.88	813	162	51.70
	Total/Average	1,000,035	31,054	$1,310,708	$42.20	$1,638,375	$1638	$2,047,959	2048	4.85	19.30	$314,708	$315	100.00%

[a] Based on net sales assuming a 2.1% return rate.

Exhibit 15-10 Mail Plan—Notes

Exhibit 15-10 shows a sample mail plan which would be put together before a mailing. The primary purpose of putting together such a plan is to build the sales and profit projection for the total mailing by estimating the performance of each list separately.

Column 1 contains the key code used on the response device to indicate the list from which each order is obtained.

Column 2 contains a written description of the list.

Column 3 shows the mail quantity of each list.

Columns 4 through 6 detail the expected average order size, response rate, and resulting gross sales per thousand for each list. These results applied to the mail quantity provide the expected total gross sales for each list, which are displayed in column 7.

Column 8 contains the expected net sales per thousand which is estimated from the gross sales by applying a return factor.

Column 9 indicates the total catalog mailing cost, while column 10 expresses that selling cost as a percentage of net sales.

Column 11 displays the expected pre-tax profit which is derived by subtracting the merchandise cost, operating cost, fixed cost allocation and selling cost from the expected net sales. All of these calculations can be approximated readily using the procedure shown in Exhibits 15-1 and 15-2.

Column 12 gives the resulting profit per thousand and the final column shows profit as a percent of net sales.

Exhibit 15-11 Mail Report—Notes

Exhibit 15-11 shows a sample mail report which would be generated during the course of a mailing.

Columns 1 through 3 include the source code, list description and actual mail quantity, respectively.

Columns 4 and 5 display the actual cumulative orders and sales as of the date of the report.

Column 6 contains the average order size derived by dividing the cumulative sales by the cumulative orders.

Column 7 displays the adjusted sales, which are obtained by adding a pro-rata allocation of the uncoded sales to each list. The adjusted sales per thousand in Column 8 are derived by dividing the adjusted sales by the mail quantity.

Column 9 shows projected sales which are derived by dividing the adjusted sales by the estimated percentage done for the catalog at the time of the report. Historic order response patterns are applied to the mail dates for each list to determine the percent done. Column 10 divides column 9 by the mail quantity in thousands.

Column 11 contains the projected response rate which is obtained by projecting cumulative orders to completion in the same way that sales were projected, and dividing the projected orders by the mail quantity.

Column 12 contains the estimated selling cost percent of net sales obtained by dividing the promotional cost by the projected net sales for each list.

The projected profit and profit per thousand in columns 13 and 14 are derived by applying the relevant costs to the projected sales.

The last column contains the probability of meeting the 10% profit target. This figure is derived by comparing the projected response rate with the response rate required to produce a 10% profit given the average order size for each list. Taking the actual mail quantity into consideration, this figure represents the statistical probability that each list would achieve or exceed the target response rate when mailed again under similar conditions.

order cycle. Resulting profitability is based on projected results, not on orders received to date.

Basing the analysis simply on orders to date again would understate final sales and profitability very significantly. Finally, this analysis calculates the statistical probability of exceeding the minimum 10 percent target for pre-tax profit. What a handy tool this final column provides. It synthesizes into a single number the likelihood of achieving the desired profit by mailing to that list again assuming, of course, that all other conditions remain the same.

That last assumption should not be skipped over quickly. Conditions in the economy shift. Some companies make radical changes in the composition of their product line. Some companies whose lists you rent may have made important changes resulting in customers who behave differently. A direct marketer can make better use of statistics and arithmetic than can a person engaged in any other form of marketing. But it is not all science. The tools discussed in this chapter will help you, but they will not substitute for careful decision making based on good business judgment. Learn the tools well—and then apply your own good sense.

Self-Quiz

1. Variable costs are those which relate primarily to _____ _____ or_____.

2. In direct marketing the costs of placing advertisements, making mailings, or using the telephone should be considered as

☐ advertising expense   ☐ selling expense.

3. Creative expense and extra costs of producing test programs (print, broadcast, direct mail) should

☐ be included in profitability calculations

☐ be charged to overhead expense.

4. Typically, the more highly qualified an inquiry is the

☐ more costly it will be to generate

☐ less costly it will be to generate.

5. In the short run, it is profitable to continue making conversion mailings to an inquiry list until the _____ of the last mailing is _____ the contribution it generates.

6. What are the three factors that determine profitability?

a. _____

b. _____

c. _____

7. Catalog marketers should not only analyze overall results, but they should analyze results for each _____ and _____ of items as well.

8. A practical way to compute return on investment is to try to simulate _____ and expenses _____ as they are expected to occur.

9. Name three strategies that might be applied to improving return on investment for a catalog operation.

a. _____

b. _____

c. _____

10. In order to continue to expand an ongoing mail order operation it is wise to utilize _____ percent to _____percent of each campaign to test new lists, or packages, or offers.

Pilot Project

You have a mail order item that sells for $45. Your total cost, including product cost, shipping and handling costs, estimated returned goods, and overhead is $29. Your mailing cost is $350 per thousand.

Considering your unit profit per sale and your cost per thousand mailed, perform the following calculations.

a. Number of orders required per thousand to break even.
b. Number of orders required per thousand to make a 10 percent profit.

Chapter Sixteen

Idea Development and Testing

"We've got to develop ideas with breakthrough potential and test their validity" is an oft-repeated statement in direct marketing circles. The never-ending thirst for the breakthrough is motivated by fantastic pay-off potentials. "Book-of-the-Month Club" was a breakthrough concept. It led to billions of dollars of book sales. Newspaper and magazine inserts. The "Gold Box" concept. TV support for other media. Ink-jet imaging. Each a gigantic breakthrough.

But how does one develop breakthrough ideas? Are there techniques to be applied? Yes.

Brainstorming

Brainstorming, first popularized in the 1950s by Alex Osborne of BBD&O, continues to be one of the most effective methods of finding new creative solutions to difficult problems. Scores of examples could be cited of breakthroughs that have resulted from brainstorming, but a few will suffice. First, some house rules for brainstorming.

House Rules for Brainstorming

Select a leader. Let the leader take all responsibility for contact with reality; everyone else in the brainstorming meeting is to "think wild." In the brainstorming meeting, the leader plays a low-key role. It's important to avoid an influence on the participants. The duties of the leader are:

- To see that detailed notes are taken on all ideas expressed
- To see that the agenda and time schedule are adhered to
- To admonish any critical thinkers in the group—no negative thinking is allowed during the brainstorming session

- To see that the group takes time to "build up" each idea
- To keep all participants involved and contributing

Rules During Brainstorming

1. Suspend all critical judgment of your own—or other people's—ideas. Don't ask yourself if this is a *good idea* or a *bad idea*. Accept it and rack your brain for ways to improve the concept.
2. Welcome "free wheeling," off-the-wall thinking. Wild, crazy, funny, far-out ideas are important. Why? Because they frequently shock us into a totally new viewpoint of the problem.
3. Quantity, not quality, is the objective during the brainstorm session. This may sound contradictory. It's not. Remember, every member of the group has been briefed on the problem in advance. You have a carefully planned agenda of material to cover. Consequently, your group is well directed toward the right problem. Therefore we can say, "Go for quantity in the idea session."
4. Build up each idea. Here's where most so-called brainstorm sessions fail. They just collect ideas as fast as they come and let it go at that. The leader should carefully slow the group down so they stop with each idea and help build it up. Enhance each idea, no matter how crazy or off-beat it may seem.

It's the leader's responsibility to see that these four guidelines are adhered to in every meeting, but he or she should do this in a very low-key, informal manner. It is important that the leader does not become a dominant, authority figure in meetings.

Brainstorming is part of a three-phase process.

1. Before you start, create an agenda and carefully define problem(s) in writing.
2. Set quotas for ideas and a time limit for each section of the agenda.
3. Review the house rules with participants before each brainstorming session.

After the session is over, then—and only then—use your normal everyday judgment to logically select ideas with the most potential from all available alternatives.

Brainstorming Example 1

The problem: Insurance companies are not allowed to give free gifts as an incentive for applying for an insurance policy. How can we offer a free gift and stay within the law? That was the brainstorming problem. Sounds like an impossible problem. Right? Wrong. Brainstorming participants broke through with a positive solution, a blockbuster.

The breakthrough: The brainstorming idea that hit pay dirt was: offer the free gift to everyone, whether they apply for the policy or not.

Results: A 38 percent increase in applications.

| Brainstorming Example 2 | The problem: How can we avoid paying postage for sending prizes to "no" entrants in an "everybody wins" sweepstakes? (Possible savings in postage to the marketer—if the problem could be solved—was about $250,000.) |

The breakthrough: We asked "no" entrants to provide a stamped, self-addressed envelope. We included a prize in the shipping carton for those who said "yes." (The Post Office Department approved the requirement at the time.)

Results: This was the most successful sweepstakes contest the sponsor ever conducted. The sponsor also enjoyed savings of $250,000 in postage.

| Brainstorming Example 3 | The problem: We have 36 competitors selling to schools. They all promise "prompt shipment" of their pompons. How can we dramatize the fact that we ship our pompons in 24 hours and thus capture the bulk of the market? |

The breakthrough: We inserted a Jiffy Order Card in the catalog, in addition to the regular order form, featuring Guaranteed Shipment Within 24 hours.

Result: Pompon sales increased a dramatic 40 percent!

| Brainstorming Example 4 | The problem: A leading agricultural chemical company manufactures both a corn herbicide and corn insecticide. Each product has its own positioning in the farm market, and each product has a different share of market in various geographic areas across the nation. How can new users for each product be won over from competition? |

The breakthrough: Create a combination rebate program. Since the ratio of herbicide to insecticide remains relatively constant regardless of farm size, offer a rebate on *both* products when purchased at the same time.

Result: A significant number of farmers who had planned to purchase the two products from different manufacturers took advantage of the rebate offer and purchased both products from our manufacturer, with an average order of $25,000.

Fantasy Games

Of all the games creative people play, my favorites are fantasy games. These can be defined as games that enable one to reach out for satisfaction of his or her most fervent wishes. Here's a fantasy game anyone can play in a group or alone. The rules are simple: before you charge into the solution to a direct marketing problem, write three words on the top of a piece of paper—"I wish that. . . ." Then complete the sentence with your most fervent wish. Let's take some examples:

Fantasy 1. Some time ago, someone probably said, "I wish I could find a way to spread my advertising sales cost over several books rather than one." Out of it came the negative option and the Book-of-the-Month Club. A marketing triumph.

Fantasy 2. A client recently expressed this wish: "I wish we could cut our bad debts in half." A fantasy? Not at all. Brainstorming provided a way to cut the client's bad debts by 80 percent!

Fantasy 3. "I wish that we could find a way to contact customers just one week before their supplies are depleted." A unique computer system to accomplish exactly that came out of this wish.

Lateral Thinking

Recently I sent a memo to all of our writers, asking the question, "What do you do when your creative process turns blah?" Here is the reply of one of our senior writers: "I use the principles of random word technique and lateral thinking. I also like to use the Think Tank, a piece of gadgetry, designed by Savo Bojicic of University of Ontario. It forces the user to break the habit of logical, vertical thinking and opens the mind to creative, uninhibited lateral thought. Here's how I use the Think Tank:

> First, I twist the dials on the sides of the Think Tank to jumble up the words inside. Second, I copy down six random words that appear in the window of the Think Tank. Third, I spend at least five minutes with each word, using word associations and so forth, that relate to the problem I'm trying to solve. Usually one or more of the words will "trigger" an idea. Here's an example:
>
> My problem was to come up with some new ideas on how to get more credit card holders for Amoco. I twirled the dial on the Think Tank and the word "water" popped into the window. In a matter of milliseconds my free, stream-of-consciousness thinking was set in motion and led to a unique idea. Water made me think of boats. Boats need gasoline, just as cars do (a good-size cruiser may spend $75 to $100 or more for a fill-up). There are Amoco gas pumps at marinas on the water. Why not send our regular credit card solicitation package with a special letter and special appeal to a list of boat owners? (Credit the lateral thinking process with this breakthrough idea.)

Creative Stimulators

The degree of truly creative output is directly related to two factors: clear and specific definitions of problems to be solved and the right "atmosphere" for developing creative solutions.

Frank Daniels, a creative director with Stone & Adler, has a system for stimulating creative people. Using a long-established technique for idea stimulation, he provides creative people with eight "stimulators" designed to expand their thinking. The examples that follow were applied to the Lanier Company, manufacturers of dictating equipment. Creativity was being stimulated for promoting a minirecorder, Lanier's Pocket Secretary. Each of the eight stimulators is accompanied by a key thought and a series of questions designed to promote creative solutions.

Can We COMBINE?

Combining two or more elements often results in new thought processes. These questions are designed to encourage brainstorming participants to think in terms of combinations.

Key thought: Combine appropriate parts of well-known things to emphasize the benefits of our product. "Think of owning a Rolls-Royce the size of a Volkswagen" (Lanier Pocket Secretary).

- What can be combined physically or conceptually to emhasize product benefits?
- Can the product be combined with another so that both benefit?
- Where in the product offer would a combination of thoughts be of most help?
- What opposites can be combined to show a difference from competitive products?
- What can we combine with our product to make it more fun to own, use, look at?
- Can part of one of our benefits be combined with part of another to enhance both?
- Can newness be combined with tradition?
- Can a product benefit be combined with a specific audience need through visual devices? Copy devices?
- What can we combine from the advertising and sales program to the benefit of both? Can salespersons' efforts be combined into advertising?
- Can we demonstrate product advantages by using "misfit" combination demonstration?
- Can we combine manufacturing information performance tests with advertising to demonstrate advantages?

TIME ELEMENTS

Saving time and having extra time are conventional human wants. This series of questions is designed to expand one's thinking toward making time a plus factor in the product offer.

Key thought: Alter time factor(s) in present offer, present schedules, and present product positioning to motivate action.

- Does seasonal timing have an effect on individual benefits?
- Can present seasonal timing be reversed for special effect?

- Can limited offers be effective?
- Can early buyers be given special consideration?
- Can off-season offers be made?
- Are there better days, weeks, or months for our offers?
- Can we compress or extend present promotional sequencing?
- Can our price be keyed to selected times of the week, month, year?
- Can we feature no-time-limit offers?
- Can we feature limited time offers?
- Can we feature fast delivery or follow-up?

Can We ADD?

An axiom of selling is that the customer often unconsciously compares the added benefits of a competitor's product with those of your product. The products with the most added benefits traditionally sell better. These questions are designed to ferret out added benefits for a particular product.

Key thought: Look for ways to express benefits by relating functional advantages of unrelated products or things. "We've taken all the best cassette recorder features and added one from the toaster" (pop-out delivery).

- What has been added to our product that's missing from others?
- Do we have a deficiency due to excess that can be turned into advantage?
- Is our product usable in many different ways aside from the intended use?
- Is our product instantly noticeable? Is it unusual in terms of size, shape, color? What unrelated symbols can we use to emphasize this unique characteristic?
- Does our product make something easier? What have we added by taking this something away?
- Does our product make order out of chaos or meaningful chaos out of total chaos? What have we added by taking this something away?
- What does the purchase of our product add to the buyer's physical situation, mental condition, subconscious condition, present condition, future condition?
- Where would the buyer be if he does not purchase? What would be missing from his life?
- Does our product give its full benefit to the buyer immediately or does he build up (add to) his well-being through continued possession?

Can We SUBTRACT?

Taking away can often be as appealing as adding to. Less weight, less complexity, less fuss, less bother are fundamental appeals. These questions steer brainstorming participants in that direction.

Key thought: Subtract from the obvious to focus attention on benefits of our product/service. "We've weighed all the minirecorders and made ours lighter."

- What deficiencies does our product have competitively?
- What advantage do we have?
- What features are the newest? The most unusual?
- How can our product use/cost be "minimized" over time?
- Can a buyer use less of another product if he buys ours?
- Can the evidence of total lack of desire for our product be used to illustrate benefits?
- Can the limitations of our benefits be used as an appeal?
- What does lack of our product in the buyer's living habits do to him?
- Does our product offer a chance to eliminate any common element in all competitive products?
- Does our product reduce or eliminate (subtract) anything in the process of performing its work?
- Will our product deflate (subtract from) a problem for the buyer?

Can We Make ASSOCIATIONS? Favorable associations are often the most effective way to emphasize product benefits. "Like Sterling on silver," a classic example of a favorable association, is an [observation] [saying] [remark] [comment] that accrues to the benefit of the product being compared with other products.

Key thought: Form a link with unrelated things or situations to emphasize benefits:

- Can we link our product to another already successful product to emphasize benefits?
- Can we appeal to popular history, literature, poetry, art to emphasize benefits?
- What does the potential buyer associate with our product? How can we use this association to advantage?
- When does the potential buyer associate our product with his potential use?
- Can associations be drawn with present or future events?
- Can associations be made with abstractions that can be expressed visually, musically, with words and so forth?
- Can funny, corny, challenging associations be made?
- Can associations be made with suppliers of component parts?

- Is our product so unique it needs no association?
- Can our product be associated with many different situations?

Can We SIMPLIFY?

What is the simple way to describe and illustrate our major product benefit? As sophisticated as our world is today, the truism persists that people relate best to simple things. These questions urge participants to state benefits with dramatic simplicity.

Key thought: Dramatize benefits individually or collectively with childishly simple examples, symbols, images.

- Which of our appeals is strongest over our competition? How can we simplify to illustrate?
- Is there a way to simplify *all* our benefits for emphasis?
- Where is most of the confusion about our product in the buyer's mind?
- Can we illustrate by simplification?
- Is our appeal abstract? Can we substitute simple, real visualizations to emhasize?
- Could a familiar quotation, picture, be used to make our appeal more understandable?
- Is our product complex? Can we break it up (literally) into more understandable pieces to emphasize benefits?
- Can I overlap one benefit with another to make product utility more understandable?
- Can I contrast an old way of doing something with the confusing part of our product to create understanding?
- Is product appeal rigidly directed at too small a segment of the market? Too broad a segment?
- Can we emphasize benefits by having an unskilled person or child make good use of the product in a completely out-of-context situation.

Can We SUBSTITUTE?

The major product benefit for our product is often so similar to major product benefits of competitive products that it is difficult for the consumer to perceive the difference. Substituting another theme, such as Avis did when the company changed its theme to "We Try Harder," can often establish a point of difference. These questions inspire participants to think in terms of substitution.

Key thought: Substitute the familiar for another familiar theme for emphasis; substitute the unfamiliar for the familiar for emphasis.

- Can a well-known theme for another product be substituted for our theme, or can a well-known benefit for another product be substituted for our benefit?

- Can an incongruous situation be used to focus emphasis on our theme or benefits.
- Can a series of incongruous situations be found for every benefit we have? Can they be used in one ad? Can they form a continuity series of ads?
- What can be substituted for our product appeal that will emphasize the difference between us and our competitors?
- Can an obviously dissimilar object be substituted for the image of our product?
- Can a physical object be used to give more concrete representation of a product intangible?
- Is our product replacing a process rapidly becoming dated? Can we substitute the past for the present, the future for the past or the present?
- Can we visualize our product where the competitor's product is normally expected to be?
- Can we visualize our product as the only one of its kind in the world, as if there were no other substitutes for our product?

Can We Make a REVERSAL? The ordinary can become extraordinary as normal situations are reversed. A man doing the wash. A cute miss pumping gas. A trained bear pushing a power mower. These questions are designed to motivate participants to think in terms of reversing normal situations.

Key thought: Emphasize a benefit by completely reversing the normal situation.

- What are the diametrically opposed situations for each of our product benefits?
- For each copy point already established, make a complete reverse statement.
- How would a totally uninformed person describe our product?
- Can male- and female-oriented roles be reversed?
- Can art and copy be totally reversed to emphasize a point?
- How many incongruous product situations can be shown graphically? Verbally?
- Can we find humor in the complete reversal of anticipated product uses or benefits?

Test the Big Things

Whether testable ideas come out of pure research, brainstorming, or self-developed creativity, the same picture applies: *test the big things.* Trivia testing, e.g., testing the tilt of a postage stamp or testing the effect of various colors of paper stock, are passé. Breakthroughs are possible only when you test the big things. Six big areas from which break-throughs emerge are:

1. The products or services you offer
2. The media you use (lists, print, and broadcast)
3. The propositions you make
4. The copy platforms you use
5. The formats you use
6. The timing you choose

Five of the areas for testing appear on most published lists these days. But testing new products and new product features is rarely recommended. Yet everything starts with the product or service you offer.

Many direct marketers religiously test new ads, new mailing packages, new media, new copy approaches, new formats, and new timing schedules season after season with never a thought to testing new product features. Finally, the most imaginative of creative approaches fails to overcome the waning appeal of the same old product. And still another product bites the dust.

This need not happen. For example, consider the most common-place of mail order items, the address label. Scores of firms offer them in black ink on standard white stock. Competition is keen: prices all run about the same. From this variety of competitive styles, however, a few emerge with new product features: gold stock, colored ink, seasonal borders, and so forth. Tests are made to determine appeal. The new product features appeal to a bigger audience.

Projectable Mailing Sample Sizes

Determining mail sample sizes for testing purposes was covered thoroughly in Chapter 5—Mailing Lists. As we pointed out, a 5,000 test of a given list is usually adequate to get a "feel" of responsiveness but continuations are almost certain to vary because of time lapse, seasonality, change in list sources, economics, weather conditions, consumer behavior, and a host of other factors.

Some direct marketers live by probability tables that tell the mailer what the sample size must be at various response levels within a specified error limit, such as 5 or 10 percent. No one argues the statistical validity of probability tables. Probability tables can't be relied on too heavily because it is impossible to construct a truly scientific sample. However, such tables, within limits, can be helpful. Table 16-1 is based on a 95 percent confidence level at various limits of error.

Testing Components Vs. Testing Mailing Packages

In the endless search for breakthroughs, the question continually arises: In direct mail, should we test components or mailing packages? There are two schools of thought on this. The prevailing one is that the big breakthroughs come about through the testing of completely different mailing packages as opposed to testing individual components within a mailing package. Something can be learned from each procedure, of course. In my opinion, however, the more logical procedure is to first find the big difference in mailing packages and then follow with tests of individual components in the losing packages, which can often make the winning packages even better.

In package testing, one starts with a complete concept and builds all the components to fit the image of the concept. Consider the differences between these two package concepts:

	Package 1	Package 2
Envelope:	9 x 12	#10
Letter:	8-page, stapled	4-sheet (two sides) computer written
Circular:	None	4-page, illustrated
Order form:	8½ x 11, perforated stub	8½ x 3⅔

The differences between these two package concepts are considerable. Chances are great that there will be a substantial difference in response. Once the winning package evolves, component tests make excellent sense. Let us say the 9 x 12 package is the winner. A logical subsequent test would be to fold the same inserts into a 6 x 9 envelope. A reply envelope may be considered as an additional test. Computerizing the first page of the eight-page letter could be still another test.

How to Test Print Advertising

For direct marketing practitioners who are multimedia users, testing print advertising is just as important as testing direct mail. And, as with direct mail, it is important that the tests be constructed in such a way as to produce valid results.

Gerald Schreck, media director of Doubleday Advertising Company, New York, gave the following pointers on A-B split tests in an *Advertising Age* feature article.

The split helps you determine the relative strengths of different ads. For example, you can run two ads, A and B, in a specific issue or edition of a publication so that two portions of the total run are equally divided and identical in circulation. The only difference is that ad A will run in

Table 16-1. Test Sample Sizes Required for 95 Percent Confidence Level for Mailing Response Levels from 0.1 to 4.0 Percent.

R (Response)	LIMITS OF ERROR (EXPRESSED AS PERCENTAGE POINTS)														
	.02	.04	.06	.08	.10	.12	.14	.16	.18	.20	.30	.40	.50	.60	.70
.1	95,929	23,982	10,659	5,995	3,837	2,665	1,957	1,499	1,184	959	426	240	153	106	78
.2	191,666	47,916	21,296	11,979	7,667	5,324	3,911	2,994	2,366	1,917	852	479	307	213	156
.3	287,211	71,803	31,912	17,951	11,488	7,978	5,861	4,487	3,546	2,872	1,276	718	459	319	234
.4	382,564	95,641	42,507	23,910	15,303	10,627	7,807	5,977	4,723	3,826	1,700	956	612	425	312
.5	477,724	119,431	53,080	29,858	19,109	13,270	9,749	7,464	5,987	4,777	2,123	1,194	764	530	390
.6	572,693	143,173	63,632	35,793	22,908	15,908	11,687	8,948	7,070	5,727	2,545	1,432	916	636	467
.7	667,470	166,867	74,163	41,717	26,699	18,541	13,622	10,429	8,240	6,675	2,966	1,669	1,068	741	545
.8	762,054	190,514	84,673	47,628	30,482	21,168	15,552	11,907	9,408	7,621	3,387	1,905	1,219	847	622
.9	856,447	214,112	95,160	53,528	34,258	23,790	17,478	13,382	10,573	8,564	3,806	2,141	1,370	951	699
1.0	950,648	237,662	105,628	59,415	38,026	26,407	19,401	14,854	11,736	9,506	4,225	2,376	1,521	1,056	776
1.1	1,044,656	261,164	116,072	65,291	41,786	29,018	21,319	16,322	12,897	10,446	4,643	2,611	1,671	1,160	853
1.2	1,138,472	284,618	126,496	71,155	45,539	31,624	23,234	17,788	14,055	11,385	5,060	2,846	1,821	1,265	929
1.3	1,232,097	308,024	136,899	77,006	49,284	34,225	25,145	19,251	15,211	12,321	5,476	3,080	1,971	1,369	1,006
1.4	1,325,529	331,382	147,280	82,845	53,021	36,820	27,051	20,711	16,364	13,255	5,891	3,314	2,121	1,473	1,082
1.5	1,418,769	354,692	157,640	88,673	56,751	39,410	28,954	22,168	17,515	14,188	6,305	3,547	2,270	1,576	1,158
1.6	1,511,818	377,954	167,980	94,489	60,473	41,995	30,853	23,622	18,664	15,118	6,719	3,780	2,419	1,680	1,234
1.7	1,604,674	401,168	178,297	100,292	64,187	44,574	32,748	25,073	19,811	16,047	7,132	4,012	2,567	1,783	1,310
1.8	1,697,338	424,334	188,592	106,083	67,894	47,148	34,639	26,521	20,955	16,973	7,543	4,243	2,716	1,886	1,385
1.9	1,789,810	447,452	198,868	111,863	71,592	49,717	36,526	27,966	22,096	17,898	7,955	4,474	2,863	1,988	1,461
2.0	1,882,090	470,523	209,121	117,631	75,284	52,280	38,410	29,407	23,235	18,821	8,365	4,705	3,011	2,091	1,536
2.1	1,974,178	493,544	219,352	123,386	78,967	54,838	40,289	30,846	24,372	19,742	8,774	4,935	3,158	2,193	1,611
2.2	2,066,074	516,518	229,564	129,129	82,643	57,391	42,165	32,282	25,507	20,661	9,182	5,165	3,306	2,295	1,686
2.3	2,157,778	539,444	239,753	134,861	86,311	59,938	44,036	33,715	26,638	21,578	9,590	5,394	3,452	2,397	1,761
2.4	2,249,290	562,322	249,920	140,581	89,972	62,480	45,903	35,145	27,769	22,493	9,997	5,623	3,599	2,499	1,836
2.5	2,340,609	585,152	260,068	146,288	93,624	65,017	47,767	36,572	28,896	23,406	10,403	5,851	3,745	2,600	1,911
2.6	2,431,737	607,934	270,192	151,983	97,269	67,547	49,627	37,996	30,021	24,317	10,807	6,079	3,891	2,702	1,985
2.7	2,522,673	630,668	280,296	157,667	100,907	70,074	51,483	39,416	31,144	25,227	11,211	6,307	4,036	2,803	2,059
2.8	2,613,416	653,354	290,380	163,339	104,537	72,595	53,335	40,834	32,264	26,134	11,615	6,534	4,181	2,904	2,133
2.9	2,703,968	675,992	300,440	168,998	108,159	75,110	55,183	42,249	33,382	27,039	12,017	6,760	4,326	3,004	2,207
3.0	2,794,328	698,582	310,480	174,645	111,773	77,620	57,026	43,661	34,497	27,943	12,419	6,986	4,471	3,105	2,281
3.1	2,884,495	721,124	320,499	180,281	115,380	80,125	58,867	45,070	35,611	28,845	12,820	7,211	4,615	3,205	2,355
3.2	2,974,470	743,618	330,496	185,904	118,979	82,623	60,702	46,476	36,721	29,745	13,220	7,436	4,759	3,305	2,428
3.3	3,064,254	766,063	340,471	191,516	122,570	85,118	62,535	47,878	37,830	30,642	13,619	7,660	4,903	3,404	2,501
3.4	3,153,845	788,461	350,427	197,115	126,154	87,607	64,364	49,278	38,936	31,538	14,017	7,884	5,046	3,504	2,574
3.5	3,243,244	810,811	360,360	202,703	129,730	90,089	66,188	50,675	40,040	32,432	14,414	8,108	5,189	3,603	2,647
3.6	3,332,452	833,113	370,271	208,278	133,298	92,568	68,009	52,069	41,141	33,325	14,811	8,331	5,332	3,702	2,720
3.7	3,421,467	855,367	380,163	213,842	136,859	95,041	69,825	53,460	42,240	34,214	15,207	8,554	5,474	3,801	2,793
3.8	3,510,290	877,572	390,031	219,393	140,412	97,507	71,638	54,848	43,336	35,103	15,601	8,776	5,616	3,900	2,865
3.9	3,598,921	899,730	399,878	224,932	143,957	99,969	73,446	56,233	44,430	35,989	15,995	8,997	5,758	3,998	2,938
4.0	3,687,360	921,840	409,706	230,460	147,494	102,426	75,252	57,615	45,522	36,874	16,388	9,218	5,900	4,097	3,010

half of the issue and ad B will run in the other half. For measuring the strength of the ads, a split includes an offer requiring your reader to act by writing or sending in a coupon. Then all you need do is compare the responses with the individual ads. If done properly this method can be accurate to two decimal points. You also have the advantage of real-world testing to find out what people actually do, not just what they say they'll do. And, because all factors are held equal, the difference in results can be attributed directly to your advertising. (See Exhibit 16-1)

A/B splits. In an ideal situation, any issue of a split-run publication will carry ad A in every other copy with ad B in the alternate copies.

Clump splits. Most often, however, publications cannot produce an exact A/B split. They will promise a clump. That is, every lift of 50 copies, for instance, will be evenly split or even every lift of 25 or 10. The clump can be very accurate when the test is done in large circulations.

Flip-flops. For publications that offer no split at all, you can create your own. Take two comparable publications, X and Y. Run ad A in X and ad B in Y for the first phase. Then for the second phase, reverse the insertions: Ad B in X and Ad A in Y. Total the respective results for A and B and compare.

The split that isn't. We recently asked one magazine publisher if he ran splits. The production manager told us, "Oh, yes, we run a perfect split. Our circulation divides exactly—one-half east of the Mississippi and one-half west." Look out. That is not a valid split.

While the A/B split can't tell you why individuals respond to your ad, the technique can tell you what they responded to. And a real bonus is that when you have completed your tests, you'll have a list of solid prospects.

In the A/B split, how can you compare one run against another run of the same ad? You can "key" coupons or response copy by:

1. *Dating.* On your coupons, try JA383NA for January 3, 1983 in *Newsweek* for ad A and JA383NB for the same insertion of ad B.

Exhibit 16-1. Variations in the Uses of Splits

A/B Split	Clump Split	Flip-Flop Split
A	A	A
B	A	B
A	A	B
B	B	A
	B	
	B	

2. *Department numbers.* Use Dept. A for ad A and Dept. B for B in your company's address.

3. *Color of coupon.* One color for A, another for B.

4. *Color of ink.*

5. *Names.* In ad A, ask readers to send correspondence to Mr. Anderson, For B, have them write to Mr. Brown.

6. *Telephone numbers.*

7. *Shape of coupon.*

8. *IBM punches.* You don't even need a computer. Just select a pattern you can read.

9. *The obvious.* Right on the coupon, use "For Readers of *Glamour*" in A and "For *Glamour* Readers" in B.

10. *Address information.* Mr., Mrs., Miss in A, Mr., Ms., for B.

11. *Abbreviations.* In your address, New York, for A, N.Y. for B.

12. *Typeface.* In coupon A, all caps for NAME, etc., and in Coupon B, upper- and lower-case for Name, etc.

The possibilities are virtually unlimited. All you need is a code that's in keeping with your ad and the publication, one you find is easy to understand and use.

Telescopic Testing

While it is certainly necessary to construct meaningful A/B split tests, they do have limitations. When the advertiser runs an A/B split test he doesn't know what would have happened if he had been able to run ad C against ads A and B and, additionally, ads D, E, F, and G—all simultaneously, all in the same edition, all under measurable conditions.

Today, testing to find the best ad among a multiplicity of ads all tested under the same conditions is quite feasible. The method is widely known as *telescopic testing.* Telescopic testing is simply the process of telescoping an entire season of test ads into one master test program. (Examples of telescopic testing were given in Chapter 13.) Regional editions of publications and other developments make telescopic testing possible. Indeed, with regional editions you can telescope a year's testing sequences into a single insertion, testing many ads simultaneously. *TV Guide* offers the best opportunity for telescopic testing. *TV Guide* publishes over 100 different editions. *Woman's Day* offers 26 regional editions. *Time*, with 8 regional editions, makes it possible to test nine different ads or ad variations simultaneously.

Tom Collins, a pioneer in telescopic testing, has established a rule of thumb for estimating the minimum circulation you should buy for your ad tests to make results meaningful. First, start by assuming you need an average of 200 responses per appeal to be statistically valid.

Then, multiply your allowable advertising cost per response by 200. Finally, multiply that figure by the number of key numbers in the test. This will give you the total minimum expenditure required to get meaningful results.

To clarify the technique further, let's say you want to test four new ads against a control ad, which we will call ad A. Your tests for the four new ads against the control ad will be structured as follows: A vs. B; A

Split 1—Ad A vs. Ad B

Edition	Circulation
San Francisco Metro	750,000
Pittsburgh	225,000
Detroit	225,000
South Georgia	67,000
Iowa	210,000
Pheonix	275,000
Western Illinois	87,000
Northern Indiana	186,000
	2,025,000

Split 2—Ad A vs. Ad C

Edition	Circulation
Northern Wisconsin	170,000
Phildelphia	230,000
Cleveland	55,000
Kansas City	230,000
Western New England	175,000
North Carolina	272,000
Colorado	139,000
Illinois/Wisconsin	225,000
Gulf Coast	125,000
Minneapolis/St. Paul	126,000
Central California	115,000
Southeast Texas	64,000
West Virginia	165,000
	2,091,000

Split 3—Ad A vs. Ad D

Edition	Circulation
Central Ohio	210,000
Michigan State	309,000
Western New York State	65,000
Central Indiana	230,000
San Diego	255,000
New Hampshire	141,000
Portland	195,000
Eastern Virginia	160,000
Kansas State	92,000
Tuscon	70,000
North Dakota	65,000
Eastern Washington St.	145,000
Evansville-Paducah	104,000
	2,041,000

Split 4—Ad A vs. Ad E

Edition	Circulation
Eastern New England	665,000
Chicago Metro	475,000
Orlando	140,000
Oklahoma State	184,000
St. Louis	235,000
Eastern Illinois	100,000
Missouri	141,000
Eugene	45,000
Idaho	57,000
	2,042,000

vs. C; A vs. D; A vs. E. Thus we have a total of five ads requiring eight different keys. (Ad A, the control ad, is being tested against a different ad in four separate instances and therefore requires four different keys.)

To read the results in this kind of test, we simply convert ad A to 100 percent, depending on the results achieved. In this way, ad C can be compared with ad E, for instance, even though they are not directly tested against one another. Now, let's say we want to test the four new ads in *TV Guide* against the control ad. Further, using the Collins formula, let's assume we need a circulation of two million to get 200 or more replies for each side of each two-way split. The type of schedule that would be placed in *TV Guide* to accomplish this objective appears on the previous page. Note that a careful review of the markets selected for each split (region) shows that all markets are balanced geographically.

Telescopic testing is not limited to regional editions of publications. Newspaper inserts serve as an ideal vehicle for such testing. The test pieces are intermixed at the printing plant before being shipped to the newspaper. All test pieces, however, must be exactly the same size. Otherwise, newspapers cannot handle them on their automatic inserting equipment.

Using full-page card inserts in magazines is still another way to test simultaneously a multiplicity of ads. Scores of magazines now accept such inserts. It is important to remember that in telescopic testing we are looking for breakthroughs, not small differences. As Collins puts it, "We are not merely testing ads, we are testing hypotheses. Then when a hypothesis appears to have been proved by the results, it is often possible to construct other, even more successful ads, on the same hypothesis."

Test hypotheses tend to fall into four main categories:

1. What is the best price and offer?
2. Who is the best prospect?
3. What is the most appealing product advantage?
4. What is the most important ultimate benefit? (By "ultimate benefit" we mean the satisfaction of such basic human needs as pride, admiration, safety, wealth, peace of mind, and so on.)

Idea development and testing are soul mates. The two things to keep uppermost in mind are: (1) strive for breakthrough ideas and (2) test the big things.

Self-Quiz

1. What are the duties of the leader in brainstorming?

a. _____

b. _____

c. _____

d. _____

e. _____

2. What are the three phases of the brainstorming process?

a. _____

_____

b. _____

_____

c. _____

_____

3. One way to solve a difficult problem is to fantasize. The first three words of your expressed desire should be: _____

_____

4. What is lateral thinking?

_____

_____

_____

_____

5. What are the six big things to test?

a. _____

b. _____

c. _____

d. _____

e. _____

f. _____

6. What is the safest rule to follow in testing mailing lists?

_____

_____

_____

_____

7. In direct mail testing, which is preferable?

☐ Testing components.   ☐ Testing complete mailing packages.

8. Name six ways to key a print ad.

a. _____

b. _____

c. _____

d. _____

e. _____

f. _____

9. Define telescopic testing.

_____

_____

_____

10. Name the four categories into which hypotheses seem to fall.

a. _____

b. _____

c. _____

d. _____

Pilot Project

You are engaged in a fantasy game. Three wishes follow. Come up with at least three solutions for each of the wishes.

1. *I wish that* I could get all my customers to suggest friends who would likewise become customers.

2. *I wish that* I could get all my customers to pay their bills within 45 days.

3. *I wish that* I could reach all the people in this country who are over 6-feet tall.

Chapter Seventeen

Research for Direct Marketers

Sophisticated direct marketers are going far beyond brainstorming and testing in an effort to increase their response levels.They are applying all the research techniques of traditional marketers.

Old-school direct marketers have traditionally scoffed at the use of marketing research. They argue, plausibly enough, that inherent in their system is the most powerful research tool of all—measurable responses. To some degree they are right. In-market testing *can* be more cost-efficient than other means in many situations. However, what in-market testing cannot do is:

- Provide an understanding of the marketing environment necessary for strategic planning
- Identify your best prospect's characteristics, wants, and needs
- Provide information that can help creative people upgrade copy before incurring production and media costs
- Determine which elements of your program are working and why
- Monitor how perceptions of your product or service are changing over time

New-school direct marketers are applying research techniques long standard among general advertisers, not because it is fashionable or intellectually stimulating to do so, but because research pays off at the bottom line.

The purpose of this chapter is to identify the major areas in which marketing research has been successfully applied to direct marketing. It will not serve as a "cookbook" of research methodologies. Because research is highly technical, its execution and analysis should be left to the professionals. But it is important for the direct response advertiser to develop a sense of when those professionals can be productively called in to aid the creative process or reduce the risk of decision-making.

Development of Marketing Research

Marketing research, as we know it, is a very new field. One simple but broad definition is that "marketing research comprises all those information gathering activities conducted to facilitate the marketing of goods or services." Research so defined has been practiced systematically since about the turn of the century. Research as we know it today, though, has only emerged since World War II.

Two series of developments are responsible for its explosive growth to what is now perhaps a two billion dollar a year business. The first developments are *technological:* They include the application of a host of techniques borrowed from such fields as psychology, sociology, economics, and statistics. They also include ready access to computers, without which much of the routine research work and most advanced techniques simply wouldn't be feasible.

Equally important to the development of research, however, is the acceptance of a concept—the *marketing concept.* Before this deceptively simple idea was adopted manufacturers were much more concerned with what they could *make* than with what they could *sell.* Henry Ford's dictum that the public could have any color car it wanted as long as it was black is perhaps the purest expression of this position.

After World War II, in the fierce competitive struggle to satisfy pent-up consumer demand, the focus of industry began to shift from manufacturing to marketing. No longer was it enough to know what one's plant was capable of producing. It became crucial to determine how well it was satisfying the public's wants and needs. This—the marketing concept—is squarely focused on the consumer. So too is marketing research, often called consumer research.

Focus on the Consumer

With the marketing concept firmly in place at most manufacturing companies, marketing research can now be loosely redefined as "those activities conducted to describe consumer behavior, characteristics and attitudes in order to facilitate the marketing of goods or services." The core of this idea is that the more you know about your prospect, the more you can sell to him or her. This is clearly just as true for direct marketers as it is in general marketing. Research, then, is simply a management tool for reducing the frequently awesome financial risk inherent in marketing decisions by gathering facts that help to predict and understand consumer behavior.

An obvious starting point in predicting consumer behavior is to develop an understanding of who the consumer is. Several means of classification, all of them useful, are used by marketers. Most basic is the use of demographics—fundamental personal characteristics such as age, sex, education, occupation, income, etc. It is rare that a direct response advertiser approaches his task without at least a rough profile of his prospect's demographic characteristics in mind. These are frequently available through syndicated data sources, in-house information, or just plain common sense.

Another frequently useful way to classify consumers is by their stage in the life cycle. Is the prospect just beginning to form a family and raise children or is he or she still single? In either case this person may share the demographics of age, sex and education, but may differ substantially in receptivity to baby food or cosmetic advertising. For many product categories, life cycle stage may be a more useful description than demographics, although the two obviously are related.

Psychographic classifications of consumers have been in use for about 15 years, but tend to be ignored by most direct response people. This tool attempts to describe consumers in terms of their psychological characteristics, particularly as they relate to the product category at hand. Psychographics are best derived from sophisticated survey research but are frequently judgmental. In such a system we could describe a prospect for a Pontiac Trans Am as "sporty," "ostentatious," or having a "zest for life." A Volkswagen Rabbit owner, on the other hand, might be "conservative," "economy minded," or "family oriented."

Psychographics are generally most useful when they serve to describe differing consumer segments that exist in a product category. If we understand the psychological mindsets that consumers—and different groups of consumers—bring to one category, we have taken a giant step toward selling them our product.

Researchers in recent years have developed a relatively new means of classifying people. They are now classifying by *lifestyles*—the deep-rooted emotional values, needs, and attitudes that determine many aspects of consumer behavior. A major lifestyle study now in progress is the Values and Lifestyles (VALS) program conducted by SRI International, formally the Stanford Research Institute. VALS has divided the adult United States population into nine segments, each with very distinct lifestyles. By understanding the individual characteristics of these segments, we can fine-tune the elements of our marketing program to maximize the responsiveness of the group or groups that we want to reach.

A familiar example of this involves Young & Rubicam's approach to the Merrill Lynch account, soon after it was acquired. The previous agency's campaign featured a large herd of bulls thundering over the landscape with the slogan "Merrill Lynch is Bullish on America." Y&R research indicated that the bulls were a memorable symbol strongly associated with the stock market.

VALS analysis, however, suggested that the campaign's symbolism most strongly appealed to a segment called the belonger, a traditional blue collar group that actually felt safest as "one of the herd." The Merrill Lynch prospect was very different—the achiever, an upscale group that prides itself in individual accomplishments. With this insight, Y&R turned the herd into a single bull, successfully negotiating mazes and china shops and changed the slogan to "Merrill Lynch, a Breed Apart." The VALS typology is now being applied to many direct marketing programs throughout the Young & Rubicam network.

In addition to these broad systems for classifying people, there are several other key types of information that should be considered in developing a direct marketing program:

- Awareness: How *familiar* is the prospect with your product?
- Needs: What attributes are most *important* in your category?
- Attitudes: What are the *perceptions* of your product relative to competition?
- Intentions: Would the prospect consider *buying* your product?
- Behavior: Does he *use* your product? How often?

The point to be made here is that knowledge of the consumer is at the very core of the marketing concept and of any successful direct response program. It is probably impossible to mount a winning campaign without at least one key insight to motivate your prospect. Research is the tool with which such insights are uncovered and developed.

Basic Research Functions

There are scores of research techniques and many ways to classify them. A very simple but commonly accepted model relates research functions to the basic business process with the following elements:

- *Business analysis and planning.* This includes a thorough assessment of the business environment and corporate resources, the setting of objectives, the development of strategies to reach those objectives, and the identification of tactical options to implement the strategies.
- *Program implementation.* This includes the actual operational steps to carry out the preferred tactics, that is, to make the business run.
- *Monitoring.* Every business has a system for evaluating its progress, sales and profits being the most commonly tracked. Such information continuously feeds back into the analysis/planning process and is a major consideration in adjusting future strategies.

The three key research functions that directly support these elements are schematized in Exhibit 17-1.

Let us take each research function in turn:

I. *Exploratory research* is conducted before strategy development to gather information about how consumers relate to your product category. Generally speaking, research conducted at this front-end stage is the most useful of all because it provides the information upon which everything else is based. It helps to answer such basic questions as:

- Who is my best prospect?
- What does he know or think about my product?
- What can I tell him about my product that is most likely to make him buy it?

Because exploratory research is so important, it tends to employ the most sophisticated and expensive techniques. It is not unusual for a comprehensive exploratory program to take over a year to complete at a cost of $500,000. On the other hand, it is possible to gain valuable insights and a broad overview of a category in one month at a small fraction of that cost.

Most direct marketers consistently tend to ignore exploratory front-end research even though it is precisely at this point that research has the greatest potential payoff. I occasionally hear the argument that it doesn't matter much what you say in a direct mail piece or a two-minute commercial because you have the space or time to say everything that seems pertinent. That is absurd. By identifying the benefits and motivations that are really important to your prospect through exploratory research, you will be able to give priority to your sales points and emphasize the ones that are most likely to generate a response. If you are going to conduct research at all, then, I urge you to do it up front!

Exhibit 17-1. Three Key Research Functions

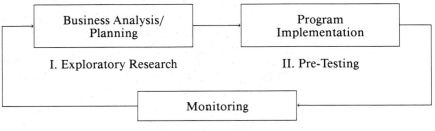

II. *Pre-testing* includes all of those procedures intended to gain insight into the potential performance of a piece of communication *before* major production or media costs are incurred. Basic advertising concepts, print ads, commercials, direct mail pieces, and catalogs are commonly subjected to some form of pre-testing.

The stimulus being tested may be in very rough form—sometimes just a statement typed on a 3 x 5 card—or it can be a finished advertisement. In every case, the stimulus is presented to consumers and their responses are elicited. Responses are then analyzed to form some judgment as to how the stimulus would perform as a finished piece in the marketplace and to identify areas for improvement.

Some of the major pre-testing techniques will be discussed shortly. None of them is perfect. They can all be misused—and often are. Despite this, more and more direct marketers are employing pre-testing productively. Such tests are frequently useful in eliminating low-potential copy ideas—more so than in picking "winners"—and thereby reducing risk. The earlier in the creative process such unpromising approaches are eliminated or opportunities for improvement are spotted, the less time and money are spent on them, the better the end product is and, therefore, the more cost-effective the research investment is.

So try to get consumer feedback from your ideas as soon as possible. Be sure, though, that you are aware of the limitations of the techniques you are using. They can only aid your marketing judgment and help to generate new ideas. They cannot predict front- or back-end response. Used correctly, they can improve that response, however.

III. *Evaluative research* is conducted to determine how effective a marketing element has been after it has been implemented. One may want to evaluate the net effect of all elements of a campaign or of just a single print ad or mailing. The distinction between pre-testing and evaluative post-testing is often in the eye of the beholder. As a rule, though, post-testing refers to that which is conducted after significant production and media commitments have been made and little flexibility remains for changing course except to abort.

Evaluation is generally much easier for direct response advertisers than it is for general advertisers, who may never really know the sales impact of their efforts. Front- and back-end responses, cost per order, and net profit are routinely and accurately tracked for every direct response campaign. While these are certainly the most important considerations, they are not the only ones. Often we need to know who is or is not responding to our program, rather than just how many are responding. Or we may want to determine the reasons why consumers responded or didn't respond. A type of evaluative research, often called responder/nonresponder studies, may be used to address these issues.

Since every direct marketing program also has the potential of performing the general advertising functions of creating product awareness and favorable attitudes, it is frequently important to measure these effects as well. Some mail order firms routinely monitor trends in awareness and attitudes via large-scale tracking studies, usually conducted once or twice a year.

In general, marketing research has less to contribute to direct marketing as an evaluative tool than it does to the exploratory and pretesting phases simply because responses are so directly accountable. Be alert, though, to situations in which a more complete understanding of consumer characteristics and reactions to a current program can provide guidance in mounting the next campaign. Evaluative research—responder/nonresponder or tracking studies—may be appropriate.

A manufacturer of very expensive console television sets, for example, instituted a tracking study a few years ago to measure sales, awareness, and attitudes among consumers over a broad cross-section of the country. Expecting to find customers for his $1,000 plus sets in the highest income brackets, he was surprised to find that they were purchased mainly by blue collar workers of modest means. Subsequent research revealed that this group placed a high value on the expensive console model as a status symbol among friends and as a focal point for family gatherings. Armed with this unique insight, he was able to tailor his direct mail traffic-building and awareness advertising program much more effectively to his real prospect with dramatic sales gains.

These, then, are the three main functions of research as applied to direct marketing:

- to *explore* the marketing environment
- to *pretest* responses to creative elements before they run
- to *evaluate* those elements after they appear in the media

Note that we have not even mentioned specific research techniques up to this point. This is because it is much more important for you, as a direct marketing practitioner, to be sensitive to situations to which research can contribute than it is to get into the mechanics of the research itself. Leave that to the professionals, but know when to call them. Nevertheless, you will be in a better position to weigh the potential contribution of research in a given situation if you have an overview of the techniques available, which we will now cover.

Research Techniques

The most basic distinction that can be made in classifying research techniques is that between *qualitative* and *quantitative* research.

Qualitative techniques usually involve interviewing consumers (called "respondents" by researchers) individually or in small groups in which a relatively unstructured discussion is used to gain insights into a topic area in depth. Qualitative research is extremely useful in the exploratory phase in which one needs to know the general ways that people relate to a category or general subject.

It is not used to generate hard facts or numerical data but, rather, to develop ideas and hypotheses that may be later confirmed by more rigorous quantitative research studies. Direct marketers are usually very familiar with qualitative research in the form of focus groups, also called focus panels. Individual depth interviews are much less frequently employed and are used when the respondents are difficult to assemble in a group or the topic is very sensitive.

Quantitative research can be used to complement or confirm qualitative, but employs very different techniques. It usually involves interviewing much larger numbers of respondents using a highly structured standard questionnaire, so that answers can be aggregated and reported numerically. Most quantitative work takes the form of surveys in which the respondent typically spends from 10 minutes to an hour answering questions.

Other forms of quantitative research, such as diary panels or physiological measures of bodily responses, are used to a very limited extent by direct response advertisers. Surveys can be employed for all three research functions—exploration, pre-testing and evaluation—though the form that they take tends to vary substantially by function.

With the key distinction in mind between qualitative and quantitative research, we will next describe the major techniques that have been successfully applied to the direct marketing process.

Focus Groups

The technique most commonly used by direct marketers is certainly the focus group. In a typical group, about 10 respondents who have been prescreened for eligibility are assembled in a research facility where, guided by a trained moderator, they participate in a free-flowing discussion of about two hours. Screening criteria for selecting respondents usually relates to the product category being examined and includes one or more demographics. For example, one might specify "men, age 18 to 30 who regularly drink the equivalent of six cans of beer per week."

While the discussion is relatively informal, it is not without structure. Prior to the focus group, great care must be put into developing a comprehensive discussion guide to steer the conversation into all key topics in a logical order. This should ideally be done in concert with all involved parties giving their input—client, agency, and moderator—although the moderator usually prefers to write the final guide. One of the major benefits of focus groups is that client and agency personnel also get an opportunity to witness the actual discussion through a one-way mirror to experience real-world consumer reactions first hand.

Sad to say, most direct response advertisers tend to use focus groups at the wrong time for the wrong reasons. The value of focus groups for exploratory research was mentioned previously. More often than not, focus groups are used to pre-test rough or finished copy, an application with several major limitations. This seems to be done for any combination of three reasons:

- Groups are usually cheaper than most other research methods, averaging about $2,500 each at this writing.
- They can be done quickly, often within a week.
- Many direct response advertisers are unfamiliar with any kind of research except focus groups.

It is almost always true that the use of focus groups for exploratory purposes is more productive than for pre-testing. This is particularly true when working in a new category or when the marketing environment of a familiar category has changed substantially. Exploratory groups are used to:

- Generate ideas and hypotheses
- Identify consumer problems and issues
- Determine perceptions of brands
- Get a feel for consumer language used in a category
- Develop a background for followup quantitative research

Exploratory focus groups have been invaluable to Young & Rubicam on numerous occasions. For example, in the beer category, Young & Rubicam researchers found that consumer nomenclature for several major beer types was completely different from that used by the brewing industry:

Trade Language	Consumer Language
Super premiums	Premium beers
Premiums	Regular beers
Price brands	Local or cheap beers

If the trade language had been used in subsequent surveys or advertising, the results could have been very misleading or disappointing.

Focus groups can be legitimately employed to pre-test advertising or other marketing elements. However, one should be particularly aware of their limitations when used for this purpose. The major limitation of all qualitative research is that it is not projectable. That is, you cannot assume that the responses of 20 people in two groups or interviewed individually are at all typical of the population you are trying to investigate. There are simply too few of them, even if you do 10 groups, for they are not selected with the degree of methodological rigor needed to apply valid statistical techniques to their responses.

Also, you have to be careful about giving consumers the opportunity to act as experts. They love to critique advertising and will gleefully give advice down to the smallest detail. The moderator must be alert to this tendency and should constantly steer them back to their reactions as consumers rather than as experts.

A third limitation that applies more to pre-testing than to exploratory groups (though to both to some degree) is bias. If I show my rough layout to a group and the first speaker says, "The whole situation looks phony. I wouldn't buy it!", how would you expect the other nine to react? Chances are few would have the courage to defend it. One useful way to get around this problem is to have the respondents commit their reactions to a piece of paper before the discussion is thrown open. Considering these limitations, it is clear that you won't necessarily get the same reactions in the real world as you did in the focus groups.

Despite all the caveats, though, groups can be useful for pre-testing. They can help to resolve issues like these:

- Do consumers generally understand the messages I am trying to get across about the product?
- Do they "track" the story line?
- Do the product messages and the story "hang together"?
- Do they react negatively to any elements of the ad, commercial, mailing piece, etc?

In some recent focus groups for a therapeutic vitamin product, for example, everybody understood the copy and easily related it to the commercial's format. However, it was found that women reacted very negatively to one phrase that had been used for years in the category—*high potency*. The expression apparently conjured up fears of overdosing with possible side effects and even appeared to have sexual connotations. High potency was dropped in subsequent advertising. It is unlikely that this reaction would have been discovered through any technique except focus groups or some other in-depth probing technique.

Groups, then, can be an extremely useful direct marketing tool, particularly for initial exploratory work. As a pre-testing technique they can also be an excellent means of gaining insights into consumer reactions to advertising, rough or finished. Use them with caution, though. And always remember that focus group "findings" are not projectable; they may allow consumers to play the role of advertising expert and they may be biased by group dynamics. The best advice is to take the time to select a well-trained and sensitive professional moderator and give him or her all the information necessary to understand your product's market environment and let that person help to interpret the reactions of the groups.

Quantitative Survey Research

The quantitative research method most commonly used by direct response advertisers is the survey. Surveys come in many shapes and sizes, but they have several elements in common:

- They gather information from a relatively small sample of a larger universe that they intend to measure. If the sample is drawn in accordance with very precise statistical guidelines, everybody in the universe has an equal probability of being included, and it will represent a true cross-section of the universe.
- Although survey samples may represent a small percentage of the corresponding universe, they nearly always include more respondents than one used in qualitative research. Large government surveys may interview 10,000 people. The majority of surveys conducted for marketing purposes have a sample size between 200 and 1,000. Smaller samples are frequently used for pre-testing and somewhat larger for full-scale segmentation studies.
- Surveys are structured. Respondents are taken through a questionnaire so that the same questions are asked in the same order. If responses were not uniform, they could not be combined to give an aggregate answer representing the whole sample. This is probably the most fundamental difference between qualitative and quantitative research.
- Because surveys ideally draw samples with great care and interview large numbers of people with a uniform questionnaire, their results are said to be projectable. That is, survey results predict the responses of the universe they represent within statistically known margins of error. Results from the 10,000 respondent government survey would be accurate to within plus or minus one percentage point. The smaller the sample, the larger the margin of error. With a sample of 200, the range would be accurate to within about plus or minus 6 points. As a rule, the bigger the risk a decision involves, the bigger the survey sample you would want to draw to investigate the issue.

Surveys may also differ in several important respects. Most obvious is sample size, as just mentioned. The questionnaire itself may be administered a number of ways:

- Questions can be asked personally by the interviewer or they may be self-administered. Generally, simple checklists can be self-administered successfully, but more complicated questionnaires require a trained interviewer.

- Personal interviews can take place in the respondent's home, over the telephone, or in a central research facility, such as those found in many shopping malls.

From the standpoint of sampling precision, statistical accuracy is best where personal interviews are conducted in the home, followed in descending order by telephone interviews or interviews in a central research facility. The trade-off is that the methods of interviewing are also ranked in descending order of cost. Mall research tends to be cheaper because the respondents come to a concentrated point where they can be readily screened and shown test stimuli. Self-administered questionnaires can be filled out in a central facility or, more commonly, are *mailed* to large numbers of people to be mailed back to the sender for tabulation. Mail surveys are often used to reach people who we know are qualified because they are on a list (such as magazine subscribers), very low incidence groups or prerecruited panels.

- Surveys differ substantially by length. A simple questionnaire meant to establish only a couple of basic facts might take a minute or two to administer. The W. R. Simmons Company conducts a syndicated annual survey of media and purchase behavior that takes about five hours to complete (for a substantial cash incentive).
- Geographic areas surveyed usually conform to a product's current or potential trading areas. A survey may cover a cross-section of the entire United States or just a single city.
- Processing and analysis of questionnaire responses can range from a simple tabulation of totals, to cross-tabs of individual segments (e.g., under age 35 vs. over 35) to sophisticated multivariate analysis by computer.

Surveys also differ widely by subject matter and basic methodology. Some of those most widely applied to direct marketing are briefly outlined next.

1. Attitude and Usage (A&U) Surveys. These are also called Usage and Attitude (U&A) Surveys or Studies and occasionally Awareness, Attitude and Usage (AAU) Surveys. They are usually regarded as major pieces of exploratory research that serve to guide many marketing decisions for a brand while they remain timely. The majority of such surveys include between 400 and 1,000 respondents interviewed in person or by telephone on a national basis. Virtually all cover the same basic information:

- Category and brand usage patterns
- Aided and unaided awareness of brands in the category and their advertising
- Importance ratings of product attributes
- Ratings of category brands on the same attributes
- Respondent demographics

Segmentation studies are simply A&U studies that include additional batteries of psychographic or lifestyle questions. Responses are computer-processed through a procedure known as cluster analysis to identify individual groups of consumers—usually three to six—whose attitudes and behavior differ significantly from those of the other groups. A segmentation study for banking services might reveal these segments, for example:

- Convenience oriented—merely looking for nearby, "hassle-free" service
- Quality oriented—impressed with the bank's prestige and decor
- Cost oriented—interested primarily in minimizing fees
- Service oriented—desiring the most complete array of banking services and facilities

By knowing which one or two segments represents your greatest profit potential, you can target your direct marketing program much more effectively than you could without knowing the key "hot buttons." A&U surveys or full-scale segmentation studies can serve as a veritable road map for strategic planning and creative work.

2. Copy Testing. Probably no area of research has been as controversial as copy testing. Well over one hundred systems are listed in the American Marketing Association's directory of services. To my knowledge, none is specifically designed to test the unique elements of direct response advertising (undoubtedly because of the greater predictability of in-market, multi-cell testing).

We have already discussed the usefulness of pre-testing rough copy or even more bare-bones copy concepts. Since we can never be as objective about our work as consumers can, it is important to get their reactions to our creative product as early as possible. We have found simple comprehension studies among small samples of target consumers to be quite valuable for about the cost of one focus group.

A typical study would screen for 50 target respondents in a shopping mall facility who would view the test stimulus one at a time. A personal interview would determine what sales messages were communicated, what elements of the execution were memorable, such things as believability and items liked or disliked. Simple surveys like this can be invaluable in helping creative people refine and upgrade the final execution.

We don't believe that any one copy pre-testing technique is best for evaluating direct response advertising. Some are useful in some situations, others in others. None of them have very good measures of nonverbal emotional response. Sometimes it is even appropriate to measure different aspects of a single advertisement's performance with more than one technique. What no copy test can do, of course, is predict response. This can only be done through sophisticated simulation techniques or limited in-market testing. Copy testing is such a quagmire of conflicting claims and methodologies that it is important to involve an experienced research person as soon as possible when it is being considered.

3. Simulation Modeling. Simulation modeling is a powerful state-of-the-art pre-testing technique. Allstate Insurance Company has been particularly successful in applying the technique to direct marketing. What the technique does essentially is to build a mathematical equation, or "model," that translates the results of survey data into a prediction of in-market response rates. This is no easy task.

Allstate Insurance Company has invested a considerable amount of time and money in the process. They began by assembling the elements of a number of alternative mailings in rough form. Next, target consumers were exposed to just one of the mailings and taken through a survey questionnaire that included a variety of purchase intent and rating scales and other measurements. From these questionnaires response rates and even potential premiums generated can be determined.

A computerized technique, known as regression analysis, was then applied to identify the mathematical relationship between the survey responses and the actual responses to the mailings. From this, a formula was developed to use the key survey responses to predict mail responses with great accuracy.

Allstate Insurance Company submits most of its new products to this survey process. It has several advantages:

- Because the packages can be produced in rough (2/C letter/brochure format), the cost is relatively inexpensive.
- Response rates to a simulator are usually quite high (30 percent as compared to .3-.5 percent on a live test). Therefore Allstate Insurance Company can mail significantly fewer packages (5,000 packages per cell on a simulator vs. 150,000 on a live test) and still get statistically significant results. Again, this saves a considerable amount of money.
- The system is particularly appealing for an insurance advertiser in that it allows for pre-testing of several product variations without having to file each product with the insurance commissioner.

● This process is also a breakthrough for pre-testing a sweepstakes offer. It allows an advertiser to ascertain if incremental sales would be generated by adding a sweepstakes offer, *without* having to actually award the prizes.

4. Responder/Nonresponder Surveys. This refers less to a specific technique than it does to the objective of determining the differences between people who do and don't respond to a direct marketing program. It is basically an evaluative process but, like all others, should be used to improve the next effort.

Suppose that you mailed a catalog with a broad array of products using a rather general compiled list. Front-end response was good, but there was no consistent pattern to indicate who was responding or why. Since you already have lists of both groups, a followup survey either by telephone or by mail would be a routine matter. It could determine the demographic or psychographic characteristics of both groups and why they did or didn't respond. Such information would serve as a guide for offering products in the future for modifying the catalog's tonality and for selecting more specific mailing lists.

5. Tracking Studies. As noted earlier, direct response advertisers are fortunate in being able to evaluate their efforts quickly and accurately simply by counting responses. When marketing objectives also include building awareness and improving attitudes towards a product, service, or fulfillment system, the program can be measured accurately by tracking studies, another evaluative research tool. Tracking studies are usually surveys that gather a limited amount of information from a large number of people, frequently 1,500 or more.

Syndicated national surveys are ideal for this purpose because you share costs with the research firm's other participating clients and can purchase as little as one question in the interview. Some syndicated systems conduct personal in-home or telephone interviews once a month or quarter. Others maintain ongoing mail panels that can be sent self-administered questionnaires as needed. Sometimes you may want to conduct your own survey among your customer list or among a list of clearly defined prospects. In that case a self-administered mail questionnaire would probably be least expensive and sufficiently accurate.

The cardinal rule of tracking studies is that they should be changed as little as possible from wave to wave to maintain the comparability of results. If an annual study were conducted in April the first year, every effort should be made to do it in April again the next year to avoid possible seasonal variations. Results from a mail survey are very probably not comparable to those from a telephone survey, even if they were conducted in successive Aprils using the same questionnaire. Resist the urge to improve tracking studies once the base wave has been launched.

6. Geodemography. A very exciting new concept that has become generally available in just the past two years appears to be tailor-made for direct response advertisers and particularly direct mail—geodemography. Its potential uses in the exploratory, pretesting, and evaluative areas seem to be limited only by the imagination. Three companies now offer very similar geodemographic services: ACORN from C.A.C.I., PRIZM from Claritas, and Cluster-Plus from Donnelley Marketing. They do not conduct primary research in the sense that they are commissioned to interview people. Rather, they analyze an existing data base—the U.S. Census. The systems are based on the principle that "birds of a feather flock together." That is, that people who live together in small geographic areas—block groups, census tracts, ZIP code units, etc.—tend to have more similar demographic characteristics than people who live elsewhere. Although you may think that you have little in common with your next door neighbor, the odds are that you have less in common with somebody drawn at random from the other side of town.

All three services started with the full base of census demographics covering all U.S. households. They used statistical techniques to reduce the thousand-plus measured variables to the hundred or so that provided the most discrimination between households. Their computers next processed the variables in a factor reduction and clustering operation that identified 40 to 44 individual population segments (like those from segmentation surveys). The output of all this statistical wizardry is a system that can specify a household's approximate demographic characteristics given only its address or ZIP code. PRIZM has given their clusters colorful names such as "Blueblood Estates," "Bunker's Neighbors," and, at the low end, "Hardscrabble." If they know your ZIP code, they can label you.

Geodemographics can be used in the exploratory sense to determine the demographics of one's best prospects. For example, using a computer list of an appliance manufacturer developed from warranty cards, names were run through one of the systems and got a detailed demographic profile as output. The analysis revealed a strong previously unknown skew toward a particular market segment. Marketing efforts were then increased against this segment.

The systems are ideal for pre-testing lists. Once your target is profiled, alternate lists need only be run through a geodemographic program to determine which one delivers the highest proportion of target clusters. They can be used for evaluation to track the demographic quality of responders, or do automatic responder/nonresponder studies, using only the addresses of each. Moreover, all three systems are now tied in to other major data bases, such as W. R. Simmons, Mediamark Research Inc. (MRI), and R. L. Polk. With such a link you can extract from a master list those households that are most likely to buy a high-priced foreign car, life insurance, or chewing tobacco.

I predict that geodemography will become a standard tool for direct marketing operations and research in the years immediately ahead.

Summary

The chart in Exhibit 17-2 groups the techniques and classifications that have been discussed.

In summary, from the research highlights presented, here are the key thoughts to keep in mind.

- Seek the help of marketing research professionals at your company, agency, or an independent research firm as soon as research issues arise.
- Concentrate research efforts in the up-front exploratory stages where they can provide the most leverage.
- Involve creative people in the research process as much as possible. It is they who can derive the most benefit from it.
- Don't reinvent the wheel. Many excellent secondary data bases may be accessible through research libraries and other sources that should be scanned before initiating primary research. VALS and W. R. Simmons are just two of such sources that have been mentioned here.
- Consider small-scale pre-tests or rough copy to guide its development. These can be focus groups or limited surveys designed to give creative people as much diagnostic feedback as possible.
- Become familiar with the new geodemographic services.

And, above all, know your prospect. That's what good marketing research is all about.

Exhibit 17-2. Research Techniques and Classifications

	Techniques	
Function	**Qualitative In-Depth**	**Quantitative Surveys**
Exploratory	• focus groups (preferred use)	• attitude and usage surveys • geodemography
Pretesting	• focus groups	• comprehension tests • simulation models • geodemography (for lists)
Evaluative	———	• tracking studies • responder/non-responder surveys • geodemography

Self-Quiz

1. Define the *marketing concept.*

_____

_____

_____

2. Define marketing research.

_____

_____

_____

3. Define psychographics.

_____

_____

_____

4. Complete this list of key types of information that should be considered in developing a direct marketing program.

1.   Awareness   4.   _____

2.   Needs   5.   _____

3.   _____

5. Exploratory research helps to answer such basic questions as:

1.   Who is my best prospect?

2.   _____

3.   _____

6. What is the purpose of pretesting?

_____

_____

_____

7. What is the purpose of evaluative research?

_____

_____

_____

8. What is the difference between qualitative and quantitative research?

_____

_____

_____

9. The use of focus groups is usually more effective for _____

_____ purposes than for

_____

10. The most common quantitative research method used by direct marketers is the _____

11. Complete this list of basic information covered by attitude and usage surveys.

1. Category and brand usage patterns
2. Aided and unaided awareness of brands in the category and their advertising
3. _____
4. _____
5. _____

12. What no copy test can do is predict _____ or

_____ response.

13. The purpose of responder/nonresponder surveys is to

_____

_____

_____

14. Why should tracking study specifications remain consistent between survey waves?

_____

_____

_____

15. What is geodemography?

_____

_____

_____

Pilot Project

Suppose that your company acquired a product line in a category with which you were totally unfamiliar. No information existed as to who used such products or why. Consumer attitudes toward the line and competitive products were unknown. Prepare a research plan that will provide the basic information necessary to market the line. This should include a statement of research objectives for each project item and the specific type of technique best suited to meet them.

Chapter Eighteen

Direct Marketing in the Total Marketing Mix

Pete Hoke, publisher of *Direct Marketing* magazine, often refers to direct marketing as "a subset of marketing," which is to say it is integral to the total marketing mix. There is a tendency by many to regard direct marketing as an isolated method of selling—mail order—but what remains to be understood and applied is the melding of direct marketing with other marketing methods.

Exhibit 18-1 graphically shows the elements involved in a total marketing situation. Company objectives relate directly to marketing objectives. Marketing objectives relate directly to market definition and marketing mix definition. And these definitions have a direct bearing on the four Ps: product, price, place, promotion.

The famous Professor Theodore Levitt, of the Graduate School of Business Administration, Harvard University, is of the school who puts businesses into one of two classes: those who are marketing driven, favoring the consumer, and those who are production driven, favoring the manufacturer. The professor and his legion of followers clearly favor businesses who are marketing driven. And they are right.

Exhibit 18-2 neatly delineates the attitudes of the two camps: marketing and production. As one can see the two camps can be poles apart. That's why marketing must have top management status in the company structure to achieve maximum success. (Exhibit 18-3).

And, finally, marketing must have a strong hand in company procedures (Exhibit 18-4). I can say, without fear of contradiction, that a major deterrent to direct marketing success where other marketing disciplines are primary is the failure to give direct marketing proper status in the marketing mix.

Perhaps the best way to dramatize opportunities for melding direct marketing with other marketing methods is to give live examples of applications.

Airlines

The primary marketing channel for the sale of airline tickets is through travel agencies, accounting for about 65 percent of total airline revenue. Secondary channels are airline ticket offices and airport ticket counters. Prime advertising mediums for driving consumers and business people

**Exhibit 18-1. The Elements of a
Total Marketing Situation**

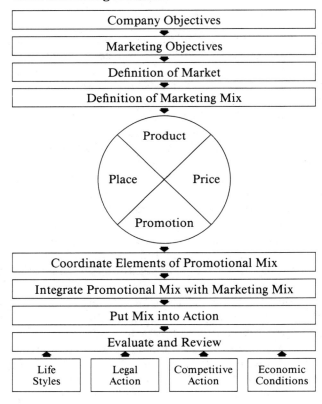

Source: *Readings in Promotion Management,*
    James U. McNeal, editor
    (New York, Appleton-Century-Crofts, 1966)

to these outlets are television, newspapers, and radio, with magazines as a secondary medium.

Newspaper advertising, in particular, is used to promote specific destinations such as ski areas, summer vacation areas, and exotic places like Hawaii. Thousands of inquiries are received annually, requesting information about specific trips. When these names are captured the airline can build a data base by specific interests: skiing, Hawaii, European destinations, etc. Data about advertising source, date of inquiry, can and should be included in the data base.

Exhibit 18-2. Marketing and Production Orientations

Marketing Orientation	Attitudes	Production Orientation
——[C O N S U M E R]——		——[M A N U F A C T U R I N G]——
Consumer forces dominate; emphasis on long-range planning.	Objectives	Internal forces dominate; emphasis on efficiency and technology in the short run.
Decision-making starts with the consideration of the consumer.	Place of the consumer	Decisions are imposed on the consumer.
Company makes what it can sell.	Product mix	Company sells what it can make.
Used to determine customer needs and test how product satisfies these needs.	Role of marketing research	Used to determine consumer reaction, if used at all.
Create new markets as well as serve present markets.	Marketing strategy	Satisfy existing markets.
Focus on market opportunities.	Innovation	Focus on technology.
Sometimes lead, sometimes follow; offensive posture.	Competition	Always follow, react; defensive posture.
An objective.	Profit	A residual, what's left over after all costs are paid.
Focus on marketing problems.	Other corporate functions	Focus on manufacturing and finance problems.

Source: Robert F. Vizera, Thomas F. Chambers and Edward J. Cook.
Adoption of the Marketing Concept—Fact or Fiction
Sales Executive Club of New York, 1967

It is the use of the data base that brings direct marketing into play. For now there can be an annual target mailing to all who raised their hands and said in effect, "We have a special interest in ski vacations." Prime prospects, to be sure. The same may be said of those who have inquired about Hawaii, or European destinations, or other special destinations.

Unique to the airline industry is the marketing fact that about 80 percent of their revenue comes from about 20 percent of their customers commonly known as "frequent flyers." It is to this choice market—frequent flyers—that the airlines give special recognition. And they employ direct marketing methods to single them out.

Direct marketing methods have been used, very successfully, to gain memberships for airline key clubs: United Airlines Red Carpet Club, American Airlines Admirals Club, and TWA Ambassador Club, for example. Club members receive trip news and special offers at frequent intervals. Other direct marketing applications by airlines in-

Exhibit 18-3. Marketing and Production Orientations

Marketing Orientation	Structure	Production Orientation
—[C O N S U M E R]—		—[M A N U F A C T U R I N G]—
Marketing personnel.	**Top management**	Production or finance personnel in top job.
On same level as heads of production, finance and personnel.	**Place of Marketing Executive**	On lower level.
Reports to top Marketing Executive.	**Sales Executive, Advertising Department, Marketing Research**	On same level, or higher, than the top Marketing Executive; sometimes not a separate department.
Reports to top Marketing Executive.	**Product planning**	Reports to engineering, production, top executive; sometimes not a separate function.
In the marketing group; seen as customer service.	**Customer credit**	In the controller's department; seen as necessary evil.
Reports to marketing department.	**Inventory function, transportation**	Reports to production department.

Source: Martin Baier, Adjunct Professor,
    University of Missouri, Kansas City.

clude mailings to travel agencies—their number one sales outlet—encouraging them to recommend their airlines over competition and mailings to their data bases encouraging consumers to go to travel agencies to inquire about passage on their airlines over competition.

But perhaps the best example of melding direct marketing with other marketing methods in the airline industry is direct marketing

Exhibit 18-4. Marketing and Production Orientations

Marketing Orientation	Procedures	Production Orientation
——[C O N S U M E R]——		——[M A N U F A C T U R I N G]——
Begins with determination of customer needs; seeks to identify a market opportunity.	**Product planning**	Begins with consideration of production and technological capacities; looks to utilize excess capacity and waste material.
Customer determines prices; price determines costs.	**Price**	Costs determine price.
A co-ordinated approach including all aspects of the Marketing Mix. Marketing integrated into all functions of the business.	**Marketing campaign**	Individual efforts by each department, often resulting in conflict and wasted effort. No integration of marketing and other functions.
Designed for customer convenience; seen as sales tool.	**Packaging**	Seen as protection and a container for the product.
Communicates need-satisfying benefits of the product; consumer motivations paramount.	**Advertising**	Emphasizes product features, quality and ego of the producer. Producer motives paramount.
Level set with customer requirements in mind.	**Inventory**	Levels set with production requirements in mind.
Seen as customer service.	**Transportation**	Seen as extension of production and storage functions.
Helps the buyer to buy; seeks to match product to customer needs; co-ordinates with advertising, promotion, distribution; determines unfilled customer needs.	**Sales**	Seeks to "sell" to the buyer; often unaware of advertising, promotion research and distribution activities.

involvement in airline bonus miles programs. Early in the 1980s one of the airlines, in an effort to develop consumer loyalty, came up with the concept of offering bonuses for total miles flown on their airline. "Accumulate 10,000 miles and get a free up-grade to a first class seat," for example. Several airlines soon followed suit. United Airlines, for example, established their "Mileage Plus" program. Using the computer for their data base, they were able to frequently tell each participant exactly how many miles they had accumulated and what rewards they were eligible for (Exhibit 18-5).

As programs matured, airlines took their loyalty incentive program a step further: they offered bonus miles for flying on given days and to given destinations. Thus, through the application of direct marketing methods, airlines found a way to improve payload on low traffic days and a way to fight competition in targeted markets.

Automobile Manufacturers

Automobiles have been marketed to the consumer in the same way for decades: from manufacturer to the dealer to the consumer. Manufacturer advertising budgets are huge. The Lincoln Mercury division of Ford Motor Company had a 1981 advertising budget in the neighborhood of $100 million, for example. The huge manufacturer budget does not include dealer association budgets or individual dealer budgets. More millions.

Manufacturer budgets are heavy in television, radio, magazines, and newspapers. Local dealer associations go heavy in TV with some newspaper and radio. Leading local dealers tend to go heavy in local TV and newspapers, while lesser dealers tend to put most of their advertising dollars into newspapers.

It is at the manufacturer and dealer association levels that direct marketing applications are most likely to be initiated. The manufacturer has the most targeted mailing list of all: he has an exact list of all owners of his cars by year, by model. And because present owners are the best prospects for future sales automobile manufacturers make it a practice to invite present owners to see the new models as introduced at their dealers each year.

Second to efforts to maintain customer loyalty are efforts to encourage car owners to switch. Direct marketing efforts in this regard are quite sophisticated.

All automobile manufacturers have available to them lists of owners of competitive makes of cars by model, by year. Applying marketing logic, manufacturers deduce that an owner of a Toyota is not likely to be a prime prospect for a Lincoln or a Cadillac. But a Toyota owner could be a good prospect for a Datsun. A Lincoln owner could be a good prospect for a Cadillac. An Oldsmobile Cutlass owner could be a good

Exhibit 18-5. Sample Award Notification

MILEAGE-PLUS

UNITED AIRLINES

AWARD NOTIFICATION

YOUR CURRENT MILEAGE PLUS BALANCE INDICATES
THAT YOU QUALIFY FOR THE MILEAGE PLUS AWARD
INDICATED BELOW.

MILEAGE PLUS ACCOUNT NO. 8771453

ACCOUNT STATUS

FLIGHTS POSTED AS OF 10/28/82

ROBERT STONE
606 LAUREL AVE
WILMETTE, IL 60091

BONUS MILES	8129
MILES FLOWN +	13187
AWARD MILES DEDUCTED −	0
CURRENT MILEAGE PLUS BALANCE	21316

The Mileage Plus Account status shown above reflects the Mileage Plus information received and recorded as of the date indicated. Normally, flights are posted to your account approximately 10 to 14 days after the actual flight date.

MILEAGE-PLUS

UNITED AIRLINES

ACCOUNT ACTIVITY

THE FOLLOWING REPRESENTS THE MOST RECENT TRANSACTIONS APPLIED TO YOUR MILEAGE PLUS ACCOUNT.

DATE	DESCRIPTION OF TRANSACTION	ITINERARY	MILES ADDED	MILES DEDUCTED
08/22/82	FLT 908	ORD JFK	722	
08/22/82	FLT 908 FIRST CLASS BONUS	ORD JFK	180	
09/22/82	FLT 556	MCI ORD	407	
09/28/82	FLT 908	ORD JFK	722	
09/28/82	FLT 908 FIRST CLASS BONUS	ORD JFK	180	
09/30/82	FLT 897	ORD MCI	407	
09/30/82	FLT 897 FIRST CLASS BONUS	ORD MCI	101	
09/30/82	FLT 209	YYZ ORD	436	
09/30/82	FLT 209 FIRST CLASS BONUS	YYZ ORD	109	
10/13/82	FLT 245	DCA ORD	595	
10/17/82	FLT 908	ORD JFK	722	
10/17/82	FLT 908 FIRST CLASS BONUS	ORD JFK	722	

MILEAGE-PLUS

UNITED AIRLINES

AWARD 20,000 MI. 25% OFF ON UA ROUND TRIP, AVIS AND WESTIN WEEKEND

***IF** you wish to receive certificates for this award, please complete the information requested, and return Copy 1 to us in the envelope provided. Retain Copy 2 for your records. Please allow two weeks for processing and mailing.*

***IF** you elect not to accept the award at this time, you don't need to return this form. As you continue to fly United, your Mileage Plus account will build toward the next mileage level.*

☐ **YES,** *please send my award certificates and deduct* **20,000** *miles* (B) *from my Mileage Plus account after I've reached that amount.*

***I**ssue Mileage Plus Award Certificates in the name(s) of:*

PLEASE PRINT FIRST NAME, OR INITIAL, MIDDLE INITIAL AND LAST NAME. ONE LETTER OR SPACE PER BOX.

XXXXXXXXXXXXXXXXXXXXXXXXXXXXXX

***C**ertificates can be issued in your name or any other name you specify, but once issued, are non-transferable. Certificates are not refundable and may not be retroactively applied to any trip already taken. Certificates will be mailed to you at the address above. See reverse side for Terms and Conditions.*

MILEAGE PLUS PARTICIPANT SIGNATURE	PHONE NUMBER	DATE
	( )	

COPY 1 *IMPORTANT: BEFORE SIGNING READ REVERSE SIDE.*

Award notification serves as incentive for flyer to remain loyal to United Airlines.

prospect for a Mercury Cougar. These matchups offer the best opportunities for encouraging switching.

Thus mailing efforts through dealer associations—names of neighborhood dealers are often featured—targeted to best prospects for switching can produce dealer traffic. Rebate certificates and free gifts for test drives are often key factors in inducing car owners to switch.

The dealer's best defense against losing customers to competition is to keep his present customers coming back to his dealership for maintenance services. And, here again, direct marketing methods are best suited to achieving the objective. Many dealers use a planned program to remind owners of various checkup periods in relation to the age of their cars. And they offer incentives to have the checkups and maintenance services done at their dealership.

Insurance Companies

Not counting merchandise sales of huge mail order companies such as Sears, Wards, J.C. Penney, and Spiegels, insurance companies lead the pack in sales via direct marketing methods. Annual sales of insurance via direct marketing methods is estimated to be in excess of four billion dollars. Leading "mail order" insurance companies include Colonial Penn, National Liberty, Physicians Mutual, and Old American Insurance Company. For these firms direct marketing is their prime marketing method. But most of them have a secondary marketing channel—an agent organization who engages in person-to-person selling.

There is a natural synergism between direct marketing and agent marketing. The millions of dollars spent by mail order insurance companies on TV, on radio, in newspapers and magazines, and in direct mail serves as "advertising" for the agent organization, thus building an "image" for agent prospects.

But astute insurance direct marketers carry the synergism a lot further than the impact of advertising. Some use their mail order policyholder list as a "prospect list" for their agent organization. For example, an agent who has a policyholder card, indicating the policyholder now has an A&H (accident and health) policy with the company, might attempt to sell a life insurance policy or an add-on to the existing A&H policy. Experience shows that the agent's closure rate is far greater when he works existing policyholders as contrasted to "cold" prospects.

Another important application of direct marketing in the insurance field is "cross-selling"—selling other policies to existing policyholders direct by mail. Some insurance companies pay a commission to agents even though they're not involved in such sales; others don't.

Most insurance companies today, whether they sell insurance direct to the consumer, or not, use direct marketing methods for "upgrading" or "downgrading" existing policyholders. Allstate Insurance Company, for example, uses direct mail to upgrade bodily injury coverage for automobile policyholders. And I have seen mailings where they use direct mail suggesting downgrading of deductibles.

But of all the applications of direct marketing methods as part of the total marketing mix of insurance companies, none is more dramatic than "third-party selling." The success of third-party selling is dependent upon the recommendation of an affinity group, such as a union, a fraternal organization, an oil company credit card group, an alumni association, or a senior citizen organization. Allegiance to the organization, and therefore respect for their recommendation, plus common interests, account for the better-than-average response to third-party selling efforts (Exhibits 18-6 and 18-7).

The most dramatic application of third-party selling has been done against the AARP (American Association of Retired People) membership list. The insurance needs of older people are unique and common to the membership list. Thus third-party insurance offers, catering to the needs of AARP's millions of members, are highly productive.

Oil Companies

Oil companies saw the advantages of adding direct marketing to their marketing mix early on—the catalyst for profiting from direct marketing methods has been, and continues to be, the oil company credit card.

The credit card grew out of a desire to have a device that would build gasoline station loyalty for a particular brand of gasoline. The credit card filled that need. So most of the oil companies—Shell, Exxon, Texaco, Amoco, Gulf and many of the smaller ones—issued their own gasoline credit cards—free. This spur to gas station marketing had its rewards, but cementing customer loyalty became muted, to a major degree, by the fact that any credit-worthy person could hold cards from all the major oil companies. Maintenance of the credit program became a financial burden for many of the oil companies.

Then in the late 1950s, direct marketing provided a way to bring added income to oil company credit card operations, thus absorbing major portions of credit file costs. Someone correctly deduced that oil company credit card holders would be ideal prospects for selected merchandise offers, particularly if payment could be made on the installment plan through the oil company credit card.

The chief exponents of this revolutionary marketing method were syndicators, many of whom underwrote test mailing costs for the oil companies. One of the pioneers in syndication was Al Sloan of Chicago, who underwrote the first syndicated mailing package test program for the $149.95 Bell & Howell movie camera outfit. Thousands and thousands of movie outfits were sold to oil company credit card holders.

But this was just the beginning of merchandise offers to oil company credit card holders. There were scores of successful offers. Wrist watches—for men and women. Flatware. China. Cameras—Polaroid

Exhibit 18-6. Third-Party Letter

"Third party" letter from Shell Oil Company, recommending hospital income plan underwritten by National Home Life Assurance Company

SHELL OIL COMPANY
SHELL CREDIT CARD CENTER
TULSA, OKLAHOMA 74102

Dear Customer:

Have you ever wondered, "Could I ever cover medical bills and day-to-day expenses for my family if I was hospitalized for any length of time?"

Now there's a Plan available for Shell Credit Card Customers that pays you regardless of what you collect from Medicare, Workers' Compensation or any other company's plans. This Group Hospital Income Plan was designed to help you pay your hospital and medical bills when you're hospitalized.

These benefits may help you to budget your other income for those every day living expenses that don't stop just because you're in the hospital.

In inflationary times like these, many good plans don't pay all the medical bills. That's why it's particularly important to consider a Group Hospital Income Plan like this.

We selected one of the leaders in the direct-to-consumer health and hospital insurance products, National Home Life Assurance Company, to underwrite and offer this Plan especially for our Credit Card Customers.

I urge you to read the enclosed letter for all the details on the many benefits of this low group rate Plan. You will then see why I recommend you consider this valuable opportunity to help protect yourself and your loved ones.

Sincerely,

E.E. Cassady

EEC:il
LY4521R

Manager, Customer Services
Shell Credit Card Center

P.S. Good News--As a Shell Credit Card Customer--you are automatically eligible for low group rates. And, you can charge it to your Shell Credit Card Account.

Exhibit 18-7. Application Form Included in Third-Party Mailing

GUARANTEED ACCEPTANCE FORM FOR THE
Group Hospital Income Plan

Medical
Emergency
Card

◀ **Your Medical Emergency Card**

**FOR SHELL
CREDIT CARD
CUSTOMERS**

LARRY STONE
CX4 004 391

LARRY STONE
606 LAUREL
WILMETTE, IL 60091

is eligible to enroll in this low-cost Group Hospital Income
Insurance Plan for only $1 for your first month—and then
continue for as little as $3.92 a month depending on the
plan you choose.

PLEASE REPLY BY AUG 13, 1982

It's So Easy To Enroll!

1. Check the Hospital Income Plan that is best for you. Then...

2. Complete and sign the form below.

3. Send no money. Mail your completed form in the postage paid envelope.

☐ 00 Plan A
$60.00 a day

☐ 01 Plan B
$30.00 a day

Plans A and B pay from the very first day for covered accident and illness.

If you would prefer to have coverage from the very first day for covered accidents and after the fifth day for illnesses, please check one of the plans at right. ☐ 02 **Plan C, $60.00 a day** ☐ 03 **Plan D, $30.00 a day**

Please see brochure for benefits, rates, limitations and renewability for all plans.

RXRBNXRMD	GROUP ENROLLMENT APPLICATION TO NATIONAL HOME LIFE ASSURANCE COMPANY	34304139

(Please Print)
Name
Address **LARRY STONE**
City **606 LAUREL**
WILMETTE
Your Date of Birth _____
Month   Day   Year

Telephone (   ) _____
State **IL**   Zip **60091**
Age _____ Male ☐ Female ☐

☐ I want coverage for children   ☐ I want coverage for maternity benefits   ☐ I want coverage for children and maternity benefits

List all dependents to be covered under this Plan: (DO NOT include name that appears above.)

Name Please print name and indicate relationship (for example husband, wife, son etc.)	Relationship	Sex M/F	Date of Birth			Age
			Month	Day	Year	
1.						
2.						
3.						
FOR ADDITIONAL DEPENDENTS: Please use separate sheet if necessary.						

Please enroll me in the Group Hospital Plan for Shell Credit Card Customers and charge my Shell account. I understand that the initial billing will be for the first two (2) months coverage.
   I understand that no insurance will be in effect until I am issued my certificate by the underwriter (National Home Life Assurance Company; Administrative Offices: Valley Forge, Pa. 19493). I also understand that injury or sickness for which I or any person listed have been medically advised or treated or where distinct symptoms were evident during the 12 month period immediately prior to the effective Date of my coverage will not be covered during the first year. Any such pre-existing conditions will, however, be covered for daily hospitalization benefits after the first year, provided that hospitalization begins more than one year from the Effective Date of coverage.

Signature x _____   Date _____

NHGA-780   **GROUP ENROLLMENT FORM**   NHGC-780-1080 60/30 EP0/5

Underwritten by National Home Life Assurance Company

LOW GROUP RATES

GUARANTEED ACCEPTANCE

SIGN & MAIL THIS FORM TODAY. SEND NO MONEY. CHARGE IT!

and others. Lounge chairs. Lawn mowers. You name it. Oil companies collected a handsome profit on each sale, plus interest on installment sales.

Syndication isn't the force today it once was because as selling costs have increased over the years there has been a profit squeeze, rarely leaving enough room for two profits: the syndicator and the oil company. However, oil companies have not gone out of the merchandise business. Their major channel for merchandise sales today is the remittance envelope enclosed with monthly statements (Exhibit 18-8). The selling cost is so nominal that when a "hot" item is offered profits are almost certain.

Double-digit inflation and the high cost of money added to the cost burden of maintaining oil company credit card operations. As a matter

Exhibit 18-8. Merchandising through Credit Card Billings

This offer was included with monthly remittance statements to Amoco credit card holders.

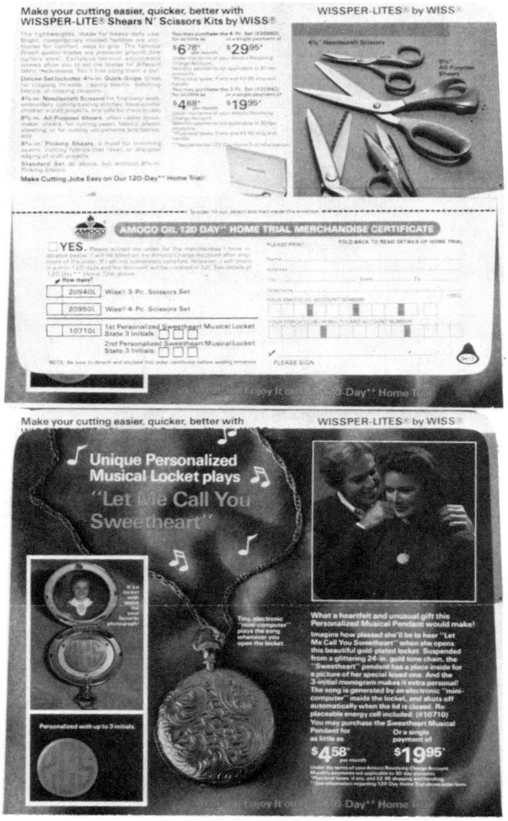

of fact one of the majors—Atlantic Richfield (Arco)—dropped its credit card operation entirely, offering a cash discount in lieu of charge privileges. But most other oil companies decided not to give up their credit card franchises, although many aped Arco's offer of a discount for cash purchases. One alternative to be considered was converting the free oil company credit card to a fee card. The only problem there was that, at best, oil companies would probably end up with no more than half of the credit card file they had had. Another alternative would be to drop the free cards in lieu of bank card privileges: VISA or MasterCard, or both. The negative to this move was loss of identity of the oil company as against competing oil companies.

Faced with these dilemmas American Oil Company (Amoco) came up with a brilliant marketing alternative: a new fee card, called "Multicard," with advantages over their regular free oil company card. Thus, using direct marketing methods, they were able to move hundreds of thousands of free card holders to the status of fee card holders.

Retailers

While most retailers have been slow to make direct marketing a part of their marketing mix, others have achieved remarkable success. The opportunity for department stores to increase store traffic and expand markets via the catalog medium was covered thoroughly in Chapter 12. But there are other opportunities. Many, in fact.

Surprisingly, many retailers who say they don't use direct marketing methods are doing so without realizing it. For example, every time a local department store runs a newspaper ad stating, "Telephone Orders Accepted," a direct marketing technique is being applied. Traditionally retailers "talk" to their publics—prospects and customers—through newspaper advertising. Retailers, as a category, do not talk to their identifiable customers—the backbone of their businesses—as effectively as they might.

The smallest of retail businesses—a neighborhood apparel store, for example—can profit by applying direct marketing methods. Direct mail and telephone are the two ideal mediums for giving special recognition to customers.

It's hard to beat the appeal of an advance announcement of a forthcoming sale, as an example. Many merchants run sales for customers only, closing the store for a given period to all who do not have a customer admittance card. This technique can be dynamite. And the telephone is a natural for personal contact with regular customers. There's the story of the leading salesman of an upscale clothing store in Kansas City, Missouri. He maintains a card file of all his customers. Knows their size, color preferences, whether they prefer vests or not, whether they prefer cuffs or not. Everything. So when the new spring line, or summer, or winter line comes in, this salesman goes through the stock and picks out suits for his customers. Then he gets on the phone. This marketing concept is easily expandable to chains like Brooks Brothers and Capper & Capper.

Retailers have three big advantages that cannot be matched by those who do not have retail stores.

1. *The advantage of local identity.* This is a big plus in the local trading area. The reluctance to order by mail from an unknown firm in a distant city is overcome when a mailing comes from a local retailer.

2. *The advantage of additional traffic.* A firm that sells solely through mail order either gets an order direct by mail or phone, or it's dead. The retailer, on the other hand, can have his cake and eat it too. Orders are generated direct by mail or by phone. And he can expect additional store traffic as well.

3. *Buying power.* Giant retailers and buying groups have buying power going for them. They have the sources of supply and the possibility of volume discounts.

There are three disadvantages which retailers must overcome.

1. *Lists.* Most retail customer lists consist of charge customers, those who have charged purchases at the retail store. They are *not*, for the most part, mail order buyers. Few retail charge lists are arranged by recency, frequency, or amount of purchase. Most retail direct mail promotions are across-the-board: metro and suburban areas alike. And you just don't sell many power mowers to apartment dwellers! The merchandise retailers stock in suburban stores is different from that in downtown stores to cater to different preferences. But retailers seem to ignore this necessity when it comes to direct mail.

2. *Installment credit.* Without installment credit, the sale of big ticket merchandise by mail is a virtual impossibility. There is a real hang-up for retailers who want to retain their identity with their own charge card—offering 30-day terms—to the exclusion of other charge cards which allow for installment payments. The answer lies in choosing one of two alternatives: instituting a revolving credit plan for the existing store credit card, or working through one of the bank credit card systems.

3. *Merchandise selection.* Selecting merchandise for mail order sales and selecting merchandise for sale over the counter can be as different as day and night. Few mail order practitioners could sit in the chair of the retail store buyer and vice versa! The types of merchandise to be selected, the manner of promotion, the economics involved, differ greatly.

Since the retailer enjoys the great advantages of store traffic resulting from his direct marketing effort, there are many objectives that can be explored.

1. *Activating existing charge customers.* The area with the most sales potential in any business is existing customers. And the charge card list is the prime list. There's no more effective way to activate a charge list than to give special recognition to charge customers and to show this recognition with special offers.

2. *Getting new customers.* Close behind the objective of activating existing customers is the goal of getting new customers. And here's where direct marketing methods can prove a bonanza. Pinpoint marketing makes it possible to seek new customers in most trading areas with the most potential around existing stores. Merchandise offers can be tied to efforts to acquire new customers, with the objective of making such efforts break even or do better.

3. *Increasing store traffic.* Store traffic is still the name of the game. Direct marketing efforts will automatically create store traffic spillover. But beyond this, the retailer can direct mail a special offer not generally advertised, designed to increase store traffic. A well-organized store traffic program can pay off big.

4. *Leveling out sales volume.* The retail sales cycle has been a fact of life ever since the early days of Wanamaker, the Penneys, and the Fields. It still is today. Direct marketing efforts can be a big factor in filling in the valleys of the cycle.

5. *Pretesting merchandise and price.* Direct marketing methods offer perhaps the most accurate means of pretesting the appeal of merchandise and the most appealing price level. I have yet to see retailers use direct marketing for this purpose, but it could prove to be imaginative and profitable.

6. *Selling a wider range of merchandise.* This can be the most desirable and most profitable objective of all. Mail order thrives on the sale of merchandise and merchandise combinations not generally available in the retail store. But who is to say that a retailer should not sell merchandise *not generally available in his retail store?* It's being done right now—successfully. Cameras, radios, dinnerware, tool sets,delicacies, paint guns, magazine subscriptions, insurance—an endless variety of merchandise and services, and all extra business.

So the time is ripe for retailers to get on the direct marketing bandwagon. The elements are all here ·for those who will grasp the opportunities and run with them.

The applications of direct marketing methods by airlines, automobile manufacturers, insurance companies, oil companies, and retailers are widely adaptable to other industries as part of their marketing mix. Here are additional direct marketing applications that can be melded into the marketing mix.

Introducing New Products

It is a fact of marketing that most manufacturers limit new product development to the restraints of their present channels of distribution. A manufacturer who markets major equipment through a small sales force does not attempt to develop low cost equipment that appeals to thousands of prospects. Nor rarely does a package goods manufacturer, whose major channel of distribution is the grocery trade, show interest in developing new products for another channel of distribution, such as department stores.

And yet the same research department that has the ability to develop a major breakthrough for a new computer might well have the ability to develop a new pocket calculator that would appeal to the masses. If the manufacturer decides against such development because the product doesn't fit his present distribution channel—a small sales force dedicated to the sale of major equipment—a big profit opportunity may be passed by.

Following is a classic case history where direct marketing made it possible for a major equipment manufacturer—Hewlett-Packard—to introduce an exciting new product that did not fit their selling mode. The year was 1970. Hewlett-Packard had just invented the first scientific pocket calculator. The basic markets were determined to be scientists and engineers. And an appropriate selling price was determined to be $395. There was no way that the small sales force of H-P, accustomed to making sales in the thousands of dollars, could cover a market of thousands of scientists and engineers. What to do?

Direct marketing proved to be the answer to the problem. The target market was scientists and engineers. There was a wide array of publications and mailing lists available to reach these target markets. So a space and direct mail campaign was developed. (See Exhibits 18-9 and 18-10). The results were sensational. About 10 percent of inquiries were converted to sales: the direct mail package pulled an incredible $40,000 in sales for every 1,000 inquiries.

Hewlett-Packard soon found other markets. And they rapidly developed other specialized pocket calculators. Direct marketing was a major factor in opening the college book store market, for example, and it proved highly successful.

But the marketing story doesn't end there. As H-P developed a complete line of specialized calculators, the development of a catalog covering the complete line became a logical extension of the solo mailing program. And this worked too. So successful was the Hewlett-

Exhibit 18-9. Space Ad Designed to Get Inquiries for the HP-35 Pocket Calculator.

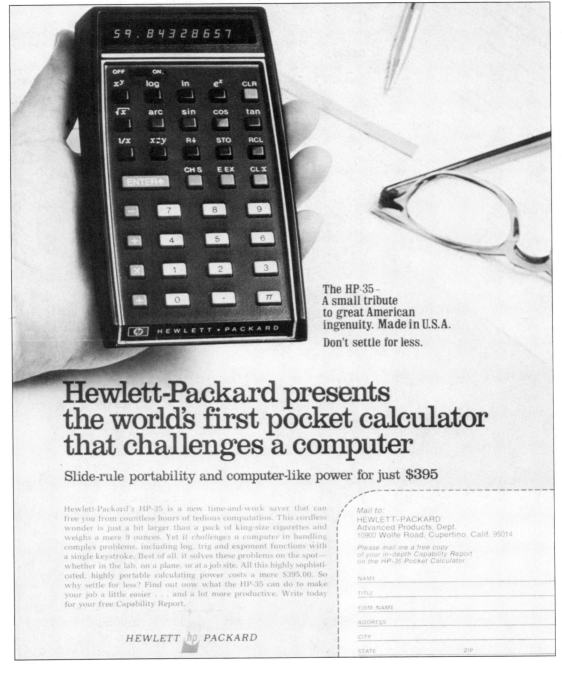

The HP-35 –
A small tribute
to great American
ingenuity. Made in U.S.A.

Don't settle for less.

Hewlett-Packard presents the world's first pocket calculator that challenges a computer

Slide-rule portability and computer-like power for just $395

Hewlett-Packard's HP-35 is a new time-and-work saver that can free you from countless hours of tedious computation. This cordless wonder is just a bit larger than a pack of king-size cigarettes and weighs a mere 9 ounces. Yet it *challenges a computer* in handling complex problems, including log, trig and exponent functions with a single keystroke. Best of all, it solves these problems on the spot—whether in the lab, on a plane, or at a job site. All this highly sophisticated, highly portable calculating power costs a mere $395.00. So why settle for less? Find out now what the HP-35 can do to make your job a little easier . . . and a lot more productive. Write today for your free Capability Report.

HEWLETT *hp* PACKARD

Mail to:
HEWLETT-PACKARD
Advanced Products, Dept.
10900 Wolfe Road, Cupertino, Calif. 95014

*Please mail me a free copy
of your in-depth Capability Report
on the HP-35 Pocket Calculator.*

NAME

TITLE

FIRM NAME

ADDRESS

CITY

STATE   ZIP

Exhibit 18-10. HP Mailing to Engineers.

Hewlett-Packard's mailing for its pocket calculator was carefully designed to appeal to engineers. Package pulled an incredible $40,000 in sales for every 1,000 inquiries.

Packard direct marketing program that they went from sales of approximately $20 million the first year to about $60 million the second year to almost $100 million the third year. A true success story.

The success of H-P, however, brought on serious competition—foreign competition and domestic competition from such prestigious firms as Texas Instruments. And with competition, lower prices. Much lower. The much lower prices greatly reduced the viability of direct marketing as the major channel of distribution.

This would be a sad ending to a great marketing story if it weren't for the fact that direct marketing popularized pocket calculators to the point where distribution through retail stores—electronic stores and department stores, in particular—became viable and successful. So H-P followed the marketing evolution.

This case history dramatizes three important points. (1) A firm need not limit product development to products which fit their present distribution mode. (2) Direct marketing can be the most effective method for introducing a new product. (3) Direct marketing can popularize a new product and lead to other channels of distribution.

After-Markets

The office equipment and computer equipment fields are classic examples of melding direct marketing into their total marketing mix. Direct marketing solves a basic marketing problem: how to capture the substantial after-market for supplies on a cost-efficient basis following the sale of the basic equipment?

Examples

The A. B. Dick Company, a pioneer in the office duplicating equipment field, found they had in excess of 200,000 users of their equipment, too small to warrant pursuing for supply sales—ink and paper primarily—by their sales force. Market research disclosed the after-market for supplies was being serviced mainly by office supply dealers who were selling supplies from competitive manufacturers.

Direct marketing helped to solve this marketing problem for A. B. Dick. A combination telephone and direct mail program was launched to small businesses, churches, and fraternal organizations who had A. B. Dick equipment. Some A. B. Dick regions got supplies orders from as much as 14 percent of those they phoned. And an unexpected bonus was the sale of thousands of dollars of new equipment to replace outmoded equipment.

The 3M Company is a major manufacturer and seller of overhead equipment for showing transparencies. Their prime markets are businesses and schools. Their modes of distribution are through dealer and company salespeople. Selling the equipment is just the first step. There is a great after-market for supplies. Supplies include not only blank transparencies for conversion to printed transparencies by the equipment owner, but complete pre-printed programs as well.

As an example, 3M has complete packaged programs for schools on subjects such as math for various grade levels, languages, safety, hygiene, and scores more. Sales in the aggregate are substantial, but there is a problem: dollar sales are small compared to dollar sales for original equipment. So salespeople tend to concentrate their efforts on the sale of original equipment.

A big answer to the marketing problem for 3M was to prepare a supplies catalog to go direct to owners of their equipment. And a plus was that the catalog produced "over-the-transom" orders for their dealers.

IBM, the huge manufacturer of computers and typewriters, today has a company-wide commitment to direct marketing as a part of their total marketing mix. Getting qualified leads for salespeople is just one of several direct marketing applications. The cost of person-to-person selling being what it is, IBM too has found they can no longer afford to have their salespeople sell after-market supplies except to the largest of customers. So today IBM has their own office and computer supply catalog. And they even sell typewriters direct to small businesses. What's more, IBM uses direct marketing methods to drive prospects into computer shows that they conduct in the U.S. and Canada.

Direct Marketing In the Advertising Mix

So, as we have seen, there are scores of ways to meld direct marketing with other marketing methods. But what about melding direct marketing advertising with general advertising? Here the opportunities for improvement are considerable.

More often than not, I've seen direct response advertising for given firms that has little resemblance to their general advertising. Different typography. Different look. Inappropriate handling of logos. No tie-in with central campaign themes. Lost opportunities, for sure.

Major general advertisers spend millions of dollars establishing their franchises, building their images. To pass up the opportunity to ride established images is to dilute the effectiveness of direct response advertising. To fail to tie in to campaign themes—"The Friendly Skies of United"—"You're In Good Hands with Allstate"—"The Knowledge Business"—is to lose identity.

The applications of direct marketing as a single marketing method or as a part of the total marketing mix are almost endless. With strategic planning and professional execution, the opportunities are almost endless. Best of success to you in all your direct marketing efforts!

Self-Quiz:

1. What are the four Ps of marketing?

a. _____

b. _____

c. _____

d. _____

2. Basically, managements dictate that their companies be:

a. _____ driven, or

b. _____ driven.

c. _____ driven is preferable.

3. Name a prime source for building a data base for airlines.

_____

4. What is an automobile dealer's best defense against losing customers to competition?

_____

_____

_____

5. Define "third-party selling" in the insurance field.

_____

_____

_____

6. What is the major advantage of an oil company credit card from the standpoint of the oil company?

_____

_____

_____

7. Using direct marketing as a part of the total marketing mix offers three big advantages to retailers over nonstore marketers. Name them.

a. _____

b. _____

c. _____

8. Why is direct marketing a logical marketing method for capturing major equipment after-markets?

_____

_____

_____

9. Why should direct response advertising ride on the coattails of general advertising used by traditional marketers?

_____

_____

_____

Pilot Project

Assume you are the Assistant Marketing Director of the Lincoln-Mercury Division of Ford Motor Company. You have been given a key task that lends itself to direct marketing applications: to switch owners of competitive cars to the Mercury Cougar.

Prepare a marketing plan that will identify:

1. Owners you consider to be your best prospects to switch, by competitive make of car.

2. Your marketing strategy for getting these prospects into Mercury dealer showrooms. (Incentives, offers, etc.).

3. Prepare a sales letter to accomplish your objective.

Glossary

Access Time: The time it takes a computer to locate a piece of information in memory or storage and to take action, i.e., the "read" time. Also, the time it takes a computer to store a piece of information and to complete action, i.e., the "write" time.

Action Devices: Items and techniques used in a mailing to initiate the response desired.

Active Buyer: A buyer whose latest purchase was made within the last twelve months. *(See Buyer).*

Active Customer: A term used interchangeably with "active buyer."

Active Member: Any member who is fulfilling the original commitment or who has fulfilled that commitment and has made one or more purchases in the last twelve months.

Active Subscriber: One who has committed for regular delivery of magazines, books or other goods for a period of time still in effect.

Actives: Customers on a list who have made purchases within a prescribed time period, usually not more than one year; subscribers whose subscriptions have not expired.

Additions: New names, either of individuals or companies, added to a mailing list.

Add-On Service: Service of Direct Marketing Assn. which gives consumers an opportunity to request that their names be added to mailing lists.

Address Coding Guide (CG): Contains the actual or potential beginning and ending house numbers, block group and/or enumeration district numbers, ZIP Codes, and other geographic codes for all city delivery service streets served by 3,154 post offices located within 6,601 ZIP Codes.

Address Correction Requested: An endorsement which, when printed in the upper left-hand corner of the address portion of the mailing piece (below the return address), authorizes the U.S. Postal Serivce, for a fee, to provide the known new address on the mailing piece.

A.I.D.A.: The most popular formula for the preparation of direct mail copy. The letters stand for Get Attention, Arouse Interest, Stimulate Desire, Ask for Action.

Alphanumeric: A contraction of "alphabetic" and "numeric." Applies to any coding system that provides for letters, numbers (digits), and special symbols such as punctuation marks. Synonymous with Alphameric.

Assigned Mailing Dates: The dates on which the list user has the obligation to mail a specific list. No other date is acceptable without specific approval of the list owner.

Audience: The total number of individuals reached by a promotion or advertisement.

Source: Direct Marketing Association.

479

Audit: Printed report of the counts involved in a particular list or file.

Back End: The activities necessary to complete a mail order transaction once an order has been received and/or the measurement of a buyer's performance after he has ordered the first item in a series offering.

Bangtail: Promotional envelope with a second flap which is perforated and designed for use as an order blank.

Batch Processing: Technique of executing a set of computer programs/selections in batches as opposed to executing each order/selection as it is received. Batches can be created by computer programming or a manual collection of data into groups.

Batched Job: A job that is grouped with other jobs as input to a computing system, as opposed to a transaction job entry where the job is done singly to completion.

Bill Enclosure: Any promotional piece or notice enclosed with a bill, an invoice or a statement not directed toward the collection of all or part of the bill, invoice or statement.

Binary: Involves a selection, choice or condition in which there are two possibilities such as the use of the symbols "0" and "1" in a numbering system.

Bingo Card: A reply card inserted in a publication and used by readers to request literature and samples from companies whose products and services are either advertised or mentioned in editorial columns.

Bit: A single character or elements in a binary number (digit). The smallest element of binary machine language represented by a magnetized spot on a recording surface or a magnetized element of a storage device.

Bounce Back: An offer enclosed with mailings sent to a customer in fulfillment of an order.

BPI (Bytes Per Inch): Characters, represented in bytes, per inch.

Broadcast Media: A direct response source that includes radio, television and cable TV.

Broadside: A single sheet of paper, printed on one side or two, folded for mailing or direct distribution, and opening into a single, large advertisement.

Brochure: Strictly, a high-quality pamphlet, with especially planned layout, typography and illustrations. Term is also used loosely for any promotional pamphlet or booklet.

Bucktag: A separate slip attached to a printed piece containing instructions to route the material to specific individuals.

Bulk Mail: A category of Third Class Mail involving a large quantity of identical pieces but addressed to different names which are specially processed for mailing before delivery to the post office.

Business List: Any compilation or list of individuals or companies based upon a business-associated interest, inquiry, membership, subscription or purchase.

Buyer: One who orders merchandise, books, records, information or services. Unless another modifying word or two is used, it is assumed that a buyer has paid for all merchandise to date.

Burst: To separate continuous form paper into discrete sheets.

Byte: Sequence of adjacent binary digits operated upon as a unit and usually shorter than a computer word. A character is usually considered a byte. (A single byte can contain either two numeric characters or one alphabetic or special character.)

Cash Buyer: A buyer who encloses payment with order.

Cash Rider: Also called "cash up" or "cash option" wherein an order form offers installment terms, but a postscript offers the option of sending full cash payment with order, usually at some saving over the credit price as an incentive.

C/A: Change of address.

Catalog: A book or booklet showing merchandise, with descriptive details and prices.

Catalog Buyer: A person who has bought products or services from a catalog.

Catalog Request (Paid or Unpaid): One who sends for a catalog (prospective buyer). The catalog may be free; there may be a nominal charge for postage and handling, or there may be a more substantial charge that is often refunded or credited on the first order.

Census Tract: Small geographical area established by local committees, and approved by the Census Bureau, which contains a population segment with relatively uniform economic and social characteristics with clearly identifiable boundaries averaging approximately 1,200 households.

Cheshire Label: Specially prepared paper (rolls, fanfold or accordion fold) used to reproduce names and addresses to be mechanically affixed, one at a time, to a mailing piece.

Circulars: General term for printed advertising in any form, including printed matter sent out by direct mail.

Cleaning: The process of correcting and/or removing a name and address from a mailing list because it is no longer correct or because the listing is to be shifted from one category to another.

Cluster Selection: A selection routine based upon taking a group of names in series, skipping a group, taking another group, etc. E.g.—a cluster selection on an nth name basis might be the first 10 out of every 100 or the first 125 out of 175, etc.; a cluster selection using limited ZIP Codes might be the first 200 names in each of the specified ZIP Codes, etc.

Coding: (1) Identifying devices used on reply devices to identify the mailing list or other source from which the address was obtained. (2) A structure of letters and numbers used to classify characteristics of an address on a list.

Collate: (1) To assemble individual elements of a mailing in sequence for inserting into a mailing envelope. (2) A program which combines two or more ordered files to produce a single ordered file. Also the act of combining such files. Synonymous with merge as in Merge-Purge.

Commission: A percentage of sale, by prior agreement, paid to the list broker, list manager, or other service arm for their part in the list usage.

Compile: The process by which a computer translates a series of instructions written in a programming language into actual machine language.

Compiled List: Names and addresses derived from directories, newspapers, public records, retail sales slips, trade show registrations, etc., to identify groups of people with something in common.

Compiler: Organization which develops lists of names and addresses from directories, newspapers, public records, registrations and other sources, identifying groups of people, companies or institutions with something in common.

Completed Cancel: One who has completed a specific commitment to buy products or services before cancelling.

Comprehensive: Complete and detailed layout for a printed piece. Also: "Comp," "Compre."

Computer: Data processor that can perform substantial computation, without intervention by a human.

Computer Compatibility: Ability to interchange the data or programs of one computer system with one or more other computers.

Computer Letter: Computer-printed message providing personalized, fill-in information from a source file in pre-designated positions. May also be full-printed letter with personalized insertions.

Computer Personalization: Printing of letters or other promotional pieces by a computer using names, addresses, special phrases, or other information based on data appearing in one or more computer records. The objective is to use the information in the computer record to tailor the promotional message to a specific individual.

Computer Program: Series of instructions or statements prepared to achieve a certain result.

Computer Record: All of the information about an individual, company, or transaction stored on a specific magnetic tape or disc.

Computer Service Bureau: An internal or external facility providing general or specific data processing services.

Consumer List: A list of names (usually at home address) compiled, or resulting, from a common inquiry or buying activity indicating a general or specific buying interest.

Continuity Program: Products or services bought as a series of small purchases, rather than all at one time. Generally based on a common theme and shipped at regular or specific time intervals.

C.T.O.: Contribution to overhead (profit).

Contributor List: Names and addresses of persons who have given to a specific fund raising effort. *(See Donor List).*

Controlled Circulation: Distribution at no charge of a publication to individuals or companies on the basis of their titles or occupations. Typically, recipients are asked from time to time to verify the information that qualifies them to receive the publication.

Controlled Duplication: A method by which names and addresses from two or more lists are matched (usually by computer) in order to eliminate or limit extra mailings to the same name and address.

Continuous Form: Paper forms designed for computer printing that are folded, and sometimes perforated, at predetermined vertical measurements. These may be letters, vouchers, invoices, cards, etc.

Conversion: (1) Process of changing from one method of data processing to another, or from one data processing system to another. Synonymous with Reformatting. (2) To secure specific action such as a purchase or contribution from a name on a mailing list or as a result of an inquiry.

Co-op Mailing: A mailing of two or more offers included in the same envelope or other carrier, with each participating mailer sharing mailing costs according to some predetermined formula.

C.P.I. (Cost Per Inquiry): A simple arithmetical formula derived by dividing the total cost of a mailing or an advertisement by the number of inquiries received.

C.P.O. (Cost Per Order): Similar to Cost Per Inquiry except based on actual orders rather than inquiries.

C.P.M. (Cost Per Thousand): Refers to total cost-per-thousand pieces of direct mail "in the mail."

Coupon: Part of an advertising promotion piece intended to be filled in by the inquirer or customer and returned to the advertiser.

Coupon Clipper: One who has given evidence of responding to free or nominal-cost offers out of curiosity, with little or no serious interest or buying intent.

Deadbeat: One who has ordered a product or service and, without just cause, hasn't paid for it.

Decoy: A unique name especially inserted in a mailing list for verifying list usage.

Delinquent: One who has fallen behind or has stopped scheduled payment for a product or service.

Delivery Date: The date a list user or a designated representative of the list user receives a specific list order from the list owner.

Demographics: Socio-economic characteristics pertaining to a geographic unit (county, city, sectional center, ZIP Code, group of households, education, ethnicity, income level, etc.).

Direct Mail Advertising: Any promotional effort using the Postal Service, or other direct delivery service, for distribution of the advertising message.

Direct Response Advertising: Advertising, through any medium, designed to generate a response by any means (such as mail, telephone, or telegraph) that is measurable.

Donor List: A list of persons who have given money to one or more charitable organizations. *(See Contributor List)*

Doubling Day: A point in time established by previous experience when 50% of all returns to a mailing will normally be received.

Dummy: (1) A mock-up giving a preview of a printed piece, showing placement and nature of the material to be printed. (2) A fictitious name with a mailable address inserted into a mailing list to check on usage of that list.

Dupe (Duplication): Appearance of identical or nearly identical entities more than once.

Duplication Elimination: A specific kind of controlled duplication which provides that: no matter how many times a name and address is on a list, and how many lists contain that name and address, it will be accepted for mailing only once by that mailer. Also referred to as "dupe elimination."

Editing Rules: Specific rules used in preparing name and address records that treat all elements the same way at all times. Also, the rules for rearranging, deleting, selecting, or inserting any needed data, symbols and/or characters.

Envelope Stuffer: Any advertising or promotional material enclosed in an envelope with business letters, statements or invoices.

Exchange: An arrangement whereby two mailers exchange equal quantities of mailing list names.

Expire: A former customer who is no longer an active buyer.

Expiration: A subscription which is not renewed.

Expiration Date: Date a subscription expires.

Field: Reserved area in a computer which services a similar function in all records of the file. Also, location on magnetic tape or disc drive which has definable limitations and meaning: e.g., Position 1-30 is the Name Field.

File Maintenance: The activity of keeping a file up-to-date by adding, changing, or deleting data (all or part). Synonymous with List Maintenance. *(See Update)*

Fill-In: A name, address or other words added to a preprinted letter.

First-Time Buyer: One who buys a product or service from a specific company for the first time.

Fixed Field: A way of laying out, or formatting, list information in a computer file that puts every piece of data in a specific position relative to every other piece of data, and limits the amount of space assigned to that data. If a piece of data is missing from an individual record, or if its assigned space is not comletely used, that space is not filled (every record has the same space and the same length). Any data exceeding its assigned space limitation must be abbreviated or contracted.

Former Buyer: One who has bought one or more times from a company with no purchase in the last twelve months.

Free-Standing Insert: A promotional piece loosely inserted or nested in a newspaper or magazine.

Frequency: The number of times an individual has ordered within a specific period of time. *(See Monetary Value* and *Recency)*

Friend-Of-A-Friend (Friend Recommendation): The result of one party sending in the name of someone considered to be interested in a specific advertiser's product or service; a third party inquiry.

Front End: Activities necessary, or the measurement of direct marketing activities, leading to an order or a contribution.

Fund Raising List: Any compilation or list of individuals or companies based on a known contribution to one or more fund raising appeals.

Geographics: Any method of subdividing a list, based on geographic or political subdivisions (ZIP Codes, sectional centers, cities, counties, states, regions).

Gift Buyer: One who buys a product or service for another.

Gimmick: Attention-getting device, usually dimensional, attached to a direct mail printed piece.

Guarantee: A pledge of satisfaction made by the seller to the buyer and specifying the terms by which the seller will make good his pledge.

Hot-Line List: The most recent names available on a specific list, but no older than three months. In any event, use of the term "hot-line" should be further modified by "weekly," "monthly," etc.

House List: Any list of names owned by a company as a result of compilation, inquiry or buyer action, or acquisition, that is used to promote that company's products or services.

House-List Duplicate: Duplication of name-and-address records between the list user's own lists and any list being mailed by him on a one-time use arrangement.

Inquiry: One who has asked for literature or other information about a product or service. Unless otherwise stated, it is assumed no payment has been made for the literature or other information. *(Note: A Catalog request is generally considered a specific type of inquiry.)*

Installment Buyer: One who orders goods or services and pays for them in two or more periodic payments after their delivery.

Inter-List Duplicate: Duplication of name and address records *between* two or more lists, other than house lists, being mailed by a list user.

Intra-List Duplication: Duplication of name and address records *within* a given list.

K: Used in reference to computer storage capacity, generally accepted as 1,000. Analogous to M in the direct marketing industry.

Key: One or more characters within a data group that can be used to identify it or control its use. Synonymous with Key Code in mailing business.

Key Code (Key): A group of letters and/or numbers, colors, or other markings, used to measure specific effectiveness of media, lists, advertisements, offers, etc., or any parts thereof.

Keyline: Can be any one of many partial or complete descriptions of past buying history coded to include name-and-address information and current status.

KBN (Kill Bad Name): Action taken with undeliverable addresses; i.e., nixies. You KBN a nixie.

Label: Piece of paper containing the name and address of the recipient which is applied to a mailing for address purposes.

Layout: (1) Artist's sketch showing relative positioning of illustrations, headlines and copy. (2) Positioning subject matter on a press sheet for most efficient production.

Letterhead: The printing on a letter that identifies the sender.

Lettershop: A business organization that handles the mechanical details of mailings such as addressing, imprinting, collating, etc. Most lettershops offer some printing facilities and many offer some degree of creative direct mail services.

List (Mailing List): Names and addresses of individuals and/or companies having in common a specific interest, characteristic or activity.

List Broker: A specialist who makes all necessary arrangements for one company to use the list(s) of another company. A broker's services may include most, or all, of the following: research, selection, recommendation and subsequent evaluation.

List Buyer: Technically, this term should apply only to one who actually buys mailing lists. In practice, however, it is usually used to identify one who orders mailing lists for one-time use; a List User or Mailer.

List Cleaning: The process of correcting and/or removing a name and/or address from a mailing list because it is no longer correct. Term is also used in the identification and elimination of house list duplication.

List Compiler: One who develops lists of names and addresses from directories, newspapers, public records, sales slips, trade show registrations and other sources for identifying groups of people or companies with something in common.

List Exchange: A barter arrangement between two companies for the use of a mailing list(s). May be: list for list, list for space, or list for comparable value—other than money.

List Maintenance: Any manual, mechanical or electronic system for keeping name-and-address records (with or without other data) up-to-date at any specific point(s) in time.

List Manager: One who, as an employee of a list owner or as an outside agent, is responsible for the use, by others, of a specific mailing list(s). The list manager generally serves the list owner in several or all of the following capacities: list maintenance (or advice thereon), list promotion and marketing, list clearance and record keeping, collecting for use of the list by others.

List Owner: One who, by promotional activity or compilation, has developed a list of names having something in common; or one who has *purchased* (as opposed to rented, reproduced, or used on a one-time basis) such a list from the developer.

List Rental: An arrangement whereby a list owner furnishes names to a mailer, together with the privilege of using the list on a one-time basis only (unless otherwise specified in advance). For this privilege, the list owner is paid a royalty by the mailer. ("List Rental" is the term most often used although "List Reproduction" and "List Usage" more accurately describe the transaction, since "Rental" is not used in the sense of its ordinary meaning of leasing property.)

List Royalty: Payment to list owners for the privilege of using their names on a one-time basis.

List Sample: A group of names selected from a list in order to evaluate the responsiveness of that list.

List Segmentation: *(See List Selection).*

List Selection: Characteristics used to define smaller groups within a list (essentially, lists within a list). Although very small, select groups may be very desirable and may substantially improve response; increased costs, however, often render them impractical.

List Sequence: The order in which names and addresses appear in a list. While most lists today are in ZIP Code sequence, some are alphabetical by name within the ZIP Code; others are in carrier sequence (postal delivery); and still others may (or may not) use some other order within the ZIP Code. Some lists are still arranged alphabetically by name or chronologically, and in many other variations or combinations.

List Sort: Process of putting a list in a specific sequence or from another sequence or no sequence.

List Test: Part of a list selected to try to determine the effectiveness of the entire list. *(See List Sample)*

List User: One who uses names and addresses on someone else's list as prospects for the user's product or service; similar to Mailer.

Load Up: Process of offering a buyer the opportunity of buying an entire series at one time after the customer has purchased the first item in that series.

Magnetic Tape: A storage device for electronically recording and reproducing, by use of a computer, defined bits of data.

Mail Date: Date a list user, by prior agreement with the list owner, is obligated to mail a specific list. No other date is acceptable without specific approval of the list owner.

Mailer: (1) A direct mail advertiser who promotes a product or service using lists of others or house lists or both. (2) A printed direct mail advertising piece. (3) A folding carton, wrapper or tube used to protect materials in the mails.

Mailgram: A combination telegram-letter, with the telegram transmitted to a postal facility close to the addressee and then delivered as first class mail.

Mailing Machine: A machine that attaches labels to mailing pieces and otherwise prepares such pieces for deposit in the postal system.

Mail Order Action Line (MOAL): A service of the Direct Marketing Association which assists consumers in resolving problems with mail order purchases.

Mail Order Buyer: One who offers, and pays for, a product or service through the mail. (Generally, an order telephoned in response to a direct response advertisement is considered a direct substitute for an order sent through postal channels.)

Mail Preference Service (MPS): A service of the Direct Marketing Association wherein consumers can request to have their names removed from, or added to, mailing lists. These names are made available to both members and non-members of the Association.

Master File: File that is of a permanent nature or regarded in a particular job as authoritative, or one that contains all sub files.

Match: A direct mail term used to refer to the typing of addresses, salutations or inserts onto letters with other copy imprinted by a printing process.

Match Code: A code determined either by the creator or the user of a file for matching records contained in another file.

MOAL: Acronym for Mail Order Action Line.

Monetary Value: Total expenditures by a customer during a specific period of time, generally twelve months.

MPS: Acronym for Mail Preference Service.

Multiple Buyer: One who has bought two or more times (not one who has bought two or more items, one time only); also a Multi-Buyer or Repeat Buyer.

Multiple Regression: Statistical technique used to measure the relationship between responses to a mailing with census demographics and list characteristics of one or more selected mailing lists. Used to determine the best types of people/areas to mail. This technique can also be used to analyze customers, subscribers, etc.

Name: Single entry on a mailing list.

Name Acquisition: Technique of soliciting a response to obtain names and addresses for a mailing list.

Name-Removal Service: Portion of Mail Preference Service offered by Direct Marketing Association wherein a consumer is sent a form which, when filled in and returned,

constitutes a request to have the individual's name removed from all mailing lists used by participating members of the association and other direct mail users.

Negative Option: A buying plan in which a customer or club member agrees to accept and pay for products or services announced in advance at regular intervals *unless* the individual notifies the company, within a reasonable time after announcement not to ship the merchandise. *(See Federal Trade Commission Regulations in Section 12).*

Nesting: Placing one enclosure within another before inserting into a mailing envelope.

Net Name Arrangement: An agreement, at the time of ordering or before, whereby the list owner agrees to accept adjusted payment for less than the total names shipped to the list user. Such arrangements can be for a percentage of names shipped or names actually mailed (whichever is greater) or for only those names actually mailed (without a percentage limitation). They can provide for a running charge or not.

Nixie: A mailing piece returned to a mailer (under proper authorization) by the Postal Service because of an incorrect, or undeliverable, name and address.

No-Pay: One who has not paid (wholly or in part) for goods or services ordered. "Uncollectable," "Deadbeat," and "Delinquent" are often used to describe the same person.

North/South Labels: Mailing labels that read from top to bottom and can be affixed with Cheshire equipment.

Novelty Format: An attention-getting direct mail format.

Nth Name Selection: A fractional unit that is repeated in sampling a mailing list. For example, in an "every tenth" sample, you would select the 1st, 11th, 21st, 31st, etc. records—or the 2nd, 12th, 22nd, 32nd, etc., records and so forth.

OCR (Optical Character Recognition): Machine identification of printed characters through use of light-sensitive devices.

Offer: The terms promoting a specific product or service.

One-Time Buyer: A buyer who has not ordered a second time from a given company.

One-Time Use Of A List: An intrinsic part of the normal list usage, list reproduction, or list exchange agreement in which it is understood that the mailer will not use the names on the list more than one time without specific prior approval of the list owner.

Open Account: A customer record that, at a specific time, reflects an unpaid balance for goods and services ordered, without delinquency.

Optical Scanner: An input device that optically reads a line of printed characters and converts each character into its electronic equivalent for processing.

Order Blank Envelopes: An order form printed on one side of a sheet, with a mailing address on the reverse. The recipient simply fills in the order, folds and seals like an envelope.

Order Card: A reply card used to initiate an order by mail.

Order Form: A printed form on which a customer can provide information to initiate an order by mail. Designed to be mailed in an envelope.

Package: A term used to describe all of the assembled enclosures (parts or elements) of a mailing effort.

Package Insert: Any promotional piece included in a product shipment. It may be for different products (or refills and replacements) from the same company or for products and services of other companies.

Package Test: A test of part or all of the elements of one mailing piece against another.

Paid Cancel: One who completes a basic buying commitment, or more, before cancelling the commitment. *(See Completed Cancel)*

Paid Circulation: Distribution of a publication to individuals or organizations which have paid for a subscription.

Paid During Service: Term used to describe a method of paying for magazine subscriptions in installments, usually weekly or monthly, and, usually, collected in person by the original sales person or a representative of that company.

Peel-Off Label: A self-adhesive label attached to a backing sheet which is attached to a mailing piece. The label is intended to be removed from the mailing piece and attached to an order blank or card.

Penetration: Relationship of the number of individuals or families on a particular list (by state, ZIP Code, S.I.C., etc.) compared to the total number possible.

Personalizing: Individualizing of direct mail pieces by adding the name of other personal information about the recipient.

Phone List: Mailing list compiled from names listed in telephone directories.

Piggy-Back: An offer that hitches a free ride with another offer.

Poly Bag: Transparent polyethylene bag used in place of envelopes for mailing.

Pop-Up: A printed piece containing a paper construction pasted inside a fold and which, when the fold is opened, "pops up" to form a three-dimensional illustration.

Positive Option: A method of distributing products and services incorporating the same advance notice technique as *Negative Option* but requiring a specific order each time from the member or subscriber. Generally, it is more costly and less predictable than Negative Option.

Postal Service Prohibitory Order: A communication from the Postal Service to a company indicating that a specific person and/or family considers the company's advertising mail to be pandering. The Order requires the company to remove from its own mailing list and from any other lists used to promote that company's products or services all names listed on the Order. Violation of the Order is subject to fine and imprisonment. Names listed on the Order are to be distinguished from those names removed voluntarily by the list owner at an individual's request.

Post Card: Single sheet self-matters on card stock.

Post Card Mailers: Booklet containing business reply cards which are individually perforated for selective return, to order products or obtain information.

Premium: An item offered to a buyer, usually free or at a nominal price, as an inducement to purchase or obtain for trial a product or service offered via mail order.

Premium Buyer: One who buys a product or service to get another product or service (usually free or at a special price), or who responds to an offer of a special product (premium) on the package or label (or sometimes in the advertising) of another product.

Preprint: An advertising insert printed in advance and supplied to a newspaper or magazine for insertion.

Private Mail: Mail handled by special arrangement outside the Postal Service.

Program: A sequence of steps to be executed by the computer to solve a given problem or achieve a certain result.

Programming: Design, writing and testing of a program.

Prospect: A name on a mailing list considered to be a potential buyer for a given product or service but who has not previously made such a purchase.

Prospecting: Mailing to get leads for further sales contact rather than to make direct sales.

Protection: The amount of time, before and after the assigned mailing date, a list owner will not allow the same names to be mailed by anyone other than the mailer cleared for that specific date.

Psychographics: Any characteristics or qualities used to denote the lifestyle(s) or attitude(s) of customers and prospective customers.

Publisher's Letter: A second letter enclosed in a mailing package to stress a specific selling point.

Purge: The process of eliminating duplicates and/or unwanted names and addresses from one or more lists.

Pyramiding: A method of testing mailing lists, in which one starts with a small quantity and, based on positive indications, follows with increasingly larger quantities of the list balance until the entire list is mailed.

Questionnaire: A printed form to a specified audience to solicit answers to specific questions.

Random Access: An access mode in which records are obtained from, or placed into, a mass storage file in a non-sequential manner so that any record can be rapidly accessed. Synonymous with Direct Access.

Recency: The latest purchase or other activity recorded for an individual or company on a specific customer list. *(See Frequency and Monetary Value).*

Reformatting: Changing a magnetic tape format from one arrangement to another, more usable format. Synonymous with Conversion (list or tape).

Renewal: A subscription that has been renewed prior to, or at, expiration time or within six months thereafter.

Repeat Buyer: *(See Multiple Buyer).*

Rental: *(See List Rental).*

Reply Card: A sender-addressed card included in a mailing on which the recipient may indicate his response to the offer.

Reply-O-Letter: One of a number of patented direct mail formats for facilitating replies from prospects. It features a die-cut opening on the face of the letter and a pocket on the reverse. An addressed reply card is inserted in the pocket and the name and address thereon shows through the die cut opening.

Reproduction Right: Authorization by a list owner for a specific mailer to use that list on a one-time basis.

Response Rate: Percent of returns from a mailing.

Return Envelopes: Addressed reply envelopes, either stamped or unstamped—as distinguished from business reply envelopes which carry a postage payment guarantee—included with a mailing.

Return Postage Guaranteed: A legend imprinted on the address face of envelopes or other mailing pieces when the mailer wishes the Postal Service to return undeliverable third class bulk mail. A charge equivalent to the single piece, third class rate will be made for each piece returned. *(See List Cleaning).*

Return Requested: An indication that a mailer will compensate the Postal Service for return of an undeliverable mailing piece.

Returns: Responses to a direct mail program.

RFMR: Acronym for Recency-Frequency-Monetary Value Ratio, a formula used to evaluate the sales potential of names on a mailing list.

Rollout: To mail the remaining portion of a mailing list after successfully testing a portion of that list.

R.O.P. (Run of Paper or Run of Press): Usually refers to color printing which can be placed on any page of a newspaper or magazine.

Rough: Dummy or layout in sketchy form with a minimum of detail.

Royalties: Sum paid per unit mailed or sold for the use of a list, imprimatur, patent, etc.

Running Charge: The price a list owner charges for names run or passed, but not used by a specific mailer. When such a charge is made, it is usually to cover extra processing costs. However, some list owners set the price without regard to actual cost.

Run Of Paper: (1) A term applied to color printing on regular paper and presses, as distinct from separately printed sections made on special color presses. (2) Sometimes used to describe an advertisement positioned by publisher's choice—in other than a preferred position—for which a special charge is made.

Salting: Deliberate placing of decoy or dummy names in a list to trace list usage and delivery. *(See Decoy and Dummy).*

Sample Buyer: One who sends for a sample product, usually at the special price or for a small handling charge, but sometimes free.

Sample Package (Mailing Piece): An example of the package to be mailed by the list user to a particular list. Such a mailing piece is submitted to the list owner for approval prior to commitment for one-time use of that list. Although a sample package may, due to time pressure, differ slightly from the actual package used, the list user agreement usually requires the user to reveal any material differences when submitting the sample package.

Scented Inks: Printing inks to which a fragrance has been added.

Sectional Center (SCF or SCF Center): A Postal Service distribution unit comprising different Post Offices whose ZIP Codes start with the same first three digits.

Selection Criteria: Definition of characteristics that identify segments or sub-groups within a list.

Self-Cover: A cover of the same paper as the inside text pages.

Self-Mailer: A direct mail piece mailed without an envelope.

Sequence: An arrangement of items according to a specified set of rules or instructions. Refers generally to ZIP Codes or customer number sequence.

S.I.C. (Standard Industrial Classification): Classification of businesses, as defined by the U.S. Department of Commerce.

Software: A set of programs, procedures and associated documentation concerned with operation of a data processing system.

Solo Mailing: A mailing promoting a single product or a limited group of related products. Usually it consists of a letter, brochure and reply device enclosed in an envelope.

Source Code: Unique alphabetical and/or numeric identification for distinguishing one list or media source from another. *(See Key Code)*

Source Count: The number of names and addresses, in any given list, for the media (or list sources) from which the names and addresses were derived.

Split Test: Two or more samples from the same list—each considered to be representative of the entire list—used for package tests or to test the homogeneity of the list.

State Count: The number of names and addresses, in a given list, for each state.

Statement Stuffer: A small, printed piece designed to be inserted in an envelope carrying a customer's statement of account.

Step Up: The use of special premiums to get a mail order buyer to increase his unit of purchase.

Stock Art: Art sold for use by a number of advertisers.

Stock Cut: Printing engravings kept in stock by the printer or publisher for occasional use.

Stock Formats: Direct mail formats with pre-printed illustrations and/or headings to which an advertiser adds his own copy.

Stopper: Advertising slang for a striking head-line or illustration intended to attract im-mediate attention.

Stuffer: Advertising enclosures placed in other media—i.e., newspapers, merchandise packages, mailings for other products, etc.

Subscriber: Individual who has paid to receive a periodical.

Swatching: Attaching samples of material to a printed piece.

Syndicated Mailing: Mailing prepared for dis-tribution by firms other than the manufac-turer or syndicator.

Syndicator: One who makes available prepared direct mail promotions for specific prod-ucts or services to a list owner for mailing to his own list. Most syndicators also offer product fulfillment services.

Tabloid: A preprinted advertising insert of four or more pages, usually about half the size of a regular newspaper page, designed for inserting into a newspaper.

Tape Density: The number of bits of informa-tion (bytes) that can be included in each of a specific magnetic tape—e.g., 556 BPI, 800 BPI, 1600 BPI, etc.

Tape Dump: A printout of data on a magnetic tape to be edited and checked for correct-ness, readability, consistency, etc.

Tape Layout: A simple "map" of the data in-cluded in each record and its relative, or specific, location.

Tape Record: All the information about an in-dividual or company contained on a spe-cific magnetic tape.

Teaser: An advertisement or promotion planned to excite curiosity about a later advertise-ment or promotion.

Telecommunications: Data transmission be-tween a computer system and remotely lo-cated devices via a unit that performs the necessary format conversion and controls the rate of transmission over telephone lines, microwaves, etc. Synonymous with Transceive.

Terminal: Any mechanism which can transmit and/or receive data through a system or communications network.

Test Panel: A term used to identify each of the parts or samples in a split test.

Test Tape: A selection of representative records within a mailing list that enables a list user or service bureau to prepare for reformat-ting or converting the list to a form more efficient for the user.

Throwaway: An advertisement or promotional piece intended for widespread free distri-bution. Generally printed on inexpensive paper stock, it is most often distributed by hand to passersby or from house-to-house.

Tie-In: Cooperative mailing effort involving two or more advertisers.

Til Forbid: An order for continuing service which is to continue until specifically can-celled by the buyer. Also "TF".

Title: A designation before (prefix) or after (suf-fix) a name to more accurately identify an individual. (Prefixes—Mr., Mrs., Dr., Sis-ter, etc.; Suffixes—M.D., Jr., President, Sales Manager, etc.)

Time Sharing: Multiple utilizations of avail-able computer time, often via terminals, usually shared by different organizations.

Tip-On: An item glued to a printed piece.

Token: An involvement device, often consisting of a perforated portion of an order card designed to be removed from its original position and placed in another designated area on the order card, to signify a desire to purchase the product or service offered.

Town Marker: A symbol used to identify the end of a mailing list's geographical unit. (Originated for "towns" but now used for ZIP Codes, Sectional Centers, etc.).

Traffic Builder: A direct mail piece intended primarily to attract recipients to the mailer's place of business.

Trial Buyer: One who buys a short-term supply of a product, or buys the product with the understanding that it may be examined, used, or tested for a specified time before deciding whether to pay for it or to return it.

Trial Subscriber: A person ordering a publication or service on a conditional basis. The condition may relate to: delaying payment, the right to cancel, a shorter than normal term and/or a special introductory price.

Uncollectable: One who hasn't paid for goods and services at the end of a normal series of collection efforts.

Unit of Sale: Description of the average dollar amount spent by customers on a mailing list.

Universe: Total number of individuals that might be included on a mailing list; all of those fitting a single set of specifications.

Update: Recent transactions and current information added to the Master (main) list to reflect the current status of each record on the list.

Up Front: Securing payment for a product offered by mail order before the product is sent.

UPS: Acronym for United Parcel Service.

Variable Field: A way of laying out for formatting list information that assigns a specific sequence to the data, but doesn't assign it specific positions. While this method conserves space on magnetic tape, it is generally more difficult to work with.

Verification: The process of determining the validity of an order by sending a questionnaire to the customer.

WATS: Acronym for Wide Area Telephone Service. A service providing a special line allowing calls within a certain zone, on a direct dialing basis, for a flat monthly charge.

White Mail: Incoming mail that is not on a form sent out by the advertiser. All mail other than orders and payments.

White Envelope: Envelope with a die-cut portion on the front that permits viewing the address printed on an enclosure. The "die cut window" may or may not be covered with a transparent material.

Wing Mailer: Label-affixing device that uses strips of paper on which addresses have been printed.

ZIP Code: A group of five digits used by the U.S. Postal Service to designate specific post offices, stations, branches, buildings or large companies.

ZIP Code Count: The number of names and addresses in a list, within each ZIP Code.

ZIP Code Sequence: Arranging names and addresses in a list according to the numeric progression of the ZIP Code in each record. This form of list formatting is mandatory for mailing at bulk third class mail rates, based on the sorting requirements of Postal Service regulations.

Index